Happy
Crossword
Hooker

NWL18 edition

©魏時明

Hi Brendan
May the Q be with U always!

Nam

Norman Wei

Table of Contents

Preface and Introduction

This book is a compilation of front and back hooks to all three to seven letter words that are valid in competitive Scrabble tournaments that use the NWL18 (New Word List 2018) in North America. It is one of the two official dictionaries used in tournaments in North America.

The book also includes list of all valid words that have the same front and back hook. Examples are MAIL and STOP with the e hook.

Chapter 7 identifies the three to seven letter NEW words that have hooks.

Hooks - front and back - are very important in Scrabble because they help the players to extend their words. Knowing or missing the appropriate hook at a critical stage of a game can often mean victory or defeat.

Happy tiles and hooking.

Chapter 1: Three letter words with hooks

With front hook A

AHS	DOS	HIS	LEE	MUS	REG	TOP	YAH
ALS	EON	HOY	LES	NEW	RES	UGH	YES
BAS	FAR	IDS	LIT	NIL	RIA	VID	YIN
BED	FRO	INS	LOW	NUS	RID	VOW	
BET	GAR	ITS	LUM	PED	RUM	WAY	
BOS	GAS	JAR	MAS	PER	SEA	WED	
BUT	GED	JEE	MEN	PES	SHY	WEE	
BYE	GEE	KIN	MID	POD	TAP	WRY	
BYS	GIN	LAR	MIR	POS	TES	XED	
DIT	HEM	LAS	MIS	QUA	TOM	XIS	

With back hook A

ACT	DIT	ILK	MAR	OBI	PUN	SOD	VAS
ALB	DON	JOT	MAS	ODE	PUP	SOL	VEG
AMI	DOS	JUG	MAY	OFF	RAG	SOM	VIG
ANT	DUM	KAT	MEG	OLE	RAI	SOY	VIN
ARE	FET	KIN	MES	ORC	RAJ	SUB	VIS
BET	FIL	KOR	MET	OUT	RAY	TAP	WET
BOT	FOR	LAM	MIC	PAC	ROT	TAX	WHO
BUN	GAG	LAV	MOL	PAP	RUG	TEL	ZED
BUR	GAL	LEV	MOR	PAR	SAG	TOE	
CHI	GAM	LIP	NAG	PIC	SER	TOG	
COD	GET	LOT	NAN	PIN	SET	TOR	
COL	GIG	LUM	NAP	PIP	SHE	TUB	
COX	HAH	LUN	NIP	PIT	SIM	TUN	
DAD	HOM	MAM	NOM	PRO	SOB	UMM	
DEV	HOY	MAN	NOT	PUL	SOC	VAR	

With front hook B

AAL	ANI	AYS	ICE	LED	OIL	RAN	UMS
AAS	ARB	EAR	IDS	LET	OLD	RAS	UNS
ABA	ARE	EAT	IFF	LIN	OLE	RAT	URB
ABY	ARF	EAU	ILK	LIP	ONE	RAW	URD
ADS	ARK	EDS	ILL	LOB	OOT	RAY	URN
AFF	ARM	ELL	INS	LOG	OPS	RED	URP
AGS	ARS	ELS	IRK	LOT	ORA	REE	UTE
AIL	ASH	END	ITS	LOW	ORE	RIG	UTS
AIT	ASK	ENS	LAB	OAR	ORT	RIM	YES
ALE	ASS	ERG	LAG	OAT	OUT	RIN	
ALL	ATE	EST	LAH	ODE	OWL	ROO	
ALS	ATT	ETA	LAM	ODS	OXY	ROW	
AND	AWL	ETH	LAT	OFF	RAD	RUT	
ANE	AWN	HUT	LAW	OHO	RAG	UMP	

With back hook B

BAR	BIB	BOO	BUR	CAR	COB	CUR	DUM

FEE	FOR	GAR	JAM	LAM	PRO	TOM
FLU	GAM	HER	JIB	NEW	SIB	

With front hook C

ABS	APO	ELS	HID	LAD	OCA	ONS	RIB
ADS	ARB	ERE	HIN	LAG	ODA	OOF	RIP
AFF	ARE	ESS	HIP	LAM	ODE	OOT	ROC
AGE	ARK	HAD	HIS	LAP	ODS	OPE	ROW
AID	ARS	HAM	HIT	LAW	OFF	OPS	UKE
AIN	ART	HAO	HON	LAY	OFT	ORE	UMS
ALL	ASH	HAP	HOP	LEG	OHO	ORS	UPS
ALS	ASK	HAT	HOW	LIP	OIL	OWL	URB
AMI	ATE	HAW	HUB	LIT	OKE	RAG	URD
AMP	AVA	HAY	HUG	LOG	OLD	RAM	URN
ANE	AVE	HEM	HUM	LOP	OLE	RAP	UTE
ANT	AYS	HEW	ION	LOT	OMA	RAW	UTS
APE	ELL	HIC	IRE	OAT	ONE	RED	

With back hook C

ALE	CHI	MAR	SYN	ZIN
BAN	DIS	PER	TOR	

With front hook D

ABS	ALS	ECO	ICE	OAT	ORE	RAY	UPS
ACE	AMP	EFT	ICK	OBE	ORS	REE	URN
ADO	ARB	EKE	IFF	OES	OSE	REG	YER
ADS	ARE	ELF	IFS	OFF	OUR	RIB	YES
AFF	ARK	ELL	ILL	OHS	OUT	RIP	
AFT	ART	ELS	INK	OLE	OWN	RUB	
AGO	ASH	EME	INS	OMS	OXY	RUG	
AGS	ATE	EMO	IRE	ONE	RAG	RUM	
AHS	AWN	ENS	IRK	ONS	RAM	UKE	
AIS	AYS	ERE	ITS	OPA	RAT	UMP	
ALE	EAR	HOW	JIN	OPE	RAW	UNS	

With back hook D

ACE	BUN	EYE	GIE	KIN	ORA	RIN	TEN
AGE	BUR	FAR	GOA	LAR	OWE	ROO	TIE
AMI	CAR	FEE	GOO	LEA	PAR	RUE	TOE
APE	CHI	FEN	HAE	LEU	PEE	SAN	USE
APO	COL	FEU	HER	LIE	PEN	SEE	VIE
AWE	COR	FIN	HIE	LOR	PIE	SEN	WAN
AXE	CRU	FON	HIN	MEL	POO	SHA	WAR
BAL	CUE	FOO	HOE	MEN	PRO	SHE	WEE
BAN	CUR	FOR	HOO	MIL	QUA	SHO	WEN
BAR	DEE	FUN	HUE	MOL	RAI	SKI	WIN
BEN	DIE	GAE	ICE	MOO	RAN	SOL	WOO
BIN	DYE	GEE	IRE	NEE	RED	SUE	WYN
BRA	EKE	GEL	JEE	OPE	REE	TEE	YAR

YON

With front hook E

ARS	DIT	GAL	MIC	NOW	POS	TIC	YEN
AVE	EEW	GIS	MIR	ONS	RAS	TUI	YER
COS	ELS	GOS	MOS	PEE	SPY	XED	YES
CRU	GAD	MES	MUS	PIC	TAS	YAS	

With back hook E

ABY	CAR	ESS	HON	LUX	NOT	ROT	TIL
ADZ	CAT	FAD	HOP	MAC	OCH	RUB	TIN
AGE	CEP	FAN	HOS	MAD	OLD	RUN	TOM
AID	COD	FAR	HOW	MAG	PAC	SAB	TON
ALA	COL	FAT	HUG	MAN	PAL	SAD	TOP
ALE	CON	FEM	HYP	MAR	PAN	SAG	TOR
AMI	COP	FER	JET	MAT	PAR	SAL	TOT
ANT	COR	FET	JIB	MEM	PAS	SAN	TUB
ARS	COT	FIL	JUT	MET	PAT	SAT	TUN
AWE	CUB	FIN	KIN	MIC	PER	SEN	TWA
BAD	CUR	FIR	KIT	MIL	PIC	SER	TYE
BAL	CUT	FLU	KOR	MIM	PIN	SHO	VAN
BAN	DAL	FOR	LAC	MIR	PIP	SIC	VAS
BAR	DAM	FRO	LAD	MIS	POL	SIN	VID
BAS	DEL	GAG	LAM	MOD	POM	SIP	VIN
BAT	DEN	GAL	LAS	MOL	POP	SIR	VIS
BEN	DIM	GAM	LAT	MOM	POS	SIT	WAD
BIB	DIN	GAN	LAV	MOP	PUL	SOL	WAG
BID	DIT	GAP	LED	MOR	PUR	SOM	WAN
BIN	DOG	GAT	LEK	MOT	RAG	SON	WAR
BIS	DOL	GEN	LIN	MUS	RAP	SPA	WIN
BIT	DOM	GIB	LIP	MUT	RAS	STY	WIS
BIZ	DON	GIT	LIT	NAB	RAT	SUP	WIT
BOD	DOR	GOR	LOB	NAM	RED	SYN	WOK
BRA	DOS	HAD	LOG	NAP	RET	TAM	YAG
BUT	DOT	HAM	LOP	NAV	RID	TAP	YAR
CAD	DUD	HAT	LOR	NIT	RIF	TAR	YIP
CAF	DUN	HEM	LOW	NIX	RIM	TAS	YOK
CAM	DUP	HER	LUD	NOD	RIP	TAT	YOW
CAN	ELS	HID	LUG	NOM	ROB	TEL	YUK
CAP	ERN	HOM	LUN	NOS	ROD	THE	ZIN

With front hook F

ABS	AIL	ASH	EDS	ERN	INK	LAT	LEY
ACE	AIN	ATE	EEL	ESS	INS	LAW	LIP
ACT	AIR	AVA	ELL	EST	IRE	LAX	LIT
ADO	ALL	AVE	EME	ETA	ITS	LAY	LOG
ADS	ANE	AWN	EMS	ICE	LAB	LEA	LOP
AFF	ARE	AYS	END	IDS	LAG	LED	LOW
AGS	ARM	EAR	ENS	ILK	LAM	LEE	LUX
AHS	ART	EAT	ERE	ILL	LAP	LEX	OES

OIL	OPS	ORT	RAG	REE	ROM	USE
OLD	ORA	OUR	RAP	RET	ROW	
ONS	ORB	OWL	RAT	RIG	RUG	
OOT	ORE	OXY	RAY	ROE	UNS	

With back hook F

ALE	CAF	CUR	GOO	LEA	PRO	ROO	WOO
BAR	CAL	DEL	GUL	LIE	REE	SEI	
BEE	COO	DIF	HOO	LOO	REI	SEL	
BUM	COR	FIE	HOW	POO	RIF	SER	

With front hook G

ABS	ALL	AVE	HAT	LED	NUS	RAM	ROW
ABY	ALS	AYS	HIS	LEE	OAT	RAN	RUB
ADS	AMA	EAR	IDS	LEG	ODS	RAT	RUE
AFF	AMP	EDS	IFS	LEY	OES	RAY	RUM
AGA	ANE	EEK	ILL	LIB	OLD	REE	UMS
AGE	APE	ELD	IMP	LOB	ONE	RID	UNS
AGS	ARB	ELS	INK	LOP	OOF	RIG	UTS
AIN	ARS	EMS	INS	LOW	ORE	RIM	
AIT	ASH	ENS	ITS	LUG	OUT	RIN	
ALA	ASP	EST	LAD	LUM	OWN	RIP	
ALE	ATE	ETA	LAM	NAW	RAD	ROT	

With back hook G

AGO	BUR	GAN	LUN	PIN	RUN	SUN	VUG
ARE	DAN	HOG	MIG	PRO	SAN	TAN	WIN
BAN	DIN	HON	MUG	PUN	SHA	TEG	ZIN
BIN	DON	HUN	MUN	QUA	SHO	TIN	
BIO	DUN	JAG	NOG	RAG	SIN	TON	
BRA	FAN	KIN	PAN	RAN	SKA	TUN	
BUN	FRO	LIN	PEA	RIN	SON	VAN	

With front hook H

AFT	ALT	ATE	ELM	ICK	OKE	OPE	UNS
AGS	AND	AVE	EME	ILL	OLD	OPS	UTS
AHA	ANT	AYS	EMS	INS	OLE	ORA	WAN
AHS	ARE	EAR	ENS	IRE	OMA	OSE	
AIL	ARK	EAT	ERE	ITS	OMS	OUR	
AIR	ARM	EEL	ERN	MMM	ONE	OWE	
AJI	ART	EFT	ERS	OAR	ONS	OWL	
ALE	ASH	ELD	EST	ODS	OOF	UMP	
ALL	ASP	ELL	ETH	OES	OOT	UMS	

With back hook H

AMA	BAT	BOS	CAP	DIS	EAT	GOS	HAT
ARC	BET	BOT	COS	DOS	FAS	GOT	HET
BAS	BIS	BUS	DAS	DOT	GAS	HAS	HUN

KIT	MAT	OAT	PIS	RAT	SIT	UMP
KOP	MES	ODA	PIT	RES	SOP	VUG
LAS	MET	OKE	POO	RUT	SOT	WAS
LAT	MOS	OPA	POS	SHA	SUK	WIS
LOT	MOT	PAS	PUG	SHH	TEC	WIT
MAC	MUS	PAT	PUS	SIG	TET	YEA
MAS	NOS	PEC	RAS	SIN	TOP	YOD

With front hook I

BIS	DOL	LEA	MAM	ONS	RES	WIS
CON	KAT	LEX	MID	RED	RID	

With back hook I

ANT	DEL	LAR	MOD	PER	ROT	TIT	ZIT
BAN	DEN	LAT	MOM	PUL	SAD	TOP	
BID	DEV	LOT	MUN	PUR	SAT	TOR	
CAD	GAD	MAG	NOD	QUA	SOL	WAD	
CAM	HAJ	MAX	NOR	RAG	SUM	YAG	
CON	IMP	MID	PAD	RAM	TAX	YET	
DEF	KEP	MIR	PAL	RAN	TIP	YON	

With front hook J

ABS	APE	AYS	EST	INK	IVY	OWL	UTE
AGS	ARS	ELL	IFF	INN	OES	UDO	UTS
AIL	AUK	EON	ILL	INS	OKE	UKE	
ANE	AVA	ESS	IMP	ISM	OLE	UMP	

With back hook J

HAD	HAJ

With front hook K

AAS	ANA	EEK	HAT	ILL	NEE	OPS	UDO
ABS	ANE	EEL	HET	INK	NEW	ORA	VAS
AIL	ART	EFS	HIS	INS	NIT	ORE	YAK
AIN	AVA	ENS	ICK	IRK	NOB	ORS	YAR
ALE	AYS	ERN	IDS	ITS	NOT	RAI	YES
AMI	BAR	ETA	IFS	NAP	NOW	RAY	

With back hook K

BAL	BUR	DAW	FOR	HON	LAC	MAR	MOS
BAN	BUS	DIN	FUN	HOO	LAR	MAS	MUS
BAR	CAL	DIS	GEE	HOW	LEA	MIC	NOO
BAS	CAR	DOC	GIN	HUN	LEE	MIL	PAC
BIS	CON	DOR	GOO	JIN	LIN	MIR	PAR
BOO	COO	DUN	GUN	JUN	LOO	MOC	PEA
BOS	COR	FIL	HAW	KIN	LUN	MON	PEC
BUN	DAN	FIN	HIC	KIR	MAC	MOO	PEE

PER	PUN	RIN	SAN	SOC	TAS	WAN	WON
PIC	RAN	ROC	SEE	SOU	TEA	WAR	YER
PIN	REC	ROO	SIC	SUN	TIC	WEE	
PUL	REE	SAC	SIN	TAN	TOO	WIN	

With front hook L

ABS	AMA	AVA	ENS	INN	ODE	OUD	UNS
ACE	AMP	AVE	ESS	INS	OFT	OUR	UTE
ADS	AND	AWN	EST	ION	ONE	OUT	YES
AGS	ANE	AYS	ICE	IRE	OOF	OWE	
AHS	ARK	EAR	ICH	ITS	OOT	OWN	
AID	ARS	EEK	ICK	OAF	OPE	UDO	
AIN	ASH	EFT	IDS	OBE	OPS	ULU	
AIR	ASS	EKE	IMP	OCA	ORE	UMP	
ALL	ATE	END	INK	OCH	OSE	UMS	

With back hook L

ANA	CEL	FAR	HOW	MOO	POL	SEA	VIA
ANI	COO	FEE	JAR	NIL	POO	SEE	WAW
AXE	COW	FIL	JOW	OPA	PUL	SEL	WEE
BAA	CUR	FOO	LEA	ORA	PUR	SOU	WOO
BAL	DAH	FOU	MAR	OVA	RAI	TAE	YAW
BEL	DEL	FUR	MEL	PAL	REE	TEA	YOW
BOW	DIE	GAL	MEW	PAW	RIA	TEE	
BUR	DOL	GOA	MIL	PEA	ROT	TEL	
CAL	DUE	GUL	MOI	PEE	SAL	TIL	
CAR	EAR	HER	MOL	PIA	SAU	TOO	

With front hook M

ACE	ALL	ART	EEK	ETA	INK	OLE	ORT
ADS	ALT	ASH	ELD	ETH	IRE	OMS	OWN
AGE	AMA	ASK	ELL	HOS	IRK	ONO	UMM
AGS	ANA	ASS	ELS	ICE	OAT	ONS	UMP
AID	ANE	ATE	EME	ICK	ODE	OOT	UMS
AIL	ANY	ATT	EMO	IDS	ODS	OPE	UNI
AIM	ARC	AWN	EMS	IFF	OHO	OPS	UNS
AIN	ARE	AYS	END	IGG	OIL	ORA	USE
AIR	ARK	EAT	ERE	ILK	OKE	ORE	UTE
ALE	ARS	EDS	ESS	ILL	OLD	ORS	UTS

With back hook M

BAL	DEE	FOR	HMM	PAL	SEE	TEE	WHO
BAR	DOR	FRO	LOO	PER	SHA	THE	ZOO
BOO	FAR	GOR	MUM	PRO	SKI	TOO	
CAL	FIL	HAE	NEE	ROO	SPA	WAR	
COR	FIR	HER	NOR	SEA	TEA	WHA	

With front hook N

ABS	ALA	AVE	ESS	IFF	OES	OPE	UNS
AFF	ANA	AYS	EST	ILL	OIL	OSE	URD
AGA	APE	EAR	EVE	ITS	OMA	OVA	UTS
AGS	ARC	EAT	ICE	ODE	OMS	OWT	YAH
AIL	ARK	EON	ICK	ODS	ONE	UKE	

With back hook N

AGO	CAR	EYE	JIN	MAW	PIA	SPA	WEE
AIR	CHI	FER	KIR	MOA	POO	SUN	WYN
ALA	CON	FIR	KOA	MOO	RAI	TAR	YAR
AMI	COO	FOH	LAR	MOR	REI	TEE	YAW
AZO	COR	GAE	LAW	MOW	SAW	THE	YEA
BAR	CUR	GIE	LEA	NOO	SEE	TOO	ZOO
BEE	DAM	GOO	LIE	OPE	SEW	TOR	
BOO	DAW	HAE	LIN	PAW	SHE	TOW	
BRA	DOW	HER	LOO	PEA	SIG	UDO	
BUN	EAR	HEW	LOR	PEE	SKI	UPO	
BUR	EVE	HIS	LOW	PHO	SOW	WAR	

With front hook O

ARS	BIT	GAM	LEA	NUS	PAS	RAD	VUM
BAS	DAH	GEE	LES	OHS	PED	RES	WED
BES	DAS	INK	MAS	OPS	PEN	TIC	YER
BEY	DOR	KAS	MEN	PAH	PES	UTA	YES
BIS	FAY	KAY	NOS	PAL	PUS	UTS	YEZ

With back hook O

ALS	CAP	FID	KAY	LOG	MON	RAT	TAR
ALT	DAD	FIL	KEN	LOT	MUS	RED	TOP
ARC	DAG	FIN	KIN	LUD	NAN	REP	TOR
BOB	DID	GOB	KOB	MAN	OLE	ROT	TOY
BOY	DIN	GYP	LEV	MAY	PEP	SAG	VET
BRO	ERG	HER	LID	MEM	PES	SEG	VIN
BUB	FAD	HOB	LIN	MEN	PIS	SHO	WIN
CAL	FAN	HOM	LIP	MIL	POL	SOL	
CAM	FAR	HYP	LOB	MIS	POM	SUM	

With front hook P

ACE	ALL	ASH	EDS	EST	ICK	LEA	ODS
ACT	ALP	ASS	EEK	HAT	ILL	LED	OKE
ADS	ALS	ATE	EEL	HEW	IMP	LEX	OLE
AGE	ANE	AVE	EKE	HIS	INK	LIE	OMS
AID	ANT	AWL	ELF	HON	INS	LOP	ONE
AIL	ARE	AWN	END	HOS	ION	LOT	ONS
AIN	ARK	AYS	ENS	HOT	ITS	LOW	OOF
AIR	ARS	EAR	EON	HUT	LAT	LUG	OOH
ALE	ART	EAT	ERE	ICE	LAY	LUM	OPE

OPS	OUR	RAT	REX	ROB	SIS	UMP	YAS
ORE	OUT	RAY	REZ	ROD	TUI	UNS	YES
ORT	OXY	REE	RIG	ROM	UGH	UPS	YIN
OSE	RAM	REP	RIM	ROW	UKE	UTS	

With back hook P

BEE	DEE	HAS	LOO	POO	SAL	TAR	WIS
BUM	DOR	HEM	LUM	PRO	SEE	TUM	YAW
BUR	DUM	HOO	MUM	PUL	SHO	VEE	YOM
CAM	GAM	HUM	NEE	RAM	SIM	WAR	
CAR	GAS	JEE	PAL	RAS	SKI	WAS	
CHI	GOO	LAM	PEE	REP	SOU	WEE	
COO	GOR	LEA	PER	ROM	SUM	WHA	
DAM	GUL	LIS	POM	RUM	TAM	WHO	

With front hook Q

AID

With front hook R

ACE	AIL	ANT	AYS	END	IFS	OES	OUT
ADS	AIN	APE	EAR	EST	ILL	OIL	UMP
AFF	AIS	APT	EDS	HOS	INK	OLE	UMS
AFT	ALE	ARE	EEK	ICE	INS	OMS	UNS
AGA	AMI	ASH	EEL	ICH	OAR	OOF	USE
AGE	AMP	ASP	EFS	ICK	OBE	OOT	UTS
AGS	AND	ATE	EFT	IDS	ODE	OPE	YAS
AID	ANI	AVE	EMS	IFF	ODS	OSE	YES

With back hook R

AGA	BOA	DOE	HOE	PEA	SEE	TYE
AGE	BOO	DOR	JEE	PEE	SOU	USE
ALA	BRR	DYE	LEA	PIE	SPA	VEE
AMI	BUR	EVE	LEE	POO	SUE	VIE
APE	CAR	EWE	LIE	PUR	TEA	WEE
AVE	CUR	EYE	MOO	RUE	TIE	YEA
BEE	DEE	FOU	PAR	SEA	TOR	YOU

With front hook S

ABS	ALP	AVE	COT	EEL	ETA	HEW	HOT
AGA	ALS	AWN	COW	EGO	HAD	HIM	HOW
AGE	ALT	AYS	CRY	ELF	HAG	HIN	HUN
AGO	AMP	CAB	CUD	ELL	HAH	HIP	HUT
AGS	AND	CAD	CUM	ELS	HAM	HIT	ICE
AID	ANE	CAM	CUP	EME	HAT	HOD	ICK
AIL	ARK	CAN	CUT	END	HAW	HOE	ILK
AIN	ASH	CAR	EAR	ERA	HAY	HOG	ILL
ALE	ASS	CAT	EAT	ERE	HEN	HOO	IMP
ALL	ATE	COP	EEK	ERS	HES	HOP	INK

INS	LAP	MEW	NUG	ONE	PAY	TAT	UNS
IRE	LAT	MOG	OAK	ONS	PEC	TAW	UPS
ITS	LAW	MUG	OAR	OOT	PED	TET	URD
KAS	LAY	MUT	OBA	OPS	PEW	TEW	WAB
KAT	LED	NAG	OCA	ORA	PIC	TOP	WAG
KEG	LID	NAP	ODA	ORB	PIN	TOT	WAN
KEP	LIP	NAW	ODS	ORE	PIT	TOW	WAP
KID	LIT	NIB	OFT	ORT	POT	TUB	WAT
KIN	LOB	NIP	OHS	OUR	PRY	TUM	WAY
KIP	LOG	NIT	OIL	OWN	PUD	TUN	WIG
KIS	LOP	NOB	OKE	PAM	PUN	TYE	WOP
KIT	LOT	NOG	OLD	PAN	PUR	UGH	WOT
LAB	LOW	NOT	OLE	PAR	TAB	ULU	
LAG	LUG	NOW	OMA	PAS	TAG	UMP	
LAM	LUM	NUB	OMS	PAT	TAR	UMS	

With back hook S

AAH	APO	BEN	CAM	DAG	DOT	ERN	FOO
AAL	APP	BET	CAN	DAH	DOW	ERR	FOP
ABA	ARB	BEY	CAP	DAK	DRY	EST	FOY
ABO	ARC	BIB	CAR	DAL	DUB	ETA	FUB
ABY	ARE	BID	CAT	DAM	DUD	ETH	FUD
ACE	ARF	BIG	CAW	DAN	DUE	EVE	FUG
ACT	ARK	BIN	CAY	DAP	DUG	EWE	FUN
ADD	ARM	BIO	CEE	DAW	DUN	EYE	FUR
ADO	ART	BIT	CEL	DAY	DUO	FAB	GAB
AGA	ASK	BOA	CEP	DEB	DUP	FAD	GAD
AGE	ASP	BOB	CHI	DEE	DYE	FAG	GAE
AHI	ATE	BOD	CIG	DEL	EAR	FAH	GAG
AID	AUK	BOG	COB	DEN	EAT	FAN	GAL
AIL	AVE	BOO	COD	DEP	EBB	FAT	GAM
AIM	AVO	BOP	COG	DEV	ECO	FAY	GAP
AIN	AWE	BOS	COL	DEW	ECU	FED	GAR
AIR	AWL	BOT	CON	DEY	EDH	FEE	GAT
AIT	AWN	BOW	COO	DIB	EEL	FEH	GAY
AJI	AXE	BOY	COP	DIE	EFF	FEM	GED
ALA	AYE	BRA	COR	DIF	EFT	FEN	GEE
ALB	BAA	BRO	COS	DIG	EGG	FES	GEL
ALE	BAD	BUB	COT	DIM	EGO	FET	GEM
ALL	BAG	BUD	COW	DIN	EKE	FEU	GEN
ALP	BAL	BUG	COY	DIP	ELD	FIB	GET
ALT	BAM	BUM	CRU	DIS	ELK	FID	GHI
AMA	BAN	BUN	CUB	DIT	ELL	FIG	GIB
AMI	BAP	BUR	CUD	DOC	ELM	FIL	GID
AMP	BAR	BUS	CUE	DOE	EME	FIN	GIE
AMU	BAS	BUT	CUM	DOG	EMO	FIR	GIF
ANA	BAT	BUY	CUP	DOH	EMU	FIT	GIG
AND	BAY	BYE	CUR	DOL	END	FLU	GIN
ANE	BED	CAB	CUT	DOM	ENG	FOB	GIP
ANI	BEE	CAD	CWM	DON	EON	FOE	GIT
ANT	BEG	CAF	DAB	DOR	ERA	FOG	GNU
APE	BEL	CAL	DAD	DOS	ERG	FON	GOA

GOB	ILK	KUE	MED	NOM	PAS	REB	SEW
GOD	ILL	KYE	MEG	NOW	PAT	REC	SHE
GOO	IMP	LAB	MEL	NUB	PAW	RED	SIB
GOY	INK	LAC	MEM	NUG	PAY	REE	SIC
GUL	INN	LAD	MES	NUN	PEA	REF	SIG
GUM	ION	LAG	MEW	NUT	PEC	REG	SIM
GUN	IRE	LAH	MHO	OAF	PED	REI	SIN
GUT	IRK	LAM	MIB	OAK	PEE	REM	SIP
GUV	ISM	LAP	MIC	OAR	PEG	REP	SIR
GUY	JAB	LAR	MID	OAT	PEH	RET	SIT
GYM	JAG	LAS	MIG	OBA	PEN	REV	SKA
GYP	JAM	LAT	MIL	OBE	PEP	RHO	SKI
HAE	JAR	LAV	MIR	OBI	PET	RIA	SOB
HAG	JAW	LAW	MIS	OCA	PEW	RIB	SOD
HAH	JAY	LAY	MOA	ODA	PHI	RID	SOH
HAM	JEE	LEA	MOB	ODD	PHO	RIF	SOL
HAP	JET	LEE	MOC	ODE	PIA	RIG	SOM
HAT	JEW	LEG	MOD	OFF	PIC	RIM	SON
HAW	JIB	LEI	MOG	OHM	PIE	RIN	SOP
HAY	JIG	LEK	MOL	OIK	PIG	RIP	SOT
HEH	JIN	LES	MOM	OIL	PIN	ROB	SOU
HEM	JOB	LET	MON	OKA	PIP	ROC	SOW
HEN	JOE	LEV	MOO	OKE	PIS	ROD	SOY
HEP	JOG	LEY	MOP	OLD	PIT	ROE	SPA
HER	JOT	LIB	MOR	OLE	POD	ROM	SRI
HET	JOW	LID	MOS	OMA	POI	ROO	SUB
HEW	JOY	LIE	MOT	ONE	POL	ROT	SUE
HIE	JUG	LIN	MOW	ONO	POM	ROW	SUK
HIM	JUT	LIP	MUD	OOH	POO	RUB	SUM
HIN	KAB	LIT	MUG	OOT	POP	RUE	SUN
HIP	KAE	LOB	MUM	OPA	POT	RUG	SUP
HIS	KAF	LOG	MUN	OPE	POW	RUM	SUQ
HIT	KAT	LOO	MUS	OPT	PRO	RUN	SUS
HOB	KAY	LOP	MUT	ORB	PSI	RUT	TAB
HOD	KEA	LOT	MYC	ORC	PUB	RYA	TAD
HOE	KEF	LOW	NAB	ORE	PUD	RYE	TAG
HOG	KEG	LUD	NAE	ORG	PUG	RYU	TAM
HOM	KEN	LUG	NAG	ORT	PUL	SAB	TAN
HON	KEP	LUM	NAN	OSE	PUN	SAC	TAO
HOP	KEY	LUN	NAP	OUD	PUP	SAG	TAP
HOT	KHI	LUV	NAV	OUR	PUR	SAL	TAR
HOW	KID	LYE	NAY	OUT	PUS	SAN	TAS
HOY	KIF	MAC	NEB	OWE	PUT	SAP	TAT
HUB	KIN	MAD	NEG	OWL	PYA	SAW	TAU
HUE	KIP	MAE	NET	OWN	PYE	SAY	TAV
HUG	KIR	MAG	NEW	OWT	QAT	SEA	TAW
HUM	KIS	MAM	NIB	PAC	RAD	SEC	TEA
HUN	KIT	MAN	NIL	PAD	RAG	SEE	TEC
HUT	KOA	MAP	NIM	PAK	RAI	SEG	TED
HYP	KOB	MAR	NIP	PAL	RAM	SEI	TEE
ICE	KOI	MAS	NIT	PAM	RAP	SEL	TEG
ICH	KOP	MAT	NOB	PAN	RAT	SER	TEL
ICK	KOR	MAW	NOD	PAP	RAW	SET	TEN
IGG	KOS	MAY	NOG	PAR	RAY	SEV	TET

TEW	TOW	UKE	VAU	WAD	WIG	YAK	YOU
TIC	TOY	ULU	VAV	WAE	WIN	YAM	YOW
TIE	TSK	UMP	VAW	WAG	WIS	YAP	YUK
TIL	TUB	UNI	VEE	WAN	WIT	YAW	YUP
TIN	TUG	URB	VET	WAP	WOE	YAY	ZAG
TIP	TUI	URD	VID	WAR	WOG	YEA	ZAP
TIT	TUM	URN	VIE	WAT	WOK	YEN	ZED
TOD	TUN	URP	VIG	WAW	WON	YEP	ZEE
TOE	TUP	USE	VIM	WAY	WOO	YEW	ZEK
TOG	TUT	UTA	VIN	WEB	WOP	YID	ZEP
TOM	TWA	UTE	VOE	WED	WOT	YIN	ZIG
TON	TWO	VAC	VOG	WEE	WOW	YIP	ZIN
TOP	TYE	VAN	VOW	WEN	WYE	YOB	ZIP
TOR	UDO	VAR	VUG	WET	WYN	YOD	ZIT
TOT	UGH	VAT	WAB	WHY	YAG	YOK	ZOO

With front hook T

ABS	ART	ERN	IFF	OMS	RAD	ROW	WIG
ACE	ASK	EST	ILL	ONE	RAM	RUE	WIN
ACT	ASS	ETH	INS	ONS	RAP	RUG	WIT
ADS	ATE	HAE	IRE	OOT	RAY	UMP	WOS
AGS	EAR	HAT	ITS	OPE	REE	UMS	YER
AIL	EAT	HAW	IVY	OPS	REF	UNS	YES
AIN	EDS	HEM	ODS	ORA	REM	UPS	YIN
ALA	EEL	HEN	OES	ORC	RES	URD	
ALE	EFF	HEW	OFF	ORE	RET	URN	
ALL	EGG	HEY	OFT	ORS	RIG	UTS	
AMP	ELL	HIN	OIL	ORT	RIM	WAE	
APE	ELS	HIS	OKE	OUR	RIP	WAS	
ARE	END	HUG	OLD	OUT	ROD	WAT	
ARS	ENS	ICK	OLE	OWN	ROT	WEE	

With back hook T

AIR	CAR	DOS	GOA	LIS	NET	RAP	TAR
BAH	CEL	DUE	HAE	LOO	NEW	REF	TAU
BAS	CHI	DUI	HAS	LUN	NOW	RES	TEA
BAT	CIS	DUN	HEN	MAR	OBI	RIF	TEN
BEE	COL	ERS	HES	MAS	PAC	ROO	TES
BEL	COO	FAR	HIN	MAT	PAN	RUN	TIL
BEN	COS	FAS	HIS	MEL	PAR	SAL	TIN
BES	CUR	FEE	HOO	MIL	PAS	SEA	TOO
BIN	DAW	FES	HOS	MIS	PEA	SEC	TOR
BIT	DEB	FIX	HUN	MIX	PEN	SEN	TWA
BOA	DEE	FON	JUS	MOA	PER	SET	UNI
BOO	DEF	FOO	KEN	MOL	PES	SEX	VAS
BOT	DEL	FOR	KEP	MOO	PHO	SHA	VEX
BRA	DEN	GAS	KIS	MOR	PIN	SHO	WAN
BUN	DIE	GEL	LAS	MOS	POS	SKA	WAR
BUS	DIN	GEN	LEE	MOT	PUN	SKI	WAS
BUT	DIP	GIF	LES	MUS	PUT	SPA	WAT
CAN	DOL	GIS	LIN	MUT	RAN	SUE	WEE

WEN	WHA	WIS	WON	WOS	YET

With front hook U

DON	DOS	NIT	PAS	SER	TAS	TES

With back hook U

BED	FUG	LEK	MEN	PUP	THO
BUB	GEN	LIE	MUM	TAB	TUT
EME	LAT	LIT	PUD	TEG	VAT

With front hook V

AIL	ALE	APE	END	ICE	ILL	LOG	ROW
AIN	AMP	ARS	ERA	IDS	INS	OES	UGH
AIR	ANE	ELD	EST	IFF	LEI	OLE	

With back hook V

PER

With front hook W

AAH	AIT	ARS	EDS	ETA	HIN	INK	ORE
ABS	ALE	ART	EEK	HAM	HIP	INS	ORT
ADS	ALL	ASH	EEL	HAP	HIT	IRE	RAP
AFF	AND	ASP	EFT	HAT	HOM	ITS	YES
AFT	ANE	ATT	ELD	HEN	HOP	OES	
AGE	ANT	AUK	ELL	HET	HUP	OKE	
AGS	ANY	AVE	END	HEW	ICH	OLD	
AIL	ARE	AWL	ENS	HEY	ICK	ONS	
AIN	ARK	AYS	ERE	HID	ILL	OOF	
AIR	ARM	EAR	EST	HIM	IMP	OPS	

With back hook W

ANE	BRA	FRO	SHA	SHO	VIE
AVO	BRO	PRO	SHE	THE	

With back hook X

APE	CAL	CRU	EAU	FLU	JEU	JIN

With front hook Y

AFF	AWL	EGG	ENS	ODS	OUR	UPS
AGE	AWN	ELD	IDS	OKE	OWE	WIS
AGS	AYS	ELK	ILL	OOF	OWL	
ARE	EAR	ELL	INS	ORE	UKE	

With back hook Y

AIR	COL	DOR	HOM	MAN	OLD	POX	TON
ALL	CON	DOT	ICK	MIR	ORB	PUN	TOR
ARM	COP	EEL	IFF	MOL	ORG	QUA	TOW
ART	COR	EGG	ILL	MON	OWL	RIM	VAR
ASH	COS	ELM	INK	MOP	PAC	RUB	VIN
AWA	COW	FOG	JOE	NAV	PAL	SAG	WAD
AWN	COZ	FOX	LAC	NIX	PAT	SEX	WAN
BOD	DEF	FUR	LAD	NOS	PIN	SHA	WAR
BOG	DEN	GAB	LEV	OAK	PIP	SPA	WAX
BOX	DEW	GAM	LIN	OAT	PIT	SUM	WIN
BRA	DEX	GAP	LOG	OBE	PIX	THE	
BUR	DID	GOB	LOR	OIL	POL	TIN	
BUS	DOG	GOR	LUN	OKA	POS	TOD	

With front hook Z

AGS	ARF	EST	ILL	ITS
ANY	EDS	ETA	INS	ONE

With back hook Z

DIT	FIZ	GEE	JEE	PHI	PUT	SPA	TIZ

Chapter 2: Four letter words with hooks

With front hook A

AHED	CRED	GAZE	LIAS	MITY	RIEL	URIC
ARGH	CUTE	GENE	LIEN	MOLE	RISE	VAIL
BACK	DEEM	GENT	LIKE	MORT	ROSE	VAST
BASE	DITS	GIST	LINE	MUCK	RUMS	VERT
BASH	DOBE	GLEE	LIST	MUSE	SCOT	VOID
BATE	DORE	GLEY	LIVE	NEAR	SHED	VOWS
BEAM	DOWN	GLOW	LOFT	NILS	SHEN	WAIT
BETS	DOZE	GONE	LOIN	NODE	SHES	WAKE
BIDE	DUST	GREE	LONE	PACE	SIDE	WARD
BLED	EGIS	HEAD	LONG	PART	SKED	WARE
BODE	EONS	HOLD	LOOF	PEAK	SKEW	WASH
BOIL	FIRE	HULL	LOUD	PEEK	SPIC	WING
BOON	FOOT	IDES	LUMS	PHIS	STIR	WOKE
BORT	FORE	IRED	MAIN	PIAN	SURA	YINS
BOUT	FOUL	ISLE	MASS	PING	SWIM	ZINE
BRIS	FRIT	ITCH	MAZE	PISH	TAPS	ZOIC
BUTS	GAIN	JUGA	MEND	PODS	TILT	
BUZZ	GAMA	LACK	MICE	PORT	TOLL	
BYES	GAPE	LAND	MIDS	PSIS	TOMS	
COCK	GARS	LANE	MINE	REAL	TONE	
COLD	GATE	LANG	MIRS	RETE	TONY	
CORN	GAVE	LATE	MISS	RIAS	TRIP	

With back hook A

BALS	DERM	GALE	LIMP	PALS	SALP	TEGU
BAND	DONG	GAMB	LING	PANG	SALS	TEST
BULL	DORS	GENU	LOOF	PARK	SANG	TINE
BURK	DOSH	GRAM	LOTS	PASH	SCOP	TONG
BURS	DOUM	GRAN	LUFF	PAST	SCUT	TORT
CALL	DOUR	HAIK	LUTE	PERE	SEPT	TREF
CELL	DRAM	HALM	MARK	PILE	SHIV	UNCI
CHIC	DURR	HERM	MASS	PINT	SIGN	VEST
CHIN	FACT	HOOK	MOOL	PLAY	SOFT	VILL
COAL	FANG	HOST	MULL	PRIM	SORT	VIOL
COCO	FAUN	JIBB	MURR	PUCK	SPIC	VOLT
COMM	FELL	KIND	NORI	PULK	SUNN	WALL
COST	FEST	LEPT	OMAS	PUNK	TANG	WISH
DELT	FOSS	LIMB	PALE	RAGG	TANK	YURT

With front hook B

AALS	ALKY	ARBS	ATES	EAUX	ESTS	ICES
ABAS	ALLS	ARES	AWLS	EERY	ETAS	IDES
AILS	ALLY	ARFS	AWNS	EGAD	ETHS	IFFY
AIRN	ALMS	ARKS	EACH	ELLS	HAJI	ILKS
AITS	ANAL	ARMS	EARS	ENDS	HANG	ILLS
ALAS	ANDS	ARMY	EAST	ERGS	HOOT	ILLY
ALES	ANES	ASKS	EATS	ESES	HUTS	IOTA

IRKS	LEAK	LOOP	OLES	RAID	RICK	RUIN
ITCH	LEAR	LOTS	ONCE	RAIL	RIDE	RUNG
LABS	LECH	LOWN	ONES	RAIN	RIGS	RUNT
LACK	LEND	LOWS	ONUS	RAKE	RILL	RUSH
LADE	LENT	LUES	OOTS	RAND	RIMS	RUSK
LAGS	LESS	LUFF	OOZE	RANK	RING	RUTS
LAHS	LEST	LUNT	OOZY	RANT	RINK	UMPH
LAIN	LETS	LUSH	ORAL	RASH	RINS	UMPS
LAME	LIMP	OARS	ORES	RATS	RISK	UNCO
LAMS	LIMY	OAST	ORTS	RAVE	ROAD	URBS
LAND	LING	OATS	OUTS	RAWS	ROCK	URDS
LANK	LINK	OCHE	OWED	RAYS	ROIL	URNS
LASE	LINY	ODES	OWLS	RAZE	ROOD	URPS
LAST	LIPS	OFFS	OWSE	READ	ROOK	URSA
LATE	LITE	OGLE	OXER	REAM	ROOM	USED
LATS	LOBS	OILS	OXES	REDE	ROOS	USES
LAWN	LOCK	OINK	RACE	REED	ROSE	UTES
LAWS	LOGS	OKEH	RADS	REES	ROSY	
LAZE	LOOM	OLDS	RAGS	RENT	ROWS	

With back hook B

BLUR	DEMO	PLUM	THRO
CUBE	MANE	SLUR	ZINE

With front hook C

ABLE	ARSE	HECK	HUMS	LEGS	LUMP	ORBY
ACHE	ARTS	HEMS	HUNK	LEPT	LUNG	ORES
AGED	ASKS	HEST	HURL	LICK	LUNK	OSES
AGER	ATES	HETH	ILIA	LIFT	OAST	OUCH
AGES	AULD	HEWS	INCH	LIMB	OATS	OVEN
AIDS	AVER	HICK	IONS	LIME	OBIA	OVER
AINS	AVES	HIDE	IRES	LINE	OCAS	OWED
AIRN	AWED	HILI	LACK	LING	ODAS	OWLS
ALIF	EASE	HILL	LADE	LINK	ODES	OXES
ALLS	ELLS	HINS	LADS	LIPS	OFFS	OYER
ALMS	EROS	HIPS	LAGS	LITS	OILS	RACK
AMAS	HAIR	HITS	LAMP	LOCK	OKES	RAFT
AMIS	HAMS	HIVE	LAMS	LOGS	OLDS	RAGS
AMPS	HANG	HOCK	LANG	LONE	OLES	RAKE
ANAL	HANT	HOKE	LANK	LOOT	OMAS	RAMP
ANES	HAPS	HOLO	LAPS	LOPS	OMER	RAMS
ANNA	HARD	HONS	LASH	LOSE	ONES	RANK
ANON	HARE	HOOK	LASS	LOTH	ONTO	RAPE
ANTS	HARK	HOPS	LAST	LOTS	ONUS	RAPS
APED	HARM	HOSE	LAVE	LOUD	OOPS	RASH
APER	HART	HOWS	LAWS	LOUR	OOTS	RATE
APES	HATS	HUBS	LAYS	LOUT	OPAL	RAVE
APOS	HAWS	HUCK	LEAN	LOVE	OPED	RAWS
ARBS	HAYS	HUFF	LEAR	LOWN	OPEN	RAZE
ARES	HEAP	HUGS	LEEK	LUCK	OPES	REAM
ARKS	HEAT	HUMP	LEFT	LUES	ORAL	REDO

REDS	REST	RIPE	ROOK	RUDE	RUST	URDS
REED	RIBS	RIPS	ROUP	RUMP	UKES	URNS
REEK	RICK	ROCK	ROWS	RUSE	UNIT	UTES
REEL	RIME	ROCS	RUCK	RUSH	URBS	

With back hook C

| ANTI | CONI | ILEA | LOTI | SERA | TOPI | YOGI |
| CODE | DURO | ILIA | MAGI | TARO | TORI | YONI |

With front hook D

ACES	EARS	ICED	OILY	RAFT	RECK	RUMS
ADOS	EATH	ICES	OLES	RAGS	REED	RUSE
AIRY	EAVE	ICKS	OOZY	RAIL	REES	RYAS
ALES	ECOS	ICKY	OPAS	RAIN	REGS	UKES
ALLY	EKED	ILLS	OPED	RAKE	REST	UMBO
AMPS	EKES	ILLY	OPES	RAMS	RIBS	UMPS
ARBS	ELLS	INKS	ORES	RANK	RIFT	URNS
ARES	EMES	INKY	OSES	RAPE	RILL	WALE
ARKS	EMIC	IRKS	OUTS	RATS	RINK	WELL
ARTS	EMIT	ITCH	OVEN	RAVE	RIPS	WELT
ASHY	EMOS	JINN	OWED	RAWS	RIVE	WINE
ATES	EVIL	JINS	OWIE	RAYS	ROLL	
AUNT	EXES	OATS	OWNS	READ	ROVE	
AWED	HOLE	OBES	OWSE	REAM	RUBS	
AWNS	HOWS	OFFS	RAFF	REAR	RUGS	

With back hook D

ABLE	BOAR	CONE	DREE	FLUE	HADE	JAPE
ACHE	BODE	COPE	DUDE	FREE	HALE	JIBE
ACNE	BONE	CORE	DUKE	FUME	HARE	JIVE
ACRE	BORE	COTE	DUPE	FUSE	HATE	JOKE
ADZE	BRAN	COVE	DURE	FUZE	HAZE	JUKE
AGUE	BREE	CROW	DYKE	GADI	HEAR	KITE
AIDE	BROO	CUBE	EASE	GAGE	HIDE	KNEE
ALAN	CAGE	CURE	EAVE	GALE	HIKE	LACE
ALKY	CAKE	DARE	ECHE	GAME	HIRE	LADE
AMEN	CANE	DATE	EDGE	GAPE	HIVE	LAIR
ANTE	CAPE	DAZE	ELAN	GATE	HOAR	LAKE
AXLE	CARE	DEKE	FACE	GAZE	HOKE	LAME
BAKE	CASE	DELE	FADE	GIBE	HOLE	LASE
BALE	CAUL	DICE	FAKE	GLEE	HOME	LATE
BANE	CAVE	DIKE	FAME	GLUE	HONE	LAVE
BARE	CEDE	DINE	FARE	GORE	HOPE	LAZE
BASE	CERE	DIVE	FATE	GRAN	HOSE	LIAR
BATE	CHAR	DOLE	FAZE	GREE	HYPE	LIKE
BEAR	CITE	DOME	FETE	GRIN	IDLE	LIME
BIDE	CLUE	DOPE	FIFE	GUAR	ILIA	LINE
BIKE	CODE	DOSE	FILE	GYBE	ISLE	LIVE
BLIN	COKE	DOTE	FINE	GYRE	IZAR	LOBE
BLUE	COLE	DOZE	FIRE	GYVE	JADE	LOPE

LOVE	MUSE	PIPE	RICE	SIZE	TONE	WAKE
LOWE	MUTE	PLEA	RILE	SKEE	TOPE	WALE
LUBE	NAME	PLIE	RIME	SLUE	TOTE	WANE
LUGE	NIDE	POKE	RIPE	SOLE	TREE	WARE
LURE	NIXE	POLE	RIVE	SOLI	TRUE	WAVE
LUTE	NOMA	PORE	ROBE	SORE	TUBE	WEAL
LYSE	NOSE	POSE	ROPE	SPAE	TUNE	WEIR
MACE	NOTE	PREE	ROSE	SPUE	TWEE	WIFE
MANE	NUKE	PUKE	ROVE	STYE	TYNE	WILE
MATE	OGEE	PULE	RULE	TAME	TYPE	WINE
MAUN	OGLE	RACE	RYKE	TAPE	TYRE	WIPE
MAZE	OOZE	RAGE	SABE	TARE	ULNA	WIRE
METE	PACE	RAKE	SANE	TASE	URGE	WISE
MIKE	PAGE	RANI	SATE	TEIN	VANE	WITE
MIME	PALE	RAPE	SAVE	THIR	VAPE	WIVE
MINE	PANE	RARE	SERE	TIDE	VICE	WYLE
MIRE	PARE	RASE	SHEN	TILE	VINE	WYTE
MIRI	PATE	RATE	SHOE	TIME	VISE	YOKE
MOPE	PAVE	RAVE	SIDE	TINE	VOLE	YOWE
MOVE	PIKE	RAZE	SIPE	TIRE	VOTE	YUKE
MULE	PILE	READ	SIRE	TOKE	WADE	ZONE
MURE	PINE	REDE	SITE	TOLE	WAGE	

With front hook E

AGER	DUCT	LATE	MAIL	NOWS	RASE	TICS
AVES	GADS	LINT	MEND	PACT	RODE	TUIS
BONY	GEST	LITE	MICS	PEES	ROSE	TWEE
BOOK	IKON	LOIN	MIRS	PICS	SCAR	VENT
CRUS	KING	LOPE	MOTE	POXY	SCOT	VERT
DITS	LAIN	LUDE	NEMA	QUID	STOP	VERY
DUCE	LAND	LUTE	NORM	QUIP	TAPE	

With back hook E

ABAS	BAST	CARL	CRIP	FLIT	GRAD	KENT
AGON	BATH	CARS	CRUD	FORM	GRAT	KERN
ALAN	BELL	CART	CRUS	FORT	GRID	KITH
ALGA	BERM	CAST	CURS	FOSS	GRIM	LAPS
AMID	BING	CHAP	CYMA	FUGU	GRIP	LATH
AMIN	BIRL	CHAR	DAUB	FUSE	GRUM	LEAS
AMUS	BLAM	CHID	DENS	FUZE	GUID	LENS
ANIL	BLAT	CHIN	DING	GAFF	HAST	LOCH
ANIS	BOMB	CLAD	DONE	GAMB	HAUT	LOCI
ANSA	BORN	CLON	DOWS	GEES	HAWS	LONG
ANTA	BOWS	COHO	EMYD	GEST	HIRE	LOOS
AQUA	BRED	COMA	ERAS	GLAD	HOLM	LOUP
AREA	BRIN	COMB	EROS	GLED	IMID	LOWS
AURA	BROS	COPS	FARL	GLIM	INBY	LUNG
AXIL	BRUT	CORS	FESS	GLOB	IRON	MACH
AXON	BURK	COUP	FILL	GLUM	JAMB	MAIL
BARB	BURS	COXA	FLAK	GLUT	JEEZ	MANS
BARD	BUTT	CRAP	FLAM	GOOS	JESS	MARS

MASS	PARS	RAGE	SETA	SOUS	TELA	UNDE
MATT	PASS	RAIS	SHAD	SPAR	TENS	UNIT
MERL	PAST	RAKE	SHAM	SPAT	TERN	UPBY
MILL	PEAG	RAMI	SHIN	SPIC	THAN	URSA
MINA	PEAS	RANG	SHIT	SPIK	THEM	VENA
MINK	PHON	RATH	SHIV	SPIN	THIN	VITA
MOOS	PLAN	RAZE	SHMO	SPIT	THRO	VOLT
MORA	PLAT	RENT	SHOT	STAG	TING	WACK
MORS	PLEB	RILL	SHUT	STAR	TOGA	WALI
MOST	PLOY	RINS	SIDH	STAT	TOIL	WAST
MOTT	PLUM	ROOS	SING	STOA	TOPE	WHIN
MURR	POIS	ROUT	SIRE	STOP	TOPH	WHIT
NEUM	PRAT	RUFF	SKAT	SUED	TORS	WITH
NOVA	PRIM	RUGA	SKIT	SUET	TORT	WRIT
OBES	PROB	SCAR	SLAT	SUIT	TRAD	YOUS
OBOL	PROS	SCOP	SLID	SWAG	TRIP	ZOEA
ODYL	PULS	SCUT	SLIM	SYCE	TROD	ZONA
OUPH	PUPA	SEIS	SLIP	TACH	TROP	
OXID	PURE	SELL	SLOP	TASS	TUBA	
OXIM	PURS	SEME	SMIT	TAWS	TWIN	
PARA	QUIT	SENT	SNIP	TEAS	ULNA	

With front hook F

ABLE	AULD	EWER	LAPS	LOCK	OOTS	RESH
ACED	AVES	EYER	LASH	LOGS	ORBS	RETS
ACES	AWNS	ICES	LATS	LONG	ORBY	RIGS
ACTA	AWNY	ILKS	LAVA	LOPS	ORDO	RILL
ACTS	AXED	ILLS	LAWS	LOSS	ORES	RISE
ADOS	AXES	ILLY	LAYS	LOTA	ORTS	RISK
AERY	EARS	INCH	LEAS	LOUR	OSSA	RITZ
AGIN	EASE	INKS	LEER	LOUT	OURS	ROCK
AILS	EAST	IRED	LEES	LOWN	OWLS	ROES
AIRS	EATS	IRES	LEET	LOWS	OXES	ROWS
AIRY	EELS	ITCH	LEYS	LUES	OYER	RUGS
ALLS	ELLS	LABS	LICK	LUFF	RACK	RUMP
ANES	EMES	LACK	LIED	LUMP	RAGS	USED
ANGA	ENDS	LAGS	LIER	LUNG	RAIL	USES
ANON	ERNS	LAIR	LIES	LUNK	RANK	
ARES	ESSE	LAKE	LING	LUSH	RAPS	
ARMS	ESTS	LAKY	LINT	LUTE	RATS	
ARTS	ETAS	LAME	LIPS	OILS	RAYS	
ATES	ETCH	LAMS	LITE	OLDS	REED	
AUGH	EVER	LANK	LITS	OLIO	REES	

With back hook F

BRIE	GONE	POUF	SHEA	TREY
GANE	HOWF	SCAR	TRAY	

With front hook G

ABBA	ABLE	AGED	AGER	AGES	AINS	AITS

ALAS	ETAS	LAND	LOOP	ORAL	RAYS	ROAN
ALES	HAST	LASS	LOPS	ORES	RAZE	ROOM
ALLS	HATS	LAZE	LORY	OUTS	REED	ROPE
ALLY	HAUT	LAZY	LOSS	OWNS	REEK	ROTS
AMAS	HOST	LEAN	LOST	OXES	REES	ROUP
AMIN	ILLS	LEDE	LOUT	RACE	RIDE	ROUT
AMPS	ILLY	LEEK	LOVE	RADS	RIDS	ROVE
APED	IMPS	LEES	LOWS	RAFT	RIFF	ROWS
APER	INCH	LEET	LUES	RAIL	RIFT	RUBS
APES	INKS	LENS	LUGS	RAIN	RIGS	RUES
ARBS	IRON	LEYS	LUMS	RAMP	RILL	RUFF
ASPS	ITCH	LIAS	LUTE	RAMS	RIME	RUMP
ATES	LACE	LIME	NOME	RAND	RIMY	RUNT
AUNT	LADE	LINT	OATS	RANT	RIND	UMBO
EARS	LADS	LOAM	OATY	RAPE	RINS	UMMA
ELDS	LADY	LOBE	OLDS	RASP	RIOT	URGE
EMMY	LAIR	LOBS	OMER	RATE	RIPE	URUS
ESTS	LAMS	LOOM	OOPS	RAVE	RIPS	WINE

With back hook G

AGIN	BLIN	CHIN	COHO	SPAN	SWAN	THIN
ALAN	BRIN	CLAN	RUIN	STUN	THAN	TYIN

With front hook H

AILS	ANTS	AWED	ELMS	IDES	OLLA	OVER
AIRS	ARES	AZAN	EMES	ILLS	OMAS	OWES
AIRY	ARKS	EARS	EMIC	ILLY	OMER	OWLS
AJIS	ARMS	EATH	ERNS	INKY	ONES	UMPH
ALES	ARTS	EATS	EROS	IRED	OOPS	UMPS
ALLS	ASPS	EAVE	ESTS	IRES	OOTS	URDS
ALMA	ATES	EDGE	ETHS	ITCH	OPED	
ALMS	AUGH	EDGY	EWER	OARS	OPES	
ALTS	AUNT	EELS	EXED	OKES	ORAL	
ANDS	AVER	EFTS	EXES	OLDS	OSES	
ANSA	AVES	ELLS	ICKS	OLES	OURS	

With back hook H

ABAS	BUMP	GIRT	MARC	PUJA	SURA	UMMA
AIRT	BURG	GRIT	MARS	RAJA	SWAT	WOOS
ALMA	CLOT	HEAT	MERC	RAYA	SYNC	WORT
ALME	CRUS	HORA	MUST	ROUT	TENT	
BAIT	EPHA	HUMP	MYNA	SANG	TILT	
BIMA	FLUS	KHET	NEAT	SLOT	TOOT	
BOOT	FORT	LAIC	PERC	SMIT	TORA	
BRAS	FRIT	LEAS	PHIS	SOOT	TORC	
BRIT	GALA	LOTA	PLUS	SUBA	TROT	

With front hook I

CONS	DEAL	DENT	DOLS	KATS	LEAL	MAGE

MAMS	MINE	RATE	RING	VIED	
MIDS	ODIC	RIDS	SLED	VIES	

With back hook I

ARCH	CELL	FILM	KORA	PARD	SERA	TOPO
BARF	COAT	FUND	LASS	PEPS	SHOG	TORI
BASS	COMB	HADJ	LATH	PIAN	SOLD	TORS
BIND	CROC	HAJJ	LICH	PILE	SOLE	VILL
BLIN	CULT	HONG	LIMB	POOR	STOA	VOLT
BUFF	DASH	HOUR	LOGO	PRIM	SWAM	XYST
CAMP	DEMO	IAMB	LUNG	PUTT	TARS	
CARP	DISC	JINN	OBOL	SCUD	TEMP	
CEIL	DOSA	KIBE	PALP	SENT	TOPH	

With front hook J

AGER	APES	EMMY	IMMY	OKES	OWLS	UMPS
AILS	AUKS	ESSE	INKS	OLES	OWLY	UNCO
ANES	AUNT	ESTS	INNS	ONES	UDOS	UNTO
APED	AWED	IFFY	ISMS	OUST	UKES	UPON
APER	ELLS	ILLS	NANA	OWED	UMBO	UTES

With front hook K

AILS	BARS	EVIL	ICKS	LICK	NEED	RAIS
AINS	EDGE	EXES	ICKY	LONG	NITS	RAYS
ALES	EELS	EYED	ILLS	LOOF	NOBS	RILL
ALIF	ERNE	EYER	INKS	LUGE	NOCK	UDOS
ANAS	ERNS	HATS	INKY	LUTZ	NOWS	URUS
ANES	ETAS	HETH	IRKS	NAPS	NURL	YACK
ARTS	ETCH	HETS	IWIS	NAVE	RAFT	YAKS

With back hook K

BLIN	CAUL	CLON	GREE	SHOO	SPUN	THAN
BLOC	CHAR	CROC	KAMI	SKIN	STAR	THIN
BRAN	CHIC	FLAN	PLAN	SPAN	STIR	TORS
BRIN	CHIN	FLIC	PULI	SPAR	STUN	TWIN
BRIS	CHOC	FLOC	REIN	SPEC	SWAN	
BROO	CLAN	GLEE	SAME	SPIC	TARO	

With front hook L

ACED	ANDS	AVER	EARS	EGER	INKS	OCHE
ACES	ANES	AVES	EASE	EGGY	INKY	ODES
AGER	APSE	AWED	EAST	ENDS	INNS	OOPS
AIRS	ARCH	AWNS	EAVE	ESES	IONS	OOTS
AIRY	ARES	AWNY	EDGE	ETCH	ISLE	OPED
ALLS	ARKS	AXES	EDGY	EVER	LAMA	OPES
AMAS	ARUM	AYIN	EERY	EXES	OAFS	ORAL
AMIA	AUGH	EACH	EFTS	ICKS	OATH	ORES
AMPS	AURA	EARN	EGAL	IMPS	OBES	OSES

OTIC	OUTS	OWES	OXES	UMPS
OTTO	OVER	OWLY	UDOS	UTES
OURS	OWED	OWSE	ULUS	YARD

With back hook L

ALGA	CRAW	HORA	MAIL	PERI	SHEA	VINY
ALKY	DEVI	HOSE	META	PICA	SHOO	VITA
ALLY	DRAW	HOVE	MODE	PIPA	SORE	WHEE
ANNA	DURA	IDEA	MOLA	PROW	SURA	WHIR
AREA	DYNE	IDYL	MORA	PUPA	TEPA	YOKE
AURA	EASE	ILEA	MORE	QUAI	THIO	ZOEA
BABE	FETA	ILIA	MOTE	RATE	THIR	ZONA
BABU	FUSE	JUGA	MURA	RAVE	TRIO	ZORI
BORA	GAVE	JURA	NAVE	RUBE	TUBA	
BRAW	GLIA	KETO	NOTA	RUGA	UREA	
CAME	GNAR	KNEE	OFFA	SCOW	UVEA	
CECA	GROW	KNUR	PANE	SERA	VASA	
COMA	GRUE	LOCA	PAPA	SETA	VENA	
COXA	HAZE	LOSE	PEAR	SHAW	VINA	

With front hook M

ACED	ALES	ANUS	AXED	ICKY	ODES	ORTS
ACES	ALLS	ARCH	AXES	IFFY	OILS	OTTO
ACHE	ALMS	ARCS	AXIS	IGGS	OKES	OUCH
ACRO	ALTS	ARES	EATS	ILIA	OLDS	OVER
AGES	AMAS	ARIA	ELDS	ILKS	OLDY	OWED
AGMA	AMBO	ARKS	ELLS	ILLS	OLES	UMPS
AIDS	AMIE	ARSE	EMES	INKS	ONOS	UNIS
AILS	ANAS	ARTS	EMOS	IRED	OOTS	USED
AIMS	ANES	ASHY	ENDS	IRES	OPED	USER
AINS	ANGA	ASKS	ESNE	IRID	OPES	USES
AIRS	ANNA	ATES	ETHS	IRKS	ORAL	UTES
ALAR	ANTA	AWED	ICKS	OATS	ORES	

With back hook M

ABYS	DENI	HAUL	PASH	SATE	THRU
ALAR	FLEA	MAXI	REAL	SEIS	TOTE
BROO	FORA	MINI	REAR	SHAW	
CHAR	HARE	MODE	RETE	SPAS	

With front hook N

ACRE	APES	AVES	ESTS	IFFY	OMEN	UKES
AGAS	ARCO	EARS	EVER	ILLS	ONCE	URDS
AILS	ARCS	EATH	EVES	ODES	ONES	
ALAS	ARES	EATS	EWER	OILS	OPAL	
ANAS	ARKS	EDDY	ICKS	OILY	OSES	
ANNA	ATES	EONS	IDES	OMAS	OWTS	

With back hook N

ATMA	DEMO	GROW	LINE	RAMI	SHOO	TOYO
BLAW	DIVA	GYRO	LIVE	RAVE	SHOW	TREE
BLOW	DJIN	HALO	LODE	REDO	SHUL	TWEE
BRAW	DOVE	HAVE	LOGO	RIPE	SIRE	VEGA
BROW	DOZE	HERO	MAYA	RISE	SKEE	WAKE
BURA	DRAW	HOSE	MIRI	RIVE	SOLA	WHEE
CAPO	FANO	KNOW	NOME	ROUE	SOLO	WIDE
CHAI	FLOW	LADE	OLDE	ROVE	SOMA	WOKE
CODE	FROW	LATE	OWSE	SARI	SPUR	WOVE
CONI	GIRO	LEAR	PARE	SATI	TABU	YEAR
COPE	GIVE	LIKE	PATE	SEME	TAKE	YOGI
COVE	GNAW	LIMA	PREE	SHAW	TOKE	YOUR
CROW	GREE	LIME	PURI	SHEW	TOLA	

With front hook O

AVES	DORS	GIVE	MASA	PING	SCAR	ZONE
BEYS	DOUR	GLED	MEGA	RACY	VARY	
BIAS	FAYS	INKS	OHED	RANG	VERT	
BITS	GAMS	KAYS	PALS	RATE	VINE	
BOLE	GEED	LIVE	PENS	READ	VOID	
DAHS	GEES	LOGY	PINE	RIEL	WING	

With back hook O

AMID	CACA	COMP	GUST	MOLT	PIAN	SEXT
AMIN	CAME	CRED	HALL	MOSS	PING	SICK
BANC	CAMP	CRUD	HELL	MOTT	PINK	SKIM
BASS	CANS	CUSS	HILL	MUCH	PINT	SOCK
BEAN	CANT	CYAN	HULL	MUNG	PONG	SOLD
BENT	CARB	DING	IMID	NARC	PORN	TANG
BING	CELL	DIPS	JELL	NUTS	PRIM	TASS
BOFF	CENT	DISC	JOCK	PANT	PROM	TEMP
BONG	CHEM	DUMB	LASS	PARE	PROS	TORS
BUCK	CHIA	FATS	LENT	PASE	PULA	TRIG
BUFF	CHIC	FILL	LIMB	PERV	PUNT	VIDE
BUNK	CHIN	FORD	LING	PEST	PUTT	WACK
BURR	COMB	GECK	MACH	PHON	RODE	WHAM
BUTE	COMM	GUAN	MIME	PHOT	SCUD	ZINC

With front hook P

ACED	AIRS	APER	AVER	EARS	ESTS	ILLS
ACES	ALES	ARCH	AVES	EASE	HONE	IMPS
ACTS	ALLS	ARES	AVID	EATS	HONS	INCH
AEON	ALLY	ARKS	AWED	EELS	HOTS	INKS
AGED	ALMS	ARSE	AWLS	EERY	HUTS	INKY
AGER	ALPS	ARTS	AWNS	EKES	HYLA	INTO
AGES	ANES	ARTY	AXES	ENDS	ICKS	IONS
AILS	ANGA	ARVO	EACH	EONS	ICKY	ITCH
AINS	ANTS	ATES	EARL	EPOS	ILEA	LACE

LACK	LIER	OKES	OTTO	REED	RISE	RUNE
LAID	LIES	OLES	OUCH	REES	ROBE	SHAW
LAIN	LINK	OLIO	OURS	REPS	ROBS	UKES
LANE	LOPS	ONCE	OUTS	REST	RODS	UMPS
LANK	LOTS	ONES	OXES	RICE	ROLE	UNTO
LASH	LOWS	OOHS	RAMS	RICK	ROMS	UPAS
LATE	LUCK	OOPS	RANG	RIDE	ROOF	URGE
LATS	LUGS	OPES	RANK	RIGS	ROSE	USES
LAYS	LUMP	ORES	RASE	RILL	ROSY	YINS
LEAD	LUMS	ORGY	RATE	RIME	ROVE	
LEAS	LUNK	ORTS	RATS	RIMS	ROWS	
LIED	LUSH	OSES	RAYS	RINK	RUDE	

With back hook P

BICE	CRAM	PLUM	SCAM	SLUR	SWAM	WHOM
CHAM	CRIS	POLY	SCAR	STIR	TRAM	
CHUM	GRAM	PRIM	SKIM	STOW	TWEE	
CLAM	GRUM	SALE	SLUM	STUM	WHEE	

With front hook Q

AIDS

With front hook R

ACED	AKEE	ANTS	AXES	EPOS	ILLS	OPED
ACES	ALES	APED	AYAH	ESES	INKS	OPES
AGAS	ALLY	APER	EACH	ESTS	OARS	OSES
AGED	AMEN	APES	EARS	ETCH	OAST	OUST
AGEE	AMIE	ARES	EAVE	EXES	OBES	OUTS
AGER	AMIN	ASPS	EDDY	HEME	ODES	OVEN
AGES	AMPS	ATES	EELS	ICED	OILS	OVER
AIDS	AMUS	AVER	EGAL	ICES	OILY	OWED
AILS	ANDS	AVES	EMIT	ICKS	OLES	UMPS
AINS	ANIS	AXED	ENDS	IDES	OOTS	USES

With back hook R

ABLE	BORE	COPE	DIRE	FIFE	GIBE	HONE
AIDE	BRIE	CORE	DIVE	FILA	GIVE	HOPE
AURA	CAGE	COVE	DOPE	FILE	GLUE	HOSE
BAKE	CANE	CUBE	DOSE	FINE	GNAR	HOVE
BALE	CAPE	CURE	DOTE	FIRE	GONE	HUGE
BARE	CARE	CUTE	DOZE	FIVE	HALE	HYPE
BASE	CATE	CYMA	DUPE	FLEE	HATE	IDLE
BIDE	CAVE	DARE	EASE	FREE	HAVE	JAKE
BIKE	CEDE	DATE	EDGE	FUME	HAZE	JAPE
BINE	CHAI	DECO	EIDE	GAGE	HIDE	JIBE
BITE	CHAR	DICE	FACE	GAME	HIKE	JIVE
BLUE	CITE	DIKE	FADE	GAPE	HILA	JOKE
BOLA	CODE	DIME	FAKE	GATE	HIRE	KITE
BONE	COME	DINE	FARE	GAZE	HOME	KNUR

LACE	MACE	NINE	RACE	SABE	TAPE	WADE
LADE	MAKE	NITE	RAGE	SAFE	TASE	WAGE
LAKE	MANO	NOTE	RAKE	SAGE	TATE	WAKE
LAME	MATE	NUDE	RAPE	SAKE	TILE	WALE
LASE	MAYO	OCHE	RARE	SANE	TIME	WAVE
LATE	MAZE	OGLE	RASE	SAVE	TOKE	WHIR
LAVE	MERE	OLDE	RATE	SERE	TOLA	WIDE
LIFE	METE	PACE	RAVE	SHEA	TONE	WIPE
LIKE	MILE	PAGE	RAZE	SHOE	TOPE	WIRE
LINE	MIME	PALE	RICE	SIKE	TOTE	WISE
LITE	MINE	PARE	RIDE	SIMA	TRUE	WIVE
LIVE	MISE	PATE	RIFE	SIZE	TUBE	WOKE
LONE	MITE	PAVE	RIME	SOFA	TUNE	YAGE
LOPE	MOLA	PIKE	RIPE	SOLA	TWEE	YARE
LOSE	MOPE	PIPE	RISE	SORE	ULNA	ZONE
LOVE	MOVE	PLIE	RIVE	SUPE	UNDE	
LOWE	MUSE	POKE	ROPE	SURE	URGE	
LUGE	MUTE	POLE	ROTO	TAKE	VAPE	
LUNA	NAME	POSE	ROVE	TALA	VELA	
LURE	NEVE	PULE	RUDE	TALE	VILE	
LUXE	NICE	PURE	RULE	TAME	VOTE	

With front hook S

ABED	CANS	CULL	HALL	HITS	IMPS	LATE
ABLE	CANT	CUMS	HALT	HIVE	INKS	LATS
AGAS	CAPE	CUPS	HAME	HOCK	IRED	LAVE
AGER	CARE	CURF	HAMS	HOED	IRES	LAWS
AGES	CARP	CUTE	HANK	HOER	IZAR	LAYS
AIDS	CARS	CUTS	HARD	HOES	KATS	LEEK
AILS	CART	EARS	HARE	HOGS	KEEN	LEET
AINS	CATS	EATS	HARK	HONE	KEET	LEPT
ALES	CENT	EDGE	HARP	HOOK	KEGS	LICE
ALLY	CION	EDGY	HAUL	HOOT	KELP	LICK
ALPS	COFF	EELS	HAVE	HOPS	KEPS	LIER
ALTS	COLD	EELY	HAWS	HORN	KIDS	LILY
AMBO	CONE	EGOS	HAYS	HOTS	KIER	LIME
AMPS	COOP	ELLS	HEAL	HOVE	KILL	LIMY
ANDS	COOT	EMES	HEAR	HOWS	KINK	LING
ANES	COPE	ENDS	HELL	HUCK	KINS	LINK
ANGA	COPS	EPIC	HENT	HUNS	KIPS	LIPE
ARKS	CORE	EVEN	HERD	HUNT	KITE	LIPS
ATES	CORN	EVER	HERO	HUSH	KITS	LITS
AUGH	COTS	EWER	HEWN	HUTS	LABS	LOBS
AVER	COWL	EXED	HEWS	ICES	LACK	LOGS
AVES	COWS	EXES	HIED	ICKS	LAGS	LOID
AWED	CRAG	HACK	HIES	ICKY	LAIN	LOOP
AXES	CRAM	HADE	HILL	IDES	LAKE	LOPE
CABS	CRAP	HAFT	HIMS	IDLE	LAMS	LOPS
CADS	CREW	HAGS	HINS	ILEX	LANG	LOTH
CALL	CRIP	HAHS	HIPS	ILKS	LANK	LOTS
CAMP	CUDS	HAKE	HIRE	ILLS	LAPS	LOWS
CAMS	CUFF	HALE	HIST	ILLY	LASH	LUES

LUFF	NICK	PAMS	PINY	TARS	TORE	WANK
LUGS	NIDE	PANG	PITS	TART	TORY	WANS
LUMP	NIFF	PANS	PLAT	TATE	TOSS	WAPS
LUMS	NIPS	PARE	PLAY	TATS	TOTS	WARD
LUNG	NITS	PARK	POKE	TEAK	TOUR	WARE
LUNK	NOBS	PARS	POOF	TEAL	TOUT	WARM
LUSH	NOGS	PATE	POOL	TEAM	TOWS	WART
MACK	NOOK	PATS	POON	TEED	TRAP	WASH
MALL	NOWS	PAWN	POOR	TEEL	TRAY	WATS
MALT	NUBS	PAYS	PORE	TEIN	TRIP	WAYS
MART	NUFF	PEAK	PORT	TELA	TROP	WEAR
MASH	NUGS	PEAN	POTS	TELE	TROW	WEEP
MAZE	OAKS	PEAR	POUT	TENT	TROY	WEER
MEEK	OARS	PECK	PRAT	TERN	TUBS	WEET
MELL	OBAS	PECS	PRAY	TETS	TUCK	WELL
MELT	OCAS	PEED	PREE	TEWS	TUFF	WEPT
MERK	ODAS	PEEL	PRIG	TICK	TUMP	WIGS
MEWS	ODIC	PEER	PROG	TIED	TUMS	WILE
MILE	OILS	PELT	PUDS	TIES	TUNG	WILL
MIRK	OKES	PEND	PUNK	TIFF	TUNS	WINE
MITE	OLES	PENT	PURS	TILE	TYES	WING
MOCK	OMAS	PERM	QUAD	TILL	UGHS	WINK
MOGS	ONES	PEWS	QUID	TILT	ULUS	WIPE
MOKE	ONLY	PICA	TABS	TIME	UMMA	WISH
MOLT	OOTS	PICE	TACK	TING	UMPS	WISS
MOTE	ORBS	PICK	TAGS	TINT	URDS	WITH
MUSH	ORES	PICS	TAIN	TOCK	URGE	WIVE
MUTS	ORTS	PIED	TAKE	TOKE	USED	WOPS
NAGS	OURS	PIER	TALE	TOLE	USES	WORD
NAIL	OWED	PIES	TALK	TONE	WABS	WORE
NAPS	PACE	PIKE	TALL	TONY	WAGE	WORN
NARK	PACY	PILE	TAMP	TOOK	WAGS	WOTS
NEAP	PAIL	PILL	TANG	TOOL	WAIL	
NECK	PALE	PINE	TANK	TOPE	WAIN	
NIBS	PALL	PINS	TARE	TOPS	WALE	

With back hook S

ABBA	ACYL	AIDE	ALUM	ANIL	ARSE	AXLE
ABBE	ADIT	AIRN	AMAH	ANKH	ARUM	AXON
ABET	ADZE	AIRT	AMAS	ANNA	ARVO	AYAH
ABLE	AEON	AKEE	AMBO	ANOA	ARYL	AYIN
ABRI	AFAR	ALAN	AMEN	ANTA	ATAP	AZAN
ABUT	AFRO	ALBA	AMIA	ANTE	ATMA	AZON
ABYE	AGAR	ALEC	AMID	ANTI	ATOM	BAAL
ABYS	AGER	ALEF	AMIE	APER	AUNT	BABA
ACAI	AGHA	ALFA	AMIN	APOD	AURA	BABE
ACHE	AGIO	ALGA	AMIR	APSE	AUTO	BABU
ACID	AGLU	ALIF	AMIS	AQUA	AVER	BACK
ACME	AGMA	ALMA	AMMO	ARAK	AVOW	BAFF
ACNE	AGON	ALME	AMOK	AREA	AWOL	BAHT
ACRE	AGRO	ALOE	AMYL	ARIA	AXEL	BAIL
ACRO	AGUE	ALTO	ANGA	ARIL	AXIL	BAIT

BAKE	BHUT	BOLE	BULL	CARN	CLAG	CORD
BALD	BIBB	BOLL	BUMF	CARP	CLAM	CORE
BALE	BIBE	BOLO	BUMP	CARR	CLAN	CORK
BALK	BICE	BOLT	BUNA	CART	CLAP	CORM
BALL	BIDE	BOMB	BUND	CASA	CLAW	CORN
BALM	BIDI	BOND	BUNG	CASE	CLAY	COST
BANC	BIER	BONE	BUNK	CASK	CLEF	COTE
BAND	BIFF	BONG	BUNN	CAST	CLEG	COUP
BANE	BIKE	BONK	BUNT	CATE	CLEW	COVE
BANG	BILE	BOOB	BUOY	CAUL	CLIP	COWL
BANK	BILK	BOOK	BURA	CAVA	CLIT	CRAB
BARB	BILL	BOOM	BURB	CAVE	CLOD	CRAG
BARD	BIMA	BOON	BURD	CEDE	CLOG	CRAM
BARE	BIND	BOOR	BURG	CEDI	CLON	CRAP
BARF	BINE	BOOT	BURK	CEIL	CLOP	CRAW
BARK	BINT	BORA	BURL	CELL	CLOT	CRED
BARM	BIOG	BORE	BURN	CELT	CLOY	CREW
BARN	BIRD	BORK	BURP	CENT	CLUB	CRIB
BASE	BIRK	BORT	BURR	CEPE	CLUE	CRIP
BASK	BIRL	BOSK	BUSK	CERE	COAL	CRIT
BAST	BIRO	BOTA	BUST	CERO	COAT	CROC
BATE	BIRR	BOTT	BUTE	CERT	COBB	CROP
BATH	BISE	BOUT	BUTT	CETE	COCA	CROW
BATT	BISK	BOWL	BYRE	CHAD	COCK	CRUD
BAUD	BITE	BOYO	BYRL	CHAI	COCO	CUBE
BAWD	BITT	BOZO	BYTE	CHAM	CODA	CUFF
BAWK	BIZE	BRAD	CACA	CHAO	CODE	CUIF
BAWL	BLAB	BRAE	CADE	CHAP	COED	CUKE
BAWN	BLAG	BRAG	CADI	CHAR	COFF	CULL
BEAD	BLAH	BRAN	CAFE	CHAT	COHO	CULM
BEAK	BLAM	BRAS	CAFF	CHAW	COIF	CULT
BEAL	BLAT	BRAT	CAGE	CHAY	COIL	CUNT
BEAM	BLAW	BRAW	CAID	CHEF	COIN	CURB
BEAN	BLEB	BRAY	CAIN	CHEM	COIR	CURD
BEAR	BLET	BREE	CAKE	CHEW	COKE	CURE
BEAT	BLIP	BREN	CALF	CHIA	COLA	CURF
BEAU	BLOB	BREW	CALK	CHIC	COLD	CURL
BECK	BLOC	BRIE	CALL	CHIN	COLE	CURN
BEEF	BLOG	BRIG	CALM	CHIP	COLT	CURR
BEEP	BLOT	BRIM	CALO	CHIT	COMA	CUSK
BEER	BLOW	BRIN	CAME	CHOC	COMB	CUSP
BEET	BLUB	BRIO	CAMI	CHON	COME	CUTE
BELL	BLUE	BRIS	CAMO	CHOP	COMM	CYAN
BELT	BLUR	BRIT	CAMP	CHOW	COMP	CYMA
BEMA	BOAR	BROO	CANE	CHUB	CONE	CYME
BEND	BOAT	BROW	CANT	CHUG	CONK	CYST
BENE	BOBO	BRUT	CAPE	CHUM	CONN	CZAR
BENT	BOCK	BUBU	CAPH	CINE	COOF	DACE
BERG	BODE	BUCK	CAPO	CINQ	COOK	DADA
BERK	BOFF	BUFF	CARB	CION	COOL	DADO
BERM	BOHO	BUHL	CARD	CIRE	COON	DAFF
BEST	BOIL	BUHR	CARE	CIST	COOP	DAGO
BETA	BOLA	BULB	CARK	CITE	COOT	DAHL
BETH	BOLD	BULK	CARL	CLAD	COPE	DALE

DAME	DIFF	DRAG	EDGE	FARO	FLAW	FULL
DAMN	DIKE	DRAM	EDIT	FART	FLAY	FUME
DAMP	DILL	DRAT	EGAD	FAST	FLEA	FUND
DANG	DIME	DRAW	EGER	FATE	FLEE	FUNK
DARB	DINE	DRAY	EKKA	FAUN	FLEW	FURL
DARE	DING	DREE	ELAN	FAVA	FLEY	FUSE
DARK	DINK	DREG	EMEU	FAVE	FLIC	FUZE
DARN	DINO	DREK	EMIC	FAWN	FLIP	FYCE
DART	DINT	DRIB	EMIR	FAZE	FLIR	FYKE
DATE	DIOL	DRIP	EMIT	FEAR	FLIT	GADI
DATO	DIRK	DROP	EMMY	FEAT	FLOC	GAFF
DAUB	DIRL	DRUB	EMYD	FECK	FLOE	GAGE
DAUT	DIRT	DRUG	ENOL	FEEB	FLOG	GAIN
DAWK	DISC	DRUM	ENOW	FEED	FLOP	GAIT
DAWN	DISK	DUAD	EPEE	FEEL	FLOW	GALA
DAWT	DITA	DUAL	EPHA	FELL	FLUB	GALE
DAZE	DITE	DUCE	EPIC	FELT	FLUE	GALL
DEAD	DIVA	DUCK	ERNE	FEME	FOAL	GAMA
DEAL	DIVE	DUCT	ERUV	FEND	FOAM	GAMB
DEAN	DJIN	DUDE	ESNE	FEOD	FOHN	GAME
DEAR	DOAT	DUEL	ESSE	FERE	FOIL	GAMP
DEBT	DOBE	DUET	ETIC	FERN	FOIN	GANG
DECK	DOCK	DUFF	ETNA	FEST	FOLD	GAOL
DECO	DODO	DUIT	ETUI	FETA	FOLK	GAPE
DEED	DOER	DUKE	EURO	FETE	FOND	GARB
DEEM	DOFF	DULL	EVEN	FEUD	FONT	GASP
DEEP	DOGE	DUMA	EVIL	FIAR	FOOD	GAST
DEER	DOIT	DUMB	EWER	FIAT	FOOL	GATE
DEET	DOJO	DUMP	EXAM	FICE	FOOT	GAUD
DEFI	DOLE	DUNE	EXEC	FIDO	FORB	GAUM
DEIL	DOLL	DUNG	EXIT	FIEF	FORD	GAUR
DEKE	DOLT	DUNK	EXON	FIFE	FORE	GAWK
DELE	DOME	DUNT	EXPO	FILE	FORK	GAWP
DELF	DONA	DUPE	EYAS	FILK	FORM	GAZE
DELI	DONG	DURA	EYER	FILL	FORT	GEAN
DELL	DOOB	DURE	EYRA	FILM	FOUL	GEAR
DELT	DOOM	DURN	EYRE	FILO	FOUR	GECK
DEME	DOOR	DURO	FACE	FIND	FOWL	GEEK
DEMO	DOPA	DURR	FACT	FINE	FRAG	GELD
DENE	DOPE	DUSK	FADE	FINK	FRAP	GELT
DENT	DORE	DUST	FADO	FINO	FRAT	GENE
DERM	DORK	DYAD	FAFF	FIRE	FRAY	GENT
DESI	DORM	DYER	FAIL	FIRM	FREE	GENU
DESK	DORP	DYKE	FAIR	FIRN	FRET	GERM
DEVA	DORR	DYNE	FAKE	FISC	FRIG	GEST
DEVI	DOSA	EARL	FALL	FIST	FRIT	GETA
DHAK	DOSE	EARN	FAME	FIVE	FROE	GEUM
DHAL	DOTE	EASE	FANE	FLAB	FROG	GHAT
DHOW	DOUM	EAST	FANG	FLAG	FROW	GHEE
DIAL	DOUT	EAVE	FANO	FLAK	FRUG	GIBE
DICE	DOVE	EBON	FARD	FLAM	FUCK	GIFT
DICK	DOWN	ECHE	FARE	FLAN	FUEL	GIGA
DIDO	DOZE	ECHO	FARL	FLAP	FUGU	GILD
DIET	DRAB	ECRU	FARM	FLAT	FUJI	GILL

GILT	GRAD	HALT	HINT	HYPO	JIVE	KELT
GIMP	GRAM	HAME	HIRE	IAMB	JOCK	KEMP
GINK	GRAN	HAND	HIST	ICON	JOEY	KENO
GIRD	GRAY	HANG	HIVE	IDEA	JOHN	KEPI
GIRL	GREE	HANK	HOAR	IDLE	JOIN	KERB
GIRN	GREY	HANT	HOBO	IDOL	JOKE	KERF
GIRO	GRID	HARD	HOCK	IDYL	JOLE	KERN
GIRT	GRIG	HARE	HOER	IGLU	JOLT	KETA
GIST	GRIN	HARK	HOGG	IKAT	JOOK	KHAF
GITE	GRIP	HARL	HOKE	IKON	JOTA	KHAN
GIVE	GRIT	HARM	HOLD	IMAM	JOUK	KHAT
GLAD	GROG	HARP	HOLE	IMID	JOWL	KHET
GLAM	GROK	HART	HOLK	IMPI	JUBA	KIBE
GLED	GROT	HASP	HOLM	INFO	JUBE	KICK
GLEE	GROW	HATE	HOLO	INTI	JUCO	KIEF
GLEN	GRUB	HAUL	HOLT	IOTA	JUDO	KIER
GLEY	GRUE	HAVE	HOMA	IRID	JUJU	KIKE
GLIA	GUAN	HAWK	HOME	IRON	JUKE	KILL
GLIM	GUAR	HAZE	HOMO	ISBA	JUKU	KILN
GLOB	GUCK	HEAD	HONE	ISLE	JUMP	KILO
GLOM	GUDE	HEAL	HONG	ITEM	JUNK	KILT
GLOP	GUFF	HEAP	HONK	IXIA	JUPE	KINA
GLOW	GUID	HEAR	HOOD	IZAR	JUST	KIND
GLUE	GULF	HEAT	HOOF	JACK	JUTE	KINE
GLUG	GULL	HEBE	HOOK	JADE	KADI	KING
GLUM	GULP	HECK	HOOP	JAGG	KAGU	KINK
GLUT	GUNK	HEED	HOOT	JAIL	KAIF	KINO
GNAR	GURU	HEEL	HOPE	JAKE	KAIL	KIRK
GNAT	GUST	HEFT	HORA	JAMB	KAIN	KIRN
GNAW	GYBE	HEIL	HORK	JANE	KAKA	KIST
GOAD	GYNO	HEIR	HORN	JAPE	KAKI	KITE
GOAL	GYPO	HELL	HOSE	JARL	KALE	KITH
GOAT	GYRE	HELM	HOST	JATO	KAME	KIVA
GOBO	GYRO	HELO	HOUR	JAUK	KANA	KIWI
GOER	GYVE	HELP	HOWE	JAUP	KANE	KLIK
GOGO	HAAF	HEME	HOWF	JAVA	KAON	KNAP
GOJI	HAAR	HEMP	HOWK	JEAN	KAPA	KNAR
GOLD	HABU	HENT	HOWL	JEEP	KAPH	KNEE
GOLF	HACK	HERB	HOYA	JEER	KAPU	KNIT
GONG	HADE	HERD	HUCK	JEFE	KARN	KNOB
GOOD	HAEM	HERE	HUFF	JEHU	KART	KNOP
GOOF	HAET	HERL	HULA	JELL	KATA	KNOT
GOOK	HAFT	HERM	HULK	JERK	KAVA	KNOW
GOON	HAHA	HERN	HULL	JEST	KAYO	KNUR
GOOP	HAIK	HERO	HUMP	JETE	KBAR	KOAN
GORE	HAIL	HEST	HUNK	JIBB	KECK	KOBO
GORM	HAIR	HETH	HUNT	JIBE	KEEF	KOEL
GORP	HAJI	HICK	HURL	JIFF	KEEK	KOHL
GOTH	HAKE	HIDE	HURT	JILL	KEEL	KOJI
GOUT	HAKU	HIGH	HUSK	JILT	KEEN	KOLA
GOWD	HALE	HIKE	HWYL	JINK	KEEP	KOLO
GOWK	HALL	HILL	HYLA	JINN	KEET	KONK
GOWN	HALM	HILT	HYMN	JIRD	KEIR	KOOK
GRAB	HALO	HIND	HYPE	JISM	KELP	KOPH

KORA	LEVA	LOOT	MALT	MIGG	MOTH	NEIF
KOTO	LIAR	LOPE	MAMA	MIKE	MOTT	NEMA
KRAI	LICK	LORD	MANA	MILD	MOUE	NENE
KRAY	LIDO	LORE	MANE	MILE	MOVE	NEON
KUDO	LIEN	LOSE	MANO	MILK	MOXA	NERD
KUDU	LIER	LOTA	MARA	MILL	MOZO	NEST
KUFI	LIEU	LOTO	MARC	MILO	MUCK	NETT
KURU	LIFT	LOUP	MARE	MILT	MUFF	NEUK
KVAS	LIKE	LOUR	MARK	MIME	MUGG	NEUM
KYAK	LILO	LOUT	MARL	MINA	MULE	NEVE
KYAR	LILT	LOVE	MART	MIND	MULL	NEWB
KYAT	LIMA	LOWE	MASA	MINE	MUMM	NEWT
KYTE	LIMB	LUAU	MASK	MINI	MUMP	NEXT
LACE	LIME	LUBE	MAST	MINK	MUMU	NICK
LACK	LIMN	LUCE	MATE	MINT	MUNG	NIDE
LADE	LIMO	LUCK	MATH	MIRE	MUNI	NIFF
LAIC	LIMP	LUDE	MATT	MIRK	MUON	NIGH
LAIR	LINE	LUDO	MAUD	MISE	MURA	NILL
LAKE	LING	LUFF	MAUL	MISO	MURE	NINE
LAKH	LINK	LUGE	MAUT	MIST	MURK	NIPA
LALL	LINN	LULL	MAXI	MITE	MURR	NITE
LAMA	LINO	LULU	MAYA	MITT	MUSE	NIXE
LAMB	LINT	LUMA	MAYO	MOAN	MUSK	NOCK
LAME	LION	LUMP	MAZE	MOAT	MUSO	NODE
LAMP	LIPA	LUNA	MEAD	MOCK	MUST	NOEL
LAND	LIPO	LUNE	MEAL	MODE	MUTE	NOGG
LANE	LIRA	LUNG	MEAN	MOFO	MUTT	NOIL
LARD	LISP	LUNK	MEAT	MOHO	MYNA	NOIR
LARI	LIST	LUNT	MECH	MOIL	MYTH	NOLO
LARK	LITE	LURE	MEED	MOJO	NAAN	NOMA
LARN	LIVE	LURK	MEET	MOKE	NABE	NOME
LASE	LOAD	LUST	MELD	MOLA	NADA	NONA
LAST	LOAF	LUTE	MELL	MOLD	NAFF	NONE
LATH	LOAM	LUXE	MELT	MOLE	NAGA	NONI
LAUD	LOAN	LWEI	MEME	MOLL	NAIF	NOOK
LAVA	LOBE	LYRE	MEMO	MOLT	NAIL	NOON
LAVE	LOBO	LYSE	MEND	MOLY	NALA	NORI
LAWN	LOCH	MAAR	MENU	MOME	NAME	NORM
LAZE	LOCI	MABE	MEOU	MONK	NANA	NOSE
LEAD	LOCK	MACE	MEOW	MONO	NANO	NOTE
LEAF	LOCO	MACH	MERC	MOOD	NAPA	NOUN
LEAK	LODE	MACK	MERE	MOOK	NAPE	NOVA
LEAN	LOFT	MAGE	MERK	MOOL	NARC	NOWT
LEAP	LOGE	MAID	MERL	MOON	NARD	NUDE
LEAR	LOGO	MAIL	MESA	MOOR	NARK	NUFF
LEDE	LOID	MAIM	METE	MOOT	NAVE	NUKE
LEEK	LOIN	MAIN	METH	MOPE	NAZI	NULL
LEER	LOLL	MAIR	MEWL	MORA	NEAP	NUMB
LEET	LONG	MAKE	MEZE	MORE	NEAR	NURD
LEFT	LOOF	MAKI	MICA	MORN	NEAT	NURL
LEHR	LOOK	MAKO	MICK	MORT	NECK	OAST
LEND	LOOM	MALE	MIDI	MOSK	NEED	OATH
LENO	LOON	MALL	MIEN	MOST	NEEM	OBEY
LEUD	LOOP	MALM	MIFF	MOTE	NEEP	OBIA

OBIT	PAIR	PHON	PONE	PUNT	RAZE	ROOD
OBOE	PALE	PHOT	PONG	PUPA	READ	ROOF
OBOL	PALI	PHUT	POOD	PUPU	REAL	ROOK
OCHE	PALL	PIAN	POOF	PURI	REAM	ROOM
ODAH	PALM	PICA	POOH	PURL	REAP	ROOT
ODOR	PALP	PICK	POOL	PURR	REAR	ROPE
ODYL	PANE	PIER	POON	PUTT	RECK	ROSE
OFAY	PANG	PIKA	POOP	PYIN	REDD	ROTA
OGAM	PANT	PIKE	POPE	PYRE	REDE	ROTE
OGEE	PAPA	PIKI	PORE	PYRO	REDO	ROTI
OGLE	PARA	PILE	PORK	QADI	REED	ROTL
OGRE	PARD	PILI	PORN	QAID	REEF	ROTO
OHIA	PARE	PILL	PORT	QOPH	REEK	ROUE
OINK	PARK	PIMA	POSE	QUAD	REEL	ROUP
OKAY	PARR	PIMP	POST	QUAG	REIF	ROUT
OKEH	PART	PINA	POUF	QUAI	REIN	ROVE
OKRA	PASE	PINE	POUR	QUAY	REND	RUBE
OLEO	PAST	PING	POUT	QUEY	RENO	RUCK
OLIO	PATE	PINK	PRAM	QUID	RENT	RUDD
OLLA	PATH	PINT	PRAO	QUIN	REPO	RUER
OMEN	PAUA	PION	PRAT	QUIP	REPP	RUFF
OMER	PAVE	PIPA	PRAU	QUIT	REST	RUIN
OMIT	PAWL	PIPE	PRAY	QUOD	RHEA	RUKH
OOZE	PAWN	PIRN	PREE	RACE	RIAL	RULE
OPAH	PEAG	PISO	PREP	RACK	RICE	RUMP
OPAL	PEAK	PITA	PREY	RAFF	RICK	RUNE
OPEN	PEAL	PITH	PRIG	RAFT	RIDE	RUNG
ORAL	PEAN	PLAN	PRIM	RAGA	RIEL	RUNT
ORCA	PEAR	PLAT	PROA	RAGE	RIFF	RUSE
ORDO	PEAT	PLAY	PROB	RAGG	RIFT	RUSK
ORLE	PECH	PLEA	PROD	RAGI	RILE	RUST
ORZO	PECK	PLEB	PROF	RAIA	RILL	RUTH
OTTO	PEEK	PLEW	PROG	RAID	RIME	RYKE
OUPH	PEEL	PLIE	PROM	RAIL	RIND	RYND
OUST	PEEN	PLOD	PROP	RAIN	RING	RYOT
OUZO	PEEP	PLOP	PROS	RAJA	RINK	SABE
OVAL	PEER	PLOT	PROW	RAKE	RIOT	SACK
OVEN	PEIN	PLOW	PUCE	RAKI	RIPE	SADE
OVER	PEKE	PLOY	PUCK	RAKU	RISE	SADI
OWIE	PELE	PLUG	PUDU	RALE	RISK	SAFE
OXER	PELF	PLUM	PUFF	RAMP	RITE	SAGA
OXID	PELT	POCK	PUJA	RAND	RIVE	SAGE
OXIM	PEND	POEM	PUKE	RANG	ROAD	SAGO
OYER	PEON	POET	PULA	RANI	ROAM	SAID
PAAN	PEPO	POGO	PULE	RANK	ROAN	SAIL
PACA	PERC	POKE	PULI	RANT	ROAR	SAIN
PACE	PERE	POLE	PULK	RAPE	ROBE	SAKE
PACK	PERI	POLL	PULL	RARE	ROCK	SAKI
PACT	PERK	POLO	PULP	RASE	RODE	SALE
PADI	PERM	POLY	PUMA	RASP	ROIL	SALP
PAGE	PERP	POME	PUMP	RATE	ROLE	SALT
PAIK	PERV	POMO	PUNA	RATO	ROLF	SAMP
PAIL	PESO	POMP	PUNG	RAVE	ROLL	SAND
PAIN	PEST	POND	PUNK	RAYA	ROMP	SANE

SARD	SHEW	SKOL	SOJU	STOW	TALE	TIFF
SARI	SHIM	SKUA	SOKE	STUB	TALK	TIKE
SARK	SHIN	SLAB	SOLA	STUD	TALL	TIKI
SATE	SHIP	SLAG	SOLE	STUM	TAME	TILE
SATI	SHIT	SLAM	SOLO	STUN	TAMP	TILL
SAUL	SHIV	SLAP	SOMA	STYE	TANG	TILT
SAVE	SHOE	SLAT	SONE	SUBA	TANK	TIME
SCAB	SHOG	SLAW	SONG	SUCK	TAPA	TINE
SCAD	SHOO	SLAY	SOOK	SUDD	TAPE	TING
SCAG	SHOP	SLED	SOOT	SUER	TARE	TINT
SCAM	SHOT	SLEW	SOPH	SUET	TARN	TIPI
SCAN	SHOW	SLIM	SORA	SUGH	TARO	TIRE
SCAR	SHRI	SLIP	SORB	SUIT	TARP	TIRL
SCAT	SHUL	SLIT	SORD	SUKH	TART	TIRO
SCOP	SHUN	SLOB	SORE	SULK	TASE	TITI
SCOT	SHUT	SLOE	SORN	SULU	TASK	TIYN
SCOW	SHWA	SLOG	SORT	SUMI	TATE	TOAD
SCUD	SIAL	SLOP	SOTH	SUMO	TAUT	TOCK
SCUM	SIBB	SLOT	SOUK	SUMP	TAXI	TOCO
SCUP	SICE	SLOW	SOUL	SUNN	TEAK	TOEA
SCUT	SICK	SLUB	SOUP	SUPE	TEAL	TOFF
SEAL	SIDE	SLUE	SOUR	SURA	TEAM	TOFT
SEAM	SIFT	SLUG	SOYA	SURD	TEAR	TOFU
SEAR	SIGH	SLUM	SPAE	SURF	TEAT	TOGA
SEAT	SIGN	SLUR	SPAM	SWAB	TECH	TOIL
SECT	SIKA	SLUT	SPAN	SWAG	TEEL	TOIT
SEED	SIKE	SMEW	SPAR	SWAN	TEEM	TOKE
SEEK	SILD	SMOG	SPAT	SWAP	TEEN	TOLA
SEEL	SILK	SMUT	SPAY	SWAT	TEFF	TOLE
SEEM	SILL	SNAG	SPEC	SWAY	TEGG	TOLL
SEEP	SILO	SNAP	SPEW	SWIG	TEGU	TOLT
SEER	SILT	SNAW	SPIC	SWIM	TEIN	TOLU
SEGO	SIMA	SNED	SPIK	SWOB	TELE	TOMB
SEIF	SIMP	SNIB	SPIN	SWOP	TELL	TOME
SELF	SINE	SNIP	SPIT	SWOT	TEMP	TONE
SELL	SING	SNIT	SPIV	SYCE	TEND	TONG
SEME	SINH	SNOB	SPOT	SYKE	TENT	TOOL
SEMI	SINK	SNOG	SPUD	SYLI	TEPA	TOON
SEND	SIPE	SNOT	SPUE	SYNC	TERM	TOOT
SENE	SIRE	SNOW	SPUR	SYPH	TERN	TOPE
SENT	SITE	SNUB	STAB	TABU	TEST	TOPH
SEPT	SIZE	SNUG	STAG	TACE	TETH	TOPI
SERE	SKAG	SNYE	STAR	TACH	TEXT	TOPO
SERF	SKAT	SOAK	STAT	TACK	THAW	TORA
SETT	SKED	SOAP	STAY	TACO	THEN	TORC
SEXT	SKEE	SOAR	STEM	TACT	THEW	TORE
SHAD	SKEG	SOBA	STEP	TAEL	THIN	TORO
SHAG	SKEP	SOCA	STET	TAHR	THOU	TORR
SHAH	SKEW	SOCK	STEW	TAIL	THUD	TORT
SHAM	SKID	SODA	STIR	TAIN	THUG	TOSA
SHAW	SKIM	SOFA	STOA	TAKA	TIAN	TOTE
SHAY	SKIN	SOFT	STOB	TAKE	TICK	TOUR
SHEA	SKIP	SOIL	STOP	TALA	TIDE	TOUT
SHED	SKIT	SOJA	STOT	TALC	TIER	TOWN

TOYO	TWIT	VEIN	WAIT	WHAT	WORD	YOGA
TRAD	TYEE	VELD	WAKE	WHEN	WORK	YOGH
TRAM	TYER	VEND	WALE	WHET	WORM	YOGI
TRAP	TYKE	VENT	WALI	WHEW	WORT	YOKE
TRAY	TYNE	VERB	WALK	WHEY	WRAP	YOLK
TREE	TYPE	VERT	WALL	WHID	WREN	YOMP
TREK	TYPO	VEST	WAME	WHIG	WRIT	YONI
TREM	TYPP	VIAL	WAND	WHIM	WYLE	YOOF
TRES	TYRE	VIBE	WANE	WHIN	WYND	YORE
TRET	TYRO	VICE	WANK	WHIP	WYNN	YOUR
TREY	TZAR	VIER	WANT	WHIR	WYTE	YOWE
TRIG	UDON	VIEW	WARD	WHIT	XYST	YOWL
TRIM	ULAN	VIFF	WARE	WHOP	YACK	YUAN
TRIO	ULNA	VIGA	WARK	WHUP	YAFF	YUCA
TRIP	ULVA	VILL	WARM	WICK	YAGE	YUCK
TROG	UMBO	VINA	WARN	WIDE	YAGI	YUGA
TROT	UMMA	VINE	WARP	WIFE	YANG	YUKE
TROW	UMPH	VINO	WART	WIKI	YANK	YULE
TROY	UNAI	VIOL	WASP	WILD	YARD	YURT
TRUE	UNAU	VIRL	WAST	WILE	YARN	YUZU
TRUG	UNCO	VISA	WATT	WILL	YAUD	ZARF
TSAR	UNDO	VISE	WAUK	WILT	YAUP	ZEAL
TUBA	UNIT	VIVA	WAUL	WIMP	YAWL	ZEBU
TUBE	UPDO	VLEI	WAVE	WIND	YAWN	ZEDA
TUCK	UREA	VLOG	WAWL	WINE	YAWP	ZEIN
TUFA	URGE	VOID	WEAL	WING	YEAH	ZERK
TUFF	USER	VOLE	WEAN	WINK	YEAN	ZERO
TUFT	UVEA	VOLK	WEAR	WINO	YEAR	ZEST
TULE	VAIL	VOLT	WEED	WIPE	YECH	ZETA
TUMP	VAIR	VOTE	WEEK	WIRE	YEGG	ZILL
TUNA	VALE	VROW	WEEN	WISE	YELK	ZINC
TUNE	VAMP	VUGG	WEEP	WISP	YELL	ZINE
TUNG	VANE	VUGH	WEET	WIST	YELP	ZING
TURD	VANG	VULN	WEFT	WITE	YERK	ZITI
TURF	VAPE	WACK	WEIR	WIVE	YETI	ZOEA
TURK	VARA	WADE	WEKA	WOAD	YETT	ZONE
TURN	VASE	WADI	WELD	WOLD	YEUK	ZONK
TURR	VAST	WAFF	WELL	WOLF	YILL	ZOOM
TUSK	VATU	WAFT	WELT	WOMB	YIPE	ZOON
TUTU	VEAL	WAGE	WEND	WONK	YIRD	ZORI
TWAE	VEEP	WAIF	WEST	WONT	YIRR	ZOUK
TWAT	VEER	WAIL	WETA	WOOD	YLEM	ZYME
TWIG	VEGA	WAIN	WHAM	WOOF	YOCK	
TWIN	VEIL	WAIR	WHAP	WOOL	YODH	

With front hook T

ABLE	AKIN	ALLY	APES	AUNT	AXON	EELS
ACES	ALAR	AMIS	ARES	AWED	EACH	EFFS
ACHE	ALAS	AMPS	ARTS	AWNY	EARS	EGGS
ACTS	ALES	ANGA	ARTY	AXED	EASE	ELLS
AILS	ALKY	APED	ASKS	AXES	EATS	ENDS
AINS	ALLS	APER	ATES	AXIS	EDDY	EPEE

ERNE	HILL	OILS	OYER	REND	ROWS	WAIN
ERNS	HINS	OKAY	RACE	RETS	RUCK	WATS
ESTS	HOLE	OKES	RACK	RIAL	RUED	WEAK
ETHS	HONG	OLES	RADS	RICE	RUER	WEED
HACK	HORN	ONES	RAGI	RICK	RUES	WEEN
HANG	HOSE	ONUS	RAIL	RIGS	RUGS	WEEP
HANK	HUGS	OOTS	RAIN	RILL	RULY	WEER
HARM	HUMP	OPED	RAMP	RIMS	RUMP	WEET
HAWS	HUNK	OPES	RAMS	RIPE	RUST	WIGS
HEBE	HURL	ORCS	RANK	RIPS	RUTH	WILL
HEFT	ICKS	ORES	RAPS	RITE	SADE	WINE
HEIR	IDES	ORTS	RAPT	ROCK	SADI	WINK
HEME	ILLS	OUCH	RASH	RODE	SKED	WINS
HENS	IMID	OURS	RAVE	ROLL	SUBA	WINY
HERE	IRED	OUTS	RAYS	ROMP	UMPS	WIST
HERM	IRES	OWED	READ	ROPE	URDS	WITS
HEWS	ITCH	OWIE	REED	ROTS	URNS	
HICK	OAST	OWNS	REES	ROUT	URPS	
HIGH	OFFS	OXIC	REMS	ROVE	WAES	

With back hook T

ALAN	CAPO	ERGO	HEAR	MIDS	SAIN	STOT
AMEN	CARE	EVEN	HELO	MOTE	SAUL	STUN
AUGH	CHAP	EVER	HIGH	NIGH	SAYS	TACE
AVER	CHAR	FACE	ISLE	NONE	SCAN	TAIN
BEAU	CLAP	FAIN	JOIN	ONCE	SCAR	TARO
BIDE	CLEF	FILE	JURA	OVER	SCAT	TEMP
BLUE	CLIP	FIRS	KAPU	PAIN	SHEN	TORO
BLUR	COME	FLEE	KEMP	PALE	SHOO	TRAP
BOAR	COMP	FLIR	KORA	PEAR	SHOT	TROU
BOAS	COOP	FRIT	KRAI	PIPE	SHUN	TWEE
BOOS	COVE	FUME	LARN	PLAN	SIGH	VALE
BRAN	CRUS	GAUN	LEAN	PLEA	SKEE	VELD
BREN	CURE	GEES	LEAP	PROS	SKIN	VIVA
BRIT	CURS	GENE	LEAS	QUIN	SLIP	WEES
BUND	DEAL	GLEE	LICH	REES	SPEC	WHIP
BURN	DELF	GOES	LUNE	REPO	SPUR	WRAP
BURS	DOES	GRAN	MANA	RIVE	STAR	YEAS
CADE	DRIP	GREE	MAYS	ROOS	STOA	
CANS	DROP	GRIP	MEAN	ROSE	STOP	

With front hook U

DONS	NITE	RARE	REAL	SAGE	TILE
LAMA	NITS	RASE	REDO	SERS	VEAL
NARY	PEND	RATE	RIAL	SING	

With back hook U

BATT	CORN	HAIK	QUIP	VEND
CENT	FOND	PARE	TEND	VERT

With front hook V

AGUE	ANES	AUNT	ESTS	ICES	LOGS	OWED
AILS	APED	EERY	ETCH	ILLS	OLES	ROOM
AIRS	APER	ELDS	EXED	IRES	OMER	ROWS
ALES	APES	ENDS	EXES	IRID	OMIT	UGHS
AMPS	ARIA	ERST	ICED	LEIS	OUCH	ULVA

With back hook V

GANE

With front hook W

AGED	ANTS	AXED	HALE	HIMS	ILLY	RACK
AGER	ARES	AXES	HAMS	HINS	IMPS	RANG
AGES	ARKS	EARS	HANG	HIPS	INCH	RAPS
AGON	ARMS	EAVE	HAPS	HIST	INKS	RAPT
AILS	ARTS	ECHT	HATS	HITS	IRED	RATH
AINS	ARTY	EDGE	HEAL	HOLE	IRES	RECK
AIRS	ASHY	EDGY	HEAT	HOOF	ITCH	REST
AITS	ASPS	EFTS	HEEL	HOOP	OLDS	RICK
ALES	ATAP	ELDS	HELM	HOPS	OMEN	RING
ALLS	AUGH	ELLS	HELP	HOSE	OOPS	RITE
ALLY	AUKS	ENDS	HENS	HUMP	OOZY	ROTE
AMUS	AVER	ESTS	HERE	ICKS	ORTS	RUNG
ANDS	AVES	ETAS	HETS	IDES	OVEN	
ANES	AWLS	HACK	HEWS	ILLS	OWED	

With back hook W

KOTO	PAPA	SINE	THRO

With front hook X

YLEM

With back hook X

BEAU	CARE	FORE	LATE	MIRE	PYRE	TELE
BORA	CODE	GALA	LURE	MURE	REDO	

With front hook Y

AGER	AULD	CLAD	EGGS	ILLS	OURS	OWLS
AGES	AWED	EARN	ELKS	OGEE	OWED	UKES
AMEN	AWLS	EARS	ELLS	OKES	OWES	ULAN
ARAK	AWNS	EAST	ESES	ORES	OWIE	UPON

With back hook Y

ABBE	AGON	ANTS	ARTS	ATOP	BAFF	BALK
ACID	ALAR	APER	ATOM	AUNT	BALD	BALL

BALM	COCK	FAWN	GYPS	LACE	MIST	PICK
BAND	COMM	FELL	HAIR	LAIR	MOLD	PINE
BARK	CONE	FELT	HAND	LAMB	MOLL	PINK
BARM	CONK	FERN	HANK	LANK	MOOD	PISS
BARN	COOK	FILL	HARD	LARD	MOON	PITH
BASS	COOL	FILM	HARP	LARK	MOOR	PLAT
BATT	COPS	FISH	HAST	LASS	MOPE	PLUM
BAWD	CORK	FIZZ	HEAD	LATH	MORA	POCK
BEAD	CORN	FLAK	HEAP	LAWN	MOSS	POKE
BEAK	COVE	FLAM	HEFT	LEAD	MOTE	PONG
BEAM	CULL	FLAW	HEMP	LEAF	MOTH	POOF
BEEF	CURD	FLAX	HERB	LEAK	MUCK	POOP
BEER	CURL	FOAM	HILL	LEAR	MUGG	POPS
BELL	CURR	FOLK	HISS	LEER	MULE	PORK
BEND	CUTE	FOOT	HOAR	LEFT	MUMM	PORN
BIFF	DAFF	FORA	HOKE	LIMB	MUMS	POSE
BILL	DAIS	FORB	HOLE	LIME	MURK	POTS
BITS	DARK	FORK	HOME	LINE	MURR	POUT
BITT	DASH	FORT	HONE	LING	MUSH	PREX
BLIN	DAUB	FUBS	HONK	LINK	MUSK	PROS
BLOW	DEAR	FULL	HOOD	LINN	MUSS	PUFF
BLUE	DECO	FUNK	HOOK	LINT	MUST	PUKE
BONE	DEED	FUSS	HOOT	LOAM	MYTH	PULP
BOOB	DELL	FUZZ	HORN	LOFT	NARK	PUNK
BOOM	DICE	GALL	HOSE	LOLL	NEED	PUNT
BOOT	DICK	GAMA	HUFF	LOOK	NERD	PURS
BORT	DIKE	GAME	HULK	LOON	NETT	PUSH
BOSK	DILL	GAUD	HUMP	LOOP	NEWS	PUSS
BOSS	DING	GAWK	HUNK	LOSS	NIFF	PUTT
BOTH	DINK	GEEK	HURL	LOUR	NOIL	RAGG
BRIN	DIRT	GERM	HUSK	LOVE	NOOK	RAIN
BROS	DISH	GILL	IRON	LUCK	NOSE	RAND
BUFF	DITS	GIMP	ITCH	LUMP	NUTS	RANG
BULK	DITZ	GIPS	JACK	LUST	PACE	RASP
BULL	DOGE	GIRL	JAGG	MALM	PALL	RAVE
BUMP	DOLL	GLAD	JAZZ	MALT	PALM	READ
BUNN	DONS	GLUE	JELL	MARL	PALS	REDD
BURL	DOOM	GOAT	JERK	MASH	PANS	REED
BURR	DOPE	GOOD	JIFF	MASS	PANT	REEF
BUSH	DORK	GOOF	JIMP	MATE	PARD	REEK
BUST	DORM	GOOK	JIVE	MEAL	PARK	REIF
BUTT	DOWN	GOON	JOCK	MEAN	PARR	RILE
BUZZ	DUCK	GOOP	JOKE	MEAT	PART	RIND
CAGE	DULL	GOOS	JOLT	MELT	PAST	RISK
CAKE	DUMP	GOUT	JOWL	MERC	PATS	RITZ
CAMP	DUNG	GRIM	JUMP	MESH	PEAK	ROCK
CANT	DUSK	GRIP	JUNK	MESS	PEAT	ROIL
CARN	DUST	GULF	KELP	MICK	PECK	ROOK
CARR	DYKE	GULL	KEMP	MIFF	PEER	ROOM
CASK	EARL	GULP	KICK	MILK	PEON	ROOT
CHAR	EBON	GUNK	KILT	MILT	PERK	ROPE
CHEW	EVER	GUSH	KINK	MINT	PERV	ROUP
COAL	FAIR	GUST	KISS	MIRK	PEST	RUDD
COBB	FAKE	GUTS	KOOK	MISS	PHON	RUNT

37

RUSH	SILK	STUD	TEEN	UNCO	WEED	WOOL
RUST	SILL	SUCK	TELL	UNIT	WEEN	WORD
SALL	SILT	SUDS	TENT	VAMP	WEEP	WORM
SALT	SLAT	SUET	TEST	VAST	WELL	WUSS
SAME	SLIM	SULK	THEW	VEAL	WHIN	YECH
SAND	SNOW	SUNN	TIPS	VEER	WHIT	YEUK
SARK	SOAP	SURF	TIZZ	VEIN	WIFE	YOLK
SASS	SOFT	SWAM	TOAD	VIEW	WILL	YUCK
SCAR	SONS	TACK	TOFF	VUGG	WIMP	ZEST
SEAM	SOOT	TALC	TONE	WACK	WIND	ZINC
SEED	SOPH	TALK	TOWN	WALL	WINE	ZING
SEEL	SOUP	TALL	TUFT	WANE	WING	
SEEP	SPIC	TANG	TURF	WART	WISP	
SHAD	SPIK	TANS	TUSH	WASH	WITH	
SHIN	SPIN	TART	TUSK	WASP	WOMB	
SHOW	STAG	TEAR	TWIN	WAVE	WONK	
SICK	STEW	TECH	TYPE	WEAR	WOOD	

With front hook Z

AMIA	AXES	EROS	ETAS	INKY	OWIE
ARFS	AYIN	ESTS	ILLS	ONES	

With back hook Z

BORT	FRIZ	PLOT	SPIT	WHIZ
FRIT	PHIZ	SPAZ	WARE	

Chapter 3: Five letter words with hooks

With front hook A

AHING	CHING	GENTS	MAZED	RILED	SURAS	VERTS
BASED	CORNS	GHAST	MAZES	RISEN	SWARM	VOIDS
BASER	CROSS	GISTS	MENDS	RISES	SWIRL	VOUCH
BASES	CUTER	GLARE	MENTA	ROUND	SWOON	VOWED
BATED	CUTES	GLEAM	MIDST	ROUSE	TELIC	VOWER
BATES	DEEMS	GOUTY	MINES	RUANA	TOLLS	WAITS
BIDED	DOBES	GREED	MOLES	SCEND	TONAL	WAKED
BIDER	DORES	GREES	MORAL	SCENT	TONED	WAKEN
BIDES	DRIFT	HOLDS	MOUNT	SCOTS	TONER	WAKES
BLATE	DROIT	HORSE	MUCKS	SHIER	TONES	WARDS
BLAZE	EDILE	IRING	MUSED	SHINE	TONIC	WEARY
BLEST	ERUGO	ISLED	MUSER	SHORE	TOPIC	WEIGH
BLOOM	ETHER	ISLES	MUSES	SIDES	TRIAL	WHILE
BLUSH	FIELD	LANDS	NEARS	SLANT	TWAIN	WHIRL
BOARD	FLAME	LARUM	NODAL	SLEEP	TWEEN	WOKEN
BODED	FLOAT	LATED	NODES	SLOPE	TYPIC	XENIC
BODES	FRESH	LEVIN	PHONY	SLOSH	UNTIE	ZINES
BORAL	FRITS	LIENS	PICAL	SPECT	URATE	ZONAL
BORTS	GAMAS	LIGHT	PIECE	SPICS	VAILS	
BOUND	GAMIC	LINED	RABIC	SPIRE	VAUNT	
BROAD	GAPES	LINER	RIDER	STERN	VENGE	
BUSED	GATES	LINES	RIELS	STONY	VENUE	
BUSES	GENES	LOINS	RIGHT	STRAY	VERSE	

With back hook A

AMENT	CAMIS	EXACT	HULLO	ORGAN	RHUMB	TREYF
AMRIT	CHARK	GLOSS	KORUN	PAGOD	SANGH	TUNIC
ARGAL	CHORE	GOTCH	MAXIM	PATIN	SENOR	WATCH
BERTH	CONCH	GRAMP	MIASM	PENNI	SPIRE	WHIRR
BIFID	CORNU	HALAL	MINIM	PLASM	STERN	
BILBO	EGEST	HALLO	NYMPH	QUANT	STRUM	
BOCCI	EJECT	HILLO	OBELI	QUINT	TALUK	
CABAL	ENTER	HOLLO	OCHRE	QUOTH	TARSI	

With front hook B

ABOON	ANGER	EATEN	IONIC	LASTS	LINGS	LOTTO
ACHED	ANGLE	EATER	IOTAS	LAWED	LINKS	LOUSE
ACHES	ARROW	EGGAR	ITCHY	LAZED	LITES	LOUSY
ADDER	ASHED	EGGED	LACKS	LAZES	LITHE	LOWED
ADMAN	ASHES	ENDED	LADED	LEACH	LOBBY	LOWER
ADMEN	ASKED	ENDER	LADER	LEAKS	LOCKS	LUFFS
AGGER	ASSES	HAJIS	LADES	LEARS	LOGGY	LUNGE
AGGIE	ASSET	HANGS	LAMED	LEARY	LOOEY	LUNTS
AILED	ASTER	HOOTS	LAMER	LENDS	LOOIE	OASTS
AIRNS	ATMAN	ICKER	LAMES	LIGHT	LOOMS	OATER
ALDER	EAGLE	ILLER	LANCH	LIMEY	LOOPS	OCHES
ALLOT	EASTS	INNED	LARES	LIMPS	LOOPY	OFFED

OGLES	OUNCE	RAKES	RAZER	RICKS	ROILS	UNCOS
OILED	OVINE	RANCH	RAZES	RIDES	ROODS	UNION
OILER	OWING	RANDS	REACH	RIDGE	ROOKS	URGER
OINKS	OXERS	RANDY	READS	RIGHT	ROOMS	URIAL
OKEHS	RACED	RANKS	READY	RILLS	ROOMY	URPED
OLDER	RACER	RANTS	REAMS	RINGS	ROSES	URSAE
OMBER	RACES	RATTY	REDES	RINKS	ROWED	USHER
OOZED	RAGGY	RAVED	REEDS	RISES	RUINS	USING
OOZES	RAIDS	RAVER	REEKS	RISKS	RUNTS	UTTER
ORALS	RAILS	RAVES	REGMA	ROACH	RUSHY	
ORATE	RAINS	RAWER	RENTS	ROADS	UDDER	
ORDER	RAINY	RAWLY	REVET	ROAST	UMMED	
OTHER	RAISE	RAYED	REWED	ROCKS	UMPED	
OUGHT	RAKED	RAZED	RIBES	ROGUE	UMPHS	

With back hook B

SUPER

With front hook C

ABLED	AVERS	HICKS	IVIES	LOSES	OUTER	REEKS
ABLER	AWING	HIDED	LACKS	LOUGH	OVARY	REELS
ABLES	EASED	HIDER	LADES	LOURS	OVENS	RESTS
ACHED	EASES	HIDES	LAMPS	LOUTS	OVERS	REWED
ACHES	ENTER	HILLS	LANKY	LOVER	OVERT	RICKS
AGERS	ESSES	HILLY	LASSY	LOVES	OVINE	RIMES
AGING	HAIRS	HINKY	LASTS	LUCKS	OWING	RIPES
AIRNS	HAMMY	HINTS	LAVER	LUMPS	RACKS	RISES
ALIFS	HANCE	HIPPY	LAVES	LUMPY	RAFTS	ROCKS
ALLEE	HANGS	HIVES	LAWED	LUNKS	RAGGY	ROOKS
ALLOW	HANTS	HOCKS	LAYED	OASTS	RAKES	ROTCH
AMASS	HARDS	HOKED	LEANS	OATER	RAMPS	ROUPS
AMBER	HARED	HOKES	LEARS	OBIAS	RANCH	ROUPY
AMPED	HARES	HOKEY	LEAVE	OCKER	RANKS	ROUSE
ANKLE	HARKS	HOLLA	LEEKS	ODDER	RAPED	ROUTE
ANNAS	HARMS	HOLOS	LEFTS	OFFER	RAPES	ROWDY
ANTED	HARRY	HOOKS	LEVER	OILED	RASES	ROWED
ANTIC	HARTS	HOPPY	LEVIS	OILER	RATCH	ROWER
ANYON	HASTE	HORAL	LICKS	OLDER	RATED	RUCKS
APERS	HAUNT	HOSEN	LIFTS	OLLIE	RATER	RUDDY
APING	HAWED	HOSES	LIMBS	OMBER	RATES	RUDER
APISH	HAZAN	HOUSE	LIMES	OMERS	RAVED	RUMMY
ARLES	HEAPS	HUBBY	LINES	ONIUM	RAVEN	RUMPS
ARSES	HEATS	HUCKS	LINGS	OPALS	RAVER	RURAL
ARTEL	HECKS	HUFFS	LINGY	OPENS	RAVES	RUSES
ASHED	HEDER	HUFFY	LINKS	OPING	RAWLY	RUSTS
ASHES	HEMIC	HUMPS	LOCHE	ORALS	RAYON	RUSTY
ASKED	HERRY	HUNKS	LOCKS	ORDER	RAZED	UMBER
ASTER	HESTS	HUNKY	LOGGY	OSIER	RAZES	UNITS
AUDAD	HETHS	HURLS	LONER	OSMIC	REAMS	UPPED
AUGHT	HEWED	ILIUM	LOOTS	OTTAR	REDOS	UPPER
AURIS	HEWER	ITHER	LOSER	OTTER	REEDS	URARE

URARI   URATE   URIAL   UTTER   YESES

With back hook C

ACINI	CULTI	FUNGI	LIMBI	PIANI
CAPRI	FILMI	IAMBI	MANIA	THYMI
COCCI	FUNDI	KALPA	PARSE	TRAGI

With front hook D

ADDLE	EARTH	HOOLY	JINNS	RAFFS	REARS	RUSES
AFTER	EAVED	ICIER	OCKER	RAFTS	RECKS	UMBER
AGGER	EAVES	ICING	ODDER	RAGEE	RIFTS	UMBOS
AMPED	EDUCE	ICKER	OFFED	RAGGY	RILLS	UMPED
AMPLY	EDUCT	IGGED	OFFER	RAILS	RINKS	UNITE
ANGER	EJECT	IMPLY	OILED	RAINS	RIVEN	UPPED
ANGLE	EKING	INGLE	OPING	RAKES	RIVER	WALES
APPLE	ELATE	INKED	ORMER	RAPED	RIVES	WELLS
ASHED	ELUDE	INNED	OTTER	RAPER	ROGUE	WINED
ASHES	ELVER	INNER	OUGHT	RAPES	ROLLS	WINES
AUNTS	ELVES	IRKED	OUTED	RAWER	ROUTH	
AVENS	EMITS	ITHER	OVENS	RAWLY	ROVED	
AWING	EMOTE	JEBEL	OWING	RAYED	ROVER	
AWNED	EVILS	JIBBA	OWNED	READS	ROVES	
EARLY	HOLES	JINNI	OWNER	REAMS	RUMLY	

With back hook D

ABASE	BARBE	BRAZE	CHIEL	DANCE	EMOTE	FLITE
ABATE	BARDE	BRIAR	CHIME	DAUBE	ENDUE	FLUKE
ABIDE	BARGE	BRIBE	CHINE	DEAVE	ENSUE	FLUME
ABODE	BARRE	BRINE	CHOKE	DEICE	ENURE	FLUTE
ABUSE	BASTE	BRUTE	CHORE	DELVE	ERASE	FLYTE
ACARI	BATHE	BUDGE	CHUSE	DEUCE	ERODE	FORCE
ADDLE	BELIE	BUGLE	CHUTE	DINGE	EVADE	FORGE
ADORE	BELLE	BULGE	CLEPE	DODGE	EVITE	FORME
AERIE	BERME	BURKE	CLONE	DONNE	EVOKE	FRAME
AGREE	BILGE	BUTLE	CLOSE	DORSA	EXILE	FUDGE
AISLE	BINGE	BUTTE	COCCI	DOUSE	EXUDE	FUGLE
ALATE	BIRLE	CABLE	COMBE	DOWSE	FABLE	FUGUE
ALINE	BLADE	CACHE	COOEE	DRAPE	FADGE	GABLE
AMAZE	BLAME	CADGE	COSIE	DRONE	FARCE	GAFFE
AMBLE	BLARE	CALVE	COUPE	DROVE	FEASE	GAUGE
AMUSE	BLAZE	CANOE	COZIE	DROWN	FEAZE	GLACE
ANELE	BLUME	CARTE	CRANE	DWINE	FEEZE	GLARE
ANGLE	BOMBE	CARVE	CRAPE	EAGLE	FENCE	GLAZE
ANKLE	BOOZE	CAUSE	CRATE	EDUCE	FESSE	GLIDE
ARGLE	BOUSE	CEASE	CRAVE	ELATE	FIBRE	GLIME
ARGUE	BOWSE	CENSE	CRAZE	ELIDE	FIDGE	GLOBE
ATONE	BOYAR	CHAFE	CREPE	ELOPE	FILLE	GLOVE
AWAKE	BRACE	CHARE	CURSE	ELUDE	FLAKE	GLOZE
AZOTE	BRAKE	CHASE	CURVE	ELUTE	FLAME	GOOSE
BADGE	BRAVE	CHIDE	CYCLE	EMCEE	FLARE	GORGE

GOUGE	KNIFE	OCHRE	QUEUE	SEGUE	SOUSE	TETRA
GRACE	KYTHE	OLLIE	QUIRE	SEINE	SPACE	THEME
GRADE	LADLE	OPINE	QUOTE	SEISE	SPADE	THOLE
GRATE	LANCE	ORATE	RAISE	SEIZE	SPARE	TINGE
GRAVE	LAPSE	PANNE	RANGE	SENSE	SPICE	TITHE
GRAZE	LATHE	PARGE	RAZEE	SERGE	SPIKE	TITLE
GRIDE	LEASE	PARLE	REAVE	SERVE	SPILE	TOGAE
GRIME	LEAVE	PARSE	RECCE	SHADE	SPINE	TOILE
GRIPE	LEDGE	PASSE	REDYE	SHALE	SPIRE	TOUSE
GROPE	LENSE	PASTE	REEVE	SHAME	SPITE	TRACE
GROVE	LEVEE	PAUSE	REIVE	SHAPE	SPOKE	TRADE
GUIDE	LIGAN	PEACE	REMAN	SHARE	SPORE	TRICE
GUILE	LODGE	PEEVE	RENTE	SHAVE	SPUME	TRINE
GUISE	LONGE	PEISE	RESEE	SHIEL	STAGE	TROKE
GUNGE	LOOSE	PENNE	RETIE	SHINE	STAKE	TRUCE
GURGE	LOTTE	PHASE	RETRO	SHORE	STALE	TWINE
HALVE	LOUPE	PHONE	REUSE	SHOVE	STANE	TYTHE
HASTE	LOUSE	PIECE	REWIN	SHREW	STARE	UNITE
HEAVE	LUNGE	PIQUE	RHYME	SHUTE	STATE	UNTIE
HEDGE	MACLE	PLACE	RIDGE	SIDLE	STAVE	VALUE
HEEZE	MAILE	PLANE	RIFLE	SIEGE	STIPE	VALVE
HELVE	MASSE	PLATE	RILLE	SIEVE	STOKE	VARVE
HINGE	MATTE	PLOYE	RINSE	SINGE	STOLE	VENGE
HOISE	MEDIA	PLUME	ROGUE	SKATE	STONE	VERGE
HORDE	MENSE	POISE	ROOSE	SKITE	STOPE	VERSE
HORSE	MERGE	PONCE	ROTTE	SKIVE	STORE	VOGUE
HOUSE	METRE	PRATE	ROUGE	SLAKE	STOVE	VOICE
IMAGE	MICHE	PRICE	ROUSE	SLATE	STYLE	VOLTE
IMBUE	MILLE	PRIDE	ROUTE	SLAVE	SUEDE	WACKE
INDUE	MINCE	PRIME	RUCHE	SLICE	SUITE	WAIVE
INURE	MITRE	PRISE	RUFFE	SLIME	SURGE	WASTE
IRONE	MONIE	PRIZE	SABRE	SLIPE	SWAGE	WEAVE
ISSUE	MOUSE	PROBE	SALVE	SLOPE	SWIPE	WEDGE
JAMBE	NACRE	PROSE	SAUCE	SMILE	SWIVE	WHALE
JESSE	NAPPE	PROVE	SAUTE	SMOKE	SWOUN	WHILE
JUDGE	NERVE	PRUNE	SCALE	SNAKE	TABLE	WHINE
JUICE	NICHE	PULSE	SCAPE	SNARE	TARRE	WHITE
KEDGE	NOISE	PUREE	SCARE	SNIPE	TASTE	WHORE
KERNE	NOOSE	PURGE	SCOPE	SNORE	TAWSE	WINCE
KITHE	NUDGE	PURSE	SCORE	SOLAN	TEASE	WITHE
KLUGE	NURSE	QUAKE	SCREE	SOLVE	TENSE	YODLE

With front hook E

AGERS	DUCTS	LICIT	LUTES	PATER	RODES	SPRIT
AGLET	GESTS	LINTS	MAILS	PICAL	ROSES	STATE
ASTER	IKONS	LITES	MENDS	POSES	SCAPE	STOPS
BOOKS	ITHER	LOINS	MERGE	QUATE	SCARP	STRAY
CARTE	LANDS	LOPED	MOTES	QUIDS	SCARS	STRUM
CHARD	LAPSE	LOPER	NATES	QUIPS	SCOTS	TALON
CHING	LATED	LOPES	NEMAS	RASED	SCUDO	TAPES
CLOSE	LATER	LUDES	PACTS	RASER	SPIED	TERNE
DUCES	LEGIT	LUTED	PARCH	RASES	SPIES	THANE

TOILE   TRIER   VENTS   VERTS   VILER

With back hook E

AGORA	CHOWS	FONDU	INDOL	OSMOL	SABIN	THECA
ALMUD	CLOTH	FORBY	IODID	OUTBY	SAITH	THEIN
ALULA	CNIDA	FORME	IODIN	PALEA	SALPA	THERM
AMEBA	COIGN	FOSSA	KARAT	PARDI	SALUT	THORP
AMPUL	COLON	FOVEA	KINAS	PAROL	SAROD	TIBIA
ANCON	CONGE	FRISE	LAMIA	PASSE	SAVIN	TOLAN
ANNEX	CONIN	FURAN	LARVA	PATIN	SCHMO	TOROS
ANYON	COOMB	FUROR	LASSI	PAVAN	SCOPA	TOUCH
AORTA	CORPS	FUSIL	LAURA	PAVIS	SCRAP	TOXIN
AVERS	COSTA	GALEA	LIBRA	PENNA	SERIN	TRIOS
BACCA	COTTA	GAMIN	LIPAS	PERDU	SEVER	TROMP
BARGE	COVIN	GAUCH	LIPID	PETIT	SILVA	TRYST
BATTU	CROSS	GEMMA	LOATH	PHYLA	SKEAN	TUYER
BLEND	CROUP	GEMOT	LOCAL	PINNA	SNATH	UMBRA
BLOND	CULPA	GENOM	LUNGE	PLEAS	SOOTH	UNCIA
BOCCI	CURIA	GLAIR	LUPIN	PLICA	SOZIN	UNCUT
BOURN	DECAN	GLEBA	LYSIN	POINT	SPARS	UNRIP
BRIBE	DEMUR	GOURD	LYTTA	POUFF	SPICA	URBAN
BROCH	DERAT	GRIFF	MADAM	PSYCH	SPRIT	UREAS
BROWS	DEVIS	GRILL	MALIC	PURIN	STELA	UVULA
BUBAL	DILDO	GROSZ	MAMMA	PUTTI	STING	VENDU
BULLA	DONNE	GUTTA	MEDIA	QUART	STOUR	VENIN
BURSA	EMERG	GYROS	MENSA	QUINT	STRIA	VERST
CAMIS	ENZYM	HALID	MERGE	RALLY	STRIP	VILLA
CAPOT	EOSIN	HEARS	MONGO	RAVIN	SUMMA	VIRGA
CARAT	EXPOS	HERMA	MORAL	RECIT	SWATH	VIRTU
CELLA	FACET	HEXAD	MUSCA	REDIA	SWING	VITTA
CHAIN	FACIA	HOARS	NUCHA	REDON	SWITH	VULVA
CHAIS	FARCI	HORST	OCREA	REGAL	SYLVA	WATAP
CHANG	FAUNA	HUMAN	OCTAN	REPIN	TAMAL	ZOMBI
CHELA	FERIA	HYDRA	OLEIN	REPOS	TEETH	
CHILD	FILOS	HYPHA	ORACH	RESID	TENIA	
CHINS	FINAL	IMPED	ORANG	RESIT	TERRA	
CHIRR	FLORA	INCUS	ORPIN	ROTCH	TESTA	

With front hook F

ABLED	ANGAS	EARED	INKED	LANES	LENSE	LONGS
ABLER	ANION	EASED	INNED	LARES	LETCH	LOOEY
ABLES	ARCED	EASES	IRING	LAVAS	LEXES	LOOIE
ACING	ARLES	EASTS	ITCHY	LAWED	LICKS	LOPPY
ACTOR	ARMED	EATER	LACKS	LAXES	LIERS	LORAL
AERIE	ARMER	ENDED	LAIRS	LAYED	LIGHT	LOSSY
AILED	ARROW	ENDER	LAKED	LAYER	LINGS	LOTAS
AIRED	ASHED	ESSES	LAKER	LEDGE	LINTS	LOURS
AIRER	ASHES	ESTER	LAKES	LEDGY	LINTY	LOURY
ALLOW	ASTER	IGGED	LAMED	LEECH	LIPPY	LOUTS
ALTER	AWNED	ILIAL	LAMER	LEERS	LITES	LOWED
AMINE	AXING	ILLER	LAMES	LEETS	LOCKS	LOWER

43

LUFFS	LUXES	OLIOS	RAILS	REEST	RISES	RUGAL
LUMPS	LYING	ORMER	RAISE	RIDGE	RISKS	RUMPS
LUNKS	ODDER	OUGHT	RANKS	RIGHT	RISKY	UNDER
LUTED	OILED	OYERS	RATER	RIGID	RITES	USING
LUTES	OLDER	RACKS	RAYED	RILLS	ROCKS	UTILE

With back hook F

BELIE	GONIF	PILAF

With front hook G

ABBAS	ASHES	LAIRY	LOSSY	RACES	REAVE	ROUSE
ABLED	ASPER	LANCE	LOUTS	RAFTS	REEDS	ROUTS
ABLES	ASSES	LANDS	LOVED	RAILS	REEDY	ROVED
ABOON	ASTER	LARES	LOVER	RAINS	RIDES	ROVES
ACHED	AUGER	LASSY	LOVES	RAINY	RIFFS	ROWER
ACHES	EARED	LAZED	LOWED	RAMPS	RIFTS	ROWTH
ADDED	ELATE	LAZES	LOWER	RANDS	RILLE	RUBBY
ADDER	ELDER	LEANS	LUMPY	RANGE	RILLS	RUFFS
AGERS	EMOTE	LEDES	LUNCH	RANTS	RIMED	RUMPS
AGGER	ENDER	LEEKS	LUTES	RAPES	RIMES	RUNTS
AGING	ENTRY	LEETS	NATTY	RASPS	RINDS	UMBOS
ALLEY	HARRY	LIMED	NOMES	RATED	RIOTS	UMMAS
AMBIT	HOSTS	LIMES	NOSES	RATER	RIPED	UMMED
AMBLE	IGGED	LINTS	OBOES	RATES	RIPER	UNITE
AMINE	ILLER	LINTY	OFFER	RAVED	RIPES	UNMAN
AMINS	IMPED	LOAMS	OLDEN	RAVEL	RIVET	URGED
ANGER	INNED	LOBBY	OLDER	RAVEN	ROANS	URGES
ANGLE	INNER	LOBED	OMERS	RAVER	ROOMS	USHER
APERS	IRONS	LOBES	ONION	RAVES	ROPED	UTTER
APING	LACED	LOOMS	ONIUM	RAYED	ROPER	
ARGLE	LACES	LOOPS	ORALS	RAZED	ROPES	
ASCON	LADES	LOOPY	OWNED	RAZER	ROUND	
ASHED	LAIRS	LOPPY	RACED	RAZES	ROUPS	

With back hook G

ACTIN	CONIN	LAYIN	MIRIN	PROLE	ROSIN	TAKIN
BARON	COVIN	LININ	PAVIN	RAVIN	SATIN	
BASIN	GAMIN	LYSIN	PHOTO	RICIN	SAVIN	
BELON	GOBAN	MATIN	PORIN	ROBIN	SERIN	

With front hook H

ACKEE	ALTER	ARTAL	EARTH	ELVES	ITHER	OPING
AFTER	ANGER	ASHED	EATER	EMMER	OBOES	OSIER
AILED	ANGRY	ASHES	EAVED	EWERS	OCKER	OTTER
AIRED	ANTED	AUNTS	EAVES	EXING	OLDEN	OUSEL
ALLOT	ARBOR	AVENS	EDGED	ICKER	OLDER	OVERS
ALLOW	ARMED	AVERS	EDGER	ILLER	OLLAS	OWLET
ALMAS	ARMER	AWING	EDGES	INTER	OMBRE	UMMED
ALOES	ARROW	AZANS	EIGHT	IRING	OMERS	UMPED

UMPHS

With back hook H

ALIYA	FELLA	HUZZA	LAVAS	PALIS	SAMEK	SUNNA
ANKUS	FINIS	IMPIS	LIROT	PARIS	SCARP	SWART
ASPIS	GANJA	JIBBA	LOOFA	PERIS	SCOUT	TOROT
COHOS	HALVA	KHEDA	MATZA	POLIS	SHEIK	TREFA
COMET	HAMZA	KIBBE	MATZO	PRUTA	SHIVA	WALLA
COPRA	HEART	KIBLA	MIKVA	PUKKA	SHOOS	WHYDA
DELIS	HIGHT	KIPPA	MINIS	PUNKA	SIRRA	ZIBET
DOURA	HIJRA	KURUS	MOOLA	PURDA	SPILT	ZIZIT
EIGHT	HOOKA	LAMED	MULLA	RAKIS	SUMAC	

With front hook I

BICES	CONIC	LEXES	NERTS	RIDES	SLING
BISES	DEALS	MAGES	ONIUM	RISES	
CONES	DENTS	MINES	RATER	SATIN	

With back hook I

ANNUL	COLON	DJINN	HERMA	KULAK	POLYP	SMALT
ARGAL	CUBIT	EPHOR	JEHAD	MOIRA	RHOMB	SOLID
CAROL	DECAN	GARDA	JIHAD	NEROL	SCAMP	STELA
CHILL	DENAR	GLUTE	KROON	PIROG	SENSE	YOGIN

With front hook J

AGERS	APERS	ASPER	ESSES	INGLE	OTTER	UDDER
AGGER	APERY	AUNTS	ESTER	INKED	OUNCE	UMBOS
AILED	APING	AUNTY	IGGED	INKER	OUSTS	UMPED
ANGLE	ARGON	AWING	IMPLY	NANAS	OWING	UNCOS

With front hook K

ABAKA	AURIS	EVILS	INKED	LUGES	NURLS	VETCH
ABAYA	EDGED	EYERS	LATCH	NAVES	RAFTS	YACKS
ALIFS	EDGES	EYING	LICKS	NIGHT	RATER	
ALONG	EGGED	HETHS	LONGS	NOBBY	RILLS	
APEEK	EGGER	ICKER	LOOFS	NOCKS	RISES	
ARRIS	ERNES	ILLER	LUGED	NUBBY	VASES	

With back hook K

ANTIC	EMBAR	MEDIC	REBEC	SQUAW	ZEBEC
DEBAR	KALPA	MUSIC	RESEE	UMIAC	

With front hook L

ACHES	AGERS	AMBER	AMPED	ARVAL	ASSES	AURAE
ACING	AGGER	AMENT	APSES	ASHED	ASTER	AURAS
ADDER	AIRED	AMIAS	ARUMS	ASHES	ATRIA	AVERS

AWFUL	EASES	EDGER	IMPED	IZARD	OPING	UMPED
AWING	EASTS	EDGES	IMPLY	LAMAS	OTTER	USHER
AWNED	EAVED	EGERS	INKED	OAVES	OTTOS	
AYINS	EAVES	EGGED	INKER	OCHES	OUTED	
EARNS	ECHED	ENDER	INTER	OCKER	OVERS	
EASED	ECHES	ICKER	ISLES	OCULI	OWING	
EASER	EDGED	IMBED	ITHER	OFTER	UMBER	

With back hook L

ACETA	BARRE	ENROL	KNAWE	PASSE	SAMBA	TELIA
AECIA	BEDEL	EXTOL	LABIA	PASTE	SANTO	TERCE
AMIDO	BURSA	FACIA	LABRA	PENCE	SEPTA	TERGA
ANIMA	CAECA	FAUNA	LARVA	PINNA	SERAI	THECA
ANTRA	CARTE	FERIA	LUTEA	PLICA	SHOVE	TIBIA
ANURA	CARVE	FESTA	MAMMA	PRIMA	SIGNA	TINEA
AORTA	CHAPE	FLORA	MANGE	RECTA	SORTA	TRAVE
APNEA	COSTA	FOVEA	MEDIA	REDIA	SPINE	UMBRA
APPAL	CRURA	GRAVE	MENSA	REFEL	STIPE	UNCIA
ARCHI	CURIA	GROVE	MENTA	REGNA	STOMA	VANDA
ASSAI	DERMA	HANSE	MONGO	RETIA	SWIVE	VESTA
ATRIA	DORSA	HOUSE	MORSE	RIDGE	TASSE	VULVA
BABOO	DRIVE	HYPHA	NUCHA	RONDE	TEASE	XENIA
BARBE	DRUPE	KERNE	PALEA	SACRA	TECTA	

With front hook M

ACHES	ALIGN	ANTES	ASSES	ESNES	OCKER	OWING
ACING	ALINE	ANTIC	ASTER	ESSES	OILED	UDDER
ACROS	ALLEE	ANTIS	AUGER	ETHYL	OILER	UMMED
ADDED	ALLOW	ANTRA	AVENS	ILIUM	OLDER	UMPED
ADDER	AMBOS	ARROW	AWING	ILLER	OLLIE	URINE
ADMAN	AMIES	ARSES	AXING	INGLE	OPING	USERS
ADMEN	ANGAS	ASCON	EAGER	INION	ORALS	USHER
AGMAS	ANGEL	ASCOT	EAGRE	INTER	ORGAN	USING
AILED	ANGER	ASHED	ELDER	IRIDS	ORRIS	UTTER
AIMED	ANGLE	ASHES	EMBER	IRING	OTHER	
AIMER	ANNAS	ASKED	ENDED	ISLED	OTTOS	
ALATE	ANTAS	ASKER	ENDER	ITHER	OVERS	

With back hook M

BALSA	CENTU	CONDO	DODGE	PURIS	SPIRE
BAZOO	CHIAS	COPAL	LINGA	SADIS	YOGIS

With front hook N

ACHES	AILED	ARROW	EATEN	ETHER	OPALS	OVATE
ACRED	AIVER	AUGHT	EATER	ICKER	OSIER	UMBER
ACRES	ANNAS	EARED	ESSES	ODDER	OTHER	UNCLE
AGGER	APERY	EARLY	ESTER	OMENS	OUGHT	UTTER

With back hook N

AMEBA	CANTO	FROZE	MACRO	RABBI	SHAVE	UNSAW
AMNIO	CARBO	GLUTE	MANNA	RATIO	SILVA	UNSEE
ANURA	CARVE	GRAVE	MEDIA	RESAW	SPOKE	UNSEW
ARISE	CAVER	HASTE	MICRO	RESEE	STOLE	VODOU
ASTER	CEDAR	HEAVE	PAISA	RESEW	STREW	WEDEL
AWAKE	CHOSE	INTER	PANDA	RESOW	STROW	WHITE
AWOKE	CLOVE	INTRO	PEASE	ROTTE	SYLVA	WICCA
BABOO	COMMO	KRONE	PEPSI	SCHUL	THORO	WIVER
BARRE	CRAVE	LATTE	PHONO	SCREE	THRAW	WORSE
BRAZE	DOLMA	LEAVE	PHOTO	SEXTO	THROW	
BROKE	DRIVE	LOOSE	PLATE	SHAKE	TORTE	
CALLA	FLAME	LOUPE	PROVE	SHAPE	TRIGO	

With front hook O

BENTO	CELLI	LIVES	PINES	RANGY	SCARS	VOIDS
BLAST	EDEMA	MENTA	PUSES	RATED	STEAL	ZONES
BLATE	GIVES	OHING	RALLY	RATES	TITIS	
BOLES	INKED	OLOGY	RANGE	READS	URARI	
BOLUS	LINGO	PINED	RANGS	RIELS	VINES	

With back hook O

BRILL	CONCH	HULLO	PSEUD	ROMAN	STING	WHATS
BRONC	CRYPT	MEDIC	PSYCH	SHACK	STINK	
CHARR	DINER	MORPH	QUART	SMALT	TOLED	
CHEAP	GAUCH	NYMPH	RABAT	SOLAN	VOMIT	
CHEER	HALLO	PEDAL	RANCH	SPEED	WEIRD	
CHURR	HOLLO	PREST	RIGHT	STERE	WHACK	

With front hook P

ACING	ASHES	HONES	LACES	LOVER	OUTED	REFER
ADDED	ASSES	HONEY	LACKS	LOWED	OUTER	REFIX
ADDER	ASTER	HOOEY	LANCH	LOWER	RAISE	REMAN
ADDLE	AVERS	ICKER	LANES	LUCKS	RANCE	REMIX
AEONS	AWING	IGGED	LATED	LUCKY	RANGS	REPAY
AGERS	AWNED	ILEUM	LATEN	LUMPS	RANKS	RESET
AGING	EARLS	ILEUS	LATER	LUMPY	RASES	RESTS
AIRED	EARLY	IMPED	LAYED	LUNGE	RATED	RETAX
ALATE	EASES	IMPLY	LAYER	LUNKS	RATER	REVUE
ALTER	ECHED	INION	LEACH	LYING	RATES	REXES
ANGAS	EERIE	INKED	LEADS	ODIUM	RAXES	REZES
ANTED	EGGED	INKER	LEASE	OLDER	RAYED	RICED
APERS	ELITE	INNED	LEDGE	OLIOS	REACH	RICER
APERY	ELVES	INNER	LEXES	OOHED	REACT	RICES
ARLES	ENDED	IONIC	LIERS	OSIER	REARM	RICKS
ARSES	ERSES	IRATE	LIGHT	OTHER	REBID	RIDES
ARSON	ESTER	ITCHY	LINKS	OTTER	REBUY	RILLS
ARVOS	HONED	LACED	LINKY	OTTOS	RECUT	RIMED
ASHED	HONER	LACER	LOUGH	OUNCE	REDRY	RIMER

RIMES	ROBED	ROPER	ROVEN	RUNES	URGED	USHER
RINKS	ROBES	ROSED	ROVER	SHAWS	URGER	UTTER
RISES	ROLES	ROSES	ROVES	UMPED	URGES	
RIVET	ROOFS	ROVED	ROWER	UPPED	URINE	

With back hook P

ESCAR	SCRIM	SHLEP	THREE	TRICE

With front hook R

ACING	AMBLE	APTLY	EDUCE	ENVOI	IGGED	OUTER
ADDED	AMIES	ASHES	EGRET	EROSE	OARED	OVERS
ADDER	AMINS	ASPER	EJECT	ESTER	OASTS	OWING
ADDLE	AMPED	ASTER	ELAND	ETAPE	OCKER	UDDER
ADIOS	ANCHO	AVENS	ELATE	EVERT	OILED	UNLET
AFTER	ANGER	AVERS	EMAIL	EVERY	OLLIE	URBAN
AGERS	ANKLE	AXING	EMEND	EVOKE	ONION	USHER
AGING	ANTED	AYAHS	EMITS	EXINE	OPING	UTILE
AIDED	APERS	EARED	EMOTE	HEMES	OSIER	
AIDER	APHIS	EAVED	ENDED	ICING	OTTER	
AILED	APING	EAVES	ENDER	ICTUS	OUSTS	
AKEES	APPEL	EBOOK	ENTER	IDENT	OUTED	

With back hook R

ABASE	BOMBE	CENSE	DELVE	FLUTE	IMAGE	MANGE
ABATE	BONZE	CHAFE	DENSE	FOLIA	INANE	MATTE
ABIDE	BOOZE	CHASE	DINGE	FORCE	IRATE	MENTO
ABUSE	BOWSE	CHIDE	DODGE	FORGE	IRONE	MERGE
ACUTE	BRACE	CHIME	DOUCE	FORME	ISSUE	MILLE
ADORE	BRAVE	CHOKE	DOUSE	FRAME	JUDGE	MINCE
AERIE	BRAZE	CLAVE	DOWSE	GAFFE	JUICE	MOUSE
ALINE	BRIBE	CLONE	DRAPE	GAUGE	KNIFE	NAIVE
ALULA	BRINE	CLOSE	DRIVE	GLAZE	KRONE	NAPPE
AMBLE	BROKE	CLOVE	DRONE	GLIDE	LADLE	NOBLE
AMPLE	BRUTE	COMBE	DROVE	GLOVE	LANCE	NOOSE
AMUSE	BUDGE	CONDO	EERIE	GORGE	LAPSE	NUDGE
ANCHO	BUGLE	CONGE	ELATE	GOUGE	LARGE	NURSE
ANGLE	BULGE	COSIE	ELOPE	GRADE	LATHE	PANNE
ARGUE	BURKE	COSTA	ELUDE	GRATE	LATTE	PARSE
ATONE	BURSA	COTTA	EMOTE	GRAVE	LEASE	PASSE
BADGE	BUTLE	COZIE	ERASE	GRAZE	LEAVE	PASTE
BARBE	BUTTE	CRATE	EVADE	GRIPE	LEDGE	PAUSE
BASTE	CABLE	CRAVE	EVOKE	GROPE	LIEVE	PENNE
BATHE	CADGE	CROZE	EXILE	GUIDE	LITHE	PHASE
BEIGE	CANOE	CRUDE	FABLE	HAUTE	LODGE	PHONE
BELIE	CANTO	CURSE	FALSE	HAWSE	LONGE	PHYLA
BINGE	CARTE	CYCLE	FARCE	HEAVE	LOOSE	PIECE
BIRLE	CARVE	DANCE	FENCE	HEDGE	LOTTE	PLACE
BLADE	CASTE	DAUBE	FILLE	HINGE	LUNGE	PLANE
BLAME	CAUSE	DEBUR	FLAKE	HOMIE	MACHE	PLATE
BLAZE	CELLA	DEICE	FLAME	HOUSE	MAILE	POISE

PRATE	RECTO	SEINE	SLATE	SPIKE	TASTE	VOGUE
PRICE	REIVE	SEISE	SLAVE	STAGE	TEASE	VOICE
PRIME	RENTE	SEIZE	SLICE	STAKE	TENNE	VULVA
PRIZE	RHYME	SELLE	SLIDE	STALE	TENSE	WACKE
PROBE	RIFLE	SERGE	SLOPE	STARE	TERSE	WAIVE
PRONE	RINSE	SERVE	SMILE	STATE	TITHE	WASTE
PROSE	ROOSE	SHADE	SMITE	STELA	TOILE	WEAVE
PROVE	ROTTE	SHAKE	SMOKE	STOKE	TONNE	WHALE
PRUNE	ROUSE	SHAPE	SNARE	STONE	TRACE	WHINE
PULSE	ROUTE	SHARE	SNIDE	STOPE	TRADE	WHITE
PURGE	SABLE	SHAVE	SNIPE	STORE	TRITE	WINCE
PURSE	SALVE	SHINE	SNORE	STOVE	TROVE	WITHE
QUAKE	SALVO	SHIVE	SOLVE	STYLE	TWINE	WORSE
QUEUE	SAMBA	SHOVE	SONDE	SUAVE	UNITE	WRITE
QUOTE	SANGA	SIDLE	SOUSE	SUITE	UVULA	YODLE
RAISE	SAUCE	SINGE	SPACE	SURGE	VAGUE	
RANGE	SCALE	SKATE	SPADE	SWAGE	VALUE	
RATHE	SCARE	SKIVE	SPARE	SWILE	VERGE	
REAVE	SCORE	SLAKE	SPICE	SWIPE	VERSE	

With front hook S

ABLER	CAPES	CREAK	EWERS	HELLS	INNED	LEEKS
ABLES	CARED	CREAM	EXING	HELVE	INNER	LEETS
ACRED	CARER	CREED	EXIST	HERDS	INTER	LICKS
ADDER	CARES	CREWS	HACKS	HERRY	IRING	LIEVE
ADDLE	CARPS	CRIED	HADED	HEUCH	IZARS	LIGHT
AGGER	CARRY	CRIES	HADES	HEUGH	KEENS	LIMED
AILED	CARTS	CRIMP	HAFTS	HEWED	KEETS	LIMES
ALARY	CATTY	CRIPS	HAKES	HEWER	KELPS	LINGS
ALINE	CENTS	CRYER	HALED	HILLS	KERRY	LINKS
ALLOW	CIONS	CUFFS	HALES	HINNY	KETCH	LINKY
ALTER	COFFS	CULCH	HAMAL	HIRES	KIDDY	LIPPY
AMBOS	COLDS	CULLS	HAMES	HISTS	KIERS	LIVER
AMPLE	CONES	CURFS	HAMMY	HIVES	KILLS	LOBBY
ANGAS	COOCH	CURRY	HANDY	HOCKS	KINKS	LOGAN
ANGER	COOPS	CURVY	HANKS	HOERS	KITED	LOIDS
ASHED	COOTS	CUTCH	HARDS	HOOKS	KITES	LOOPS
ASHES	COPED	CUTES	HARED	HOOTS	LACKS	LOPED
ASSES	COPES	EARED	HARES	HOPPY	LAHAL	LOPER
AUGER	CORED	EATER	HARKS	HOVEL	LAKED	LOPES
AVANT	CORER	EDGES	HARPS	HOVER	LAKER	LOPPY
AVERS	CORES	EDILE	HARPY	HUCKS	LAKES	LOUGH
AWING	CORIA	EDUCE	HAUGH	HUNTS	LATCH	LOWED
AXMAN	CORNS	EGGAR	HAULS	HYING	LATED	LOWER
AXMEN	COUTH	ELECT	HAVEN	ICKER	LATER	LOWLY
CABBY	COWED	ELVES	HAVER	IDLED	LAVED	LUFFS
CALLS	COWLS	ENATE	HAVES	IDLER	LAVER	LUMPS
CAMPI	CRAGS	ENDED	HAWED	IDLES	LAVES	LUMPY
CAMPS	CRAMS	ENDER	HEALS	ILLER	LAYED	MACKS
CANTS	CRAPE	ENTRY	HEARS	IMPLY	LAYER	MALLS
CANTY	CRAPS	EVENS	HEATH	INGLE	LEAVE	MALTS
CAPED	CRAWL	EVERY	HEAVE	INKER	LEDGE	MARTS

49

MAZES	OARED	PEERS	PRIER	TEAKS	TOURS	WAGER
MELLS	OAVES	PEISE	PRIGS	TEALS	TOUTS	WAGES
MELTS	ODIUM	PELTS	PRINT	TEAMS	TOWED	WAILS
MERKS	OFTEN	PENCE	PROGS	TEELS	TRAIN	WAINS
MIDGE	OFTER	PENDS	PRYER	TEINS	TRAIT	WALES
MILER	OILED	PERMS	PUNKS	TELAE	TRAPS	WANKS
MILES	OLDER	PICAS	PUNKY	TELES	TRASS	WARDS
MIRKS	OMBER	PICKS	PURGE	TELIC	TRAYS	WARMS
MIRKY	OMBRE	PIERS	QUADS	TENCH	TRESS	WARTY
MITER	ORBED	PIKED	QUARE	TENTS	TREWS	WATCH
MITES	OUGHT	PIKER	QUARK	TERES	TRICK	WEARS
MOCKS	OUTER	PIKES	QUASH	TERNS	TRIKE	WEENY
MOGGY	OWING	PILED	QUIDS	TEWED	TRINE	WEEPS
MOKES	PACED	PILES	QUILL	TICKS	TRIPE	WEEPY
MOLTS	PACER	PILLS	QUINT	TIFFS	TRIPS	WEETS
MOOCH	PACES	PINED	QUIRE	TILES	TRODE	WELLS
MUTCH	PACEY	PINES	QUIRT	TILLS	TROKE	WILES
NAGGY	PAILS	PINNY	TABLE	TILTS	TROLL	WILLS
NAILS	PALES	PINTO	TACKS	TIMES	TROVE	WINES
NAKED	PALLS	PLASH	TAINS	TINGE	TROWS	WINGS
NAPPY	PARED	PLATS	TAKER	TINGS	TROYS	WINGY
NARES	PARER	PLAYS	TAKES	TINTS	TRUCK	WINKS
NARKS	PARES	POKED	TALER	TITCH	TUBBY	WIPED
NARKY	PARGE	POKES	TALES	TOCKS	TUFFS	WIPER
NATCH	PARKS	PONGY	TALKS	TOKED	TUMPS	WIPES
NEAPS	PARKY	POOFS	TALKY	TOKER	TYING	WITCH
NECKS	PARRY	POOFY	TALLS	TOKES	UMMAS	WITHE
NICKS	PARSE	POOLS	TAMPS	TOLED	UMMED	WIVED
NIFFS	PATES	POONS	TANGS	TOLES	UNDER	WIVES
NIFFY	PAVIN	PORED	TANKS	TONED	UNLIT	WOOPS
NIPPY	PAWNS	PORES	TAPES	TONER	UNSET	WOOPY
NITTY	PAYED	PORTS	TARED	TONES	UPPED	WOOSH
NOBBY	PEAKS	POTTY	TARES	TONEY	UPPER	WORDS
NOOKS	PEANS	POUTS	TARRY	TOOLS	URGED	WOUND
NOOSE	PEARS	PRANG	TARTS	TOPED	URGER	
NUBBY	PECKS	PRATS	TASES	TOPER	URGES	
NUFFS	PECKY	PRAYS	TATER	TOPES	USING	
OAKED	PEELS	PREES	TATES	TORES	WAGED	

With back hook S

AALII	ABIDE	ACTIN	ADMIT	AGATE	AGLOO	AIVER
ABACA	ABMHO	ACTOR	ADOBE	AGAVE	AGONE	AJIVA
ABAKA	ABODE	ACUTE	ADOBO	AGENE	AGORA	AJUGA
ABAMP	ABOHM	ADAGE	ADOPT	AGENT	AGREE	AKELA
ABASE	ABOMA	ADAPT	ADORE	AGGER	AGRIA	AKENE
ABATE	ABORT	ADBOT	ADORN	AGGIE	AHOLD	ALAMO
ABAYA	ABOVE	ADDER	ADULT	AGGRO	AIDER	ALAND
ABBES	ABUSE	ADDLE	AERIE	AGING	AIMER	ALANT
ABBEY	ABYSM	ADEEM	AFRIT	AGISM	AIOLI	ALARM
ABBOT	ACKEE	ADEPT	AFTER	AGIST	AIRER	ALATE
ABELE	ACORN	ADIEU	AGAMA	AGITA	AIRTH	ALBUM
ABHOR	ACROS	ADMIN	AGAPE	AGLET	AISLE	ALCID

ALDER	AMUSE	AROID	AZOTE	BEGIN	BIONT	BOGEY
ALDOL	ANCHO	AROMA	AZOTH	BEGUM	BIOTA	BOGIE
ALEPH	ANDRO	ARPEN	AZUKI	BEIGE	BIPED	BOGLE
ALERT	ANEAR	ARRAY	AZURE	BEING	BIPOD	BOHEA
ALGIN	ANELE	ARROW	BABEL	BELAY	BIRLE	BOING
ALGOR	ANGEL	ARSON	BABKA	BELGA	BIRSE	BOINK
ALGUM	ANGER	ARTEL	BABOO	BELIE	BIRTH	BOITE
ALIBI	ANGLE	ASANA	BABUL	BELLE	BISON	BOKEH
ALIEN	ANGLO	ASCON	BACON	BELON	BITER	BOMBE
ALIGN	ANGST	ASCOT	BADGE	BELOW	BLACK	BONCE
ALINE	ANIMA	ASDIC	BAGEL	BENDY	BLADE	BONER
ALIYA	ANIME	ASIDE	BAIRN	BENNE	BLAFF	BONGO
ALKIE	ANIMI	ASKER	BAIZA	BENNI	BLAIN	BONNE
ALKYD	ANION	ASPEN	BAIZE	BENTO	BLAME	BONZE
ALKYL	ANISE	ASPER	BAKER	BERET	BLANK	BOOST
ALLAY	ANKLE	ASPIC	BALER	BERME	BLARE	BOOTH
ALLEE	ANNAL	ASSAI	BALSA	BERTH	BLAST	BOOZE
ALLEY	ANNOY	ASSAY	BALTI	BERYL	BLAZE	BORAL
ALLOD	ANNUL	ASSES	BANCO	BESET	BLEAK	BORER
ALLOT	ANODE	ASSET	BANDA	BESOM	BLEAR	BORON
ALLOW	ANOLE	ASTER	BANJO	BESOT	BLEAT	BOSOM
ALLOY	ANTIC	ASURA	BARBE	BETEL	BLEED	BOSON
ALLYL	ANTRE	ATIGI	BARCA	BETON	BLEEP	BOSUN
ALMAH	ANVIL	ATMAN	BARDE	BETTA	BLEND	BOTEL
ALMEH	ANYON	ATOLL	BARFI	BEVEL	BLIMP	BOUGH
ALMUD	AORTA	ATONE	BARGE	BEVOR	BLIND	BOULE
ALMUG	APHID	ATTAR	BARON	BEWIG	BLING	BOULT
ALOHA	APNEA	ATTIC	BARRE	BEZEL	BLINI	BOUND
ALOIN	APPAL	AUDAD	BARYE	BEZIL	BLINK	BOURG
ALPHA	APPEL	AUDIO	BASIC	BHAJI	BLITE	BOURN
ALTAR	APPLE	AUDIT	BASIL	BHANG	BLOAT	BOUSE
ALTER	APRON	AUGER	BASIN	BHOOT	BLOCK	BOVID
ALVAR	ARAME	AUGHT	BASSO	BIALI	BLOKE	BOWEL
ALWAY	ARBOR	AUGUR	BASTE	BIALY	BLOND	BOWER
AMAZE	ARDEB	AURUM	BATHE	BIBLE	BLOOD	BOWSE
AMBER	ARDOR	AUXIN	BATIK	BICEP	BLOOM	BOXER
AMBIT	ARECA	AVAIL	BATON	BIDER	BLOOP	BOXLA
AMBLE	ARENA	AVERT	BAULK	BIDET	BLUET	BOYAR
AMEBA	ARENE	AVIAN	BAYOU	BIELD	BLUEY	BOYLA
AMEER	AREPA	AVION	BAZAR	BIGHT	BLUFF	BRACE
AMEND	ARETE	AVISO	BAZOO	BIGOT	BLUME	BRACH
AMENT	ARGAL	AVOID	BEANO	BIJOU	BLUNT	BRACT
AMICE	ARGIL	AWAIT	BEARD	BIKER	BLURB	BRAID
AMIDE	ARGLE	AWAKE	BEAST	BIKIE	BLURT	BRAIL
AMIGA	ARGOL	AWARD	BEAUT	BILBO	BLYPE	BRAIN
AMIGO	ARGON	AXIOM	BEBOP	BILGE	BOARD	BRAKE
AMINE	ARGOT	AXION	BECAP	BIMAH	BOART	BRAND
AMINO	ARGUE	AXITE	BEDEL	BIMBO	BOAST	BRANK
AMNIO	ARHAT	AXONE	BEDEW	BINDI	BOCCE	BRANT
AMOLE	ARIEL	AYAYA	BEDIM	BINER	BOCCI	BRAVA
AMOUR	ARISE	AZIDE	BEFIT	BINGE	BOCHE	BRAVE
AMPUL	ARMER	AZINE	BEFOG	BINGO	BOEUF	BRAVO
AMRIT	ARMET	AZLON	BEGEM	BINIT	BOFFO	BRAWL
AMUCK	ARMOR	AZOLE	BEGET	BIOME	BOGAN	BRAWN

BRAZA	BUNYA	CAPOT	CHART	CHUMP	CLOVE	COOEY
BRAZE	BURAN	CAPRI	CHASE	CHUNK	CLOWN	COOMB
BREAD	BURET	CARAT	CHASM	CHURL	CLOZE	COOPT
BREAK	BURFI	CARBO	CHEAP	CHURN	CLUCK	COPAL
BREAM	BURGH	CARER	CHEAT	CHURR	CLUMP	COPAY
BREDE	BURIN	CARES	CHECK	CHUSE	CLUNK	COPEN
BREED	BURKA	CARET	CHEEK	CHUTE	COACT	COPER
BRENT	BURKE	CARGO	CHEEP	CHYLE	COADY	COPRA
BREVE	BURQA	CARLE	CHEER	CHYME	COALA	COPSE
BRIAR	BURRO	CAROB	CHELA	CIBOL	COAPT	COQUI
BRIBE	BURSA	CAROL	CHEMO	CIDER	COAST	CORAL
BRICK	BURSE	CAROM	CHERT	CIGAR	COATI	CORER
BRIDE	BURST	CARSE	CHEST	CISCO	COBIA	CORGI
BRIEF	BUTEO	CARTE	CHETH	CITER	COBLE	CORNU
BRIER	BUTLE	CARVE	CHICA	CIVET	COBRA	CORSE
BRILL	BUTOH	CASTE	CHICK	CIVIC	COCOA	COSEC
BRINE	BUTTE	CATER	CHICO	CIVIE	CODEC	COSET
BRING	BUTUT	CAULD	CHIDE	CLACH	CODEN	COSEY
BRINK	BUTYL	CAULK	CHIEF	CLACK	CODER	COSIE
BRISK	BUYER	CAURI	CHIEL	CLADE	CODON	COTAN
BRITH	BWANA	CAUSE	CHILE	CLAIM	COGON	COTTA
BRITT	BYLAW	CAVER	CHILI	CLAMP	COHOE	COUDE
BROAD	BYWAY	CAVIE	CHILL	CLANG	COHOG	COUGH
BROCH	CABAL	CAVIL	CHIMB	CLANK	COIGN	COUNT
BROCK	CABER	CEASE	CHIME	CLARO	COLBY	COUPE
BROIL	CABIN	CEBID	CHIMP	CLASP	COLIC	COURT
BROME	CABLE	CEDAR	CHINA	CLAST	COLIN	COUTH
BROMO	CABOB	CEDER	CHINE	CLAVE	COLOG	COVEN
BRONC	CACAO	CEIBA	CHING	CLEAN	COLON	COVER
BROOD	CACHE	CEILI	CHINK	CLEAR	COLOR	COVET
BROOK	CADET	CELEB	CHINO	CLEAT	COLZA	COVEY
BROOM	CADGE	CELLO	CHIRK	CLEEK	COMBE	COVIN
BROSE	CADRE	CELOM	CHIRM	CLEFT	COMBI	COWER
BROTH	CAGER	CENSE	CHIRO	CLEPE	COMBO	COYAU
BROWN	CAHOW	CENTO	CHIRP	CLERK	COMER	COYPU
BRUGH	CAIRD	CEORL	CHIRR	CLICK	COMET	COZEN
BRUIN	CAIRN	CERCI	CHIRU	CLIFF	COMIC	COZEY
BRUIT	CALIF	CERIA	CHIVE	CLIFT	COMMA	COZIE
BRUME	CALLA	CESTA	CHOCK	CLIMB	COMMO	CRAAL
BRUNT	CALVE	CHAFE	CHOIL	CLIME	COMPO	CRACK
BRUTE	CAMAS	CHAFF	CHOIR	CLINE	COMPT	CRAFT
BUBAL	CAMEL	CHAIN	CHOKE	CLING	COMTE	CRAKE
BUBBA	CAMEO	CHAIR	CHOLA	CLINK	CONCH	CRAMP
BUBBE	CAMPO	CHALK	CHOLI	CLOAK	CONDO	CRANE
BUCKO	CANAL	CHAMP	CHOLO	CLOCK	CONEY	CRANK
BUDGE	CANER	CHANA	CHOMP	CLOMP	CONGA	CRAPE
BUFFO	CANID	CHANG	CHOOK	CLONE	CONGE	CRATE
BUGLE	CANNA	CHANT	CHORD	CLONK	CONGO	CRAVE
BUILD	CANOE	CHAPE	CHORE	CLOOT	CONIC	CRAWL
BULGE	CANON	CHARD	CHOSE	CLOSE	CONIN	CRAZE
BUMPH	CANSO	CHARE	CHOTT	CLOTH	CONTE	CREAK
BUNCO	CANTO	CHARK	CHUCK	CLOUD	CONTO	CREAM
BUNDT	CAPER	CHARM	CHUFA	CLOUR	COOEE	CREDO
BUNKO	CAPON	CHARR	CHUFF	CLOUT	COOER	CREED

CREEK	CUSSO	DEKKO	DIVOT	DRILL	EDILE	ENSUE
CREEL	CUTEY	DELAY	DIWAN	DRINK	EDUCE	ENTER
CREEP	CUTIE	DELFT	DIXIT	DRIVE	EDUCT	ENURE
CREME	CUTIN	DELTA	DIZEN	DROID	EEJIT	ENVOI
CREPE	CUTUP	DELVE	DJINN	DROIT	EGEST	ENVOY
CREST	CUVEE	DEMIT	DOBIE	DROKE	EGGAR	ENZYM
CRICK	CYCAD	DEMOB	DOBLA	DROLL	EGGER	EOSIN
CRIER	CYCLE	DEMON	DOBRA	DRONE	EGRET	EPACT
CRIME	CYCLO	DEMUR	DOBRO	DROOL	EIDER	EPHAH
CRIMP	CYDER	DENAR	DODGE	DROOP	EIGHT	EPHOD
CRIPE	CYMAR	DENIM	DOGAN	DROUK	EIKON	EPHOR
CRISP	CYMOL	DEPOT	DOGEY	DROVE	EJECT	EPOCH
CROAK	CYNIC	DEPTH	DOGIE	DROWN	EJIDO	EPODE
CROCK	CYTON	DERAT	DOGMA	DRUID	ELAIN	EQUAL
CROFT	DACHA	DERAY	DOING	DRUNK	ELAND	EQUID
CRONE	DAGGA	DERMA	DOLMA	DRUPE	ELATE	EQUIP
CROOK	DAMAN	DESHI	DOLOR	DRUSE	ELBOW	ERASE
CROON	DAMAR	DETER	DONEE	DRYAD	ELDER	ERECT
CRORE	DANCE	DEUCE	DONGA	DRYER	ELECT	ERGOT
CROUP	DANIO	DEVEL	DONNA	DUCAT	ELEMI	ERICA
CROWD	DARER	DEVIL	DONOR	DULCE	ELFIN	ERODE
CROWN	DARIC	DEVON	DONUT	DULIA	ELIDE	EROSE
CROZE	DASHI	DEWAN	DOPER	DULSE	ELINT	ERROR
CRUCK	DATER	DEWAR	DOSER	DUMBO	ELITE	ERUCT
CRUDE	DATTO	DEXIE	DOSHA	DUMKA	ELOIN	ERUGO
CRUDO	DATUM	DHIKR	DOTER	DUNAM	ELOPE	ERUPT
CRUET	DAUBE	DHOBI	DOUBT	DUNCE	ELUDE	ERVIL
CRUFT	DAUNT	DHOLE	DOUGH	DUOMO	ELUTE	ESCAR
CRUMB	DAVEN	DHOLL	DOULA	DUPER	ELVER	ESCOT
CRUMP	DAVIT	DHOTI	DOUMA	DURES	EMAIL	ESKAR
CRUNK	DEAIR	DHUTI	DOURA	DUROC	EMBAR	ESKER
CRUOR	DEATH	DIAZO	DOUSE	DURRA	EMBAY	ESSAY
CRUSE	DEAVE	DICER	DOVEN	DURUM	EMBED	ESTER
CRUST	DEBAG	DICOT	DOWEL	DUVET	EMBER	ESTOP
CRWTH	DEBAR	DIDIE	DOWER	DWALE	EMBOW	ETAPE
CRYER	DEBIT	DIENE	DOWSE	DWARF	EMCEE	ETHER
CRYPT	DEBUG	DIGHT	DOXIE	DWEEB	EMEER	ETHIC
CUBEB	DEBUR	DIGIT	DOYEN	DWELL	EMEND	ETHYL
CUBER	DEBUT	DIKER	DOZEN	DWINE	EMERG	ETUDE
CUBIC	DEBYE	DILDO	DOZER	DYING	EMMER	ETWEE
CUBIT	DECAF	DIMER	DRAFF	DYNEL	EMMET	EVADE
CULET	DECAL	DINAR	DRAFT	EAGER	EMOJI	EVENT
CUMIN	DECAN	DINER	DRAIL	EAGLE	EMOTE	EVERT
CUNIT	DECAY	DINGE	DRAIN	EAGRE	EMYDE	EVICT
CUPEL	DECOR	DINGO	DRAKE	EARTH	ENACT	EVITE
CUPID	DECOY	DIODE	DRAMA	EASEL	ENATE	EVOKE
CUPPA	DEFAT	DIPSO	DRAPE	EASER	ENDER	EXACT
CURER	DEFER	DIRAM	DRAWL	EATER	ENDOW	EXALT
CURET	DEFOG	DIRGE	DREAD	EBBET	ENDUE	EXCEL
CURIE	DEGUM	DISCO	DREAM	EBOOK	ENEMA	EXERT
CURIO	DEICE	DISME	DREAR	ECLAT	ENJOY	EXILE
CURSE	DEIGN	DITTO	DRECK	EDEMA	ENNUI	EXINE
CURVE	DEISM	DIVAN	DRIER	EDGER	ENOKI	EXIST
CUSEC	DEIST	DIVER	DRIFT	EDICT	ENROL	EXOME

EXPAT	FERMI	FLOAT	FRISE	GAUGE	GLEEK	GRAPE
EXPEL	FESSE	FLOCK	FRISK	GAULT	GLEET	GRAPH
EXTOL	FESTA	FLONG	FRITH	GAUZE	GLIDE	GRASP
EXTRA	FETOR	FLOOD	FRITT	GAVEL	GLIFF	GRATE
EXUDE	FEUAR	FLOOR	FROCK	GAVOT	GLIME	GRAVE
EXULT	FEVER	FLORA	FROND	GAYAL	GLINT	GRAZE
EXURB	FIBER	FLOTA	FRONT	GAZAR	GLOAM	GREAT
EYRIE	FIBRE	FLOUR	FROST	GAZER	GLOAT	GREBE
FABLE	FICHE	FLOUT	FROTH	GAZOO	GLOBE	GREED
FACER	FICHU	FLUFF	FROWN	GECKO	GLOGG	GREEN
FACET	FICIN	FLUID	FRUIT	GEEST	GLOOM	GREET
FACIA	FIDGE	FLUKE	FRUMP	GELEE	GLOOP	GREGO
FADER	FIELD	FLUME	FRYER	GEMOT	GLOST	GRIDE
FADGE	FIEND	FLUMP	FUDGE	GENET	GLOUT	GRIEF
FAENA	FIFER	FLUNK	FUGIO	GENIE	GLOVE	GRIFF
FAGIN	FIFTH	FLUOR	FUGLE	GENIP	GLOZE	GRIFT
FAGOT	FIGHT	FLUTE	FUGUE	GENOA	GLUER	GRILL
FAINT	FILER	FLUYT	FUMER	GENOM	GLUME	GRIME
FAITH	FILET	FLYBY	FUMET	GENRE	GLUON	GRIND
FAKER	FILLE	FLYER	FUNGO	GENRO	GLUTE	GRIOT
FAKIE	FILLO	FLYTE	FURAN	GEODE	GLYPH	GRIPE
FAKIR	FILMI	FOEHN	FUROR	GEOID	GNARL	GRIST
FANGA	FILTH	FOGEY	FURZE	GERAH	GNARR	GRITH
FANON	FINAL	FOGIE	FUSEE	GESTE	GNOME	GROAN
FANUM	FINCA	FOIST	FUSEL	GETUP	GOBAN	GROAT
FAQIR	FIORD	FOLEY	FUSIL	GHAUT	GODET	GROIN
FARAD	FIQUE	FOLIO	FUTON	GHAZI	GOFER	GROOM
FARCE	FIRER	FONDU	FUZEE	GHOST	GOING	GROPE
FARER	FIRST	FORAM	FUZIL	GHOUL	GOLEM	GROUP
FARLE	FIRTH	FORAY	FYTTE	GHYLL	GOMBO	GROUT
FARRO	FIVER	FORCE	GABBA	GIANT	GOMER	GROVE
FATSO	FIXER	FORGE	GABLE	GIBER	GONAD	GROWL
FATWA	FIXIT	FORME	GADDI	GIGOT	GONEF	GRRRL
FAULD	FJELD	FORTE	GADID	GIGUE	GONER	GRUEL
FAULT	FJORD	FORUM	GAFFE	GIMEL	GONIF	GRUFF
FAUNA	FLACK	FOSSA	GAGER	GIMME	GONOF	GRUME
FAUVE	FLAIL	FOSSE	GALAH	GIPON	GOOSE	GRUMP
FAVOR	FLAIR	FOUND	GALEA	GIRON	GOPIK	GRUNT
FEASE	FLAKE	FOUNT	GALOP	GIRTH	GORAL	GUACO
FEAST	FLAME	FOVEA	GAMAY	GISMO	GORGE	GUANO
FEAZE	FLANK	FOYER	GAMBA	GIVEN	GORSE	GUARD
FEEZE	FLARE	FRACK	GAMBE	GIVER	GOUGE	GUAVA
FEIGN	FLASK	FRAIL	GAMER	GIZMO	GOURD	GUEST
FEINT	FLAVA	FRAME	GAMIN	GLACE	GOWAN	GUIDE
FEIST	FLEAM	FRANC	GAMMA	GLADE	GRAAL	GUILD
FELID	FLECK	FRANK	GAMUT	GLAIR	GRACE	GUILE
FELLA	FLEER	FRAUD	GANEF	GLAND	GRADE	GUILT
FELON	FLEET	FREAK	GANEV	GLARE	GRAFT	GUIRO
FEMME	FLICK	FREER	GANJA	GLAZE	GRAIL	GUISE
FEMUR	FLIER	FREON	GANOF	GLEAM	GRAIN	GULAG
FENCE	FLING	FRERE	GAPER	GLEAN	GRAMA	GULAR
FEOFF	FLINT	FRIAR	GARTH	GLEBE	GRAMP	GUMBO
FERAL	FLIRT	FRIER	GATER	GLEDE	GRAND	GUMMA
FERIA	FLITE	FRILL	GATOR	GLEED	GRANT	GUMMI

GUNGE	HELLO	HOSEY	INFER	JOCKO	KELEP	KOMBU
GURGE	HELOT	HOSTA	INGLE	JOINT	KELIM	KOPEK
GUSTO	HELVE	HOTEL	INGOT	JOIST	KENAF	KOPJE
GUYOT	HEMIN	HOUND	INION	JOKER	KENDO	KOPPA
GYNIE	HENGE	HOURI	INKER	JORAM	KENTE	KORAT
GYOZA	HENNA	HOUSE	INKLE	JORUM	KERNE	KORMA
GYPPO	HENRY	HOVEL	INLAY	JOUAL	KETOL	KOTOW
GYRON	HERON	HOVER	INLET	JOULE	KEVEL	KRAAL
HABIT	HEUCH	HOWFF	INNER	JOUST	KEVIL	KRAFT
HACEK	HEUGH	HOYLE	INPUT	JOWAR	KEYER	KRAIT
HADJI	HEVEA	HULLO	INRUN	JUDGE	KHADI	KRAUT
HAICK	HEWER	HUMAN	INSET	JUGUM	KHAKI	KREEP
HAIKU	HEXAD	HUMOR	INTER	JUICE	KHAPH	KREWE
HAINT	HEXER	HUMPH	INTRO	JULEP	KHEDA	KRILL
HAJJI	HEXYL	HURST	INURE	JUMAR	KHETH	KROON
HAKIM	HIDER	HUZZA	INURN	JUMBO	KHOUM	KRUBI
HALAL	HIGHT	HYDRA	INVAR	JUNCO	KIACK	KUBIE
HALER	HIJAB	HYDRO	IODID	JUNTA	KIANG	KUDZU
HALID	HIJRA	HYENA	IODIN	JUNTO	KIBBE	KUGEL
HALLO	HIKER	HYMEN	IONIC	JUPON	KIBBI	KUKRI
HALMA	HILLO	HYOID	IRADE	JURAT	KIBEI	KULAK
HALON	HIMBO	HYPER	IROKO	JUREL	KIBLA	KULFI
HALVA	HINGE	HYSON	IRONE	JUROR	KIDDO	KUMIS
HALVE	HIPPO	ICHOR	ISLET	JUVIE	KILIM	KURTA
HALWA	HIREE	ICING	ISSEI	KABAB	KININ	KUSSO
HAMAL	HIRER	ICKER	ISSUE	KABAR	KIOSK	KVELL
HAMZA	HOARD	IDEAL	ISTLE	KABOB	KIPPA	KYACK
HANCE	HODAD	IDENT	IXORA	KAFIR	KITER	KYLIN
HANSA	HOGAN	IDIOM	IXTLE	KAIAK	KITHE	KYRIE
HANSE	HOICK	IDIOT	IZARD	KALAM	KLICK	KYTHE
HAOLE	HOISE	IDLER	JABOT	KALIF	KLIEG	LAARI
HAPPI	HOIST	IDYLL	JACAL	KALPA	KLONG	LABEL
HAREM	HOKUM	IGLOO	JAGER	KAMIK	KLOOF	LABOR
HASTE	HOLLA	IHRAM	JAGRA	KANJI	KLUGE	LACER
HATER	HOLLO	ILIAD	JALAP	KANZU	KNACK	LADEN
HAUGH	HOLME	IMAGE	JALOP	KAPOK	KNAUR	LADER
HAULM	HOMER	IMAGO	JAMBE	KAPOW	KNAVE	LADLE
HAUNT	HOMEY	IMAUM	JAPAN	KAPPA	KNAWE	LAGAN
HAVEN	HOMIE	IMBED	JAPER	KARAT	KNEAD	LAGER
HAVER	HONAN	IMBUE	JAUNT	KARMA	KNEEL	LAHAL
HAVOC	HONDA	IMIDE	JAWAN	KAROO	KNELL	LAHAR
HAWSE	HONER	IMINE	JEBEL	KARRI	KNIFE	LAICH
HAYER	HONEY	IMPEL	JEHAD	KARST	KNOCK	LAIGH
HAZAN	HONOR	IMPRO	JELLO	KASHA	KNOLL	LAIRD
HAZEL	HOOEY	INANE	JERID	KAURI	KNOSP	LAKER
HAZER	HOOKA	INARM	JESSE	KAVAS	KNOUT	LAMED
HEART	HOPAK	INCOG	JETON	KAYAK	KNOWN	LAMIA
HEATH	HOPER	INCUR	JEWEL	KAZOO	KNURL	LANAI
HEAVE	HORAH	INDIE	JIBBA	KEBAB	KNURR	LANCE
HEDER	HORDE	INDOL	JIBER	KEBAR	KOALA	LAPEL
HEDGE	HORSE	INDOW	JIHAD	KEBOB	KOFTA	LAPIN
HEEZE	HORST	INDRI	JINNI	KEDGE	KOINE	LAPSE
HEIST	HOSEL	INDUE	JIVER	KEEVE	KOKAM	LAREE
HELIO	HOSER	INERT	JNANA	KEFIR	KOKUM	LARGE

LARGO	LIEGE	LOTTE	MAMBA	MERIT	MONDO	MUZAK
LARUM	LIFER	LOTTO	MAMBO	MERLE	MONEY	MYLAR
LARVA	LIGAN	LOUGH	MAMEE	MESNE	MONGO	MYNAH
LASER	LIGER	LOUIE	MAMEY	MESON	MONIE	MYOMA
LASSI	LIGHT	LOUMA	MAMIE	METAL	MONTE	MYOPE
LASSO	LIKEN	LOUPE	MAMMA	METER	MONTH	MYRRH
LATEN	LIKER	LOUSE	MANAT	METOL	MOOLA	MYSID
LATHE	LILAC	LOVAT	MANEB	METRE	MOPED	NABOB
LATHI	LIMAN	LOVER	MANGA	METRO	MOPER	NACHO
LATKE	LIMBA	LOVEY	MANGE	MEZZO	MORAL	NACRE
LATTE	LIMBO	LOWER	MANGO	MIAOU	MORAS	NADIR
LAUAN	LIMEN	LUCRE	MANIA	MIAOW	MORAY	NAIAD
LAUGH	LIMEY	LUFFA	MANIC	MIASM	MOREL	NAIRA
LAURA	LIMIT	LUGER	MANNA	MIAUL	MORON	NAIRU
LAVER	LIMPA	LUMEN	MANOR	MICHE	MORPH	NAIVE
LAYER	LINAC	LUNAR	MANSE	MICRO	MORRO	NAKFA
LAYIN	LINEN	LUNET	MANTA	MIDGE	MOSEY	NALED
LAYUP	LINER	LUNGE	MAPLE	MIDST	MOTEL	NAMER
LAZAR	LINGA	LUNGI	MAQUI	MIGHT	MOTET	NANCE
LEARN	LINGO	LUPIN	MARGE	MIKVA	MOTIF	NANNA
LEASE	LININ	LURER	MARKA	MILER	MOTOR	NAPPA
LEAST	LINUM	LYASE	MARSE	MILLE	MOTTE	NAPPE
LEAVE	LIPID	LYCEE	MASER	MILPA	MOTTO	NARCO
LEBEN	LIPIN	LYCRA	MASON	MIMEO	MOULD	NASAL
LEDGE	LISLE	LYING	MASSA	MIMER	MOULT	NAVAR
LEGAL	LITER	LYMPH	MASSE	MIMIC	MOUND	NAVEL
LEGER	LITHO	LYRIC	MATER	MINCE	MOUNT	NAWAB
LEGIT	LITRE	LYSIN	MATEY	MINER	MOURN	NEIGH
LEHUA	LIVEN	LYSSA	MATIN	MINIM	MOUSE	NEROL
LEMAN	LIVER	LYTTA	MATTE	MINKE	MOUTH	NERVE
LEMMA	LIVRE	MACAW	MATZA	MINOR	MOVER	NETOP
LEMON	LLAMA	MACER	MATZO	MIRID	MOVIE	NEUME
LEMUR	LLANO	MACHE	MAUND	MIRIN	MOWER	NEWEL
LENSE	LOCAL	MACHO	MAUVE	MIRTH	MOXIE	NEWIE
LENTO	LOCHE	MACLE	MAVEN	MIRZA	MUCIN	NGWEE
LEONE	LOCIE	MACON	MAVIE	MISER	MUCOR	NICAD
LEPER	LOCUM	MACRO	MAVIN	MITER	MUCRO	NICHE
LESBO	LODEN	MADAM	MAXIM	MITRE	MUDRA	NICOL
LETHE	LODGE	MADRE	MAYBE	MIXER	MUFTI	NIECE
LETUP	LOGAN	MAFIA	MAYOR	MIXUP	MUJIK	NIEVE
LEVEE	LOGIC	MAGIC	MAZER	MIZEN	MULCT	NIGHT
LEVEL	LOGIN	MAGMA	MBIRA	MOCHA	MULEY	NIHIL
LEVER	LOGON	MAGOT	MECCA	MOCHI	MULIE	NIKAH
LEVIN	LONER	MAHOE	MEDAL	MODAL	MULLA	NINER
LIANA	LONGE	MAHUA	MEDIA	MODEL	MUNGO	NINJA
LIANE	LOOEY	MAHWA	MEDIC	MODEM	MURAL	NINON
LIANG	LOOFA	MAILE	MELEE	MOGUL	MURID	NINTH
LIARD	LOOIE	MAILL	MELON	MOHEL	MURRA	NIQAB
LIBEL	LOOSE	MAIST	MENAD	MOHUR	MURRE	NISEI
LIBER	LOPER	MAIZE	MENSA	MOIRE	MUSER	NITER
LIBRA	LORAN	MAJOR	MENSE	MOLAR	MUSIC	NITON
LICHI	LOSEL	MAKAR	MENTO	MOMMA	MUSTH	NITRE
LICHT	LOSER	MAKER	MERDE	MONAD	MUTHA	NITRO
LIDAR	LOTAH	MALAR	MERGE	MONDE	MUTON	NIXIE

NIZAM	OLEUM	OXTER	PEACE	PIPIT	POMBE	PROSO
NOBLE	OLIVE	OZONE	PEAGE	PIQUE	PONCE	PROVE
NOISE	OLLIE	PACER	PEARL	PISCO	PONGO	PROWL
NOMAD	OMBER	PACHA	PEASE	PISTE	PONZU	PRUDE
NOMEN	OMBRE	PADLE	PECAN	PITON	POOJA	PRUNE
NONCE	OMEGA	PADRE	PEDAL	PITOT	POOKA	PRYER
NONET	ONION	PAEAN	PEDRO	PITTA	POORI	PSALM
NONYL	ONLAY	PAEON	PEEVE	PIVOT	POOVE	PSEUD
NOOSE	ONSET	PAGAN	PEISE	PIXEL	POPPA	PSHAW
NOPAL	OOMPH	PAGER	PEKAN	PIXIE	PORIN	PSYCH
NORIA	OOTID	PAGOD	PEKIN	PIZZA	PORNO	PUDGE
NORTH	OPERA	PAINT	PEKOE	PLACE	POSER	PUJAH
NOTER	OPINE	PAISA	PELAU	PLACK	POSIT	PULAO
NOVEL	OPIUM	PALET	PENGO	PLAGE	POSSE	PULER
NOWAY	OPSIN	PALSA	PENNE	PLAID	POTTO	PULKA
NUBIA	OPTIC	PAMPA	PENNI	PLAIN	POUFF	PULSE
NUDGE	ORANG	PANDA	PEPSI	PLAIT	POULT	PUNJI
NUDIE	ORATE	PANEL	PERDU	PLANE	POUND	PUNKA
NURSE	ORBIT	PANGA	PERIL	PLANK	POWER	PUNTO
NUTSO	ORCIN	PANIC	PERSE	PLANT	POYOU	PUPIL
NYALA	ORDER	PANNE	PERVO	PLASM	PRAAM	PURDA
NYLON	OREAD	PANTO	PESTO	PLATE	PRAHU	PUREE
NYMPH	ORGAN	PAPAW	PETAL	PLATY	PRANA	PURGE
OAKUM	ORIBI	PAPER	PETER	PLAYA	PRANG	PURIN
OATER	ORIEL	PAREN	PEWEE	PLAZA	PRANK	PURSE
OBEAH	ORLON	PAREO	PEWIT	PLEAD	PRASE	PUTON
OBJET	ORLOP	PARER	PHAGE	PLEAT	PRATE	PYLON
OBOLE	ORMER	PAREU	PHASE	PLEBE	PRAWN	PYRAN
OCCUR	ORPIN	PARGE	PHIAL	PLEON	PREEN	PYXIE
OCEAN	OSCAR	PARGO	PHONE	PLICA	PREOP	QAJAQ
OCHER	OSIER	PARKA	PHONO	PLIER	PREST	QANAT
OCHRE	OSMIC	PARLE	PHOTO	PLINK	PRICE	QAPIK
OCKER	OSMOL	PAROL	PIANO	PLONK	PRICK	QIBLA
OCREA	OTHER	PARSE	PIBAL	PLOYE	PRIDE	QUACK
OCTAD	OTTAR	PARVO	PICOT	PLUCK	PRIER	QUAFF
OCTAN	OTTER	PASEO	PICUL	PLUMB	PRILL	QUAIL
OCTET	OUGHT	PASHA	PIECE	PLUME	PRIMA	QUAKE
OCTYL	OUNCE	PASHM	PIETA	PLUMP	PRIME	QUALM
ODEON	OUPHE	PASKA	PIKER	PLUNK	PRIMO	QUANT
ODEUM	OUSEL	PASSE	PILAF	PLUOT	PRIMP	QUARK
ODIST	OUTER	PASTA	PILAU	PLYER	PRINK	QUART
ODIUM	OUTRO	PASTE	PILAW	POBOY	PRINT	QUBIT
ODOUR	OUZEL	PATEN	PILOT	POGEY	PRION	QUEAN
ODYLE	OVINE	PATER	PINGO	POILU	PRIOR	QUEEN
OFFAL	OVOID	PATIN	PINKO	POIND	PRISE	QUEER
OFFER	OVOLO	PATIO	PINNA	POINT	PRISM	QUELL
OGHAM	OVULE	PAUSE	PINON	POISE	PRIZE	QUERN
OGIVE	OWLET	PAVAN	PINOT	POKER	PROBE	QUEST
OGLER	OWNER	PAVER	PINTA	POKEY	PROEM	QUEUE
OGRES	OXBOW	PAVIN	PINTO	POLAR	PROLE	QUICK
OILER	OXEYE	PAWER	PINUP	POLER	PROMO	QUIET
OKAPI	OXIDE	PAYEE	PIPAL	POLIO	PRONG	QUIFF
OLDIE	OXIME	PAYER	PIPER	POLKA	PROOF	QUILL
OLEIN	OXLIP	PAYOR	PIPET	POLYP	PROSE	QUILT

QUINT	READD	REPEL	ROBLE	SADHE	SCALL	SEDER
QUIPU	REALM	REPIN	ROBOT	SADHU	SCALP	SEDGE
QUIRE	REARM	REPOT	RODEO	SAHIB	SCAMP	SEDUM
QUIRK	REATA	REPRO	ROGER	SAICE	SCANT	SEGNO
QUIRT	REAVE	RERIG	ROGUE	SAIGA	SCAPE	SEGUE
QUOIN	REBAR	RERUN	ROMAN	SAINT	SCARE	SEINE
QUOIT	REBBE	RESAW	ROMEO	SAJOU	SCARF	SEISE
QUOLL	REBEC	RESAY	RONDE	SAKER	SCARP	SEISM
QUOTA	REBEL	RESEE	RONDO	SAKTI	SCART	SEIZA
QUOTE	REBID	RESET	RONIN	SALAD	SCATT	SEIZE
RABAT	REBOP	RESEW	ROOSE	SALAL	SCAUP	SELAH
RABBI	REBUT	RESID	ROOST	SALAT	SCAUR	SELLE
RACER	REBUY	RESIN	ROPER	SALEP	SCENA	SELVA
RACON	RECAP	RESIT	ROQUE	SALMI	SCEND	SEMEN
RADAR	RECCE	RESOD	ROSET	SALOL	SCENE	SENNA
RADIO	RECIT	RESOW	ROSHI	SALON	SCENT	SENOR
RADON	RECON	RETAG	ROSIN	SALPA	SCHAV	SENSE
RAGEE	RECTO	RETEM	ROSTI	SALSA	SCHMO	SEPAL
RAGER	RECUR	RETIE	ROTOR	SALVE	SCHUL	SEPIA
RAGGA	RECUT	RETRO	ROTTE	SALVO	SCHWA	SEPOY
RAISE	REDAN	REUSE	ROUEN	SAMBA	SCION	SERAC
RAITA	REDIA	REVEL	ROUGE	SAMBO	SCOFF	SERAI
RAJAH	REDIP	REVET	ROUGH	SAMEK	SCOLD	SERGE
RAKEE	REDON	REVUE	ROUND	SAMFU	SCONE	SERIF
RAKER	REDUB	REWED	ROUSE	SANGA	SCOOP	SERIN
RALPH	REDYE	REWET	ROUST	SANGH	SCOOT	SEROW
RAMEE	REEST	REWIN	ROUTE	SANTO	SCOPE	SERUM
RAMET	REEVE	RHEME	ROUTH	SAPOR	SCORE	SERVE
RAMIE	REFEL	RHEUM	ROVER	SARAN	SCORN	SERVO
RAMIN	REFER	RHINO	ROWAN	SAREE	SCOUR	SETON
RANCE	REFIT	RHOMB	ROWEL	SARGE	SCOUT	SETUP
RANEE	REGIE	RHUMB	ROWEN	SARGO	SCOWL	SEVEN
RANGE	REHAB	RHYME	ROWER	SARIN	SCRAG	SEVER
RANID	REHEM	RIATA	ROWTH	SAROD	SCRAM	SEWAN
RAPER	REIGN	RICER	ROYAL	SASIN	SCRAN	SEWAR
RAPHE	REIKI	RICIN	RUANA	SATAY	SCRAP	SEWER
RAPID	REINK	RIDER	RUBEL	SATIN	SCREE	SEXER
RASER	REIVE	RIDGE	RUBLE	SATYR	SCREW	SEXTO
RATAL	REJIG	RIFLE	RUCHE	SAUCE	SCRIM	SHACK
RATAN	REKEY	RIGHT	RUFFE	SAUCH	SCRIP	SHADE
RATEL	RELAY	RIGOR	RULER	SAUGH	SCROB	SHAFT
RATER	RELET	RILLE	RUMBA	SAULT	SCROD	SHAKE
RATIO	RELIC	RIMER	RUMEN	SAUNA	SCRUB	SHAKO
RAVEL	REMAN	RINSE	RUMOR	SAUTE	SCRUM	SHALE
RAVEN	REMAP	RIOJA	RUPEE	SAVER	SCUBA	SHAME
RAVER	REMIT	RIPEN	RUTIN	SAVIN	SCUFF	SHANK
RAVIN	RENEW	RISER	SABAL	SAVOR	SCULK	SHAPE
RAWIN	RENIG	RISHI	SABER	SAVOY	SCULL	SHARD
RAYAH	RENIN	RIVAL	SABIN	SAWER	SCULP	SHARE
RAYON	RENTE	RIVER	SABIR	SAYED	SCURF	SHARK
RAZEE	REOIL	RIVET	SABLE	SAYER	SCUTE	SHARN
RAZER	REORG	RIYAL	SABOT	SAYID	SEBUM	SHARP
RAZOR	REPAY	ROAST	SABRA	SCALD	SECCO	SHAUL
REACT	REPEG	ROBIN	SABRE	SCALE	SEDAN	SHAVE

SHAWL	SHURA	SKULK	SNARE	SPAIL	SPREE	STICK
SHAWM	SHUTE	SKULL	SNARF	SPAIT	SPRIG	STIFF
SHEAF	SHYER	SKUNK	SNARK	SPALE	SPRIT	STILE
SHEAL	SIBYL	SLACK	SNARL	SPALL	SPROG	STILL
SHEAR	SICKO	SLAKE	SNATH	SPANK	SPRUE	STILT
SHEEN	SIDLE	SLANG	SNEAK	SPARE	SPRUG	STIME
SHEER	SIEGE	SLANT	SNEAP	SPARK	SPUME	STING
SHEET	SIEUR	SLATE	SNECK	SPASM	SPUNK	STINK
SHEIK	SIEVE	SLAVE	SNEER	SPATE	SPURN	STINT
SHELL	SIGHT	SLEEK	SNELL	SPAWN	SPURT	STIPE
SHEND	SIGIL	SLEEP	SNICK	SPEAK	SQUAB	STIRK
SHEOL	SIGMA	SLEET	SNIFF	SPEAN	SQUAD	STIRP
SHERD	SILVA	SLICE	SNIPE	SPEAR	SQUAT	STOAT
SHIEL	SIMAR	SLICK	SNOOD	SPECK	SQUAW	STOCK
SHIER	SINEW	SLIDE	SNOOK	SPECT	SQUEG	STOIC
SHIFT	SINGE	SLIME	SNOOL	SPEED	SQUIB	STOKE
SHILL	SIREE	SLING	SNOOP	SPEEL	SQUID	STOLE
SHINE	SIREN	SLINK	SNOOT	SPEER	STACK	STOMA
SHIRE	SIRRA	SLIPE	SNORE	SPEIL	STADE	STOMP
SHIRK	SIRUP	SLOID	SNORT	SPEIR	STAFF	STONE
SHIRR	SISAL	SLOJD	SNOUT	SPELL	STAGE	STONK
SHIRT	SITAR	SLOMO	SNUFF	SPELT	STAIG	STOOK
SHIST	SITUP	SLOOP	SOAVE	SPEND	STAIN	STOOL
SHITE	SIVER	SLOPE	SOBER	SPERM	STAIR	STOOP
SHIVA	SIXER	SLOTH	SOCLE	SPICA	STAKE	STOPE
SHIVE	SIXMO	SLOYD	SODOM	SPICE	STALE	STORE
SHLEP	SIXTE	SLUFF	SOFAR	SPICK	STALK	STORK
SHLUB	SIXTH	SLUMP	SOFTA	SPIEL	STALL	STORM
SHMOE	SIZAR	SLURB	SOKOL	SPIER	STAMP	STOTT
SHOAL	SIZER	SLURP	SOLAN	SPIFF	STAND	STOUP
SHOAT	SKALD	SLYPE	SOLAR	SPIKE	STANE	STOUR
SHOCK	SKANK	SMACK	SOLID	SPILE	STANG	STOUT
SHOER	SKATE	SMALL	SOLON	SPILL	STANK	STOVE
SHOGI	SKEAN	SMALT	SOLUM	SPINE	STAPH	STOWP
SHOJI	SKEEN	SMARM	SOLVE	SPIRE	STARE	STRAP
SHOOK	SKEET	SMART	SOMAN	SPIRT	START	STRAW
SHOOL	SKEIN	SMAZE	SONAR	SPITE	STATE	STRAY
SHOOT	SKELL	SMEAR	SONDE	SPLAT	STAVE	STREP
SHORE	SKELM	SMEEK	SONIC	SPLAY	STEAD	STREW
SHORL	SKELP	SMELL	SOOTH	SPLIT	STEAK	STRIP
SHORT	SKENE	SMELT	SOPOR	SPODE	STEAL	STROP
SHOTE	SKIER	SMERK	SOREL	SPOIL	STEAM	STROW
SHOTT	SKIFF	SMILE	SORGO	SPOKE	STEED	STROY
SHOUT	SKILL	SMIRK	SOTOL	SPOOF	STEEK	STRUM
SHOVE	SKIMO	SMITE	SOUGH	SPOOK	STEEL	STRUT
SHOYU	SKIMP	SMITH	SOUND	SPOOL	STEEP	STUFF
SHRED	SKINK	SMOCK	SOUSE	SPOON	STEER	STULL
SHREW	SKIRL	SMOKE	SOUTH	SPOOR	STEIN	STUMP
SHRUB	SKIRR	SMOLT	SOWAR	SPORE	STELE	STUNT
SHRUG	SKIRT	SMORG	SOWER	SPORT	STENO	STUPA
SHTIK	SKITE	SNACK	SOZIN	SPOUT	STENT	STUPE
SHTUP	SKIVE	SNAFU	SPACE	SPRAG	STERE	STURT
SHUCK	SKOAL	SNAIL	SPADE	SPRAT	STERN	STYLE
SHUNT	SKORT	SNAKE	SPAHI	SPRAY	STICH	SUBAH

59

SUBER	SYNCH	TEASE	THONG	TOOTH	TRIPE	TWIRP
SUCRE	SYNOD	TEGUA	THORN	TOPEE	TROAK	TWIST
SUDOR	SYNTH	TEIID	THORP	TOPER	TROCK	TWYER
SUEDE	SYREN	TEIND	THRAW	TOPHE	TROKE	TYTHE
SUETE	SYRUP	TELCO	THREE	TOPIC	TROLL	UDDER
SUGAR	SYSOP	TELLY	THRIP	TOQUE	TROMP	UHLAN
SUINT	TABER	TEMPO	THROB	TORAH	TRONA	UKASE
SUITE	TABLA	TEMPT	THROE	TORIC	TRONE	ULAMA
SULFA	TABLE	TENDU	THROW	TORSE	TROOP	ULCER
SUMAC	TABOO	TENET	THRUM	TORSK	TROPE	ULEMA
SUMMA	TABOR	TENGE	THUJA	TORSO	TROTH	ULTRA
SUNNA	TABUN	TENIA	THUMB	TORTA	TROUT	UMAMI
SUNUP	TACAN	TENNE	THUMP	TORTE	TROVE	UMBEL
SUPER	TACHE	TENNO	THUNK	TOTAL	TRUCE	UMBER
SURAH	TAFIA	TENON	THURL	TOTEM	TRUCK	UMBRA
SURGE	TAIGA	TENOR	THUYA	TOTER	TRULL	UMIAC
SURRA	TAIKO	TENSE	THYME	TOUGH	TRUMP	UMIAK
SUSHI	TAINT	TENTH	TIARA	TOUSE	TRUNK	UMIAQ
SUTRA	TAKER	TEPAL	TIBIA	TOWEL	TRUST	UMMAH
SUTTA	TAKIN	TEPEE	TICAL	TOWER	TRUTH	UNARM
SWAGE	TALAR	TEPOY	TIGER	TOWIE	TRYST	UNBAN
SWAIL	TALER	TERAI	TIGHT	TOXIC	TSADE	UNBAR
SWAIN	TALON	TERCE	TIGON	TOXIN	TSADI	UNCAP
SWALE	TALUK	TERNE	TIKKA	TOYER	TSUBA	UNCLE
SWAMI	TAMAL	TERRA	TILAK	TOYON	TSUBO	UNFIT
SWAMP	TAMER	TESLA	TILDE	TRACE	TUBER	UNHAT
SWANK	TANGA	TETRA	TILER	TRACK	TUILE	UNION
SWARD	TANGO	TETRI	TILTH	TRACT	TULIP	UNITE
SWARF	TANKA	THACK	TIMER	TRADE	TULLE	UNJAM
SWARM	TANTO	THALI	TINCT	TRAIK	TULSI	UNLAY
SWATH	TAPER	THANE	TINEA	TRAIL	TUMOR	UNMAN
SWEAR	TAPIR	THANG	TINGE	TRAIN	TUNER	UNMEW
SWEAT	TARGA	THANK	TITAN	TRAIT	TUNIC	UNPEG
SWEDE	TARGE	THARM	TITER	TRAMP	TUPIK	UNPEN
SWEEP	TAROC	THEBE	TITHE	TRANK	TUQUE	UNPIN
SWEET	TAROK	THEFT	TITLE	TRANQ	TURBO	UNRIG
SWELL	TAROT	THEGN	TITRE	TRAVE	TUTEE	UNRIP
SWIFT	TARRE	THEIN	TIYIN	TRAWL	TUTOR	UNSAY
SWILE	TASER	THEIR	TOAST	TREAD	TUTTI	UNSEE
SWILL	TASSE	THEME	TODAY	TREAT	TUYER	UNSET
SWINE	TASSO	THERE	TOGUE	TREEN	TWAIN	UNSEW
SWING	TASTE	THERM	TOILE	TREND	TWANG	UNTIE
SWINK	TATAR	THESE	TOKAY	TRIAC	TWEAK	UNWIT
SWIPE	TATER	THESP	TOKEN	TRIAD	TWEED	UNZIP
SWIRL	TAUNT	THETA	TOKER	TRIAL	TWEEN	UPBOW
SWIVE	TAUON	THICK	TOLAN	TRIBE	TWEEP	UPEND
SWOON	TAUPE	THIGH	TOLAR	TRICE	TWEET	UPPER
SWOOP	TAWER	THILL	TOLYL	TRICK	TWERK	UPSET
SWORD	TAWSE	THING	TOMAN	TRIER	TWERP	URARE
SWOUN	TAXER	THINK	TONDO	TRIGO	TWIER	URARI
SYCEE	TAXOL	THIOL	TONER	TRIKE	TWILL	URASE
SYCON	TAXON	THIRD	TONGA	TRILL	TWINE	URATE
SYLPH	TAYRA	THIRL	TONIC	TRINE	TWINK	URBIA
SYLVA	TAZZA	THOLE	TONNE	TRIOL	TWIRL	UREDO

URGER	VENIN	VOCAB	WATER	WHOLE	WRACK	YIELD
URIAL	VENOM	VOCAL	WAVER	WHOMP	WRANG	YIRTH
URINE	VENUE	VODKA	WAVEY	WHOOF	WRATH	YOBBO
URSID	VERGE	VODOU	WAXER	WHOOP	WREAK	YODEL
USAGE	VERSE	VODUN	WAZOO	WHORE	WRECK	YODLE
USHER	VERSO	VOGUE	WEALD	WHORL	WREST	YOGEE
USNEA	VERST	VOICE	WEAVE	WHORT	WRICK	YOGIN
USQUE	VERTU	VOILE	WEBER	WHUMP	WRING	YOKEL
USUAL	VERVE	VOLTE	WECHT	WHYDA	WRIST	YOUNG
USURP	VESTA	VOLVA	WEDEL	WICCA	WRITE	YOUTH
UTILE	VEXER	VOMER	WEDGE	WIDEN	WRONG	YOWIE
UTTER	VEXIL	VOMIT	WEIGH	WIDOW	WURST	YUCCA
UVULA	VIAND	VOTER	WEIRD	WIDTH	WUSHU	YULAN
VAKIL	VICAR	VOWEL	WHACK	WIELD	XEBEC	YUPON
VALET	VIDEO	VOWER	WHALE	WIFEY	XENIA	ZAIDA
VALOR	VIGIA	VOXEL	WHANG	WIGAN	XENON	ZAIRE
VALSE	VIGIL	VROOM	WHARF	WIGHT	XYLAN	ZAKAT
VALUE	VIGOR	VROUW	WHAUP	WINCE	XYLEM	ZAMIA
VALVE	VILLA	VULVA	WHEAL	WINZE	XYLOL	ZANZA
VANDA	VINAL	WACKE	WHEAT	WIPER	XYLYL	ZAYIN
VAPER	VINCA	WACKO	WHEEL	WIRER	YACHT	ZAZEN
VAPOR	VINYL	WADER	WHEEN	WITAN	YAGER	ZEBEC
VAREC	VIOLA	WAFER	WHEEP	WITHE	YAHOO	ZEBRA
VARIA	VIPER	WAGER	WHELK	WIVER	YAIRD	ZENDO
VARNA	VIREO	WAGON	WHELM	WIZEN	YAMEN	ZIBET
VARVE	VIRGA	WAHOO	WHELP	WOALD	YAMUN	ZINCO
VAULT	VIRTU	WAIST	WHERE	WODGE	YAPOK	ZINEB
VAUNT	VISIT	WAIVE	WHIFF	WOMAN	YAPON	ZIPPO
VEENA	VISOR	WAKEN	WHILE	WOOER	YARAK	ZIRAM
VEGAN	VISTA	WAKER	WHINE	WORLD	YEARN	ZLOTY
VEGIE	VITAL	WALER	WHIRL	WORSE	YEAST	ZOMBI
VELAR	VIVAT	WALIE	WHIRR	WORST	YECCH	ZONER
VELDT	VIXEN	WALLA	WHISK	WORTH	YENTA	ZOOID
VENDU	VIZIR	WASTE	WHIST	WOUND	YENTE	ZORIL
VENGE	VIZOR	WATAP	WHITE	WOVEN	YERBA	ZUPPA

With front hook T

ABLED	ASSES	EASES	HANKS	HOLED	INNER	OUTED
ABLES	ASSET	ECHED	HARMS	HOLES	INTER	OUTER
ACHES	ASTER	EENSY	HATCH	HOLOS	IRADE	OWIES
AGGER	AUGHT	ENDED	HAWED	HONGS	IRING	OWING
AILED	AUNTS	ENDER	HEBES	HORNS	ISSUE	OYERS
ALKIE	AWING	ENTER	HEFTS	HORNY	ITCHY	RACED
ALLOW	AXING	ENURE	HEIRS	HUMPS	ITHER	RACER
AMPED	AXITE	EPEES	HEIST	HUNKS	OASTS	RACES
ANGAS	AXMAN	ERNES	HEMES	HURLS	OCHER	RACKS
ANGLE	AXMEN	ERROR	HENCE	ICKER	OILED	RAILS
ANNOY	AXONS	ESTER	HERES	ILLER	OILER	RAINS
ANTRA	EARED	ETHER	HERMS	INGLE	OKAYS	RAMPS
APERS	EASED	HACKS	HICKS	INKER	OPING	RANCE
APING	EASEL	HALER	HIGHS	INKLE	OTHER	RANKS
ASKED	EASER	HANGS	HILLS	INNED	OTTER	RAPES

RAVEL	RICES	ROLLS	ROWEL	RUTHS	URBAN	WEETS
RAVES	RICKS	ROMPS	ROWTH	SADES	WAINS	WIGGY
READS	RIFLE	ROPES	RUCKS	SADIS	WEEDS	WILLS
RENDS	RILLS	ROUGH	RUFFE	SORES	WEEDY	WINED
REVET	RIMER	ROUTS	RUING	SUBAS	WEENS	WINES
RIALS	RIPES	ROVER	RUMPS	UMPED	WEENY	WINKS
RIBES	RIVET	ROVES	RUSTS	UNICA	WEEPS	WISTS
RICED	ROCKS	ROWED	RUSTY	UPPED	WEEST	WITCH

With back hook T

ABLES	CACHE	EAGLE	KAPUT	OCTAN	ROQUE	TOILE
ADMIX	CHICO	FAKES	LAMES	PALES	SADIS	TOQUE
AGHAS	CLASP	FIDGE	LANCE	PAREN	SAFES	TRUES
AMIDS	CLOSE	FILLE	LATEN	PARGE	SAGES	TURBO
ANKLE	COHOS	FINES	LAXES	PATEN	SANES	UNFIX
APPLE	CORSE	FLIES	LEARN	PIQUE	SCRIP	UNMIX
ARPEN	COVER	FORES	LIKES	PLACE	SCULP	UNPEN
AURIS	CRUSE	FORGE	LITES	PLAIN	SERES	VERSE
BARBE	CURVE	FORGO	LIVES	PLANE	SHIES	VERVE
BARES	CUTES	FREES	LOCUS	POSSE	SORES	WAUGH
BARRE	DECAN	FROWS	LOWES	PRESE	SOUGH	WEIGH
BASAL	DELIS	GAINS	LUXES	PRIES	SPINE	WHISH
BASES	DESIS	GAMES	MATZO	PURIS	SPOIL	WIDES
BEMIX	DIVER	GORGE	MERES	RABBI	STRIP	WISES
BENNE	DIVES	HALES	MIDGE	RARES	STYLE	WORSE
BLUES	DOPES	HALLO	MILLE	REDIP	SWIVE	WRIES
BONNE	DOUGH	HEIGH	MODES	REFEL	TABLE	
BOUGH	DREAM	HONES	MOLES	RELIC	TAMES	
BREVE	DRIES	IDLES	MUSCA	REMIX	TARGE	
BUDGE	DULCE	JAKES	MUTES	RILLE	TASSE	
CABLE	DUPLE	JIVES	NUDES	RIPES	TERCE	

With front hook U

LAMAS	PASES	PRATE	RARES	REDIA	RUSES	SURER
NITER	PENDS	PRISE	RASES	REDOS	SABLE	TILES
NITES	PLINK	PROSE	RATES	RIALS	SAGES	

With back hook U

CONGO	HALER

With front hook V

AGILE	AMPED	AUNTS	ENDED	EXING	OMITS
AILED	APERS	AUNTY	ENDER	ICING	OWING
ALINE	APING	AWARD	ENDUE	IDIOT	ROOMS
ALLEY	ARIAS	EGGED	ENTER	IZARD	ULVAS
ALVAR	ASTER	ELATE	ERSES	OMERS	

With back hook V

IMPRO

With front hook W

ADDED	AMBLE	EASEL	HALED	HERRY	IMPED	OVENS
ADDER	ANGLE	EAVED	HALER	HINGE	INDOW	OWING
ADDLE	ANION	EAVES	HALES	HINNY	INKED	RACKS
AFTER	ANTED	EBBED	HAMMY	HIPPY	INKER	RANGS
AGERS	ARMED	EDGED	HANGS	HISTS	INKLE	RECKS
AGGER	ARMER	EDGES	HEALS	HOLES	INNED	RESTS
AGING	ASHED	EENSY	HEATS	HOLLY	INNER	RETCH
AGONS	ASHES	EIGHT	HEELS	HOOFS	INTER	RICKS
AILED	ASTER	ELDER	HEEZE	HOOPS	IRING	RIGHT
AIRED	ATAPS	ENDED	HELMS	HUMPS	ITCHY	RINGS
AIVER	AUGHT	ESTER	HELPS	ICKER	ITHER	RITES
ALLEY	AVERS	ETHER	HENCE	IGGED	IZARD	
ALLOW	AXING	HACKS	HERES	ILLER	ORMER	

With back hook W

BURRO	FARRO	HALLO	HOLLO	MORRO	OUTRO

With front hook X

YLEMS

With back hook X

ADIEU	BIJOU	DUPLE	NOYAU

With front hook Y

AGERS	ARAKS	AWNED	EARNS	ESTER	OWING
AMENS	ARROW	CLEPT	EASTS	OGEES	ULANS
ANTRA	AWING	EARLY	ESSES	OWIES	

With back hook Y

AMBER	BETON	BOWER	BROTH	CHANT	CHUNK	CRAFT
ANGST	BITCH	BRAIN	BROWN	CHARR	CLANK	CRAMP
APPLE	BLAST	BRAND	BRUSH	CHASM	CLASS	CRANK
ARMOR	BLEAR	BRASH	BUNCH	CHEEK	CLIFF	CRAWL
ARROW	BLOCK	BRASS	BURST	CHEER	CLING	CREAK
AUGUR	BLOKE	BRAWL	CAIRN	CHERT	CLONK	CREAM
BAKER	BLOOD	BRAWN	CARBO	CHEST	CLOUD	CREEP
BALLS	BLOOM	BREAD	CATCH	CHILL	CLUMP	CREPE
BARON	BLOOP	BRIAR	CAUSE	CHINK	CLUNK	CRESS
BAULK	BLOWS	BRICK	CEDAR	CHIRP	COLON	CRIMP
BEACH	BLUES	BRIER	CHAFF	CHOKE	CONCH	CRISP
BEAUT	BOSOM	BROOD	CHALK	CHUCK	COUNT	CROAK
BEECH	BOTCH	BROOM	CHAMP	CHUFF	CRACK	CROON

CROUP	FLOUR	HORSE	PLUSH	SKANK	SPUNK	TREAT
CROWD	FLUFF	HOUSE	POACH	SKIMP	STAGE	TREND
CRUMB	FLUKE	HUMUS	POINT	SKUNK	STALK	TRESS
CRUST	FLUNK	JALOP	PONCE	SLANG	STEAD	TRICK
CURVE	FLUTE	JAPER	POUCH	SLANT	STEAM	TROLL
CUTES	FOLKS	JAUNT	POUFF	SLATE	STEEL	TROUT
DANCE	FOOTS	JUDGE	PRICE	SLAVE	STICK	TRUST
DEATH	FREAK	KLUTZ	PRICK	SLEEK	STIFF	TWANG
DENAR	FRIAR	KNOLL	PRIOR	SLEEP	STILL	TWEAK
DINGE	FRILL	KNURL	PRISS	SLEET	STING	TWEED
DJINN	FRISK	KORUN	PRUNE	SLIMS	STINK	TWEEN
DOUGH	FRIZZ	LEACH	PUNCH	SLINK	STOCK	TWERP
DOWER	FROST	LEMON	QUACK	SLOSH	STOMP	TWINK
DRAFF	FROTH	LIMPS	QUALM	SLUMP	STONE	TWIRL
DRAFT	FROWN	LINEN	QUEEN	SLURP	STORE	TWIST
DRAPE	FROWS	LIVER	QUINS	SLUSH	STORM	UNSEX
DRAWL	FRUIT	LOWER	QUIRK	SMARM	STOUR	VAPOR
DREAM	FRUMP	MANGE	RATAN	SMART	STRAW	VAULT
DREAR	GALAX	MARSH	RESIN	SMEAR	STRIP	VAUNT
DRECK	GHOST	MAUND	RHEUM	SMELL	STUFF	VOMIT
DRESS	GLAIR	MELON	RIGHT	SMILE	STUMP	WAFER
DRIFT	GLASS	MIGHT	ROOTS	SMIRK	SUGAR	WATER
DROLL	GLEAM	MISER	ROPER	SMITH	SWAMP	WAVER
DROOL	GLEET	MOPER	ROSIN	SMOKE	SWANK	WEENS
DROOP	GLINT	MOULD	ROUGH	SNACK	SWART	WEIRD
DROPS	GLITZ	MOUSE	RUDER	SNAKE	SWEAT	WHACK
DROSS	GLOOM	MOUTH	SATIN	SNARK	SWEEP	WHELK
DUPER	GLOOP	MUNCH	SAUGH	SNARL	SWING	WHIFF
DWEEB	GLOSS	MURRE	SAVOR	SNEAK	SWIRL	WHIMS
EARTH	GNARL	MYRRH	SCANT	SNEER	SWISH	WHINE
EATER	GOOSE	NIGHT	SCARE	SNIFF	SWOON	WHIRL
EIGHT	GOWAN	NITER	SCATT	SNOOP	SWOOP	WHIRR
FAKER	GRAIN	NOTCH	SCREW	SNOOT	SYLPH	WHISK
FAULT	GRAMP	OCHER	SCURF	SNOUT	SYRUP	WHITE
FEIST	GRAPE	ONION	SCUZZ	SNUFF	TEENS	WHIZZ
FELON	GRASS	ORANG	SEVER	SODOM	THING	WIELD
FILTH	GREED	PAINT	SHACK	SOREL	THONG	WINCE
FINER	GREEN	PAPER	SHALE	SPACE	THORN	WITCH
FITCH	GRIPE	PARLE	SHARN	SPARK	THYME	WOODS
FIXIT	GROSZ	PATCH	SHARP	SPECK	TITCH	WORTH
FLAKE	GROUT	PEACH	SHEEN	SPEED	TOAST	WRATH
FLASH	GROWL	PEARL	SHELL	SPEND	TOOTH	WRIST
FLECK	GRUFF	PHONE	SHIFT	SPICE	TOOTS	YEAST
FLESH	GRUMP	PITCH	SHIRT	SPIFF	TORCH	
FLINT	GUILT	PLASH	SHOAL	SPIKE	TOUCH	
FLIRT	HAULM	PLINK	SHORT	SPOOF	TOUGH	
FLOAT	HEART	PLUCK	SHOUT	SPOOK	TOWER	
FLOCK	HEATH	PLUMP	SINEW	SPOON	TRAMP	
FLOSS	HERES	PLUNK	SIRUP	SPORT	TRASH	

With front hook Z

AMIAS	AYINS	ESTER	IGGED	ITHER

With back hook Z

PIZZA   QUART   SPELT   SPRIT

Chapter 4: Six letter words with hooks

With front hook A

BASHED	CANTHI	GROUND	NEARED	SHAMED	TONICS
BASHES	CAUDAL	ITCHES	NOTHER	SHIEST	TONING
BASING	CERATE	LARUMS	PHASIC	SOCIAL	TROPHY
BATING	CEROUS	LEVINS	PHONIC	SPECTS	TROPIN
BETTED	CHIRAL	LIASES	PHOTIC	SPIRED	UNTIES
BETTER	CLINIC	LIGHTS	PLENTY	SPIRES	VAILED
BETTOR	CORNED	LINERS	QUIVER	SPRAWL	VENGED
BIDERS	CUTELY	LINING	REALLY	SQUINT	VENGES
BIDING	CUTEST	LUMINA	RISING	STATIC	VENUES
BIOTIC	CYCLIC	MASSED	ROUSED	STOUND	VIATIC
BLINGS	DEEMED	MASSES	ROUSER	STRICT	VIATOR
BODING	EDILES	MAZING	ROUSES	STRIDE	VOIDED
BOUGHT	EGISES	MENDED	RUANAS	STYLAR	VOIDER
BOUNDS	EOLIAN	MENDER	RUGOLA	SUNDER	VOWERS
BREAST	EONIAN	MENTUM	SCARED	TACTIC	VOWING
BRIDGE	ERUGOS	MERCER	SCENDS	TAXIES	WAITED
BROACH	ETHERS	MERCES	SCENTS	THEISM	WAITER
BUBBLE	FEARED	MONGST	SCRIBE	THEIST	WAKENS
BUSING	GAINST	MOTION	SEPSES	THIRST	WAKING
BUTTED	GAMETE	MOUNTS	SEPSIS	THWART	WARDED
BUTTER	GENTRY	MUSERS	SEPTIC	TINGLE	WARDER
BYSSAL	GINNER	MUSING	SEXUAL	TONERS	

With back hook A

ABOMAS	CHIMER	EROTIC	KHALIF	PAISAN	SHIKAR
ADDEND	CHOLER	EXOTIC	LOCUST	PERSON	SIGNOR
ALUMIN	CHRISM	FENING	LOMENT	PROPYL	SQUILL
ARABIC	CODEIN	FORMIC	MADRAS	QUININ	SULTAN
ASHRAM	CORTIN	GALLET	MANIOC	ROBUST	TAMBUR
BUZUKI	COTING	GALLIC	MARKKA	ROSACE	TARTAN
CANDID	CURIOS	GRAVID	MICELL	ROTUND	TAVERN
CANTAL	DEJECT	GUNNER	MOMENT	SENHOR	TEMPER
CEMENT	DEODAR	INFANT	NANDIN	SEQUEL	TYMPAN
CHIASM	DRACHM	INGEST	OSMUND	SERING	VIATIC

With front hook B

ABACUS	ANGLES	EARING	IGGING	LAGGER	LAZING
ABYING	ARISTA	EATERS	INNING	LAMING	LEAKER
ACHING	ARRACK	EATING	IONICS	LAMMED	LENDER
ADLAND	ARROWS	EERIER	ITCHED	LANDER	LESSER
AGGERS	ASHING	EERILY	ITCHES	LANKER	LIGHTS
AGGIES	ASKING	EGGARS	LACKED	LANKLY	LINKED
AILING	ASSETS	EGGING	LACKER	LASTED	LINKER
ALLIES	ASSIST	ELATED	LADDER	LASTER	LIPPED
ALLOTS	ASTERS	ENDERS	LADERS	LATHER	LISTER
ANALLY	EAGLED	ENDING	LADING	LATTER	LITHER
ANGERS	EAGLES	ICKERS	LAGGED	LAWING	LOBBED

LOCKED	LUNGES	OOZING	RAIDER	REAMED	ROOKIE
LOCKER	LUNTED	ORATED	RAILED	REVETS	ROOMED
LOGGED	LUSHED	ORATES	RAINED	RICKED	RUSHED
LOGGER	LUSHER	ORDERS	RAISED	RIDGED	RUSHER
LOOMED	LUSHES	ORDURE	RAISES	RIDGES	RUSHES
LOOPED	LUSTER	OTHERS	RAKING	RIGHTS	UDDERS
LOOPER	OATERS	OUNCES	RAMBLE	RIMMED	UMBLES
LOTTED	OFFING	OVINES	RASHER	RIMMER	UMMING
LOTTER	OILERS	OXLIKE	RASHES	RINDED	UMPING
LOUSED	OILING	RABBLE	RASHLY	RINGER	UNIONS
LOUSES	OINKED	RACERS	RATTLE	RISKED	URGERS
LOWERS	OLDEST	RACHET	RAVERS	RISKER	URIALS
LOWING	OMBERS	RACING	RAVING	ROASTS	URPING
LUBBER	ONUSES	RACKET	RAWEST	ROCKET	USHERS
LUFFED	OODLES	RADDED	RAYING	ROGUES	UTTERS
LUNGED	OOZIER	RAGGED	RAZERS	ROILED	
LUNGER	OOZILY	RAIDED	RAZING	ROOKED	

With back hook B

POTHER   PROVER

With front hook C

ACHING	HARING	HOLLAS	LASSES	LOGGER	ORDERS
ALLEES	HARKED	HOPPED	LASSIS	LONERS	OTTARS
AMBERS	HARMED	HOPPER	LATTER	LOPPED	OTTERS
AMPING	HARMER	HORDED	LAVERS	LOSERS	OUCHED
ANKLES	HASTEN	HOUSED	LAWING	LOSING	OUCHES
ANTING	HATTED	HOUSER	LAYING	LOTTED	OUTERS
ANYONS	HATTER	HOUSES	LEANED	LOUGHS	OVERED
AROUSE	HAUNTS	HUCKLE	LEANER	LOURED	OVINES
ARRACK	HAWING	HUFFED	LEANLY	LOUTED	RACKED
ARTELS	HAZANS	HUGGED	LEAVED	LOVERS	RACKER
ARTFUL	HAZZAN	HUGGER	LEAVER	LUBBER	RACKLE
ASHIER	HEAPER	HUMMED	LEAVES	LUCKED	RAFTED
ASHING	HEATED	HUMPED	LICHES	LUMBER	RAFTER
ASKING	HEATER	HUNTER	LICKED	LUMPED	RAGGED
ASTERS	HEDERS	HUPPAH	LICKER	LUMPER	RAMMED
EASING	HEWERS	HUTZPA	LIMBED	LUNKER	RAMMER
ENSURE	HEWING	INCHED	LIMBER	LUSTER	RAMPED
ENTERS	HIDDEN	INCHES	LINGER	OATERS	RANKED
EROTIC	HIDERS	LACKED	LINKED	OCKERS	RANKER
HAIRED	HIDING	LACKER	LINKER	OFFERS	RANKLE
HALLAH	HILLED	LAGGED	LIPPED	OFFING	RANKLY
HALLOT	HILLER	LAMBER	LIPPER	OILERS	RAPING
HALUTZ	HIPPED	LAMMED	LITTER	OILING	RAPPED
HAMPER	HIPPER	LAMPED	LIVERS	OLDEST	RAPPER
HANCES	HIPPIE	LAPPED	LOBBER	OLDISH	RASHER
HANGED	HITTER	LAPPER	LOCHES	OLLIED	RASHES
HANGER	HOCKED	LASHED	LOCKED	OLLIES	RATERS
HANTED	HOKIER	LASHER	LOCKER	OMBERS	RATING
HAPPED	HOKING	LASHES	LOGGED	ORACLE	RAUNCH

RAVENS	REMATE	RINGED	ROQUET	RUMBLY	UMMING
RAVERS	RESTED	RINGER	ROSIER	RUMPLE	UPPERS
RAVING	RIBBED	RIPPLE	ROUTES	RUMPLY	UPPING
RAYONS	RIBBER	RITTER	ROWERS	RUSHED	URARES
RAZING	RICKED	ROCHET	ROWING	RUSHER	URARIS
REAMED	RICKEY	ROCKED	RUDELY	RUSHES	URATES
REAMER	RIMMER	ROCKET	RUDEST	RUSTED	UTTERS
REELED	RIMPLE	ROOKED	RUMBLE	UMBERS	

With back hook C

ALKALI	CARDIA	EMBOLI	ISTHMI	PRIAPI	RHOMBI
CANTHI	COLONI	EPHEBI	PHALLI	PYLORI	THALLI

With front hook D

ADDLED	EJECTA	IMPLED	OODLES	RAPING	ROUTHS
ADDLES	EJECTS	INGLES	ORMERS	RATTED	ROVERS
AGGERS	ELATED	INKIER	OTTERS	RAYING	ROVING
ALLIED	ELATES	INKING	OUCHED	READER	RUBBED
ALLIES	ELUDED	INNERS	OUCHES	REAMED	RUBBER
AMPING	ELUDER	INNING	OUTING	REAMER	RUGGED
ANGERS	ELUDES	IREFUL	OWNERS	REARER	RUMBLE
ANGLED	ELVERS	IRKING	OWNING	RIBBED	RUMMER
ANGLER	EMERGE	ITCHED	RABBET	RIBLET	RUTHER
ANGLES	EMOTED	ITCHES	RABBLE	RIFTED	UBIETY
APPLES	EMOTES	JEBELS	RAFTED	RILLED	UMPING
ASHIER	EPOSES	JIBBAH	RAFTER	RIPPED	UNITES
ASHING	EVOLVE	JIBBAS	RAGEES	RIPPER	UPPING
AWNING	ICIEST	OCKERS	RAGGED	RIVERS	WELLED
EARTHS	ICKERS	OFFERS	RAGGLE	RIVING	WINDLE
EDUCED	ICKIER	OFFING	RAINED	ROGUES	WINING
EDUCES	IGGING	OLLIED	RAMMED	ROLLED	
EDUCTS	IGNIFY	OLLIES	RAPERS	ROLLER	

With back hook D

ABDUCE	ALLEGE	AVENGE	BERIME	BRAISE	BYLINE
ABJURE	ALLUDE	AVIATE	BETIDE	BREEZE	CACKLE
ABLATE	ALLURE	AVULSE	BEWARE	BRIDGE	CADDIE
ABRADE	AMERCE	BABBLE	BIRDIE	BRIDLE	CAJOLE
ACCEDE	ANNEXE	BAFFLE	BISTRE	BRONZE	CALQUE
ACCRUE	ANSATE	BATTLE	BLENDE	BROWSE	CANDLE
ACCUSE	APPOSE	BEAGLE	BLOUSE	BRUISE	CASQUE
ADDUCE	ARCADE	BEETLE	BLUDGE	BUBBLE	CASTLE
ADHERE	AROUSE	BEGAZE	BLUNGE	BUCKLE	CENTRE
ADJURE	ARRIVE	BEHAVE	BOBBLE	BUMBLE	CERATE
ADMIRE	ASPIRE	BEHOVE	BOGGLE	BUNDLE	CESTOI
ADVISE	ASSUME	BEMIRE	BOODLE	BUNGLE	CHAINE
AERATE	ASSURE	BEMUSE	BOOGIE	BURBLE	CHANCE
AFFINE	ATTIRE	BENAME	BORATE	BURGLE	CHANGE
AGNIZE	ATTUNE	BERAKE	BOTTLE	BUSTLE	CHARGE
ALCOVE	AURATE	BERATE	BOUNCE	BUTTLE	CHASSE

CHEESE	DEFACE	ENCASE	GANGLE	ICICLE	KLUDGE
CHINSE	DEFAME	ENCODE	GARAGE	IDEATE	LALLAN
CHIRRE	DEFILE	ENCORE	GARBLE	IGNITE	LANATE
CHOUSE	DEFINE	ENDITE	GARGLE	IGNORE	LANGUE
CHOWSE	DEFUSE	ENDURE	GAROTE	ILLUDE	LEAGUE
CHROME	DEFUZE	ENFACE	GAUCHE	ILLUME	LEGATE
CIRCLE	DEGREE	ENGAGE	GELATE	IMBIBE	LENITE
CLEAVE	DELATE	ENGINE	GENTLE	IMBRUE	LIAISE
CLICHE	DELETE	ENISLE	GIGGLE	IMMURE	LIGATE
CLIQUE	DELIME	ENLACE	GILLIE	IMPALE	LOATHE
CLOTHE	DELUDE	ENRAGE	GIRDLE	IMPEDE	LOBATE
COBBLE	DELUGE	ENROBE	GLAIRE	IMPONE	LOCATE
COCKLE	DEMISE	ENSILE	GLAIVE	IMPOSE	LOCULE
CODDLE	DEMODE	ENSURE	GLANCE	IMPUTE	LOUNGE
COERCE	DEMOTE	ENTICE	GOATEE	INCAGE	LOUVRE
COFFLE	DENOTE	EQUATE	GOBBLE	INCASE	LUNATE
COHERE	DENUDE	ERMINE	GOGGLE	INCISE	LUSTRE
COIFFE	DEPONE	ESCAPE	GOITRE	INCITE	LUXATE
COIGNE	DEPOSE	ESTATE	GOOGLE	INCUSE	LYRATE
COLLAR	DEPUTE	EUCHRE	GREASE	INDITE	MACKLE
COLLIE	DERATE	EVINCE	GREAVE	INDUCE	MACULE
CONGEE	DERIDE	EVOLVE	GRIEVE	INFUSE	MANAGE
COSTAR	DERIVE	EVULSE	GRILLE	INHALE	MANGLE
COUPLE	DESIRE	EXCIDE	GRIPPE	INHERE	MANTLE
COURSE	DETUNE	EXCISE	GROOVE	INHUME	MANURE
CRADLE	DEVISE	EXCITE	GROUSE	INJURE	MARBLE
CREASE	DEVOTE	EXCUSE	GRUDGE	INLACE	MATURE
CREATE	DIBBLE	EXHALE	GUGGLE	INSURE	MEASLE
CRINGE	DIDDLE	EXHUME	GURGLE	INTONE	MEDDLE
CROSSE	DILATE	EXPIRE	GUSSIE	INVADE	MENACE
CRUISE	DILUTE	EXPOSE	GUTTLE	INVITE	METTLE
CUDDLE	DIMPLE	FACETE	GUZZLE	INVOKE	MIDDLE
CURATE	DINDLE	FERULE	GYRATE	IODATE	MINGLE
CURDLE	DISUSE	FETTLE	HACKLE	IODISE	MINUTE
CURRIE	DIVIDE	FIDDLE	HAGGLE	IODIZE	MISCUE
CUTTLE	DIVINE	FIGURE	HANDLE	IONISE	MISUSE
DABBLE	DONATE	FIXATE	HASSLE	IONIZE	MIZZLE
DADDLE	DOODLE	FIZZLE	HEARSE	JANGLE	MOTIVE
DAGGLE	DOUBLE	FLANGE	HECKLE	JAUNCE	MOTTLE
DAMAGE	DOUCHE	FLEDGE	HIGGLE	JIGGLE	MOUSSE
DANDLE	DREDGE	FLEECE	HINNIE	JIMMIE	MUDDLE
DANGLE	DROMON	FLENSE	HIRPLE	JINGLE	MUFFLE
DAPPLE	DROWSE	FONDLE	HIRSLE	JOGGLE	MUMBLE
DARKLE	DRUDGE	FONDUE	HOBBLE	JOSTLE	MUSCLE
DARTLE	ECLOSE	FOOTLE	HOGTIE	JOUNCE	MUTATE
DAWDLE	EFFACE	FOOZLE	HOMAGE	JUGGLE	MUTINE
DAZZLE	EFFUSE	FORAGE	HONDLE	JUMBLE	MUZZLE
DEBASE	ELAPSE	FRAPPE	HOPPLE	JUNGLE	NANNIE
DEBATE	EMBRUE	FRINGE	HOWDIE	JUSTLE	NATURE
DEBONE	EMERGE	FUDDLE	HUDDLE	KECKLE	NEEDLE
DECIDE	EMERSE	FUMBLE	HUMBLE	KIBBLE	NEGATE
DECODE	EMPALE	GABBLE	HURDLE	KINDLE	NESTLE
DECREE	ENABLE	GAGGLE	HURTLE	KIRTLE	NETTLE
DEDUCE	ENCAGE	GAMBLE	HUSTLE	KITTLE	NIBBLE

69

NICKLE	PROTEI	REPAVE	SECURE	STYMIE	UNCAKE
NIDATE	PSYCHE	REPINE	SEDATE	SUBDUE	UNCASE
NIGGLE	PUDDLE	REPOSE	SEDUCE	SUCKLE	UNFREE
NIPPLE	PUMICE	REPUTE	SEETHE	SUPPLE	UNGLUE
NOBBLE	PUNGLE	RESCUE	SETTLE	SUTURE	UNLACE
NODDLE	PUPATE	RESHOE	SEVERE	SWATHE	UNLADE
NOODGE	PURFLE	RESIDE	SHEAVE	SWERVE	UNLIKE
NOODLE	PURPLE	RESILE	SHELVE	SWINGE	UNLIVE
NOTATE	PURSUE	RESITE	SHOPPE	TACKLE	UNPILE
NOTICE	PUTTIE	RESIZE	SHRINE	TANGLE	UNROBE
NOVATE	PUZZLE	RESOLE	SHRIVE	TATTLE	UNROPE
NUANCE	RABBLE	RESUME	SICKLE	TEAZLE	UNTAME
NUTATE	RACEME	RETAPE	SINGLE	TEETHE	UNTUNE
NUZZLE	RADDLE	RETILE	SIZZLE	TEMPLE	UNYOKE
OBLIGE	RAFFLE	RETIME	SLEAVE	TENURE	UPDATE
OPAQUE	RAMBLE	RETIRE	SLEAZE	THIEVE	UPDIVE
OPIATE	RANKLE	RETUNE	SLEDGE	THRIVE	UPGAZE
OPPOSE	RASSLE	RETYPE	SLEEVE	THRONE	UPPILE
OSMOSE	RATTLE	REVERE	SLUDGE	TICKLE	UPRATE
OUTVIE	RAVAGE	REVILE	SLUICE	TIERCE	UPSIZE
OUTWAR	RAVINE	REVISE	SMUDGE	TINGLE	VACATE
PADDLE	REBASE	REVIVE	SNEEZE	TINKLE	VAMOSE
PALACE	REBATE	REVOKE	SNOOZE	TIPPLE	VELURE
PARADE	REBORE	REVOTE	SOLACE	TIPTOE	VISAGE
PAROLE	REBUKE	REWAKE	SOLATE	TISSUE	VITTLE
PATINE	RECANE	REWIRE	SOOTHE	TODDLE	VOLUME
PEBBLE	RECEDE	REZONE	SOPITE	TOGATE	VOLUTE
PEDDLE	RECITE	RIDDLE	SORTIE	TOGGLE	VOYAGE
PEOPLE	RECODE	RIFFLE	SOURCE	TONGUE	WABBLE
PERUKE	RECUSE	RIMPLE	SPARGE	TOODLE	WADDIE
PERUSE	REDATE	RIPPLE	SPATHE	TOOTLE	WADDLE
PESTLE	REDDLE	ROOTLE	SPHERE	TOPPLE	WAFFLE
PETTLE	REDUCE	ROTATE	SPLICE	TORQUE	WAGGLE
PHRASE	REFACE	RUBBLE	SPLINE	TOUCHE	WAMBLE
PIAFFE	REFILE	RUCKLE	SPONGE	TOUSLE	WANGLE
PICKLE	REFINE	RUDDLE	SPOUSE	TOUZLE	WARBLE
PIDDLE	REFIRE	RUFFLE	SPRUCE	TRANCE	WARSLE
PIERCE	REFUGE	RUMBLE	SQUARE	TREBLE	WATTLE
PIFFLE	REFUSE	RUMPLE	SQUIRE	TRIAGE	WEEWEE
PIMPLE	REFUTE	RUNKLE	STABLE	TRIFLE	WHEEZE
PIRATE	REGALE	RUSTLE	STAPLE	TRIPLE	WHINGE
PLAGUE	REGLUE	SADDLE	STARVE	TROMPE	WIDDLE
PLEASE	REHEAR	SAGGAR	STATUE	TROUPE	WIGGLE
PLEDGE	REHIRE	SALUTE	STEEVE	TRUDGE	WILLIE
PLUNGE	RELACE	SAMPLE	STEPPE	TRYSTE	WIMBLE
POINTE	RELATE	SAVAGE	STIFLE	TUMBLE	WIMPLE
POLICE	RELINE	SCATHE	STODGE	TURTLE	WINDLE
POMADE	RELIVE	SCHEME	STOOGE	TUSSLE	WINKLE
POPPLE	RELUME	SCONCE	STRAFE	TWEEZE	WINTLE
POUFFE	REMATE	SCRAPE	STRAKE	TWINGE	WOBBLE
POUNCE	REMISE	SCRIBE	STRIPE	ULLAGE	WRITHE
PRAISE	REMOVE	SCRIVE	STRIVE	UMPIRE	ZIZZLE
PRANCE	RENAME	SCYTHE	STROBE	UNBALE	ZONATE
PREVUE	RENEGE	SECEDE	STROKE	UNCAGE	

With front hook E

AGLETS	LAPSED	MENDED	RASING	SPRITS	TOILES
ASTERN	LAPSES	MENDER	RASURE	SPYING	TRIERS
ASTERS	LECTOR	MERGED	RECTOR	SQUIRE	UPHROE
CARTES	LEGIST	MERGES	RODENT	STATED	VANISH
CHARDS	LEGITS	MOTION	SCAPED	STATES	VENTER
CLOSED	LOPERS	MOTIVE	SCAPES	STRAYS	VICTOR
CLOSES	LOPING	NATION	SCARPS	STRUMS	VILEST
COTYPE	LUTING	PATERS	SERINE	TALONS	VOLUTE
IRENIC	MAILED	RASERS	SPOUSE	THANES	

With back hook E

ABOLLA	CAROCH	EMETIN	HYALIN	MUCOSA
ADVISE	CARPAL	EMPLOY	HYDRAS	MYELIN
AFFAIR	CASERN	ENNUYE	HYDRIA	NARCOS
ALANIN	CATENA	EPIGON	HYDRID	NEBULA
ALEXIN	CAVIAR	EPIMER	IMPING	NEURON
ALIDAD	CESURA	ESCAPE	IMPROV	NITRID
ALUMIN	CHAETA	ETAMIN	INFANT	NITRIL
ALUMNA	CHIMER	EXEDRA	INFULA	NOVENA
AMIDIN	CHOANA	EXTERN	INSULA	NYMPHA
AMOEBA	CHOPIN	EXUVIA	INTERN	OBLIGE
ANILIN	CHORAL	FACULA	INTIMA	OCHREA
APHTHA	CICADA	FASCIA	INVITE	OLEFIN
AREOLA	CINEOL	FECULA	ISATIN	PANGEN
ARISTA	CITRIN	FERULA	ISOBAR	PAPULA
ARTIST	CLEANS	FIANCE	ISOGON	PAROLE
ASPERS	CLOACA	FIBULA	JASMIN	PARVIS
ATTACH	COCAIN	FLAMBE	JUBILE	PATINA
ATTRIT	CODEIN	FLAVIN	KAINIT	PENSIL
AURORA	COELOM	FOLIOS	KAOLIN	PEPSIN
AXILLA	COMPOS	FORBAD	LACUNA	PEPTID
BAGASS	CONCHA	FOREBY	LADRON	PEROGI
BALLAD	CONSOL	FORMAT	LAMINA	PICKAX
BEGRIM	COPULA	FRIJOL	LEGATE	PINKEY
BELDAM	CORONA	GALOSH	LEUCIN	PISTOL
BENZIN	CRISTA	GENTIL	LIGULA	PLANCH
BENZOL	CUPULA	GERMAN	LINGUA	PLATAN
BERLIN	CYANID	GLOSSA	LISSOM	PLEDGE
BICORN	CYANIN	GLYCIN	LORICA	PLEURA
BLINTZ	DENTIN	GOLOSH	LUCERN	POLEAX
BREATH	DETENT	GOODBY	LUNULA	PRECIP
BROMID	DEVISE	GOYISH	LURDAN	PRECIS
BROMIN	DEVOTE	GRADIN	MACULA	PROTYL
BRUCIN	DHOOTI	GRATIN	MARLIN	PURLIN
CAMERA	DIAMIN	GUANIN	MARQUE	PYRROL
CANULA	DIAZIN	HALTER	MEDUSA	QUININ
CAPRIC	DIOXAN	HAPTEN	MEGASS	RADIAL
CARDIA	DIOXID	HARMIN	MICELL	RADULA
CARINA	DIVERS	HERNIA	MODERN	RATLIN
CARLIN	DOMAIN	HEROIN	MORULA	RECOUP

REFUGE	SCORIA	SPRING	TEGULA	UNGULA
REGINA	SECOND	SQUAMA	TIMBAL	URTEXT
RESCUE	SECRET	STATIC	TOLUID	VAGINA
RETINA	SEROSA	STRANG	TOLUOL	VERSIN
RETIRE	SHEATH	STRUMA	TORULA	VESICA
REVERS	SIGNOR	SULFID	TRITON	VOLANT
RIPOST	SKATOL	SYLVIN	TROCHE	VOMICA
SAFROL	SMOOTH	SYNURA	TROPIN	WALLEY
SCALAR	SOIGNE	TAENIA	TUNICA	WREATH
SCLERA	SPIREM	TARTAR	TUSSOR	ZONULA

With front hook F

ACTION	EARING	LAMING	LIGHTS	LUNKER	RAPPED
ACTORS	EASING	LAMMED	LINGER	LUSHED	RATERS
ACTUAL	EASTER	LANKER	LINTED	LUSHER	RAYING
AERIES	EELING	LAPPED	LIPPED	LUSHES	RAZZLE
AILING	ENDERS	LAPPER	LIPPER	LUSTER	RESHES
AIREST	ENDING	LASHED	LITTER	LUTING	RETTED
AIRIER	ESTERS	LASHER	LOCKED	LUTIST	RIDGES
AIRING	ETCHED	LASHES	LOGGED	LYINGS	RIGGED
AIRWAY	ETCHER	LATTEN	LOGGER	OILING	RIGHTS
ALLOWS	ETCHES	LATTER	LOPPED	OLLIES	RILLED
ALTERS	IGGING	LAWING	LOPPER	ORGONE	RINGED
AMINES	INCHES	LAYERS	LOSSES	ORMERS	RISKED
ANIONS	INKING	LAYING	LOURED	OXLIKE	RISKER
ARCING	INNING	LECHES	LOUTED	OXTAIL	RITTER
ARMERS	ITCHES	LEDGED	LOWERS	RACKED	RITZES
ARMING	LACKED	LEDGES	LOWERY	RAGGED	ROCKED
ARROWS	LAGGED	LEERED	LOWING	RAILER	RUGGED
ASHING	LAGGER	LENSED	LUBBER	RAISES	UMBLES
ATTEST	LAKERS	LENSES	LUFFED	RANKED	UNFAIR
AWNING	LAKIER	LICKED	LUMMOX	RANKER	
EARFUL	LAKING	LICKER	LUMPED	RANKLY	

With back hook F

SHERIF

With front hook G

ACHING	AMBLES	ASTRAL	IGGING	LANCED	LIMMER
ADDERS	AMINES	AUGERS	IMMIES	LANCER	LINTED
ADDING	ANGERS	AUNTLY	IMPING	LANCES	LISTEN
AGGERS	ANGLED	EARING	INCHES	LASSES	LISTER
ALLEYS	ANGLES	ELATED	INNERS	LASSIE	LITTER
ALLIED	ARGLED	ELATES	INNING	LAZIER	LOBATE
ALLIES	ARGLES	ELDERS	ITCHES	LAZILY	LOBULE
ALLIUM	ASCONS	EMOTES	IZZARD	LAZING	LOOMED
ALLOWS	ASHING	ENDERS	LACIER	LEANED	LOPPED
AMBITS	ASKING	ESTATE	LADDER	LEANER	LORIES
AMBLED	ASPERS	HOSTED	LAIRED	LIBBER	LOSSES
AMBLER	ASTERS	HOSTLY	LAMMED	LIMING	LOUTED

LOVERS	RAFTER	RAVERS	RILLES	ROPING	RUFFLY
LOVING	RAINED	RAVING	RIMIER	ROUNDS	RUMBLE
LOWERS	RANGER	RAYING	RIMING	ROUPED	RUMBLY
LOWING	RANGES	RAZERS	RIMMER	ROUSED	RUMMER
LUGGED	RANTED	RAZING	RINDED	ROUSER	UMMING
LUTEAL	RANTER	REAVED	RIPING	ROUSES	UNITES
OATIER	RAPIER	REAVES	RIPPED	ROUTED	UNLESS
OFFERS	RASPED	RIDDED	RIPPER	ROUTER	UNLOCK
OLDEST	RASPER	RIDDER	RIPPLE	ROWERS	UNSHIP
OWNING	RATERS	RIDDLE	RITTER	ROWING	URGING
RABBLE	RATIFY	RIDING	RIVETS	ROWTHS	USHERS
RACING	RATINE	RIEVER	ROOMED	RUBBED	UTTERS
RACKLE	RATING	RIFTED	ROOMER	RUBBER	
RAFTED	RAVELS	RILLED	ROPERS	RUFFED	

With back hook G

BIFFIN	CODLIN	GLOBIN	MARTIN	PARKIN	SEIZIN
BIGGIN	COFFIN	GRADIN	MATTIN	PIGGIN	STATIN
BOBBIN	CUMMIN	GRATIN	MUFFIN	PIPPIN	TANNIN
BOFFIN	CYCLIN	HARMIN	MUNTIN	POSTIN	TIFFIN
BUSKIN	CYMLIN	HARPIN	NOGGIN	PUFFIN	TREPAN
CALKIN	DENTIN	HOISIN	OUTRAN	PURLIN	VERSIN
CARLIN	DUBBIN	JERKIN	OUTRUN	RAISIN	WITHIN
CATALO	GASKIN	LEGGIN	OUTSIN	ROBBIN	
CATLIN	GITTIN	MARLIN	OVERDO	SEISIN	

With front hook H

ACKEES	ANGERS	ARROWS	EDGIER	INTERS	OUSELS
AFTERS	ANTING	ASHING	EDGING	ITCHED	OVERED
AGGADA	APLITE	AUTEUR	EELING	ITCHES	OWLETS
AILING	ARBORS	EARING	EIGHTH	OCKERS	UMBLES
AIRIER	ARBOUR	EARTHS	EIGHTS	OLLIES	UMMING
AIRILY	ARMERS	EATERS	EMMERS	OMBRES	UMPING
ALLOWS	ARMFUL	EATING	ERRING	OSIERS	
ALTERS	ARMING	EDGERS	INKIER	OSTLER	

With back hook H

AARRGH	CHALLA	HALALA	MEZUZA	SABBAT	TALLIT
AGGADA	CHALOT	HALLOT	MIKVOT	SHANTI	TEREFA
AGOROT	CHUPPA	HEIGHT	OUTWIT	SHARIA	TURBIT
ALIYOT	COMMIS	HUTZPA	POORIS	SHIKSE	WHOOMP
BUSHWA	DJIBBA	MATZOT	PRUTOT	SUKKOT	
CADDIS	HAGGIS	MEGILP	QABALA	TALLIS	

With front hook I

RISING	SATINS	SOLATE

73

With back hook I

ABOMAS	DACTYL	EPIGON	OBLAST	SANTIM	SIGNOR
AFGHAN	DEMENT	HELLER	PAESAN	SECOND	TENNES
CHIASM	DENARI	MARTIN	PANDAN	SHIKAR	TYMPAN

With front hook J

AGGERS	ANGLES	IGGING	OCULAR	OUNCES	UMBLES
AGGIES	ARGONS	IMMIES	OLLIED	OUSTED	UMPING
AILING	ASPERS	INGLES	OLLIES	OUSTER	
ANGLED	AWLESS	INKERS	OSTLER	OWLIER	
ANGLER	ESTERS	INKING	OTTERS	UDDERS	

With front hook K

ABAKAS	EGGERS	ICKERS	LISTER	NAPPER	RATERS
ABAYAS	EGGING	ICKIER	LUGING	NIGHTS	RIMMER
EDGING	ENOSIS	INKIER	LUTZES	NOCKED	
EELING	ETCHES	INKING	NAPPED	NURLED	

With back hook K

AMAUTI	CALPAC	OOMIAC	TOMBAC
AMTRAC	GWEDUC	OUTRAN	

With front hook L

ADDERS	ASTERS	EDGERS	ETCHES	IONISE	OTTERS
AGGERS	AUDING	EDGIER	ICKERS	IONIZE	OUTING
AIRIER	AWLESS	EERIER	IGNIFY	IZARDS	OVERLY
AIRING	AWNING	EERILY	IGNITE	OBELIA	OWLIER
AMBERS	EARNED	EGGIER	IMPING	OCKERS	UMBERS
AMENTS	EARNER	EGGING	INDIES	OCULAR	UMPING
AMPING	EASERS	ENDERS	INKERS	OCULUS	
ARCHES	EASING	ENDING	INKING	OLLIES	
ASHING	ECHING	ETCHED	INTERS	OMENTA	

With back hook L

ADNEXA	CHANCE	ELUVIA	INSTIL	MAXIMA	QUINTA
ALODIA	CHOREA	ENCINA	INTIMA	MEDUSA	REGINA
ANGINA	CHROMY	ENTERA	ISCHIA	METICA	RETINA
APNOEA	CLOACA	ETHOXY	JEJUNA	MIASMA	ROSTRA
AURORA	COLONE	EXUVIA	JINGAL	MINIMA	RUMINA
BARBEL	CONCHA	FASCIA	LACUNA	MUCOSA	SCLERA
CAMBIA	CORNEA	FEMORA	LAMINA	NOMINA	SCROTA
CAMERA	CORNUA	FULFIL	LEXICA	NYMPHA	SEMINA
CAPITA	CORONA	GENERA	LIMINA	OMENTA	SEROSA
CARINA	CORYZA	GINGAL	LINGUA	OPTIMA	SHRIVE
CARREL	CRANIA	GLOSSA	LOCHIA	PALLIA	STERNA
CENTRA	CRISSA	HERNIA	LUMINA	PLEURA	STIGMA
CHAETA	DISTIL	INSTAL	LUSTRA	QUANTA	STRATA

STROMA	TIERCE	TRAMEL	UREDIA	VIMINA
TAPETA	TIMBRE	TRIVIA	VAGINA	WADMOL
THERME	TOPFUL	TWIBIL	VESICA	ZOARIA

With front hook M

ADDERS	ALLOWS	ARROWS	EMBERS	INTERS	OUCHED
ADDING	ANGELS	ARROWY	EMETIC	OCKERS	OUCHES
AGNATE	ANGERS	ASCONS	ENDERS	OILERS	UDDERS
AILING	ANGLED	ASCOTS	ENDING	OILING	UMBLES
AIMERS	ANGLER	ASHING	ETHANE	OLLIES	UMMING
AIMING	ANGLES	ASKERS	ETHOXY	OMENTA	UMPING
ALATES	ARCHED	ASKING	ETHYLS	ORALLY	URINES
ALIGNS	ARCHER	ASTERS	IFFIER	ORGANS	USEFUL
ALINES	ARCHES	AXILLA	INGLES	ORPHIC	USHERS
ALLEES	ARGENT	ELDERS	INIONS	OTHERS	UTTERS

With back hook M

ANIMIS	BUCKRA	MANTRA	MISTER	PREWAR

With front hook N

AGGERS	ASCENT	EDDIES	EOLITH	ONUSES	UMBLES
AILING	ATRIUM	EITHER	ESTERS	OODLES	UNCLES
APHTHA	AUGHTS	EMESES	ICKERS	OUGHTS	UNLIKE
ARROWS	EARING	EMESIS	IFFIER	UMBERS	UTTERS

With back hook N

ABELIA	EASTER	PAPAYA	REGIVE	SIERRA	UPGROW
ALKALI	EMBRYO	PASTER	REGROW	SILVER	UPRISE
AMOEBA	ENVIRO	PATTER	RERISE	SMIDGE	UTOPIA
ANLAGE	GELATI	POSTER	RESHOW	STRIVE	VIBRIO
BETAKE	GODDAM	PREWAR	RETAKE	TAMARI	WESTER
BITTER	HOARSE	PROTEA	REWAKE	THRIVE	WRITHE
BRAHMA	INWOVE	PROTEI	REWOKE	TRUDGE	YESTER
CHASTE	JIGSAW	QUINTA	REWOVE	UNDRAW	ZITHER
CHIRRE	MEDUSA	REDRAW	RIPSAW	UNLADE	
CITHER	NUCLEI	REFLOW	SALTER	UNROVE	
COARSE	OUTSEE	REGIME	SHRIVE	UNWOVE	

With front hook O

BENTOS	EDEMAS	MENTAL	PINING	REBODY	VERSET
BLASTS	ESTRIN	MENTUM	PINION	ROTUND	YESSES
CARINA	ESTRUM	MICRON	POSSUM	URARIS	ZONATE
CELLAR	ESTRUS	MIKRON	RANGES	UTMOST	
CREATE	INKING	NANISM	RATING	VARIES	
DONATE	LINGOS	PACIFY	RATION	VERBID	

With back hook O

BANDIT	MOMENT	PAISAN	PUMMEL	TYMPAN
BRACER	NITROS	PAMPER	REVERS	VERISM
MAGNET	PAESAN	PRIMER	SECOND	

With front hook P

ACTION	ICKERS	LIABLE	RANCES	REMEET	REWRAP
ADDERS	ICKIER	LIGHTS	RANGED	REMISE	RICERS
ADDING	IGGING	LINKED	RANKED	REMISS	RICING
ADDLED	IMPING	LINKER	RATERS	REMIXT	RICKED
ADDLES	IMPLED	LOPPED	RATING	REMOLD	RIDING
AEONIC	INCHED	LOTTED	RATTLE	RENAME	RIGGED
AGINGS	INCHER	LOTTER	RAYING	REPACK	RILLED
AIRING	INCHES	LOUGHS	REACTS	REPAID	RIMERS
ALATES	INFOLD	LOVERS	REARMS	REPAVE	RIMING
ALLIUM	INIONS	LOWBOY	REAVER	REPAYS	RIMMED
ALTERS	INKERS	LOWERS	REBIDS	REPLAN	RIMMER
ANELED	INKIER	LOWING	REBILL	REPOSE	RISING
ANTHER	INKING	LUCKED	REBIND	REPPED	RIVETS
ANTING	INNATE	LUGGED	REBOIL	RESALE	ROBAND
APPOSE	INNERS	LUGGER	REBOOK	RESELL	ROBING
ARABLE	INNING	LUMBER	REBUYS	RESENT	RODDED
ARCHED	ITCHED	LUMPED	RECAST	RESETS	ROOFED
ARCHES	ITCHES	LUMPEN	RECEDE	RESHIP	ROOFER
ARISES	LACERS	LUMPER	RECENT	RESHOW	ROPERS
ARSONS	LACING	LUNGED	RECEPT	RESIDE	ROSIER
ARTIER	LANATE	LUNGER	RECESS	RESIFT	ROSILY
ASHING	LANNER	LUNGES	RECIPE	RESOAK	ROSING
ASTERN	LASHED	LUNKER	RECODE	RESOLD	ROVERS
ASTERS	LASHER	LUSHED	RECOOK	RESORT	ROVING
ATTEST	LASHES	LUSHER	RECOUP	RESTER	RUDERY
AWNING	LASTER	LUSHES	RECUTS	RESUME	SALTER
ECHING	LATENS	LUSHLY	REDATE	RETAPE	SHAWED
EELING	LATINA	ODIUMS	REDIAL	RETELL	UMPING
EGGING	LATTER	OODLES	REEDIT	RETEST	UNTIES
ELITES	LAYERS	OOHING	REFACE	RETOLD	UPPING
ENATES	LAYING	ORGIES	REFECT	RETRIM	URANIC
ENDING	LAYOFF	OTHERS	REFERS	RETYPE	URGERS
ENSILE	LEADED	OTTERS	REFILE	REVERB	URGING
EONISM	LEADER	OUCHED	REFIRE	REVIEW	URINES
ESTERS	LEASED	OUCHES	REFORM	REVISE	USHERS
HARMER	LEASER	OUNCES	REFUND	REVUES	UTTERS
HATTER	LEASES	OUTERS	REHEAT	REWARM	
HONERS	LEDGED	OUTING	RELATE	REWASH	
HONEYS	LEDGER	RAISED	RELOAD	REWIRE	
HONIED	LEDGES	RAISER	REMADE	REWORK	
HONING	LESSOR	RAISES	REMAKE	REWORN	

With back hook P

BEDLAM	MANTRA	SCHLEP

With front hook R

ADDING	AMPING	EELING	EMOTES	EVOKER	OUCHES
ADDLED	ANCHOS	EFFING	ENDERS	EVOKES	OUSTED
ADDLES	ANGERS	EGRESS	ENDING	EVOLVE	OUSTER
AFTERS	ANKLED	EGRETS	ENTERS	EXINES	OUTERS
AGGIES	ANKLES	EJECTS	ENVOIS	IGGING	OUTING
AIDERS	ANTING	ELANDS	EPOSES	IMPLED	OYSTER
AIDING	APPELS	ELAPSE	ESTATE	INNING	UDDERS
AILING	ASPERS	ELATED	ESTERS	OARING	UMBLES
ALLIED	ASPISH	ELATER	ETAPES	OCKERS	UNLESS
ALLIES	ASTERS	ELATES	ETCHED	OILIER	USHERS
AMBLED	EARING	EMAILS	ETCHES	OILING	UTILES
AMBLER	EBOOKS	EMENDS	EVERTS	OLLIES	
AMBLES	EDUCED	EMERGE	EVILER	ONIONS	
AMENTA	EDUCES	EMOTER	EVOKED	OTTERS	

With back hook R

ABJURE	BLUDGE	CHOUSE	DECIDE	ENDURE	GARBLE
ABRADE	BLUNGE	CHUKKA	DECODE	ENGAGE	GARGLE
ACCEDE	BOGGLE	CIRCLE	DECREE	ENROBE	GAUCHE
ACCUSE	BONNIE	CLAQUE	DEFACE	ENSURE	GENTLE
ADDUCE	BOODLE	CLEAVE	DEFAME	ENTICE	GIGGLE
ADHERE	BOTTLE	COARSE	DEFILE	ESCAPE	GIRDLE
ADJURE	BOUNCE	COBBLE	DEFINE	EVOLVE	GIRLIE
ADMIRE	BRIDLE	CODDLE	DEFUSE	EXCITE	GLANCE
ADVISE	BRONZE	COERCE	DELUDE	EXCUSE	GOBBLE
ALLEGE	BROWSE	COHERE	DEMURE	EXHUME	GOGGLE
ALLURE	BRUISE	COLLIE	DENUDE	EXPIRE	GOONIE
AMERCE	BUBBLE	COMAKE	DEPOSE	EXPOSE	GRAMMA
APPOSE	BUCKLE	COPULA	DERIDE	FACULA	GRANGE
AREOLA	BUMBLE	COUPLE	DERIVE	FEEBLE	GREASE
AROUSE	BUNDLE	COURSE	DESIRE	FETTLE	GRIEVE
ARRIVE	BUNGLE	CRADLE	DEVISE	FIBULA	GRILLE
ARTSIE	BURBLE	CREASE	DIBBLE	FICKLE	GRIPPE
ASPIRE	BUSTLE	CRINGE	DICKIE	FIDDLE	GROOVE
ASSUME	BYLINE	CROSSE	DIDDLE	FIERCE	GROUSE
ASSURE	CACKLE	CRUISE	DILATE	FIGURE	GRUDGE
AVENGE	CAJOLE	CUDDLE	DILUTE	FLANGE	GRUNGE
AXILLA	CANDLE	CUPULA	DIVIDE	FLEECE	GUTTLE
BABBLE	CANNIE	CURDLE	DIVINE	FLENSE	GUZZLE
BAFFLE	CANULA	CURRIE	DOGGIE	FOLKIE	HACKLE
BAGGIE	CATTIE	DABBLE	DOODLE	FONDLE	HAGGLE
BARMIE	CHAINE	DAMAGE	DOUBLE	FOOTIE	HANDLE
BATTLE	CHANCE	DANDLE	DREDGE	FOOTLE	HECKLE
BEAGLE	CHANGE	DANGLE	DRUDGE	FOOZLE	HEMPIE
BEETLE	CHARGE	DAWDLE	DUCKIE	FORAGE	HIGGLE
BEHAVE	CHASTE	DAZZLE	EFFACE	FREEZE	HIPPIE
BLENDE	CHEQUE	DEBASE	EMPALE	FUMBLE	HOARSE
BLITHE	CHOICE	DEBATE	ENABLE	GABBLE	HOBBLE
BLONDE	CHOOSE	DEBONE	ENCODE	GAMBLE	HOMAGE

HOODIE	LAMINA	OBLIGE	REBATE	SHELVE	TENTIE
HORSIE	LEAGUE	OBTUSE	REBUKE	SHOPPE	THRIVE
HUDDLE	LEGATO	OFFICE	RECITE	SHRIVE	TICKLE
HUMANE	LIGULA	OPAQUE	REDUCE	SILKIE	TINGLE
HUMBLE	LITTLE	OPPOSE	REFINE	SIMPLE	TINKLE
HUNKIE	LOATHE	OSCULA	REFUSE	SIZZLE	TIPPLE
HURDLE	LOCATE	OUTLIE	REFUTE	SMOKIE	TODDLE
HUSTLE	LOGGIE	PADDLE	REGALE	SNEEZE	TOGGLE
IGNITE	LOONIE	PAPULA	RELATE	SNOOZE	TOOTLE
IGNORE	LOUNGE	PARADE	REMAKE	SOCAGE	TORQUE
IMBIBE	LUCKIE	PASTIE	REMOTE	SOLACE	TOUCHE
IMMUNE	LUNULA	PAVISE	REMOVE	SOMBRE	TRIFLE
IMPALE	MACULA	PEDDLE	RENEGE	SONSIE	TROUPE
IMPEDE	MANAGE	PEOPLE	REPINE	SOOTHE	TRUDGE
IMPOSE	MANGLE	PERUSE	REPOSE	SPARGE	TRYSTE
IMPURE	MANURE	PIAFFE	RESCUE	SPARSE	TUMBLE
IMPUTE	MARBLE	PICKLE	RESIDE	SPENCE	TURTLE
INCITE	MARINE	PIDDLE	RESUME	SPLICE	TWEEZE
INCOME	MASQUE	PIERCE	RETAKE	SPONGE	UNGULA
INDITE	MATURE	PIFFLE	RETIRE	SPRUCE	UNIQUE
INDUCE	MEAGRE	PIGGIE	REVERE	SQUARE	UNMAKE
INFUSE	MEALIE	PINKIE	REVILE	STABLE	UNRIPE
INHALE	MEDDLE	PLAGUE	REVISE	STAPLE	UNSAFE
INHUME	MENACE	PLEASE	REVIVE	STARVE	UNTRUE
INJURE	MICKLE	PLEDGE	REVOKE	STELLA	UNWISE
INSANE	MIDDLE	PLUNGE	RIBBIE	STEPPE	UPDATE
INSIDE	MINGLE	POINTE	RIDDLE	STIFLE	UPRISE
INSULA	MINUTE	POLICE	RIFFLE	STINGE	URBANE
INSURE	MISUSE	POLITE	RIPPLE	STRAFE	VOYAGE
INTONE	MORULA	POUNCE	ROOKIE	STRIDE	WABBLE
INVADE	MOTTLE	PRAISE	ROOMIE	STRIKE	WADDLE
INVITE	MUCKLE	PRANCE	RUFFLE	STRIPE	WAFFLE
INVOKE	MUDDLE	PREMIE	RUMBLE	STRIVE	WANGLE
IODIZE	MUFFLE	PUDDLE	RUSTLE	STROKE	WARBLE
IONISE	MUMBLE	PUMICE	SADDLE	SUBDUE	WARSLE
IONIZE	MUSKIE	PUNKIE	SALTIE	SUBTLE	WEDGIE
JANGLE	MUZZLE	PURFLE	SALUTE	SUCKLE	WEENIE
JINGLE	NAPPIE	PURPLE	SAMPLE	SUPPLE	WEEPIE
JOCOSE	NEBULA	PURSUE	SAVAGE	SVELTE	WHEEZE
JOGGLE	NEEDLE	PUTTIE	SCARCE	SWATHE	WHINGE
JOSTLE	NEGATE	PUZZLE	SCHEME	SWERVE	WIGGLE
JUGGLE	NESTLE	QUARTE	SCRAPE	SWINGE	WINKLE
JUGULA	NETTLE	QUINTA	SCRIBE	SWITHE	WOBBLE
JUMBLE	NEWSIE	RABBLE	SECEDE	TACKLE	WOODIE
JUNKIE	NIBBLE	RADULA	SECURE	TALKIE	WOOLIE
KINDLE	NIGGLE	RAFFLE	SEDATE	TANGLE	WORDIE
KITTLE	NIMBLE	RAMBLE	SEDUCE	TATTIE	WRITHE
KOOKIE	NOBBLE	RANULA	SEMINA	TATTLE	ZONULA
LACUNA	NONUSE	RASSLE	SERENE	TECHIE	
LADDIE	NOTICE	RATTLE	SETTLE	TEETHE	
LAMBIE	NUZZLE	RAVAGE	SEVERE	TEGULA	

With front hook S

ABLEST	CRAWLS	HARING	INNERS	LIVERS	NIFFED
ADDLED	CRAWLY	HARKED	INNING	LOBBER	NIFFER
ADDLES	CREAKS	HARPED	INTERS	LOGANS	NIGGER
AGGERS	CREAKY	HARPER	KELPED	LOGGED	NIGGLE
AILING	CREAMS	HATTER	KELTER	LOGGER	NIPPED
ALINES	CREEDS	HAUGHS	KIDDED	LOPERS	NIPPER
ALLIED	CREWED	HAULED	KIDDER	LOPING	NOGGED
ALLIES	CRIMPS	HAVERS	KILLED	LOPPED	NOOSES
ALLOWS	CRIMPY	HAVING	KINKED	LOTTED	NUBBER
ALTERS	CRUMMY	HAWING	KIPPED	LOTTER	OARING
AMPLER	CRUNCH	HEARER	KIPPER	LOUGHS	ODIUMS
ANGERS	CRYERS	HEATHS	KITING	LOWEST	OFTEST
ASHING	CRYING	HEAVED	KITTLE	LOWING	OILING
AUGERS	CUFFED	HEAVES	KOOKUM	LOWISH	ORBING
CABBED	CULLED	HELLED	LACKED	LUBBER	OUTERS
CAMPED	CULLER	HELLER	LACKER	LUFFED	PACERS
CAMPER	CULTCH	HELVED	LAGGED	LUGGED	PACIER
CANNED	CUMMER	HELVES	LAHALS	LUGGER	PACING
CANNER	CUNNER	HEROES	LAKERS	LUMBER	PALLED
CANTED	CUPPER	HEUCHS	LAKING	LUMPED	PANNED
CANTER	CUTTER	HEUGHS	LAMMED	LUSHED	PANNER
CAPING	CUTTLE	HEWERS	LANDER	LUSHES	PARERS
CARERS	CUZZES	HEWING	LAPPED	MARTED	PARGED
CARING	EARING	HICKER	LAPPER	MARTEN	PARGES
CARPED	EATERS	HILLED	LASHED	MASHED	PARING
CARPER	EATING	HIPPED	LASHER	MASHER	PARKED
CARTED	EDGIER	HIPPER	LASHES	MASHES	PARKER
CARVED	EDUCED	HITTER	LATHER	MATTER	PARRED
CARVES	EDUCES	HOCKED	LAVERS	MELLED	PARSER
CATTED	EELING	HOCKER	LAVING	MELTED	PARTAN
COFFER	EGGARS	HODDEN	LAVISH	MELTER	PATTED
COLDER	ELECTS	HOEING	LAYERS	MIDGES	PATTER
COLLOP	ELFISH	HOGGED	LAYING	MILERS	PAVINS
COOPED	ENATES	HOOTER	LEAVED	MILING	PAWNED
COOPER	ENDERS	HOPPED	LEAVES	MIRKER	PAWNER
COOTER	ENDING	HOPPER	LEDGED	MITERS	PAYING
COPING	EXISTS	HOTTED	LEDGES	MITTEN	PECKED
COPULA	EXPERT	HOVELS	LENDER	MOCKED	PEELED
CORERS	EXTANT	HOVERS	LICKED	MOLDER	PEERED
CORING	HACKED	HUNTED	LICKER	MOTHER	PEISES
CORNED	HACKLE	HUNTER	LIGHTS	MUGGER	PELTER
CORNER	HADING	HUSHED	LIMIER	MUSHED	PIKERS
COUTER	HAFTED	HUSHES	LIMING	MUSHES	PIKING
COUTHS	HAGGED	IDLERS	LIMMER	NAGGED	PILING
COWING	HALIER	IDLING	LIMPSY	NAGGER	PILLED
COWLED	HALLOT	IGNIFY	LINGER	NAILED	PINIER
CRAGGY	HALLOW	IGNORE	LINKED	NAPPED	PINNER
CRAPED	HAMALS	ILEXES	LIPPED	NAPPER	PINTOS
CRAPES	HAMMED	INGLES	LIPPER	NIBBED	PITTED
CRAPPY	HAMMER	INKERS	LITHER	NICKED	PLASHY
CRATCH	HANKED	INKING	LITTER	NICKER	PLAYED

79

POKING QUIRES TICKED TORIES UNSETS WEEPER
PONGED QUIRTS TICKER TOTTED UNWISE WELLED
POOLED TABBED TICKLE TOUTER UPPERS WELTER
POOLER TABLED TIFFED TOWAGE UPPING WIGGED
POORER TABLES TILLED TOWING URGERS WIGGER
PORING TACKED TILLER TRAINS URGING WILING
PORTED TACKER TILTED TRAITS WACKED WILLED
PORTER TAGGED TINGES TRICKS WADDLE WILLER
POTTED TAGGER TINKER TRIKES WAGERS WINDLE
POTTER TAKERS TINTED TRINES WAGGED WINGED
POUTED TAKING TINTER TRIPES WAGGER WINGER
POUTER TALKED TIPPLE TROKED WAGING WINISH
PRANGS TALKER TOCKED TROKES WALLOW WINKED
PRAYED TAMPED TOKERS TROLLS WANKED WIPERS
PRAYER TAMPER TOKING TROWED WANKER WIPING
PRIEST TANGED TONERS TUBBED WANNED WISHED
PRINTS TANNIC TONIER TUMBLE WAPPED WISHER
PUNKIE TARING TONING TUMPED WARDED WISHES
PURGES TARRED TONISH TUNNED WARMED WISSES
PURRED TARTED TOOLED ULLAGE WARMER WITHER
PUTTER TARTER TOPERS UMMING WASHED WIVING
QUARKS TATERS TOPING UNBELT WASHER WOTTED
QUILLS TEAMED TOPPED UNLESS WASHES WOUNDS
QUINTS TEWING TOPPER UNLIKE WATTER
QUIRED TIBIAL TOPPLE UNROOF WEARER

With back hook S

ABASER ACCENT ADJURE AFFIRM AIRVAC ALINER
ABASIA ACCEPT ADJUST AFFORD AIRWAY ALIPED
ABATER ACCORD ADLAND AFFRAY AJOWAN ALIYAH
ABATOR ACCOST ADMIRE AFGHAN AKEBIA ALKALI
ABDUCE ACCRUE ADNOUN AFREET ALANIN ALKANE
ABDUCT ACCUSE ADORER AFTOSA ALANYL ALKENE
ABELIA ACEDIA ADSORB AGAMID ALARUM ALKINE
ABIDER ACETAL ADSUKI AGARIC ALASKA ALKYNE
ABJURE ACETIN ADVECT AGEING ALBATA ALLEGE
ABLATE ACETYL ADVENT AGEISM ALBEDO ALLELE
ABLAUT ACHENE ADVERB AGEIST ALBINO ALLIAK
ABOUND ACNODE ADVERT AGENDA ALBITE ALLIUM
ABRADE ACQUIT ADVICE AGGADA ALCADE ALLUDE
ABSEIL ACTING ADVISE AGNAIL ALCAIC ALLURE
ABSENT ACTION ADWARE AGNATE ALCOOL ALMNER
ABSORB ACTIVE ADZUKI AGNIZE ALCOVE ALMOND
ABSURD ACUMEN AEDILE AGOUTI ALDOSE ALMUCE
ABULIA ADAGIO AERATE AGRAFE ALDRIN ALMUDE
ABUSER ADDEND AERIAL AGYRIA ALEGAR ALNICO
ABVOLT ADDICT AEROBE AHIMSA ALEVIN ALPACA
ABWATT ADDUCE AERUGO AIGLET ALEXIA ALPHYL
ACACIA ADDUCT AETHER AIGRET ALEXIN ALPINE
ACAJOU ADENYL AFFAIR AIKIDO ALFAKI ALSIKE
ACARID ADHERE AFFECT AIRBAG ALIDAD ALTHEA
ACCEDE ADJOIN AFFINE AIRING ALIGHT ALUDEL

ALUMIN	ANTHEM	ARMFUL	ATLATL	BADDIE	BARHOP
AMADOU	ANTHER	ARMING	ATOMIC	BADGER	BARITE
AMATOL	ANTHRO	ARMLET	ATONER	BAFFLE	BARIUM
AMAUTI	ANTIAR	ARMOUR	ATONIA	BAGFUL	BARKER
AMAZON	ANTICK	ARMPIT	ATONIC	BAGGER	BARLEY
AMBAGE	ANTIFA	ARMURE	ATRIUM	BAGGIE	BARLOW
AMBARI	ANTING	ARNICA	ATTACK	BAGNIO	BARNEY
AMBEER	ANTLER	AROINT	ATTAIN	BAGUET	BARONG
AMBLER	ANTRUM	AROUSE	ATTEND	BAGWIG	BARQUE
AMERCE	ANURAN	AROYNT	ATTEST	BAIDAR	BARREL
AMIDIN	ANURIA	ARPENT	ATTIRE	BAILEE	BARREN
AMIDOL	ANYWAY	ARRACK	ATTORN	BAILER	BARRET
AMMINE	AORIST	ARREAR	ATTRIT	BAILEY	BARRIO
AMNION	AOUDAD	ARREST	ATTUNE	BAILIE	BARROW
AMOEBA	APACHE	ARRIVE	AUBADE	BAILOR	BARTER
AMOUNT	APERCU	ARROBA	AUBURN	BAITER	BARYON
AMPERE	APICAL	ARROYO	AUCUBA	BAKING	BARYTA
AMPULE	APLITE	ARSHIN	AUDILE	BALATA	BARYTE
AMRITA	APLOMB	ARSINE	AUDING	BALBOA	BASALT
AMTRAC	APNOEA	ARTIGI	AUDISM	BALDIE	BASHAW
AMTRAK	APOGEE	ARTIST	AUDIST	BALEEN	BASHER
AMULET	APOLLO	ARTSIE	AUGEND	BALING	BASION
AMUSER	APOLOG	ARUANA	AUGITE	BALKER	BASKET
AMUSIA	APORIA	ASARUM	AUKLET	BALLAD	BASQUE
AMYLUM	APPALL	ASCEND	AUNTIE	BALLER	BASSET
ANADEM	APPEAL	ASCENT	AURIST	BALLET	BASTER
ANAGEN	APPEAR	ASHCAN	AURORA	BALLON	BATARD
ANALOG	APPEND	ASHLAR	AUSUBO	BALLOT	BATATA
ANANDA	APPLET	ASHLER	AUTEUR	BALSAM	BATBOY
ANANKE	APPOSE	ASHPAN	AUTHOR	BAMBOO	BATHER
ANARCH	ARABLE	ASHRAM	AUTISM	BANANA	BATTEN
ANATTO	ARAMID	ASIAGO	AUTIST	BANDER	BATTER
ANCHOR	ARBOUR	ASKARI	AUTUMN	BANDIT	BATTIK
ANCONE	ARBUTE	ASKING	AVATAR	BANDOG	BATTLE
ANEMIA	ARCADE	ASPECT	AVENGE	BANGER	BATTUE
ANGINA	ARCHER	ASPIRE	AVENUE	BANGLE	BAUBEE
ANGLER	ARCHIL	ASRAMA	AVIATE	BANIAN	BAUBLE
ANGORA	ARCHON	ASSAIL	AVIDIN	BANKER	BAWBEE
ANILIN	ARCING	ASSENT	AVOCET	BANKIT	BAWLER
ANIMAL	ARCTIC	ASSERT	AVOSET	BANNER	BAWTIE
ANKLET	ARDOUR	ASSIGN	AVOWAL	BANNET	BAYAMO
ANLACE	AREOLA	ASSIST	AVOWER	BANTAM	BAYARD
ANLAGE	AREOLE	ASSIZE	AVULSE	BANTER	BAYWOP
ANNEAL	ARGALA	ASSOIL	AWAKEN	BANYAN	BAZAAR
ANNEXE	ARGALI	ASSORT	AWNING	BANZAI	BAZOOM
ANNONA	ARGENT	ASSUME	AXILLA	BAOBAB	BEACON
ANNUAL	ARGUER	ASSURE	AXSEED	BARBEL	BEADER
ANOINT	ARGYLE	ASTHMA	AZALEA	BARBER	BEADLE
ANOMIE	ARGYLL	ASTRAL	BABACU	BARBET	BEAGLE
ANONYM	ARIOSO	ASYLUM	BABBLE	BARBIE	BEAKER
ANOPIA	ARISTA	ATABAL	BABOOL	BARBOT	BEANIE
ANORAK	ARISTO	ATAMAN	BABOON	BARBUT	BEARER
ANOXIA	ARKOSE	ATAXIA	BACKER	BAREGE	BEATER
ANSWER	ARMADA	ATAXIC	BACKUP	BARGEE	BEAVER

BECALM	BEMIRE	BICORN	BLOWER	BOPEEP	BRAZER
BECKET	BEMIST	BICRON	BLOWUP	BOPPER	BRAZIL
BECKON	BEMOAN	BIDDER	BLUDGE	BORAGE	BREAST
BECLOG	BEMOCK	BIFACE	BLUING	BORANE	BREATH
BECOME	BEMUSE	BIFFIN	BLUNGE	BORATE	BREEZE
BEDAMN	BENAME	BIFOLD	BOATEL	BORDEL	BREGMA
BEDAUB	BENDAY	BIGEYE	BOATER	BORDER	BREVET
BEDBUG	BENDEE	BIGGIE	BOBBER	BOREEN	BREWER
BEDDER	BENDER	BIGGIN	BOBBIN	BORIDE	BRIARD
BEDECK	BENNET	BIGWIG	BOBBLE	BORING	BRIBEE
BEDELL	BENUMB	BIKINI	BOBCAT	BORROW	BRIBER
BEDLAM	BENZIN	BILBOA	BOCCIA	BORSHT	BRIDAL
BEDPAN	BENZOL	BILKER	BOCCIE	BORZOI	BRIDGE
BEDRUG	BENZYL	BILLER	BODEGA	BOSKET	BRIDIE
BEDSIT	BERAKE	BILLET	BODICE	BOSQUE	BRIDLE
BEDUIN	BERATE	BILLIE	BODING	BOSTON	BRIGHT
BEDUMB	BERBER	BILLON	BODKIN	BOTHER	BRILLO
BEEBEE	BERIME	BILLOW	BOFFIN	BOTHIE	BRINER
BEEPER	BERLIN	BIMINI	BOGART	BOTNET	BROAST
BEETLE	BERTHA	BINDER	BOGGLE	BOTTLE	BROGAN
BEEZER	BESEEM	BINDLE	BOHUNK	BOTTOM	BROGUE
BEFALL	BESIDE	BINGER	BOILER	BOUBOU	BROKER
BEFLAG	BESMUT	BIOGEN	BOKKEN	BOUCLE	BROLGA
BEFLEA	BESNOW	BIONIC	BOLERO	BOUDIN	BROMAL
BEFOOL	BESTIE	BIOPIC	BOLETE	BOUFFE	BROMID
BEFOUL	BESTIR	BIOTIC	BOLIDE	BOUGIE	BROMIN
BEFRET	BESTOW	BIOTIN	BOLSON	BOULLE	BRONCO
BEGALL	BESTUD	BIPACK	BOLTER	BOUNCE	BRONZE
BEGAZE	BETAKE	BIRDER	BOMBER	BOURNE	BROWSE
BEGGAR	BETHEL	BIRDIE	BONACI	BOURSE	BRUCIN
BEGIRD	BETIDE	BIREME	BONBON	BOUTON	BRUISE
BEGLAD	BETIME	BIRKIE	BONDER	BOVINE	BRULOT
BEGRIM	BETISE	BIRLER	BONDUC	BOVVER	BRUNET
BEGULF	BETRAY	BISECT	BONITA	BOWFIN	BUBALE
BEHAVE	BETTER	BISHOP	BONITO	BOWING	BUBBIE
BEHEAD	BETTOR	BISQUE	BONNET	BOWLEG	BUBBLE
BEHEST	BEWAIL	BISTER	BONNIE	BOWLER	BUCKER
BEHIND	BEWARE	BISTRE	BONOBO	BOWPOT	BUCKET
BEHOLD	BEWEEP	BISTRO	BOOBIE	BOWSAW	BUCKLE
BEHOOF	BEWORM	BITMAP	BOOBOO	BOWSER	BUCKRA
BEHOVE	BEWRAP	BITTER	BOOCOO	BOWWOW	BUDDER
BEHOWL	BEWRAY	BIZJET	BOODLE	BOWYER	BUDDHA
BEIGNE	BEYLIC	BIZONE	BOOGER	BOXCAR	BUDDLE
BEKNOT	BEYLIK	BLADER	BOOGEY	BOXFUL	BUDGER
BELAUD	BEYOND	BLAGUE	BOOGIE	BOXING	BUDGET
BELDAM	BEZANT	BLAMER	BOOHOO	BOYARD	BUDGIE
BELEAP	BEZOAR	BLAZER	BOOJUM	BRACER	BUFFER
BELIEF	BHAKTA	BLAZON	BOOKER	BRAHMA	BUFFET
BELIER	BHAKTI	BLENDE	BOOKIE	BRAISE	BUGEYE
BELLOW	BHARAL	BLEWIT	BOOKOO	BRAIZE	BUGGER
BELONG	BIBBER	BLIGHT	BOOMER	BRASIL	BUGLER
BELTER	BIBLES	BLONDE	BOOTEE	BRAVER	BUGOUT
BELUGA	BICARB	BLOUSE	BOOTIE	BRAYER	BUGSHA
BEMEAN	BICKER	BLOWBY	BOOZER	BRAZEN	BULBEL

BULBIL	BUSHWA	CALKER	CARACK	CATGUT	CHALET
BULBUL	BUSING	CALKIN	CARAFE	CATION	CHALLA
BULGAR	BUSKER	CALLAN	CARATE	CATKIN	CHANCE
BULGER	BUSKIN	CALLEE	CARBON	CATLIN	CHANGE
BULGUR	BUSTEE	CALLER	CARBOY	CATNAP	CHAPEL
BULKER	BUSTER	CALLET	CARCEL	CATNIP	CHARGE
BULLET	BUSTIC	CALPAC	CARDER	CATSUP	CHARKA
BULLEY	BUSTLE	CALQUE	CARDIA	CATTIE	CHARRO
BUMBAG	BUTANE	CAMAIL	CARDIO	CAUDLE	CHASER
BUMBLE	BUTENE	CAMBER	CARDON	CAUSAL	CHASSE
BUMBOY	BUTLER	CAMERA	CAREEN	CAUSER	CHAUNT
BUMKIN	BUTTER	CAMION	CAREER	CAUSEY	CHAWER
BUMMER	BUTTLE	CAMISA	CARFUL	CAVEAT	CHAZAN
BUMPER	BUTTON	CAMISE	CARHOP	CAVERN	CHEAPO
BUMWAD	BUYOFF	CAMLET	CARIBE	CAVIAR	CHEBEC
BUNDLE	BUYOUT	CAMMIE	CARINA	CAVING	CHEDER
BUNGEE	BUZUKI	CAMPER	CARING	CAVORT	CHEERO
BUNGLE	BUZZER	CANAPE	CARLES	CAYMAN	CHEESE
BUNION	BYELAW	CANARD	CARLIN	CAYUSE	CHEGOE
BUNKER	BYGONE	CANCAN	CARNET	CEBOID	CHEMIC
BUNKIE	BYLINE	CANCEL	CARNEY	CEDULA	CHEQUE
BUNKUM	BYNAME	CANCER	CARNIE	CEILER	CHERUB
BUNTER	BYPATH	CANCHA	CARPAL	CELIAC	CHETAH
BUNYIP	BYPLAY	CANDID	CARPEL	CELLAR	CHEVET
BUPPIE	BYRNIE	CANDLE	CARPER	CEMENT	CHEVRE
BUQSHA	BYROAD	CANDOR	CARPET	CENOTE	CHEWER
BURBLE	BYTALK	CANFUL	CARREL	CENSER	CHIASM
BURBOT	BYWORD	CANGUE	CARROM	CENSOR	CHICHI
BURDEN	BYWORK	CANINE	CARROT	CENTAL	CHICLE
BURDIE	BYZANT	CANING	CARTEL	CENTER	CHICOT
BUREAU	CABALA	CANKER	CARTER	CENTRE	CHIDER
BURGEE	CABANA	CANKLE	CARTON	CENTUM	CHIELD
BURGER	CABBIE	CANNEL	CARVEL	CERATE	CHIGOE
BURGLE	CABLER	CANNER	CARVER	CEREAL	CHILDE
BURGOO	CABLET	CANNON	CASABA	CERIPH	CHILLI
BURIAL	CACHET	CANOER	CASAVA	CERISE	CHIMAR
BURIER	CACHOU	CANOLA	CASBAH	CERITE	CHIMER
BURKER	CACKLE	CANTAL	CASEIN	CERIUM	CHIMLA
BURKHA	CADDIE	CANTER	CASERN	CERMET	CHINSE
BURLAP	CADGER	CANTLE	CASHAW	CERUSE	CHIRRE
BURLER	CAEOMA	CANTON	CASHEW	CERVID	CHISEL
BURLEY	CAESAR	CANTOR	CASHOO	CESIUM	CHITAL
BURNER	CAFARD	CANULA	CASING	CESURA	CHITIN
BURNET	CAFTAN	CANVAS	CASINO	CETANE	CHITON
BURNIE	CAHIER	CANYON	CASITA	CHABUK	CHOICE
BURPEE	CAHOOT	CAPCOM	CASKET	CHACMA	CHOKER
BURRER	CAHOUN	CAPFUL	CASQUE	CHADAR	CHOKEY
BURROW	CAIMAN	CAPLET	CASSIA	CHADOR	CHOLER
BURSAR	CAIQUE	CAPLIN	CASTER	CHAFER	CHOLLA
BURTON	CAJOLE	CAPOTE	CASTLE	CHAINE	CHOOSE
BUSBAR	CALCAR	CAPPER	CASTOR	CHAISE	CHOPIN
BUSBOY	CALESA	CAPSID	CASUAL	CHAKRA	CHORAL
BUSHEL	CALICO	CAPTAN	CATALO	CHALAH	CHOREA
BUSHER	CALIPH	CAPTOR	CATENA	CHALEH	CHOUGH

CHOUSE	CLOTHE	COLLOP	COPALM	COUSIN	CUBOID
CHOWSE	CLOUGH	COLONE	COPECK	COUTER	CUCKOO
CHRISM	CLOVER	COLOUR	COPIER	COVERT	CUDDIE
CHROMA	COALER	COLTAN	COPING	COVINE	CUDDLE
CHROME	COATEE	COLTER	COPLOT	COVING	CUDGEL
CHROMO	COATER	COLUGO	COPOUT	COWAGE	CUEIST
CHUKAR	COAXER	COLUMN	COPPER	COWARD	CUESTA
CHUKKA	COBALT	COLURE	COPPRA	COWBOY	CUISSE
CHUPPA	COBBER	COMAKE	COPRAH	COWPAT	CULLAY
CHURRO	COBBLE	COMATE	COPTER	COWPEA	CULLER
CHYMIC	COBNUT	COMBAT	COPULA	COWPIE	CULLET
CHYRON	COBWEB	COMBER	COQUET	COWRIE	CULVER
CICADA	COCAIN	COMEDO	CORBAN	COYDOG	CUMBER
CICALA	COCCID	COMFIT	CORBEL	COYOTE	CUMBIA
CICERO	COCHIN	COMING	CORBIE	COYPOU	CUMMER
CIGGIE	COCKER	COMMIE	CORDER	CRADLE	CUMMIN
CILICE	COCKLE	COMMIT	CORDON	CRAMBE	CUNDUM
CINDER	COCKUP	COMMON	CORIUM	CRAMBO	CUNNER
CINEMA	COCOON	COMPAS	CORKER	CRATER	CUPFUL
CINEOL	CODDER	COMPEL	CORMEL	CRATON	CUPOLA
CINQUE	CODDLE	COMSAT	CORNEA	CRAVAT	CUPPER
CIPHER	CODEIA	CONCHA	CORNEL	CRAVEN	CUPRUM
CIRCLE	CODEIN	CONCHO	CORNER	CRAVER	CUPULE
CIRQUE	CODGER	CONCUR	CORNET	CRAYON	CURAGH
CITHER	CODING	CONDOM	CORONA	CREASE	CURARA
CITOLA	CODLIN	CONDOR	COROZO	CREATE	CURARE
CITOLE	COEDIT	CONFAB	CORPSE	CRECHE	CURARI
CITRAL	COELOM	CONFER	CORRAL	CREDIT	CURATE
CITRIN	COEMPT	CONFIT	CORRIE	CREESE	CURBER
CITRON	COERCE	CONGEE	CORSAC	CRENEL	CURDLE
CIVISM	COEVAL	CONGER	CORSET	CREOLE	CURFEW
CLAMOR	COFFEE	CONGOU	CORTIN	CREPON	CURITE
CLAQUE	COFFER	CONINE	CORVEE	CRESOL	CURIUM
CLARET	COFFIN	CONIUM	CORVET	CRESYL	CURLER
CLAUSE	COFFLE	CONKER	CORVID	CRETIC	CURLEW
CLAVER	COGITO	CONNER	CORYMB	CRETIN	CURRAN
CLAWER	COGNAC	CONNOR	CORYZA	CREWEL	CURRIE
CLAXON	COGWAY	CONOID	COSHER	CRINGE	CURSER
CLEAVE	COHEAD	CONSOL	COSIGN	CRINUM	CURSOR
CLEOME	COHEIR	CONSUL	COSINE	CRITIC	CURTAL
CLERIC	COHERE	CONTRA	COSMID	CROJIK	CURVET
CLERID	COHORT	CONURE	COSSET	CROSSE	CUSHAT
CLICHE	COHOST	CONVEY	COSTAR	CROTON	CUSHAW
CLIENT	COHUNE	CONVOY	COSTER	CROUPE	CUSPID
CLINIC	COIFFE	COOKER	COTEAU	CROUTE	CUSSER
CLIQUE	COIGNE	COOKEY	COTTAR	CROWER	CUSTOM
CLITIC	COILER	COOKIE	COTTER	CROZER	CUTLAS
CLIVIA	COINER	COOLER	COTTON	CRUISE	CUTLER
CLOACA	COJOIN	COOLIE	COTYPE	CRUSET	CUTLET
CLOCHE	COKING	COOLTH	COUGAR	CRYPTO	CUTOFF
CLONER	COLEAD	COOMBE	COULEE	CUATRO	CUTOUT
CLOQUE	COLLAR	COOPER	COUPLE	CUBAGE	CUTTER
CLOSER	COLLET	COOTER	COUPON	CUBISM	CUTTLE
CLOSET	COLLIE	COOTIE	COURSE	CUBIST	CYANID

CYANIN	DARKEY	DEFACE	DENUDE	DIACID	DIRDUM
CYBORG	DARKIE	DEFAME	DEODAR	DIADEM	DIRECT
CYCLER	DARKLE	DEFANG	DEPART	DIALER	DIRHAM
CYCLIN	DARNEL	DEFEAT	DEPEND	DIALOG	DIRNDL
CYGNET	DARNER	DEFECT	DEPERM	DIAMIN	DISARM
CYMBAL	DARTER	DEFEND	DEPICT	DIAPER	DISBAR
CYMENE	DARTLE	DEFIER	DEPLOY	DIAPIR	DISBUD
CYMLIN	DASHER	DEFILE	DEPONE	DIATOM	DISCUS
CYPHER	DASSIE	DEFINE	DEPORT	DIAZIN	DISEUR
CYPRES	DATCHA	DEFLEA	DEPOSE	DIBBER	DISKER
DABBER	DATING	DEFOAM	DEPUTE	DIBBLE	DISMAL
DABBLE	DATIVE	DEFORM	DERAIL	DIBBUK	DISMAY
DACITE	DATURA	DEFRAG	DERATE	DICAST	DISOWN
DACKER	DAUBER	DEFRAY	DERIDE	DICKER	DISPEL
DACOIT	DAUTIE	DEFUEL	DERIVE	DICKEY	DISTIL
DACRON	DAWDLE	DEFUND	DESALT	DICKIE	DISUSE
DACTYL	DAWTIE	DEFUSE	DESAND	DICTUM	DITHER
DADDLE	DAYBED	DEFUZE	DESEED	DIDACT	DIURON
DAEMON	DAZZLE	DEGAME	DESERT	DIDDLE	DIVERT
DAGGER	DEACON	DEGAMI	DESIGN	DIDYMO	DIVEST
DAGGLE	DEADEN	DEGERM	DESIRE	DIEOFF	DIVIDE
DAGOBA	DEAFEN	DEGREE	DESIST	DIESEL	DIVINE
DAHLIA	DEALER	DEGUST	DESMAN	DIETER	DIVING
DAHOON	DEARIE	DEHAIR	DESMID	DIFFER	DJEBEL
DAIKER	DEARTH	DEHORN	DESORB	DIGEST	DJEMBE
DAIKON	DEBARK	DEHORT	DESPOT	DIGGER	DJIBBA
DAIMIO	DEBASE	DEICER	DETAIL	DIGLOT	DOBBER
DAIMON	DEBATE	DEJECT	DETAIN	DIKDIK	DOBBIN
DAIMYO	DEBEAK	DEKARE	DETECT	DIKTAT	DOBLON
DAKOIT	DEBONE	DELATE	DETENT	DILATE	DOBSON
DALASI	DEBTOR	DELEAD	DETEST	DILDOE	DOCENT
DALEDH	DEBUNK	DELETE	DETICK	DILUTE	DOCKER
DALETH	DEBURR	DELICT	DETOUR	DIMMER	DOCKET
DALTON	DECADE	DELIME	DETUNE	DIMOUT	DOCTOR
DAMAGE	DECAMP	DELINK	DEVEIN	DIMPLE	DODDER
DAMASK	DECANE	DELIST	DEVEST	DIMWIT	DODDLE
DAMMAR	DECANT	DELUDE	DEVICE	DINDLE	DODGEM
DAMMER	DECARE	DELUGE	DEVISE	DINERO	DODGER
DAMNER	DECEIT	DELVER	DEVOIR	DINGER	DOFFER
DAMPEN	DECERN	DEMAND	DEVOTE	DINGEY	DOGDOM
DAMPER	DECIDE	DEMARK	DEVOUR	DINGLE	DOGEAR
DAMSEL	DECILE	DEMAST	DEWLAP	DINING	DOGGER
DAMSON	DECKEL	DEMEAN	DEWOOL	DINKEY	DOGGIE
DANCER	DECKER	DEMENT	DEWORM	DINKUM	DOGLEG
DANDER	DECKLE	DEMISE	DEXTER	DINNER	DOGNAP
DANDLE	DECLAW	DEMIST	DEZINC	DIOBOL	DOLLAR
DANGER	DECOCT	DEMOTE	DHARMA	DIOXAN	DOLLOP
DANGLE	DECODE	DENGUE	DHARNA	DIOXID	DOLMAN
DANSAK	DECREE	DENIAL	DHOLAK	DIOXIN	DOLMEN
DAPHNE	DEDUCE	DENIER	DHOORA	DIPLOE	DOLOUR
DAPPLE	DEDUCT	DENOTE	DHOOTI	DIPNET	DOMAIN
DARBAR	DEEJAY	DENTAL	DHURNA	DIPOLE	DOMINE
DARING	DEEPEN	DENTIL	DHURRA	DIPPER	DOMINO
DARKEN	DEEWAN	DENTIN	DHYANA	DIQUAT	DONAIR

DONATE	DROMON	EARLAP	EMOTER	ENTRAP	ETHYNE
DONGLE	DRONER	EARNER	EMPALE	ENTREE	ETOILE
DONJON	DRONGO	EARWIG	EMPIRE	ENVIER	ETRIER
DONKEY	DROUTH	EASTER	EMPLOY	ENVIRO	ETYMON
DONNEE	DROVER	EATING	ENABLE	ENWIND	EUCHRE
DONZEL	DROWND	ECARTE	ENAMEL	ENWOMB	EUNUCH
DOOBIE	DROWSE	ECHARD	ENAMOR	ENWRAP	EUPNEA
DOODAD	DRUDGE	ECHOER	ENCAGE	ENZYME	EUREKA
DOODAH	DRUPEL	ECLAIR	ENCAMP	EOLITH	EVADER
DOODLE	DRYLOT	ECLOSE	ENCASE	EONISM	EVENER
DOODOO	DUBBER	ECTYPE	ENCINA	EOSINE	EVINCE
DOOLEE	DUBBIN	ECZEMA	ENCODE	EPARCH	EVOKER
DOOLIE	DUCKER	EDGING	ENCORE	EPATER	EVOLVE
DOOWOP	DUCKIE	EDIBLE	ENCYST	EPHEBE	EVULSE
DOOZER	DUDEEN	EDITOR	ENDCAP	EPIGON	EVZONE
DOOZIE	DUELER	EFFACE	ENDEAR	EPILOG	EXACTA
DOPANT	DUELLO	EFFECT	ENDING	EPIMER	EXAMEN
DOPING	DUENDE	EFFORT	ENDITE	EPONYM	EXARCH
DORADO	DUENNA	EFFUSE	ENDIVE	EPOPEE	EXCEED
DORBUG	DUFFEL	EGGCUP	ENDRIN	EQUATE	EXCEPT
DORMER	DUFFER	EGGNOG	ENDURE	EQUINE	EXCIDE
DORMIN	DUFFLE	EGOISM	ENDURO	ERASER	EXCISE
DORPER	DUGONG	EGOIST	ENFACE	ERBIUM	EXCITE
DORSAL	DUGOUT	EIGHTH	ENFOLD	ERGATE	EXCUSE
DORSEL	DUIKER	ELAPID	ENGAGE	ERINGO	EXEDRA
DORSER	DULCET	ELAPSE	ENGILD	ERMINE	EXEMPT
DOSAGE	DUMDUM	ELATER	ENGINE	EROTIC	EXHALE
DOSSAL	DUMPER	ELDEST	ENGIRD	ERRAND	EXHORT
DOSSEL	DUNITE	ELEGIT	ENGLUT	ERRANT	EXHUME
DOSSER	DUNKER	ELEVEN	ENGRAM	ERRATA	EXILER
DOSSIL	DUNLIN	ELEVON	ENGULF	ERYNGO	EXOGEN
DOTAGE	DUOLOG	ELICIT	ENHALO	ESCAPE	EXONYM
DOTARD	DUPING	ELIXIR	ENIGMA	ESCARP	EXOTIC
DOTTEL	DUPION	ELODEA	ENISLE	ESCHAR	EXPAND
DOTTER	DUPLET	ELOIGN	ENJAMB	ESCHEW	EXPECT
DOTTLE	DURBAR	ELOPER	ENJOIN	ESCORT	EXPEND
DOUBLE	DURIAN	ELUANT	ENLACE	ESCROW	EXPERT
DOUCHE	DURION	ELUATE	ENLIST	ESCUDO	EXPIRE
DOURAH	DURRIE	ELUDER	ENNEAD	ESPIAL	EXPORT
DOUSER	DUSTER	ELUENT	ENOUGH	ESPOIR	EXPOSE
DOWNER	DUSTUP	EMBALM	ENRAGE	ESPRIT	EXSECT
DOWSER	DUYKER	EMBANK	ENROBE	ESSOIN	EXSERT
DOYLEY	DYADIC	EMBARK	ENROLL	ESTATE	EXTEND
DRACHM	DYBBUK	EMBLEM	ENROOT	ESTEEM	EXTENT
DRAGEE	DYEING	EMBOSK	ENSERF	ESTRAY	EXTERN
DRAGON	DYNAMO	EMBRUE	ENSIGN	ESTRIN	EXTOLL
DRAPER	DYNAST	EMBRYO	ENSILE	ESTRUM	EXTORT
DRAWEE	DYNEIN	EMERGE	ENSOUL	ETALON	EYEBAR
DRAWER	DYNODE	EMEROD	ENSURE	ETAMIN	EYECUP
DREDGE	DYVOUR	EMETIC	ENTAIL	ETCHER	EYEFUL
DREIDL	EAGLET	EMETIN	ENTICE	ETHANE	EYELET
DRIVEL	EARBUD	EMEUTE	ENTIRE	ETHENE	EYELID
DRIVER	EARFUL	EMIGRE	ENTOIL	ETHION	FABLER
DROGUE	EARING	EMODIN	ENTOMB	ETHNIC	FABRIC

FACADE	FELINE	FIRMER	FONDLE	FULHAM	GAMING
FACIAL	FELLAH	FISCAL	FONDUE	FULLAM	GAMMER
FACING	FELLER	FISHER	FOODIE	FULLER	GAMMON
FACTOR	FELLOE	FITTER	FOOTER	FULMAR	GANDER
FACTUM	FELLOW	FIXATE	FOOTIE	FUMBLE	GANGER
FADEIN	FEMALE	FIXING	FOOTLE	FUNDER	GANGLE
FADING	FENCER	FIXURE	FOOZLE	FUNGAL	GANGUE
FAERIE	FENDER	FIZGIG	FORAGE	FUNKER	GANJAH
FAGGOT	FENING	FIZZER	FORBID	FUNKIA	GANNET
FAILLE	FENNEC	FIZZLE	FORCER	FUNNEL	GANOID
FAJITA	FENNEL	FLACON	FOREST	FURANE	GAOLER
FAKEER	FERBAM	FLAGON	FORGER	FURLER	GARAGE
FALCON	FERLIE	FLAKER	FORGET	FURORE	GARBLE
FALLAL	FERREL	FLAMBE	FORINT	FURROW	GARCON
FALLER	FERRET	FLAMEN	FORKER	FUSAIN	GARDEN
FALLOW	FERRUM	FLAMER	FORMAL	FUSION	GARGET
FALSIE	FERULA	FLANGE	FORMAT	FUSSER	GARGLE
FALTER	FERULE	FLAUNT	FORMER	FUSTIC	GARLIC
FAMINE	FERVOR	FLAUTA	FORMOL	FUTURE	GARNER
FANBOY	FESCUE	FLAVIN	FORMYL	FYLFOT	GARNET
FANDOM	FESTER	FLAVOR	FOSSIL	GABBER	GAROTE
FANEGA	FETIAL	FLAYER	FOSTER	GABBLE	GARRET
FANFIC	FETTER	FLECHE	FOURTH	GABBRO	GARRON
FANION	FETTLE	FLEDGE	FOWLER	GABION	GARTER
FANJET	FIACRE	FLEECE	FOXING	GABOON	GARVEY
FANNER	FIANCE	FLENSE	FRAISE	GACHER	GASBAG
FANTOD	FIASCO	FLEXOR	FRAMER	GADDER	GASCON
FANTOM	FIBBER	FLIGHT	FRAPPE	GADGET	GASKET
FAQUIR	FIBRIL	FLORAL	FRATER	GADOID	GASKIN
FARCER	FIBRIN	FLORET	FRAZIL	GAFFER	GASPER
FARCIE	FIBULA	FLORIN	FREEZE	GAGAKU	GASSER
FARDEL	FIDDLE	FLOTEL	FRENUM	GAGGER	GASTER
FARFAL	FIDGET	FLOWER	FRESCO	GAGGLE	GATEAU
FARFEL	FIESTA	FLUTER	FRICOT	GAINER	GATHER
FARINA	FIGURE	FLYBOY	FRIDGE	GAITER	GATING
FARMER	FILING	FLYING	FRIEND	GALAGO	GAUCHE
FARROW	FILLER	FLYOFF	FRIEZE	GALENA	GAUCHO
FASCIA	FILLET	FLYWAY	FRIGHT	GALERE	GAUGER
FASTEN	FILLIP	FOAMER	FRINGE	GALIOT	GAVAGE
FATHER	FILMER	FODDER	FRISEE	GALLET	GAVIAL
FATHOM	FILTER	FOETOR	FRIVOL	GALLEY	GAWKER
FATTEN	FIMBLE	FOGBOW	FRIZER	GALLON	GAWPER
FAUCAL	FINALE	FOGDOG	FROLIC	GALLOP	GAYDAR
FAUCET	FINDER	FOGGER	FROWST	GALOOT	GAZABO
FAVELA	FINEST	FOIBLE	FRYPAN	GALORE	GAZEBO
FAVISM	FINGER	FOISON	FUCKER	GALYAC	GAZUMP
FAVOUR	FINIAL	FOLATE	FUCKUP	GALYAK	GEEGAW
FAWNER	FINING	FOLDER	FUCOID	GAMBIA	GEEZER
FEARER	FINITE	FOLDUP	FUCOSE	GAMBIR	GEISHA
FECIAL	FINNAN	FOLIUM	FUDDLE	GAMBIT	GELADA
FEDORA	FIPPLE	FOLKIE	FUELER	GAMBLE	GELANT
FEEDER	FIRING	FOLLOW	FUGATO	GAMBOL	GELATE
FEELER	FIRKIN	FOMENT	FUHRER	GAMETE	GELATI
FEIJOA	FIRMAN	FOMITE	FULFIL	GAMINE	GELATO

GELCAP	GLAZER	GOSSAN	GUGGLE	HALALA	HAULER
GELDER	GLIDER	GOSSIP	GUGLET	HALIDE	HAUSEN
GEMOTE	GLIOMA	GOTCHA	GUIDER	HALIER	HAVIOR
GENDER	GLISSE	GOTHIC	GUIDON	HALITE	HAWALA
GENEVA	GLOBIN	GOUGER	GUIMPE	HALLAH	HAWKER
GENOME	GLORIA	GOURDE	GUINEA	HALLAL	HAWKEY
GENTLE	GLOSSA	GOVERN	GUINEP	HALLEL	HAWKIE
GENTOO	GLOVER	GRABEN	GUITAR	HALLOA	HAWSER
GERBIL	GLOWER	GRADER	GULDEN	HALLOO	HAYING
GERENT	GLUCAN	GRADIN	GULLET	HALLOW	HAYMOW
GERMAN	GLUTEN	GRAHAM	GULLEY	HALOID	HAZARD
GERMEN	GLYCAN	GRAMMA	GULPER	HALTER	HAZING
GERUND	GLYCIN	GRAMME	GUMMER	HALVAH	HAZMAT
GETOUT	GLYCOL	GRAMPA	GUNDOG	HAMADA	HAZZAN
GETTER	GLYCYL	GRANGE	GUNITE	HAMATE	HEADER
GEWGAW	GNAWER	GRAPLE	GUNNEL	HAMAUL	HEALER
GEYSER	GNOMON	GRAPPA	GUNNER	HAMFAT	HEALTH
GHARRI	GOALIE	GRATER	GUNSEL	HAMLET	HEAPER
GHAZAL	GOANNA	GRATIN	GUNTER	HAMMAL	HEARER
GHERAO	GOATEE	GRAVEL	GURGLE	HAMMAM	HEARSE
GHETTO	GOBANG	GRAVER	GURNET	HAMMER	HEARTH
GHIBLI	GOBBET	GRAZER	GURNEY	HAMPER	HEATER
GIAOUR	GOBBLE	GREASE	GUSHER	HAMZAH	HEAUME
GIBBER	GOBLET	GREAVE	GUSSET	HANDER	HEAVEN
GIBBET	GOBLIN	GREIGE	GUSSIE	HANDLE	HEAVER
GIBBON	GODDAM	GRIEVE	GUTFUL	HANGAR	HECKLE
GIBLET	GODOWN	GRIFFE	GUTTER	HANGER	HECTIC
GIBSON	GODSON	GRIGRI	GUTTLE	HANGUP	HECTOR
GIFTEE	GODWIT	GRILLE	GUZZLE	HANKER	HEDDLE
GIGGLE	GOFFER	GRILSE	GWEDUC	HANKIE	HEDGER
GIGLET	GOGGLE	GRINGA	GYPPER	HANSEL	HEEDER
GIGLOT	GOGLET	GRINGO	GYPSUM	HANSOM	HEEHAW
GIGOLO	GOITER	GRIPER	GYRASE	HANTLE	HEELER
GILDER	GOITRE	GRIPPE	GYRATE	HAPPEN	HEFTER
GILLER	GOLFER	GRISON	GYRENE	HAPTEN	HEGARI
GILLIE	GOMUTI	GRIVET	GYTTJA	HARBOR	HEGIRA
GIMBAL	GONIFF	GROCER	HABOOB	HARDEN	HEIFER
GIMLET	GONOPH	GROOVE	HACKEE	HAREEM	HEIGHT
GIMMAL	GOOBER	GROPER	HACKER	HARKEN	HEINIE
GIMMIE	GOODBY	GROTTO	HACKIE	HARLOT	HEJIRA
GINGAL	GOODIE	GROUND	HACKLE	HARMER	HELIUM
GINGER	GOOGLE	GROUSE	HADITH	HARMIN	HELLER
GINGKO	GOOGOL	GROVEL	HADJEE	HARPER	HELMET
GINKGO	GOOLIE	GROWER	HADRON	HARPIN	HELPER
GINNER	GOONDA	GROWTH	HAEMIN	HARROW	HEMMER
GIPPER	GOONEY	GROYNE	HAFFET	HARTAL	HENBIT
GIRDER	GOONIE	GRUDGE	HAFFIT	HASLET	HENLEY
GIRDLE	GOORAL	GRUGRU	HAFTER	HASSEL	HEPCAT
GIRLIE	GOPHER	GRUNGE	HAGBUT	HASSLE	HEPTAD
GITANO	GORGER	GUAIAC	HAGDON	HASTEN	HERALD
GLAIRE	GORGET	GUANAY	HAGGLE	HATFUL	HERBAL
GLAIVE	GORGON	GUANIN	HAILER	HATPIN	HERDER
GLAMOR	GORHEN	GUENON	HAIRDO	HATRED	HERDIC
GLANCE	GOSPEL	GUFFAW	HAKEEM	HATTER	HERIOT

HERMIT	HOLLOA	HULLER	IMMURE	INFOLD	INVEST
HERNIA	HOLLOO	HULLOA	IMPACT	INFORM	INVITE
HEROIC	HOLLOW	HULLOO	IMPAIR	INFUSE	INVOKE
HEROIN	HOMAGE	HUMATE	IMPALA	INGATE	INWALL
HETERO	HOMBRE	HUMBLE	IMPALE	INGEST	INWARD
HETMAN	HONCHO	HUMBUG	IMPARK	INGULF	INWIND
HEXADE	HONDLE	HUMINT	IMPART	INHALE	INWRAP
HEXANE	HONKER	HUMMER	IMPAWN	INHAUL	IODATE
HEXONE	HONKEY	HUMOUR	IMPEDE	INHERE	IODIDE
HEXOSE	HONKIE	HUMPER	IMPEND	INHUME	IODINE
HEYDAY	HONOUR	HUMVEE	IMPHEE	INJECT	IODISE
HEYDEY	HOODIE	HUNGER	IMPING	INJERA	IODISM
HICCUP	HOODOO	HUNKER	IMPONE	INJURE	IODIZE
HICKEY	HOOFER	HUNKEY	IMPORT	INKJET	IOLITE
HICKIE	HOOKAH	HUNKIE	IMPOSE	INKLES	IONISE
HIDING	HOOKER	HUNTER	IMPOST	INKPOT	IONIUM
HIGGLE	HOOKEY	HUPPAH	IMPROV	INLACE	IONIZE
HIGHTH	HOOKUP	HURDLE	IMPUGN	INLAND	IONONE
HIJACK	HOOPER	HURLER	IMPUTE	INLIER	IPECAC
HIJRAH	HOOPLA	HURLEY	INBRED	INMATE	IRENIC
HILLER	HOOPOE	HURRAH	INCAGE	INNAGE	IRONER
HILLOA	HOOPOO	HURRAY	INCANT	INNING	IRRUPT
HINDER	HOORAH	HURTER	INCASE	INPOUR	ISATIN
HINGER	HOORAY	HURTLE	INCENT	INROAD	ISLAND
HINNIE	HOOTER	HUSKER	INCEPT	INSEAM	ISOBAR
HINTER	HOOVER	HUSSAR	INCEST	INSECT	ISOGON
HIPPIE	HOPPER	HUSTLE	INCHER	INSERT	ISOHEL
HIRPLE	HOPPLE	HUTZPA	INCISE	INSIDE	ISOLOG
HIRSEL	HORNET	HUZZAH	INCITE	INSIST	ISOMER
HIRSLE	HORROR	HYAENA	INCLIP	INSOLE	ISOPOD
HISSER	HORSIE	HYALIN	INCOME	INSOUL	ISSUER
HITTER	HORSTE	HYBRID	INCUSE	INSPAN	ITALIC
HOAGIE	HOSIER	HYDRID	INDABA	INSTAL	IXODID
HOAXER	HOSTEL	HYMNAL	INDENE	INSTAR	IZZARD
HOBBER	HOTBED	HYPHEN	INDENT	INSTEP	JABBER
HOBBIT	HOTDOG	HYPOID	INDICT	INSTIL	JABIRU
HOBBLE	HOTPOT	HYSSOP	INDIGO	INSULT	JACANA
HOBNOB	HOTROD	IAMBIC	INDITE	INSURE	JACKAL
HOCKER	HOTTIE	ICECAP	INDIUM	INTAKE	JACKER
HOCKEY	HOUDAH	ICICLE	INDOLE	INTEND	JACKET
HODDEN	HOUSEL	IDEATE	INDOOR	INTENT	JAEGER
HODDIN	HOUSER	IGNITE	INDUCE	INTERN	JAGGER
HOGGER	HOWDAH	IGNORE	INDUCT	INTIMA	JAGUAR
HOGGET	HOWDIE	IGUANA	INDULT	INTINE	JAILER
HOGNUT	HOWLER	ILLITE	INDUNA	INTOMB	JAILOR
HOGTIE	HOWLET	ILLUDE	INFALL	INTONE	JAMMER
HOIDEN	HOYDEN	ILLUME	INFANT	INTORT	JANGLE
HOISIN	HRYVNA	IMAGER	INFARE	INTRON	JANNEY
HOLARD	HUBBUB	IMARET	INFECT	INTUIT	JARFUL
HOLDER	HUBCAP	IMBALM	INFEED	INTURN	JARGON
HOLDUP	HUCKLE	IMBARK	INFEST	INULIN	JARINA
HOLISM	HUDDLE	IMBIBE	INFILL	INVADE	JARRAH
HOLIST	HUGGER	IMBRUE	INFIRM	INVENT	JARVEY
HOLLER	HUIPIL	IMMUNE	INFLOW	INVERT	JASMIN

JASPER	JOYPAD	KASBAH	KINASE	LACKER	LATIGO
JASSID	JOYPOP	KASHER	KINDLE	LACKEY	LATINA
JAUNCE	JUBBAH	KATANA	KINEMA	LACTAM	LATINO
JAYGEE	JUBHAH	KATION	KIPPAH	LACUNA	LATRIA
JAYVEE	JUBILE	KEBBIE	KIPPER	LACUNE	LATTEN
JAZZBO	JUDDER	KEBLAH	KIRPAN	LADDER	LATTER
JAZZER	JUDGER	KECKLE	KIRTLE	LADDIE	LATTIN
JEERER	JUDOKA	KEDDAH	KISHKA	LADING	LAUDER
JEHADI	JUGFUL	KEENER	KISHKE	LADINO	LAUNCE
JENNET	JUGGLE	KEEPER	KISMAT	LADLER	LAUREL
JERBOA	JUICER	KEGGER	KISMET	LADRON	LAVABO
JEREED	JUJUBE	KEGLER	KISSER	LAGEND	LAVAGE
JERKER	JUMBAL	KELOID	KITBAG	LAGGER	LAVEER
JERKIN	JUMBIE	KELPIE	KITING	LAGOON	LAWINE
JERRID	JUMBLE	KELSON	KITTEN	LAGUNA	LAWING
JERSEY	JUMPER	KELTER	KITTLE	LAGUNE	LAWYER
JESTER	JUNGLE	KELVIN	KLAXON	LAKING	LAYOFF
JESUIT	JUNIOR	KENNEL	KLEPHT	LALLAN	LAYOUT
JETLAG	JUNKER	KERMES	KLEPTO	LAMBDA	LAZULI
JETSAM	JUNKET	KERNEL	KLUDGE	LAMBER	LEADEN
JETSOM	JUNKIE	KERRIA	KNAWEL	LAMBIE	LEADER
JETTON	JURANT	KERSEY	KNIFER	LAMEDH	LEAGUE
JETWAY	JURIST	KETENE	KNIGHT	LAMENT	LEAKER
JEZAIL	JUSTER	KETONE	KNOWER	LAMINA	LEANER
JIBBAH	JUSTLE	KETOSE	KOBOLD	LAMPAD	LEAPER
JIBBER	KABAKA	KETTLE	KOCHIA	LANCER	LEASER
JICAMA	KABALA	KEWPIE	KOODOO	LANCET	LEAVEN
JIGGER	KABAYA	KEYPAD	KOOKUM	LANDAU	LEAVER
JIGGLE	KABIKI	KEYPAL	KOPECK	LANDER	LECHER
JIGSAW	KABOOM	KEYSET	KOPPIE	LANGUE	LECHWE
JIHADI	KABUKI	KEYWAY	KORUNA	LANGUR	LECTIN
JILTER	KAFFIR	KHALIF	KOSHER	LANNER	LECTOR
JIMMIE	KAFTAN	KHAZEN	KOUMIS	LANUGO	LEDGER
JIMSON	KAHUNA	KHEDAH	KOUMYS	LAOGAI	LEEWAY
JINGAL	KAINIT	KIAUGH	KOUSSO	LAPDOG	LEFTIE
JINGLE	KAISER	KIBBEH	KOWTOW	LAPFUL	LEGATE
JINKER	KAIZEN	KIBBLE	KRAKEN	LAPPER	LEGATO
JITNEY	KAKAPO	KIBLAH	KRATER	LAPPET	LEGEND
JITTER	KALIAN	KICKER	KRUBUT	LAPSER	LEGGIN
JOBBER	KALIPH	KICKUP	KUBASA	LAPTOP	LEGION
JOBBIE	KALIUM	KIDDER	KUCHEN	LARDER	LEGIST
JOCKEY	KALMIA	KIDDIE	KUDLIK	LARDON	LEGONG
JOGGER	KALONG	KIDLIT	KULTUR	LARGES	LEGUME
JOGGLE	KALPAC	KIDNAP	KUMKUM	LARIAT	LEKVAR
JOINER	KALPAK	KIDNEY	KUMMEL	LARKER	LENDER
JOJOBA	KAMALA	KIDVID	KURGAN	LARRUP	LENGTH
JOLTER	KAMSIN	KIKUYU	KWACHA	LASCAR	LENITE
JORDAN	KANAKA	KILLER	KWANZA	LASHER	LENTIL
JOSEPH	KANBAN	KILLIE	LAAGER	LASSIE	LEPTIN
JOSHER	KANTAR	KILTER	LABIAL	LASTER	LEPTON
JOSTLE	KAOLIN	KILTIE	LABOUR	LATEEN	LESION
JOTTER	KARAHI	KIMCHI	LABRET	LATENT	LESSEE
JOUNCE	KARATE	KIMONO	LABRUM	LATEST	LESSEN
JOURNO	KARROO	KINARA	LACING	LATHER	LESSON

90

LESSOR	LIPPEN	LOONEY	LYSATE	MAMZER	MASJID
LETHAL	LIPPER	LOONIE	LYSINE	MANAGE	MASKEG
LETOUT	LIQUID	LOOPER	MACACO	MANANA	MASKER
LETTER	LIQUOR	LOOSEN	MACHER	MANCHE	MASQUE
LEUCIN	LISPER	LOOTER	MACKLE	MANEGE	MASSIF
LEUCON	LISTEE	LOPPER	MACRON	MANGEL	MASTER
LEUKON	LISTEL	LOPPET	MACULA	MANGER	MASTIC
LEVANT	LISTEN	LOQUAT	MACULE	MANGLE	MATING
LEVIER	LISTER	LORICA	MADAME	MANIAC	MATRIC
LEXEME	LITCHI	LOSING	MADCAP	MANILA	MATRON
LEZZIE	LITHIA	LOTION	MADDEN	MANIOC	MATSAH
LIAISE	LITTER	LOTTER	MADDER	MANITO	MATTER
LIBBER	LITTLE	LOUDEN	MADTOM	MANITU	MATTIN
LIBIDO	LIVIER	LOUNGE	MADURO	MANNAN	MATURE
LIBLAB	LIVING	LOUVER	MAENAD	MANNER	MATZAH
LICHEE	LIVYER	LOUVRE	MAFFIA	MANTEL	MATZOH
LICHEN	LIZARD	LOVAGE	MAFTIR	MANTID	MAULER
LICKER	LOADER	LOVING	MAGGOT	MANTLE	MAUMET
LICTOR	LOAFER	LOWBOY	MAGIAN	MANTRA	MAXIXE
LIERNE	LOANEE	LOWING	MAGILP	MANTUA	MAYDAY
LIFTER	LOANER	LUBBER	MAGLEV	MANUAL	MAYHEM
LIGAND	LOATHE	LUCERN	MAGNET	MANUKA	MAYING
LIGASE	LOBBER	LUCITE	MAGNUM	MANURE	MAYPOP
LIGATE	LOBULE	LUCKIE	MAGPIE	MAPLES	MAYVIN
LIGNAN	LOCALE	LUETIC	MAGUEY	MAPPER	MAZARD
LIGNIN	LOCATE	LUGGER	MAHANT	MARACA	MAZUMA
LIGULA	LOCHAN	LUGGIE	MAHOUT	MARAUD	MEADOW
LIGULE	LOCHIA	LULLER	MAHZOR	MARBLE	MEALIE
LIGURE	LOCKER	LUMBAR	MAIDAN	MARCEL	MEANER
LIKING	LOCKET	LUMBER	MAIDEN	MARGAY	MEANIE
LIMBER	LOCKUP	LUMPEN	MAIHEM	MARGIN	MEASLE
LIMMER	LOCULE	LUMPER	MAILER	MARINA	MEDAKA
LIMNER	LOCUST	LUMPIA	MAIMER	MARINE	MEDDLE
LIMPER	LODGER	LUNATE	MAKEUP	MARKER	MEDIAL
LIMPET	LOFTER	LUNGAN	MAKING	MARKET	MEDIAN
LINAGE	LOGGER	LUNGEE	MALATE	MARKKA	MEDICK
LINDEN	LOGGIA	LUNGER	MALICE	MARKUP	MEDICO
LINEUP	LOGION	LUNGYI	MALIGN	MARLIN	MEDINA
LINGAM	LOGJAM	LUNKER	MALINE	MARMOT	MEDIUM
LINGER	LOGOFF	LUNULE	MALKIN	MAROON	MEDLAR
LINHAY	LOGOUT	LUPINE	MALLEE	MARQUE	MEDLEY
LINING	LOGWAY	LURDAN	MALLET	MARRAM	MEDUSA
LINKER	LOITER	LURKER	MALLOW	MARRER	MEETER
LINKUP	LOLLER	LUSTER	MALTED	MARRON	MEGILP
LINNET	LOLLOP	LUSTRE	MALTHA	MARROW	MEGOHM
LINNEY	LOMEIN	LUTEIN	MALTOL	MARTEN	MEGRIM
LINSEY	LOMENT	LUTING	MAMLUK	MARTIN	MEHNDI
LINTEL	LONGAN	LUTIST	MAMMAL	MARTYR	MEINIE
LINTER	LONGER	LUVVIE	MAMMEE	MARVEL	MELDER
LINTOL	LOOFAH	LUXATE	MAMMER	MASALA	MELENA
LIPASE	LOOGIE	LYCEUM	MAMMET	MASCON	MELLOW
LIPIDE	LOOKER	LYCHEE	MAMMEY	MASCOT	MELOID
LIPOID	LOOKIT	LYRISM	MAMMIE	MASHER	MELTER
LIPOMA	LOOKUP	LYRIST	MAMMON	MASHIE	MELTON

MEMBER	MIKVAH	MIZZEN	MOSAIC	MURINE	NAPKIN
MEMOIR	MIKVEH	MIZZLE	MOSHER	MURMUR	NAPPER
MENACE	MILADI	MOANER	MOSQUE	MURREY	NAPPIE
MENAGE	MILAGE	MOBBER	MOSSER	MURRHA	NARDOO
MENDER	MILDEN	MOBCAP	MOTHER	MUSCAT	NARROW
MENHIR	MILDEW	MOBILE	MOTILE	MUSCID	NARWAL
MENIAL	MILIEU	MOBLOG	MOTION	MUSCLE	NASION
MENTEE	MILING	MOCKER	MOTIVE	MUSEUM	NATION
MENTOR	MILKER	MOCKUP	MOTLEY	MUSHER	NATIVE
MENUDO	MILLER	MODERN	MOTMOT	MUSICK	NATRON
MERCER	MILLET	MODULE	MOTTLE	MUSING	NATTER
MERGEE	MILNEB	MOGGIE	MOUJIK	MUSJID	NATURE
MERGER	MILORD	MOGHUL	MOULIN	MUSKEG	NAUGHT
MERINO	MILTER	MOHAIR	MOUSER	MUSKET	NAUSEA
MERLIN	MIMBAR	MOHAWK	MOUSSE	MUSKIE	NAVAID
MERLON	MIMOSA	MOILER	MOUTON	MUSKIT	NAYSAY
MERLOT	MINBAR	MOJITO	MOVANT	MUSLIN	NEATEN
MESCAL	MINCER	MOKSHA	MOWING	MUSSEL	NEBULA
MESSAN	MINDER	MOLDER	MUCKER	MUSTEE	NECKER
MESTEE	MINGLE	MOLEST	MUCKLE	MUSTER	NECTAR
METAGE	MINING	MOLLAH	MUCLUC	MUTANT	NEEDER
METATE	MINION	MOLLIE	MUCOID	MUTASE	NEEDLE
METEOR	MINIUM	MOLOCH	MUCOSA	MUTATE	NEGATE
METEPA	MINNOW	MOLTER	MUDBUG	MUTINE	NEKTON
METHOD	MINTER	MOMENT	MUDCAP	MUTISM	NELLIE
METHYL	MINUET	MOMISM	MUDCAT	MUTTER	NELSON
METICA	MINUTE	MOMSER	MUDDER	MUTTON	NEOCON
METIER	MINYAN	MOMZER	MUDDLE	MUTUAL	NEPETA
METOPE	MIOTIC	MONGER	MUDHEN	MUTUEL	NEPHEW
METRIC	MIRAGE	MONGOE	MUDPIE	MUTULE	NEREID
METTLE	MIRROR	MONGOL	MUESLI	MUUMUU	NEROLI
METUMP	MISACT	MONISM	MUFFIN	MUZHIK	NESTER
MEWLER	MISADD	MONIST	MUFFLE	MUZJIK	NESTLE
MEZCAL	MISAIM	MONKEY	MUGFUL	MUZZLE	NESTOR
MEZUZA	MISCUE	MOOLAH	MUGGAR	MYCELE	NETFUL
MIASMA	MISCUT	MOOLEY	MUGGEE	MYELIN	NETTER
MICELL	MISEAT	MOONER	MUGGER	MYOPIA	NETTLE
MICKEY	MISFIT	MOOTER	MUGGUR	MYOSIN	NEURON
MICKLE	MISHAP	MOPOKE	MUGHAL	MYOTIC	NEUTER
MICRON	MISHIT	MOPPER	MUKLUK	MYRIAD	NEWBIE
MIDAIR	MISKAL	MOPPET	MUKTUK	MYRICA	NEWSIE
MIDDAY	MISKEY	MORALE	MULETA	MYRTLE	NEWTON
MIDDEN	MISLAY	MOREEN	MULLAH	MYSOST	NIACIN
MIDDLE	MISLIE	MORGAN	MULLEN	MYSTIC	NIBBLE
MIDGET	MISPEN	MORGEN	MULLER	MYXOMA	NIBLET
MIDGUT	MISSAL	MORGUE	MULLET	NABBER	NICKEL
MIDLEG	MISSAY	MORION	MULLEY	NAGANA	NICKER
MIDRIB	MISSEL	MORNAY	MUMBLE	NAGGER	NICKLE
MIDWAY	MISSET	MORPHO	MUMMER	NAILER	NIDATE
MIGGLE	MISTER	MORROW	MUMPER	NANDIN	NIDGET
MIGNON	MISUSE	MORSEL	MUNTIN	NANISM	NIELLO
MIHRAB	MITHER	MORTAL	MURAGE	NANKIN	NIFFER
MIKADO	MITTEN	MORTAR	MURDER	NANNIE	NIGGER
MIKRON	MIZUNA	MORULA	MUREIN	NAPALM	NIGGLE

NILGAI	NUDISM	OHMAGE	OROGEN	OXFORD	PARAMO
NILGAU	NUDIST	OILCAN	OROIDE	OXHERD	PARANG
NIMROD	NUDNIK	OILCUP	ORPHAN	OXHIDE	PARAPH
NIPPER	NUGGET	OILWAY	ORPINE	OXTAIL	PARCEL
NIPPLE	NULLAH	OLEATE	ORRICE	OXYGEN	PARDAH
NIQAAB	NUMBAT	OLEFIN	OSCINE	OYSTER	PARDON
NITRID	NUMBER	OLEINE	OSCULE	OZALID	PARENT
NITRIL	NUMDAH	OLINGO	OSETRA	PABLUM	PARGET
NITWIT	NUMNAH	OMELET	OSMIUM	PACING	PARIAH
NOBBLE	NUNCIO	OMERTA	OSMOLE	PACKER	PARIAN
NOCEBO	NUNCLE	ONAGER	OSMOSE	PACKET	PARING
NODDER	NURSER	ONLOAD	OSMUND	PACZKI	PARKER
NODDLE	NUTATE	ONWARD	OSPREY	PADAUK	PARKIN
NODULE	NUTBAR	OOCYST	OSSEIN	PADDER	PARLAY
NOGGIN	NUTJOB	OOCYTE	OSTLER	PADDLE	PARLEY
NOMISM	NUTLET	OOLITE	OTTAVA	PADNAG	PARLOR
NONAGE	NUTMEG	OOLITH	OUGIYA	PADOUK	PAROLE
NONANE	NUTRIA	OOLONG	OURANG	PAELLA	PARRAL
NONART	NUTTER	OOMIAC	OURARI	PAESAN	PARREL
NONCOM	NUZZLE	OOMIAK	OUREBI	PAGING	PARROT
NONEGO	NYMPHO	OOMPAH	OUSTER	PAGODA	PARSEC
NONFAN	OBELIA	OORALI	OUTACT	PAISAN	PARSER
NONGAY	OBENTO	OPAQUE	OUTADD	PAJAMA	PARSON
NONKIN	OBEYER	OPENER	OUTAGE	PAKEHA	PARTAN
NONUSE	OBIISM	OPERON	OUTASK	PAKORA	PARTER
NONWAR	OBJECT	OPHITE	OUTBEG	PALACE	PARTON
NOODGE	OBLAST	OPIATE	OUTBID	PALAPA	PARURA
NOODLE	OBLATE	OPIOID	OUTBUY	PALATE	PARURE
NOOGIE	OBLIGE	OPPOSE	OUTEAT	PALING	PASCAL
NOOKIE	OBLONG	OPPUGN	OUTFIT	PALLET	PASHKA
NOONER	OBOIST	OPTIME	OUTGUN	PALLOR	PASKHA
NOOSER	OBTAIN	OPTION	OUTHIT	PALMER	PASSEL
NORITE	OBTEST	ORACHE	OUTING	PALTER	PASSER
NORMAL	OBTUND	ORACLE	OUTJUT	PAMPER	PASTEL
NOSHER	OBVERT	ORANGE	OUTLAW	PANADA	PASTER
NOSING	OCCULT	ORATOR	OUTLAY	PANAMA	PASTIE
NOSTOC	OCELOT	ORCEIN	OUTLET	PANDAN	PASTIL
NOTATE	OCHREA	ORCHID	OUTLIE	PANDER	PASTOR
NOTICE	OCICAT	ORCHIL	OUTMAN	PANDIT	PATACA
NOTION	OCTANE	ORDAIN	OUTPUT	PANEER	PATENT
NOUGAT	OCTANT	ORDEAL	OUTRIG	PANFUL	PATINA
NOUGHT	OCTAVE	ORDURE	OUTROW	PANGEN	PATINE
NOVATE	OCTAVO	OREIDE	OUTRUN	PANIER	PATOOT
NOVENA	OCTROI	ORFRAY	OUTSAY	PANINI	PATROL
NOVICE	OCULAR	ORGASM	OUTSEE	PANNER	PATRON
NOYADE	OEDEMA	ORGEAT	OUTSET	PANTIE	PATTEN
NOZZLE	OEUVRE	ORGONE	OUTSIN	PANZER	PATTER
NUANCE	OFFCUT	ORIENT	OUTSIT	PAPAIN	PATTIE
NUBBER	OFFEND	ORIGAN	OUTVIE	PAPAYA	PATZER
NUBBIN	OFFICE	ORIGIN	OUTWAR	PAPISM	PAULIN
NUBBLE	OFFING	ORIOLE	OUTWIT	PAPIST	PAUPER
NUBUCK	OFFSET	ORISHA	OVISAC	PAPULA	PAUSER
NUCHAL	OGDOAD	ORISON	OVONIC	PAPULE	PAVANE
NUDGER	OGRISM	ORMOLU	OXCART	PARADE	PAVING

PAVIOR	PEPLUM	PHYSIO	PIPAGE	POETIC	POTBOY
PAVISE	PEPPER	PHYTIN	PIPING	POGROM	POTEEN
PAWNEE	PEPSIN	PHYTOL	PIPKIN	POINTE	POTFUL
PAWNER	PEPTIC	PHYTON	PIPPIN	POISER	POTHER
PAWNOR	PEPTID	PIAFFE	PIQUET	POISON	POTION
PAWPAW	PERCID	PIAZZA	PIRANA	POLACK	POTPIE
PAYDAY	PERDUE	PICARA	PIRATE	POLDER	POTSIE
PAYNIM	PEREON	PICARO	PIRAYA	POLEYN	POTTER
PAYOFF	PERIOD	PICKER	PISHER	POLICE	POTTLE
PAYOLA	PERMIT	PICKET	PISSER	POLLEE	POTZER
PAYOUT	PERNOD	PICKLE	PISTIL	POLLEN	POUFFE
PEAHEN	PEROGI	PICKUP	PISTOL	POLLER	POUNCE
PEANUT	PERRON	PICNIC	PISTON	POLYOL	POURER
PEAVEY	PERSON	PIDDLE	PISTOU	POMACE	POUTER
PEBBLE	PERUKE	PIDGIN	PITAYA	POMADE	POWDER
PECHAN	PERUSE	PIECER	PITIER	POMELO	POWTER
PECKER	PESADE	PIEING	PITMAN	POMMEL	POWWOW
PECTEN	PESETA	PIERCE	PITSAW	POMMIE	POZOLE
PECTIN	PESEWA	PIFFLE	PIZZLE	POMPOM	PRAISE
PEDALO	PESTER	PIGEON	PLACER	POMPON	PRAJNA
PEDANT	PESTLE	PIGGIE	PLACET	PONCHO	PRANCE
PEDDLE	PETARD	PIGGIN	PLAGUE	PONDER	PRATER
PEDLAR	PETITE	PIGLET	PLAICE	PONGAL	PRATIE
PEDLER	PETNAP	PIGNUT	PLAINT	PONGEE	PRAYER
PEDWAY	PETREL	PIGOUT	PLANER	PONGID	PREACT
PEELER	PETROL	PIGPEN	PLANET	PONTIL	PREAMP
PEEPBO	PETSAI	PIKAKE	PLAQUE	PONTON	PREARM
PEEPER	PETTER	PILAFF	PLASMA	POOBAH	PREBID
PEEPUL	PETTLE	PILEUP	PLATAN	POODLE	PREBUY
PEERIE	PEWTER	PILFER	PLATEN	POOLER	PRECIP
PEEWEE	PEYOTE	PILING	PLATER	POPGUN	PRECUT
PEEWIT	PEYOTL	PILLAR	PLAYER	POPLAR	PREFAB
PEGTOP	PHARMA	PILLOW	PLEASE	POPLIN	PREFER
PELAGE	PHASER	PILULE	PLEDGE	POPOUT	PRELIM
PELHAM	PHENOL	PIMPLE	PLEIAD	POPPER	PREMED
PELITE	PHENOM	PINANG	PLENUM	POPPET	PREMIE
PELLET	PHENYL	PINATA	PLEURA	POPPLE	PRENUP
PELMET	PHLEGM	PINCER	PLEXOR	POPSIE	PREPAY
PELOTA	PHLOEM	PINDER	PLIGHT	PORISM	PRESET
PELTER	PHOBIA	PINEAL	PLINTH	PORKER	PRESTO
PELVIC	PHOBIC	PINENE	PLISSE	PORTAL	PRETOR
PENANG	PHOEBE	PINGER	PLOUGH	PORTER	PREVUE
PENCEL	PHONER	PINION	PLOVER	POSADA	PREYER
PENCIL	PHONEY	PINITE	PLOWER	POSEUR	PRICER
PENNER	PHONIC	PINKEN	PLUNGE	POSOLE	PRIEST
PENNON	PHONON	PINKER	PLURAL	POSSES	PRIMER
PENSEE	PHOTIC	PINKEY	PLUTON	POSSET	PRINCE
PENSIL	PHOTOG	PINKIE	PNEUMA	POSSUM	PRISON
PENTAD	PHOTON	PINNER	POCKET	POSTAL	PRIVET
PENTYL	PHRASE	PINOLE	PODITE	POSTER	PRIZER
PENULT	PHREAK	PINTLE	PODIUM	POSTIE	PROBER
PEOPLE	PHYLLO	PINYIN	PODSOL	POSTIN	PROBIT
PEPINO	PHYSED	PINYON	PODUNK	POSTOP	PROFIT
PEPITA	PHYSIC	PIOLET	PODZOL	POTAGE	PROJET

PROLAN	PUNTER	QUELEA	RAMBLA	REASON	REDFIN
PROLEG	PUPATE	QUEUER	RAMBLE	REAVER	REDIAL
PROLOG	PUPPET	QUEZAL	RAMJET	REAVOW	REDLEG
PROMPT	PURANA	QUICHE	RAMMER	REBAIT	REDOCK
PROPEL	PURDAH	QUINCE	RAMONA	REBASE	REDOUT
PROPER	PURFLE	QUININ	RAMROD	REBATE	REDOWA
PROPYL	PURGER	QUINOA	RAMSON	REBATO	REDRAW
PROSER	PURINE	QUINOL	RAMTIL	REBECK	REDTOP
PROTEA	PURISM	QUINTA	RANCHO	REBILL	REDUCE
PROTON	PURIST	QUINTE	RANCOR	REBIND	REEARN
PROTYL	PURLIN	QUIPPU	RANDAN	REBOIL	REEBOK
PROVER	PURPLE	QUIVER	RANDOM	REBOOK	REEDIT
PRUNER	PURSER	QULLIQ	RANGER	REBOOT	REEFER
PSEUDO	PURSUE	QUOHOG	RANKER	REBORE	REEKER
PSOCID	PURVEY	QUOKKA	RANKLE	REBOZO	REELER
PSYCHE	PUSHER	QUORUM	RANSOM	REBUFF	REEMIT
PSYCHO	PUSHUP	QUOTER	RANTER	REBUKE	REFACE
PSYLLA	PUSLEY	QWERTY	RANULA	RECALL	REFALL
PSYWAR	PUTLOG	RABATO	RAPHIA	RECANE	REFECT
PTERIN	PUTOFF	RABBET	RAPIER	RECANT	REFEED
PTISAN	PUTOUT	RABBIN	RAPINE	RECAST	REFEEL
PUBLIC	PUTTEE	RABBIT	RAPIST	RECEDE	REFILE
PUCKER	PUTTER	RABBLE	RAPPEE	RECEPT	REFILL
PUDDLE	PUTTIE	RACEME	RAPPEL	RECHEW	REFILM
PUDEUR	PUZZLE	RACHET	RAPPER	RECIPE	REFIND
PUEBLO	PYEMIA	RACING	RAPTOR	RECITE	REFINE
PUFFER	PYJAMA	RACINO	RASCAL	RECKON	REFIRE
PUFFIN	PYKNIC	RACISM	RASHER	RECLAD	REFLAG
PUGGLE	PYRENE	RACIST	RASPER	RECOAL	REFLET
PUGREE	PYRITE	RACKER	RASSLE	RECOAT	REFLOW
PUISNE	PYROLA	RACKET	RASTER	RECOCK	REFOLD
PULING	PYRONE	RACOON	RASURE	RECODE	REFORM
PULLER	PYROPE	RADDLE	RATBAG	RECOIL	REFUEL
PULLET	PYRROL	RADIAL	RATINE	RECOIN	REFUGE
PULLEY	PYTHON	RADIAN	RATING	RECOMB	REFUND
PULLUP	PYURIA	RADIUM	RATION	RECOOK	REFUSE
PULPER	QABALA	RADOME	RATITE	RECORD	REFUTE
PULPIT	QIGONG	RADULA	RATLIN	RECORK	REGAIN
PULQUE	QINDAR	RAFFIA	RATOON	RECOUP	REGALE
PULSAR	QINTAR	RAFFLE	RATTAN	RECTOR	REGARD
PULSER	QIVIUT	RAFTER	RATTEN	RECTUM	REGEAR
PUMELO	QUAERE	RAGBAG	RATTER	RECUSE	REGENT
PUMICE	QUAGGA	RAGGEE	RATTLE	REDACT	REGGAE
PUMMEL	QUAHOG	RAGGLE	RATTON	REDATE	REGIFT
PUMPER	QUAICH	RAGLAN	RAVAGE	REDBAY	REGILD
PUNDIT	QUAIGH	RAGOUT	RAVINE	REDBUD	REGIME
PUNGLE	QUAKER	RAGTAG	RAVING	REDBUG	REGINA
PUNKAH	QUANGO	RAGTOP	RAZZIA	REDCAP	REGION
PUNKER	QUARTE	RAIDER	RAZZLE	REDDEN	REGIVE
PUNKEY	QUARTO	RAILER	READER	REDDER	REGLET
PUNKIE	QUASAR	RAISER	REAGIN	REDDLE	REGLOW
PUNKIN	QUATRE	RAISIN	REAMER	REDEAR	REGLUE
PUNNER	QUAVER	RALLYE	REAPER	REDEEM	REGRET
PUNNET	QUBYTE	RAMADA	REARER	REDEYE	REGROW

95

REHANG	RENOWN	RESITE	REWORD	RITARD	ROZZER
REHEAR	RENTAL	RESIZE	REWORK	RITTER	RUBACE
REHEAT	RENTER	RESKIN	REWRAP	RITUAL	RUBATO
REHEEL	RENVOI	RESOAK	REXINE	RIVAGE	RUBBER
REHIRE	REOPEN	RESOLE	REZERO	ROADEO	RUBBLE
REISHI	REPACK	RESORB	REZONE	ROADIE	RUBIGO
REIVER	REPAIR	RESORT	RHAPHE	ROAMER	RUBOFF
REJECT	REPARK	RESPOT	RHEBOK	ROARER	RUBOUT
REJOIN	REPAST	RESTER	RHETOR	ROBALO	RUBRIC
REKNIT	REPAVE	RESULT	RHUMBA	ROBAND	RUCKLE
REKNOT	REPEAL	RESUME	RHYMER	ROBATA	RUCOLA
RELACE	REPEAT	RETACK	RHYTHM	ROBBER	RUDDER
RELAND	REPENT	RETAIL	RHYTON	ROBBIN	RUDDLE
RELATE	REPERK	RETAIN	RIALTO	ROCHET	RUDIST
RELEND	REPINE	RETAKE	RIBALD	ROCKER	RUFFLE
RELENT	REPLAN	RETAPE	RIBAND	ROCKET	RUGGER
RELEVE	REPLAY	RETARD	RIBBER	ROCOCO	RUGOLA
RELICT	REPLOT	RETEAM	RIBBIE	RODENT	RUGOSA
RELIEF	REPLOW	RETEAR	RIBBIT	RODNEY	RUGRAT
RELIER	REPOLL	RETELL	RIBBON	ROLFER	RUINER
RELINE	REPORT	RETENE	RIBEYE	ROLLER	RULING
RELINK	REPOSE	RETEST	RIBIER	ROLLIE	RUMAKI
RELIST	REPOUR	RETILE	RIBLET	ROLLUP	RUMBLE
RELIVE	REPUGN	RETIME	RIBOSE	ROMAJI	RUMDUM
RELOAD	REPUMP	RETINA	RICHEN	ROMANO	RUMMER
RELOAN	REPUTE	RETINE	RICKEY	ROMPER	RUMOUR
RELOCK	REQUIN	RETINT	RICRAC	RONDEL	RUMPLE
RELOOK	RERACK	RETIRE	RIDDER	RONION	RUMPOT
RELUCT	REREAD	RETOOL	RIDDLE	RONNEL	RUNDLE
RELUME	RERENT	RETORT	RIDGEL	RONYON	RUNKLE
REMAIL	RERISE	RETRIM	RIDGIL	ROOFER	RUNLET
REMAIN	REROLL	RETUNE	RIDING	ROOFIE	RUNNEL
REMAKE	REROOF	RETURN	RIDLEY	ROOKIE	RUNNER
REMAND	RESAIL	RETYPE	RIEVER	ROOMER	RUNOFF
REMARK	RESALE	REVAMP	RIFFLE	ROOMIE	RUNOUT
REMATE	RESCUE	REVEAL	RIFLER	ROOSER	RUNWAY
REMEET	RESEAL	REVERB	RIFLIP	ROOTER	RUPIAH
REMELT	RESEAT	REVERE	RIGGER	ROOTLE	RUSHEE
REMEND	RESEAU	REVERT	RIGOUR	ROPING	RUSHER
REMIND	RESECT	REVEST	RILLET	ROQUET	RUSSET
REMINT	RESEDA	REVIEW	RIMMER	ROSACE	RUSTIC
REMISE	RESEED	REVILE	RIMPLE	ROSCOE	RUSTLE
REMOLD	RESEEK	REVISE	RINGER	ROSTER	RUTILE
REMORA	RESELL	REVIVE	RINSER	ROTATE	RYOKAN
REMOTE	RESEND	REVOKE	RIOTER	ROTCHE	SABBAT
REMOVE	RESENT	REVOLT	RIPOFF	ROTGUT	SABICU
REMUDA	RESHIP	REVOTE	RIPOST	ROTINI	SABINE
RENAIL	RESHOE	REWAKE	RIPPER	ROTTER	SABKHA
RENAME	RESHOW	REWARD	RIPPLE	ROUBLE	SACBUT
RENDER	RESIDE	REWARM	RIPRAP	ROUCHE	SACHEM
RENEGE	RESIFT	REWEAR	RIPSAW	ROUSER	SACHET
RENEST	RESIGN	REWELD	RISING	ROUTER	SACKER
RENNET	RESILE	REWIND	RISKER	ROVING	SACQUE
RENNIN	RESIST	REWIRE	RISTRA	ROWING	SACRAL

SACRUM	SANNOP	SCHISM	SECRET	SERGER	SHELVE
SADDEN	SANNUP	SCHIST	SECTOR	SERIAL	SHENAI
SADDHU	SANSAR	SCHIZO	SECURE	SERINE	SHEQEL
SADDLE	SANSEI	SCHLEP	SEDATE	SERMON	SHERIF
SADISM	SANTIM	SCHLUB	SEDUCE	SEROMA	SHERPA
SADIST	SANTIR	SCHMOE	SEEDER	SEROSA	SHEUCH
SAFARI	SANTOL	SCHOOL	SEEING	SERVAL	SHEUGH
SAFROL	SANTUR	SCHORL	SEEKER	SERVER	SHEWER
SAGBUT	SAPELE	SCHRIK	SEEMER	SESAME	SHIBAH
SAGGAR	SAPOTA	SCHROD	SEESAW	SESTET	SHIELD
SAGGER	SAPOTE	SCHTIK	SEETHE	SETOFF	SHIKAR
SAILER	SAPOUR	SCHTUP	SEGGAR	SETOUT	SHIKRA
SAILOR	SAPPER	SCHUIT	SEICHE	SETTEE	SHIKSA
SAIMIN	SARAPE	SCILLA	SEIDEL	SETTER	SHIKSE
SAIYID	SARDAR	SCLAFF	SEINER	SETTLE	SHINDY
SALAAM	SARNIE	SCLERA	SEISER	SEWAGE	SHINER
SALAMI	SARODE	SCONCE	SEISIN	SEWING	SHIVAH
SALINA	SARONG	SCORER	SEISOR	SEXISM	SHIVER
SALINE	SARSAR	SCOTER	SEITAN	SEXIST	SHLEPP
SALIVA	SARSEN	SCOTIA	SEIZER	SEXPOT	SHLOCK
SALLET	SARTOR	SCOUSE	SEIZIN	SEXTAN	SHLONG
SALLOW	SASHAY	SCOUTH	SEIZOR	SEXTET	SHLUMP
SALMON	SATANG	SCRAPE	SELECT	SEXTON	SHMEAR
SALOON	SATARA	SCRAWB	SELFIE	SHACKO	SHMEER
SALOOP	SATCOM	SCRAWL	SELKIE	SHADER	SHMUCK
SALPID	SATEEN	SCREAK	SELLER	SHADOW	SHNOOK
SALTER	SATIRE	SCREAM	SELSYN	SHADUF	SHOCHU
SALTIE	SATORI	SCREED	SEMEME	SHAHID	SHOFAR
SALUKI	SATRAP	SCREEN	SENATE	SHAIKH	SHOGUN
SALUTE	SAUCER	SCRIBE	SENDAL	SHAIRD	SHOLOM
SALVER	SAUGER	SCRIMP	SENDER	SHAIRN	SHOPPE
SALVIA	SAUREL	SCRIPT	SENDUP	SHAKER	SHORAN
SALVOR	SAVAGE	SCRIVE	SENECA	SHALOM	SHOVEL
SALWAR	SAVANT	SCROLL	SENEGA	SHAMAL	SHOVER
SAMARA	SAVATE	SCROOP	SENHOR	SHAMAN	SHOWER
SAMBAL	SAVINE	SCRUFF	SENILE	SHAMBA	SHRIEK
SAMBAR	SAVING	SCRYER	SENIOR	SHAMOY	SHRIFT
SAMBUR	SAVIOR	SCULPT	SENITI	SHANTI	SHRIKE
SAMECH	SAVOUR	SCYTHE	SENNET	SHAPER	SHRILL
SAMEKH	SAWLOG	SEABAG	SENNIT	SHARER	SHRIMP
SAMIEL	SAWNEY	SEABED	SENORA	SHARIA	SHRINE
SAMITE	SAWYER	SEADOG	SENSEI	SHARIF	SHRINK
SAMLET	SAXIST	SEALER	SENSOR	SHASTA	SHRIVE
SAMOSA	SAYING	SEAMER	SEPTET	SHAUGH	SHROFF
SAMPAN	SAYYID	SEANCE	SEPTIC	SHAVER	SHROOM
SAMPLE	SCALAR	SEASON	SEPTUM	SHAVIE	SHROUD
SAMSHU	SCALER	SEATER	SEQUEL	SHAYKH	SHTETL
SANDAL	SCARAB	SEAWAN	SEQUIN	SHEATH	SHTICK
SANDER	SCARER	SEAWAY	SERAIL	SHEAVE	SIALID
SANDHI	SCARPH	SECANT	SERAPE	SHEEVE	SICKEE
SANGAR	SCATHE	SECEDE	SERAPH	SHEIKH	SICKEN
SANGER	SCENIC	SECERN	SERDAB	SHEILA	SICKIE
SANGHA	SCHEMA	SECOND	SEREIN	SHEKEL	SICKLE
SANJAK	SCHEME	SECPAR	SERENE	SHELTA	SIDDHA

SIDDHI	SKATOL	SNOOSE	SOVRAN	SPRITE	STOLON
SIDDUR	SKEANE	SNOOZE	SOWBUG	SPROUT	STONER
SIDING	SKEWER	SNORER	SOWCAR	SPRUCE	STOOGE
SIDLER	SKIBOB	SOAKER	SOWING	SPURGE	STOPER
SIENNA	SKIDOO	SOAPER	SOZINE	SPUTUM	STORER
SIERRA	SKIING	SOARER	SPACER	SQUALL	STOREY
SIESTA	SKIVER	SOBBER	SPADER	SQUARE	STOTIN
SIFAKA	SKLENT	SOCAGE	SPAHEE	SQUARK	STOUND
SIFTER	SKYCAP	SOCCER	SPARER	SQUAWK	STOURE
SIGHER	SKYWAY	SOCIAL	SPARGE	SQUEAK	STOVER
SIGNAL	SLAHAL	SOCKET	SPARID	SQUEAL	STRAFE
SIGNEE	SLAKER	SODDEN	SPATHE	SQUILL	STRAIN
SIGNER	SLALOM	SODDIE	SPAVIE	SQUINT	STRAIT
SIGNET	SLATER	SODIUM	SPAVIN	SQUIRE	STRAKE
SIGNOR	SLAVER	SOFFIT	SPECIE	SQUIRL	STRAND
SIKSIK	SLAVEY	SOFTEN	SPEEDO	SQUIRM	STRATA
SILAGE	SLAYER	SOFTIE	SPEISE	SQUIRT	STRATH
SILANE	SLEAVE	SOIREE	SPENCE	SRADHA	STREAK
SILENT	SLEAZE	SOLACE	SPENSE	STABLE	STREAM
SILICA	SLEAZO	SOLAND	SPEWER	STACTE	STREEK
SILKIE	SLEDGE	SOLANO	SPHENE	STADIA	STREEL
SILLER	SLEEVE	SOLATE	SPHERE	STAGER	STREET
SILVAN	SLEIGH	SOLDAN	SPICER	STAKER	STRICK
SILVER	SLEUTH	SOLDER	SPIDER	STALAG	STRIDE
SIMCHA	SLICER	SOLERA	SPIGOT	STAMEN	STRIFE
SIMIAN	SLIDER	SOLION	SPIKER	STANCE	STRIKE
SIMILE	SLIEVE	SOLUTE	SPILTH	STANOL	STRINE
SIMLIN	SLIGHT	SOLVER	SPINAL	STANZA	STRING
SIMMER	SLIPUP	SOMITE	SPINEL	STAPLE	STRIPE
SIMNEL	SLIVER	SOMONI	SPINET	STARER	STRIVE
SIMOOM	SLOGAN	SONANT	SPINOR	STARVE	STROBE
SIMOON	SLOPER	SONATA	SPINTO	STATER	STROKE
SIMPER	SLOUGH	SONDER	SPIRAL	STATIC	STROLL
SIMPLE	SLOVEN	SONNET	SPIREA	STATIN	STROUD
SINGER	SLUDGE	SOONER	SPIREM	STATOR	STRUMA
SINGLE	SLUICE	SOOTHE	SPIRIT	STATUE	STRUNT
SINKER	SLURVE	SOPITE	SPITAL	STAYER	STUCCO
SINNER	SMALTO	SORBET	SPLAKE	STEEVE	STUDIO
SINNET	SMEGMA	SORDOR	SPLEEN	STELLA	STUPID
SINTER	SMIDGE	SORGHO	SPLENT	STEMMA	STUPOR
SIPHON	SMILER	SORING	SPLICE	STEPPE	STYLER
SIPPER	SMILEY	SORNER	SPLIFF	STEREO	STYLET
SIPPET	SMITER	SORREL	SPLINE	STEROL	STYMIE
SIRDAR	SMOKER	SORROW	SPLINT	STEVIA	SUBDEB
SIRRAH	SMOKEY	SORTAL	SPLORE	STIFLE	SUBDUE
SIRREE	SMOKIE	SORTER	SPLURT	STIGMA	SUBGUM
SISKIN	SMOOTH	SORTIE	SPONGE	STINGE	SUBLET
SISTER	SMRITI	SOUARI	SPOUSE	STINGO	SUBLOT
SITCOM	SMUDGE	SOUCAR	SPRAIN	STIPEL	SUBMIT
SITREP	SNARER	SOUDAN	SPRANG	STIVER	SUBNET
SITTER	SNATHE	SOURCE	SPRAWL	STODGE	SUBORN
SIZING	SNEEZE	SOUSER	SPREAD	STOGEY	SUBSET
SIZZLE	SNIPER	SOUTER	SPRING	STOGIE	SUBURB
SKATER	SNIVEL	SOVIET	SPRINT	STOKER	SUBWAY

SUCCAH	SWIPLE	TAMPAN	TECHNO	TEXTER	TINCAL
SUCCOR	SWIVEL	TAMPER	TECTUM	THAIRM	TINDER
SUCKER	SWIVET	TAMPON	TEDDER	THALER	TINEID
SUCKLE	SWOUND	TANDEM	TEDIUM	THAWER	TINFUL
SUDDEN	SYLVAN	TANGLE	TEEMER	THEINE	TINGLE
SUDOKU	SYLVIN	TANIST	TEENER	THEISM	TINKER
SUDSER	SYMBOL	TANKER	TEEPEE	THEIST	TINKLE
SUFFER	SYNCOM	TANNER	TEETER	THENAR	TINNER
SUITER	SYNDET	TANNIN	TEETHE	THERME	TINSEL
SUITOR	SYNDIC	TANNOY	TEEVEE	THETRI	TINTER
SUKKAH	SYPHER	TANREC	TEFLON	THIEVE	TIPCAT
SULDAN	SYPHON	TANTRA	TEKKIE	THIRAM	TIPOFF
SULFID	SYSTEM	TANUKI	TELEDU	THIRST	TIPPER
SULFUR	TABARD	TAPALO	TELEGA	THORIA	TIPPET
SULKER	TABLET	TAPING	TELFER	THORON	TIPPLE
SULPHA	TABOUR	TAPPER	TELLER	THORPE	TIPTOE
SULTAN	TABULI	TAPPET	TELNET	THRALL	TIPTOP
SUMACH	TACKER	TARAMA	TELOME	THRAVE	TIRADE
SUMMER	TACKET	TARGET	TELSON	THREAD	TISANE
SUMMIT	TACKLE	TARIFF	TEMPEH	THREAP	TISSUE
SUMMON	TACTIC	TARMAC	TEMPER	THREAT	TITBIT
SUNBED	TAENIA	TARPAN	TEMPLE	THREEP	TITFER
SUNBOW	TAFFIA	TARPON	TENACE	THRIFT	TITHER
SUNDAE	TAGGER	TARSAL	TENAIL	THRILL	TITIAN
SUNDER	TAGINE	TARSIA	TENANT	THRIVE	TITTER
SUNDEW	TAGRAG	TARTAN	TENDER	THROAT	TITTIE
SUNDOG	TAHINA	TARTAR	TENDON	THRONE	TITTLE
SUNKER	TAHINI	TARZAN	TENNER	THRONG	TITTUP
SUNKET	TAHSIL	TASSEL	TENOUR	THRUST	TOCHER
SUNNAH	TAILER	TASSET	TENPIN	THULIA	TOCSIN
SUNRAY	TAILLE	TASSIE	TENREC	THWACK	TODDLE
SUNSET	TAILOR	TASTER	TENSOR	THWART	TOECAP
SUNTAN	TAIPAN	TATAMI	TENTER	THYMOL	TOERAG
SUPINE	TAJINE	TATSOI	TENURE	THYRSE	TOFFEE
SUPPER	TAKAHE	TATTER	TENUTO	TICKER	TOGGLE
SUPPLE	TAKEUP	TATTIE	TEOPAN	TICKET	TOGROG
SURFER	TAKING	TATTLE	TEPHRA	TICKLE	TOILER
SURGER	TALBOT	TATTOO	TERBIA	TICTAC	TOILET
SURIMI	TALCUM	TAUTEN	TERCEL	TICTOC	TOLANE
SURREY	TALENT	TAUTOG	TERCET	TIDBIT	TOLEDO
SURVEY	TALION	TAVERN	TEREDO	TIDIER	TOLLER
SUSLIK	TALKER	TAWNEY	TERETE	TIDING	TOLUID
SUTLER	TALKIE	TAWPIE	TERMER	TIEPIN	TOLUOL
SUTTEE	TALLIT	TAXEME	TERMOR	TIERCE	TOLUYL
SUTURE	TALLOL	TAXITE	TERRET	TIFFIN	TOMBAC
SWAGER	TALLOW	TEACUP	TERRIT	TIGLON	TOMBAK
SWARTH	TALUKA	TEAPOT	TERROR	TIGNON	TOMBOY
SWATHE	TAMALE	TEAPOY	TESTEE	TILING	TOMCAT
SWAYER	TAMARI	TEARER	TESTER	TILLER	TOMCOD
SWERVE	TAMBAC	TEASEL	TESTON	TILTER	TOMTIT
SWEVEN	TAMBAK	TEASER	TETHER	TIMBAL	TONEME
SWILER	TAMBUR	TEAZEL	TETRAD	TIMBER	TONGER
SWINGE	TAMEIN	TEAZLE	TETRYL	TIMBRE	TONGUE
SWIPER	TAMMIE	TECHIE	TETTER	TIMING	TONLET

99

TONNER	TRIJET	TURACO	UNCAKE	UNREST	UPRISE
TONSIL	TRIMER	TURBAN	UNCASE	UNROBE	UPROAR
TOODLE	TRIODE	TURBIT	UNCIAL	UNROLL	UPROOT
TOOLER	TRIOSE	TURBOT	UNCLIP	UNROOF	UPSELL
TOONIE	TRIPLE	TUREEN	UNCLOG	UNROOT	UPSEND
TOOTER	TRIPOD	TURGOR	UNCOCK	UNROPE	UPSHOT
TOOTLE	TRITON	TURION	UNCOIL	UNSEAL	UPSIDE
TOPPER	TRIUNE	TURKEY	UNCORK	UNSEAM	UPSIZE
TOPPLE	TRIVET	TURNER	UNCUFF	UNSEAT	UPSOAR
TOQUET	TROCAR	TURNIP	UNCURB	UNSELL	UPSTEP
TORERO	TROCHE	TURNON	UNCURL	UNSHIP	UPSTIR
TOROID	TROGON	TURNUP	UNDINE	UNSNAG	UPTAKE
TORPID	TROIKA	TURRET	UNDOCK	UNSNAP	UPTALK
TORPOR	TROMPE	TURTLE	UNDOER	UNSTEP	UPTEAR
TORQUE	TROPIC	TUSCHE	UNDRAW	UNSTOP	UPTICK
TORULA	TROPIN	TUSHIE	UNEASE	UNTACK	UPTILT
TOSSER	TROTYL	TUSKER	UNFOLD	UNTHAW	UPTIME
TOSSUP	TROUGH	TUSSAH	UNFREE	UNTRIM	UPTOWN
TOTTER	TROUPE	TUSSAR	UNFURL	UNTUCK	UPTURN
TOUCAN	TROVER	TUSSEH	UNGIRD	UNTUNE	UPWAFT
TOUCHE	TROWEL	TUSSER	UNGLUE	UNVEIL	UPWARD
TOUPEE	TROWTH	TUSSLE	UNHAIR	UNWIND	UPWELL
TOUPIE	TRUANT	TUSSOR	UNHAND	UNWRAP	UPWIND
TOURER	TRUDGE	TUSSUR	UNHANG	UNYOKE	URACIL
TOUSLE	TRUFFE	TUXEDO	UNHASP	UPBEAR	URANIA
TOUTER	TRUISM	TUYERE	UNHELM	UPBEAT	URANYL
TOUTON	TRYOUT	TWEEZE	UNHOOD	UPBIND	URCHIN
TOUZLE	TRYSTE	TWELVE	UNHOOK	UPBOIL	UREASE
TOWAGE	TSETSE	TWIBIL	UNHUSK	UPCAST	UREIDE
TOWARD	TSKTSK	TWINER	UNICOM	UPCOIL	UREMIA
TOWHEE	TSOTSI	TWINGE	UNIPOD	UPCURL	URETER
TOWNEE	TUBBER	TWOFER	UNIQUE	UPDART	URGING
TOWNIE	TUBFUL	TYCOON	UNISON	UPDATE	URINAL
TOXINE	TUBING	TYMBAL	UNITER	UPDIVE	UROPOD
TOXOID	TUBIST	TYMPAN	UNKINK	UPFLOW	URTEXT
TRACER	TUBULE	TYPHON	UNKNIT	UPFOLD	USANCE
TRADER	TUCHUN	TYPING	UNKNOT	UPGAZE	USURER
TRAGIC	TUCKER	TYPIST	UNLACE	UPGIRD	UTMOST
TRAMEL	TUCKET	TYRANT	UNLADE	UPGROW	UTOPIA
TRANCE	TUFFET	TZETZE	UNLEAD	UPHEAP	UVULAR
TRAPAN	TUFTER	UAKARI	UNLINK	UPHILL	VACATE
TRAUMA	TUGGER	ULLAGE	UNLIVE	UPHOLD	VACUUM
TRAVEL	TUGRIK	ULSTER	UNLOAD	UPHROE	VAGINA
TREBLE	TUILLE	ULTIMA	UNLOCK	UPKEEP	VAHINE
TREMOR	TULADI	UMIACK	UNMAKE	UPLAND	VAKEEL
TREPAN	TUMBLE	UMLAUT	UNMASK	UPLEAP	VALINE
TREVET	TUMOUR	UMPIRE	UNMOLD	UPLIFT	VALISE
TRIAGE	TUMULT	UNBALE	UNMOOR	UPLINK	VALKYR
TRIBAL	TUNDRA	UNBEAR	UNNAIL	UPLOAD	VALLEY
TRICEP	TUNEUP	UNBELT	UNPACK	UPPILE	VALLUM
TRICOT	TUNING	UNBEND	UNPICK	UPPING	VALOUR
TRIENE	TUNKET	UNBIND	UNPILE	UPPROP	VALUER
TRIFLE	TUNNEL	UNBOLT	UNPLUG	UPRATE	VALUTA
TRIGON	TUPELO	UNCAGE	UNREEL	UPREAR	VAMOSE

100

VAMPER	VETTER	WAFFLE	WEAKEN	WIENER	WOOLIE
VANDAL	VIATOR	WAFTER	WEAKON	WIENIE	WOOPIE
VANNER	VIBIST	WAGGER	WEALTH	WIGEON	WORDIE
VAPOUR	VIBRIO	WAGGLE	WEANER	WIGGER	WORKER
VARIER	VICTIM	WAGGON	WEAPON	WIGGLE	WORKUP
VARLET	VICTOR	WAHINE	WEARER	WIGLET	WORMER
VAROOM	VICUNA	WAILER	WEASEL	WIGWAG	WORMIL
VARROA	VIDIOT	WAITER	WEASON	WIGWAM	WORRIT
VASSAL	VIELLE	WAIVER	WEAVER	WIKIUP	WORSEN
VATFUL	VIEWER	WAKAME	WEBCAM	WILDER	WORSET
VAWARD	VIGOUR	WAKIKI	WEBLOG	WILLER	WOWSER
VEALER	VIKING	WAKING	WEDDER	WILLET	WRAITH
VECTOR	VIOLET	WALKER	WEDELN	WILLIE	WRASSE
VEEJAY	VIOLIN	WALKUP	WEDGIE	WILLOW	WREATH
VEEPEE	VIRAGO	WALLAH	WEEDER	WIMBLE	WRIGHT
VEGGIE	VIRGER	WALLET	WEENIE	WIMPLE	WRITER
VEILER	VIRGIN	WALLEY	WEEPER	WINCER	WRITHE
VEINER	VIRION	WALLIE	WEEPIE	WINCEY	WURZEL
VELCRO	VIROID	WALLOP	WEEVER	WINDER	WUTHER
VELLUM	VIRTUE	WALLOW	WEEVIL	WINDLE	WYVERN
VELOUR	VISAGE	WALNUT	WEEWEE	WINDOW	XYLENE
VELURE	VISARD	WAMBLE	WEIGHT	WINDUP	XYLOSE
VELVET	VISION	WAMPUM	WEINER	WINGER	XYSTER
VENDEE	VISUAL	WANDER	WEIRDO	WINKER	YABBER
VENDER	VITRIC	WANGAN	WELDER	WINKLE	YABBIE
VENDOR	VITTLE	WANGLE	WELDOR	WINNER	YAFFLE
VENDUE	VIVACE	WANGUN	WELKIN	WINNOW	YAKKER
VENEER	VIZARD	WANION	WELLIE	WINTER	YAMMER
VENENE	VIZIER	WANKER	WELTER	WINTLE	YANQUI
VENINE	VIZSLA	WANTER	WESKIT	WIRING	YANTRA
VENIRE	VODOUN	WANTON	WESTER	WISDOM	YAPOCK
VENTER	VOGUER	WAPITI	WETHER	WISENT	YAPPER
VENULE	VOICER	WARBLE	WETTER	WISHER	YARDER
VERBAL	VOIDER	WARDEN	WHACKO	WITHER	YARNER
VERBID	VOLLEY	WARDER	WHALER	WITHIN	YARROW
VERDIN	VOLOST	WARMER	WHARVE	WITNEY	YASMAK
VERGER	VOLUME	WARMTH	WHEEZE	WITTER	YATTER
VERISM	VOLUTE	WARMUP	WHERVE	WITTOL	YAUPER
VERIST	VOMITO	WARNER	WHIDAH	WIVERN	YAUPON
VERITE	VOODOO	WARPER	WHINER	WIZARD	YAUTIA
VERMIN	VOTIVE	WARREN	WHINGE	WIZZEN	YAWNER
VERSAL	VOUDON	WARSAW	WHISHT	WOBBLE	YAWPER
VERSER	VOYAGE	WARSLE	WHITEN	WOGGLE	YEELIN
VERSET	VOYEUR	WASABI	WHITEY	WOLFER	YELLER
VERSIN	VULGAR	WASHER	WHOOMP	WOLVER	YELLOW
VERSTE	WABBLE	WASHUP	WHOSIT	WOMBAT	YELPER
VERVET	WADDER	WASTER	WHYDAH	WOMERA	YIPPIE
VESICA	WADDIE	WATAPE	WICCAN	WONDER	YODLER
VESPER	WADDLE	WATTLE	WICKER	WONNER	YOGINI
VESPID	WADMAL	WAUCHT	WICKET	WONTON	YOGISM
VESSEL	WADMEL	WAUGHT	WIDDER	WOODIE	YOGURT
VESTAL	WADMOL	WAXING	WIDDIE	WOOFER	YONDER
VESTEE	WADSET	WAYANG	WIDDLE	WOOLEN	YONKER
VETOER	WAFFIE	WAYLAY	WIDGET	WOOLER	YOUPON

YOWLER	ZAIKAI	ZEBRAS	ZILLAH	ZODIAC	ZYGOMA
YTTRIA	ZANANA	ZECHIN	ZINGER	ZOMBIE	ZYGOSE
YUKATA	ZANDER	ZENANA	ZINNIA	ZONING	ZYGOTE
YUPPIE	ZAPPER	ZENITH	ZIPOLA	ZONULA	ZYMASE
ZAFFAR	ZAREBA	ZEPHYR	ZIPPER	ZONULE	
ZAFFER	ZARIBA	ZESTER	ZIRCON	ZOSTER	
ZAFFIR	ZEALOT	ZEUGMA	ZITHER	ZOUAVE	
ZAFFRE	ZEATIN	ZIBETH	ZIZZLE	ZOYSIA	
ZAIDEH	ZEBECK	ZIGZAG	ZOCALO	ZYDECO	

With front hook T

ACNODE	ENABLE	HICKER	RACERS	RIGGED	RUNNEL
ACTION	ENDERS	HITHER	RACING	RIGGER	RUSTED
ACTUAL	ENDING	HOLING	RACKED	RILLED	RUTHER
AGGERS	ENFOLD	HORNED	RACKER	RIMERS	UMBLES
AILING	ENSILE	HUMPED	RAILED	RIMMED	UMPING
ALIPED	ENTERS	HUMPER	RAILER	RIMMER	UNABLE
ALKIES	ENURED	ICKERS	RAINED	RIPPED	UPPING
ALLIED	ENURES	ILLITE	RAMMED	RIPPER	URGENT
ALLIES	ERBIUM	INGLES	RAMPED	RIVETS	WADDLE
ALLOWS	ERRORS	INKERS	RANCES	ROCKED	WANGLE
AMPING	ESTATE	INKLES	RANKED	ROLLED	WATTLE
ANGLED	ESTERS	INNERS	RANSOM	ROLLER	WEENIE
ANGLER	ETCHED	INNING	RAPPED	ROMPED	WEETED
ANGLES	ETHERS	INTERS	RAPPER	ROTTED	WIDDLE
ANNOYS	HACKED	IRADES	RASHER	ROTTER	WIGGED
ANTRUM	HALERS	ISSUED	RASHES	ROUBLE	WILLED
ARTIER	HANKED	ISSUES	RAVELS	ROUGHS	WINGED
ARTILY	HANKER	ITCHES	READER	ROUPED	WINIER
ASKING	HAWING	OCHERS	REASON	ROUSER	WINING
ASSETS	HEATER	OILERS	REDDLE	ROVERS	WINKLE
ASTERS	HEISTS	OILING	RENAIL	ROWELS	WINNED
AXISES	HEREAT	OMENTA	RENDED	ROWING	WISTED
AXITES	HEREBY	ONUSES	REVETS	ROWTHS	WITCHY
EARFUL	HEREIN	OODLES	RICING	RUCKED	WITTED
EARING	HEREOF	OTTERS	RICKED	RUCKLE	WITTER
EASELS	HEREON	OUCHED	RIDENT	RUEING	ZADDIK
EASERS	HERETO	OUCHES	RIFLED	RUFFES	
EASING	HERMAE	OUTERS	RIFLER	RUFFLE	
EDDIES	HERMIT	OUTING	RIFLES	RUNDLE	

With back hook T

ACUTES	BASSET	BRUTES	CONSUL	DOUBLE	LANGUE
ADJOIN	BEIGES	BUSIES	CONTES	EASIES	LARGES
AERIES	BEIGNE	CALLAN	CORNET	GASHES	LAZIES
ALKANE	BELEAP	CHEVRE	COSIES	GRAVES	LONGES
ANIMIS	BEWRAP	CIRCLE	COUPLE	GURGLE	LOOSES
ANTIFA	BORSCH	CLOSES	COZIES	HOLIES	LUNIES
ATTAIN	BOSQUE	COMMIX	CRUDES	HOMIES	LUSHES
BABIES	BOSSES	COMPOS	CULVER	INANES	MANCHE
BASSES	BRAVES	CONGES	CURRAN	LAMBER	MANTLE

MEDIAN	QUARTE	RICHES	SEXTAN	SUBPAR	UGLIES
NAIVES	QUINTE	RIPPLE	SHARIA	TEMPLE	UPLEAP
NOBLES	RADIAN	ROOTLE	SINGLE	TENNIS	WACKES
PLEDGE	RASHES	RUBIES	SLEIGH	TENSES	WAVIES
POKIES	REALES	RUNDLE	SPARES	THOUGH	WHITES
POSIES	REPLAN	SABLES	SPAVIE	TIDIES	ZANIES
PREMIX	REWRAP	SEAWAN	STALES	TRIPLE	

With front hook U

NEATEN	PENDED	PLINKS	PRATED	PREACH	REDIAL
NITERS	PLIGHT	PRAISE	PRATES	PRISES	

With back hook U

MANITO	SANTIM	TURACO

With front hook V

ACUITY	AMPING	ENDERS	ETCHES	OUCHES
AGUISH	AUNTIE	ENDING	IDIOTS	ROOMED
AILING	AWARDS	ENDUES	IZARDS	
ALGOID	EGGING	ENTAIL	LOGGED	
ALINES	ELITES	ENTERS	LOGGER	
ALLEYS	ENATIC	ESTRAL	OUCHED	

With front hook W

ADDERS	ANIONS	EIGHTS	HEREAT	HOOPLA	INTERS
ADDING	ANTING	EIGHTY	HEREBY	HOPPED	ITCHED
ADDLED	ARMERS	ELDERS	HEREIN	HOPPER	ITCHES
ADDLES	ARMING	ENDING	HEREOF	HUMPED	IZARDS
AFTERS	ARRANT	ESTERS	HEREON	ICKERS	OORALI
AGGERS	ARTIER	ETHERS	HERETO	IGGING	OOZIER
AILING	ASHIER	HACKED	HICKER	IMPING	OOZILY
AIRING	ASHING	HACKER	HINGED	IMPISH	ORMERS
AIVERS	ASPISH	HALERS	HINGER	IMPLED	RACKED
ALKIES	ASSAIL	HALING	HINGES	INCHED	RAPPED
ALLEYS	ASTERS	HAMMED	HIPPED	INCHER	RAPPER
ALLIES	ATTEST	HANGED	HIPPER	INCHES	RASSLE
ALLOWS	AUGHTS	HAPPED	HISTED	INDIGO	RECKED
AMBLED	AXLIKE	HEELED	HITHER	INDOWS	RESTED
AMBLES	EARING	HEELER	HITTER	INKERS	RESTER
AMUSES	EASELS	HEEZED	HOLISM	INKING	RICKED
ANGLED	EBBING	HEEZES	HOOFED	INKLES	RIGHTS
ANGLER	EDGIER	HELMED	HOOPED	INNERS	RINGED
ANGLES	EDGING	HELPED	HOOPER	INNING	RINGER

With front hook X

EROSES	EROTIC

With back hook X

BATEAU	COTEAU	MILIEU	RESEAU	TRIPLE
BUREAU	GATEAU	MINIMA	SIMPLE	

With front hook Y

ARROWS	AWNING	CLEPED	EARNED	EARNER

With back hook Y

ALMOND	COTTON	GROUCH	MILDEW	RIBBON	SPLEEN
ANALOG	CRUISE	GROWTH	MOCKER	RIFLER	SPRAWL
ANARCH	CRUNCH	GUNNER	MODEST	ROBBER	SPRING
APOLOG	CURSOR	GUTTER	MORASS	ROCKER	SPRITZ
ARCHER	CUTLER	HACKER	MORTAR	RUBBER	SQUALL
ARMOUR	CYCLER	HEALTH	MOTHER	RUSSET	SQUASH
BATTER	DACOIT	HELLER	MUMMER	SALLOW	SQUEAK
BEGGAR	DAKOIT	HICCUP	MUTTON	SALMON	SQUINT
BIBBER	DAUBER	HOGGER	NAUGHT	SALTER	SQUIRM
BILLOW	DIDDLE	HONEST	NECTAR	SATRAP	SQUISH
BINDER	DITHER	HOSIER	NUGGET	SAVOUR	STARCH
BIOGEN	DODDER	IMAGER	NURSER	SCRAWL	STARTS
BLIGHT	DODGER	INDEED	ORANGE	SCREAK	STATUS
BLOTCH	DOGGER	ISOGON	ORATOR	SCRIMP	STENCH
BOBBER	DOUGHT	JAGGER	OROGEN	SCRUFF	STREAK
BOFFIN	DRAPER	JARGON	OVULAR	SEALER	STREAM
BRANCH	DROUTH	JASPER	PALMAR	SENSOR	STRING
BRAVER	DYNAST	JITTER	PARROT	SERVER	STRIPE
BREATH	EPARCH	JOBBER	PASTIL	SHADOW	SUCCOR
BREWER	EPONYM	JOINER	PAUNCH	SHIVER	SULFUR
BRIBER	EXARCH	JUDDER	PEDLAR	SHLEPP	SUMMER
BUGGER	FACTOR	KITSCH	PEDLER	SHLOCK	SURGER
BURSAR	FAGGOT	KLUDGE	PEPPER	SHLUMP	SWARTH
BUTLER	FERRET	KOLHOZ	PEWTER	SHMUCK	TALLOW
BUTTER	FIDGET	KOLKOZ	PHLEGM	SHOWER	TANNER
BUTTON	FISHER	KVETCH	PILLOW	SHRIEK	THATCH
CANNER	FLAUNT	LATHER	PIZAZZ	SHRILL	THIRST
CARROT	FLAVOR	LECHER	PLAGUE	SHRIMP	THRASH
CARVER	FLIGHT	LENGTH	POTTER	SHTICK	THREAD
CHINCH	FLOWER	LIQUID	POWDER	SIGNOR	THRIFT
CHINTZ	FORGER	LITTER	PREACH	SILVER	THROAT
CHOOSE	FROWST	LOLLOP	PROBIT	SKETCH	TIMBER
CHURCH	FULLER	LOTTER	PUCKER	SLAVER	TINDER
CINDER	FURROW	LOUNGE	PUFFER	SLOUCH	TINSEL
CIRCUS	GADGET	MAGGOT	QUAVER	SLOUGH	TISSUE
CITRUS	GARGET	MARROW	QUIVER	SMOOCH	TORQUE
CLIQUE	GEODES	MARTYR	RABBIT	SMOOTH	TOTTER
CLOVER	GINGER	MASTER	RACKET	SMUTCH	TRACER
CLUTCH	GLITCH	MATTER	RAGGED	SNATCH	TRICKS
COOKER	GOSSIP	MEADOW	RAISIN	SPICER	TRIPOD
COOPER	GRAVEL	MENSCH	RAUNCH	SPIDER	TURNER
COPPER	GROCER	MERCER	RECTOR	SPLASH	TURNIP

TWITCH	VAPOUR	WASTER	WEIGHT	WINTER
TYMPAN	VELVET	WEALTH	WIGGER	WREATH
UNHAND	VICTOR	WEASEL	WILLOW	YELLOW
UNREAD	WAGGER	WEEVIL	WINDOW	

With front hook Z

| ESTERS | IGGING | INCITE | OOGENY | OOLOGY |

With back hook Z

| PIZZAZ | SCHNOZ |

Chapter 5: Seven letter words with hooks

With front hook A

BASHING	ETHERIC	MITOSES	SPARKLE	VARICES
BEGGING	FEBRILE	MITOSIS	SPHERIC	VENGING
BETTERS	FLUTTER	MITOTIC	SPIRANT	VENTAIL
BETTING	GAMETES	MORALLY	SPIRING	VERSION
BETTORS	GENESES	MORTISE	STERNAL	VIATORS
BOUNDED	GENESIS	MOTIONS	STEROID	VOIDERS
BRACHIA	GENETIC	MOUNTED	STHENIA	VOIDING
BRIDGED	GINNERS	NEARING	STHENIC	VOUCHED
BRIDGES	GLIMMER	NODALLY	STONISH	VOUCHER
BUTTALS	GLITTER	PHONICS	STOUNDS	VOUCHES
BUTTERS	GNOSTIC	PHONIES	TECHNIC	WAITERS
BUTTING	GRAPHIC	PLASTIC	THEISMS	WAITING
CANTHUS	GREEING	PRACTIC	THEISTS	WAKENED
CAUDATE	KINETIC	PYRETIC	TONALLY	WAKENER
CAULINE	LIGHTED	ROUSERS	TREMBLE	WARDERS
CENTRIC	LOGICAL	ROUSING	TROPHIC	WARDING
CERATED	MASSING	RUGOLAS	TROPINE	WEATHER
CHROMIC	MAZEDLY	SCENDED	TROPINS	ZYGOSES
DEEMING	MENDERS	SCRIBED	TROPISM	
DYNAMIC	MENDING	SCRIBES	TWITTER	
ESTHETE	MERCERS	SEISMIC	TYPICAL	
ESTIVAL	MIDSHIP	SOCIALS	VAILING	

With back hook A

ANAPHOR	BRONCHI	DULCIAN	MONSTER	SCIATIC	TOURIST
ANGELIC	CHAMPAC	HEPATIC	PERFECT	STROBIL	UNGUENT
ANTEFIX	CHARISM	JAVELIN	PIGNOLI	SYNTAGM	
AUTOMAT	CISTERN	MARCHES	QUILLAI	TAMANDU	
BASILIC	DEMENTI	MELODIC	RANCHER	TAMBOUR	
BOTANIC	DIASTEM	MOLLUSC	SARMENT	THERIAC	

With front hook B

ADLANDS	ITCHIER	LATTERS	LOBBING	LOUSING
AILMENT	ITCHILY	LEACHED	LOCKAGE	LOWBALL
ANALITY	ITCHING	LEACHER	LOCKERS	LOWDOWN
ARISTAS	LACKING	LEACHES	LOCKING	LUBBERS
ARRACKS	LADDERS	LEARIER	LOGGERS	LUFFING
ARTISAN	LADINGS	LENDERS	LOGGIER	LUNGERS
ASSISTS	LAGGERS	LENDING	LOGGING	LUNGING
EAGLING	LAGGING	LIGHTED	LOOMING	LUNTING
EARINGS	LAMMING	LIGHTER	LOOPERS	LUSHING
EATABLE	LANCHED	LINKERS	LOOPIER	LUSTERS
EATINGS	LANCHES	LINKING	LOOPING	OARFISH
EERIEST	LANKEST	LIPPING	LOTTERS	OATLIKE
ENDWAYS	LASTERS	LISTERS	LOTTING	OINKING
ENDWISE	LASTING	LITHELY	LOUSIER	OLDNESS
ESPOUSE	LATHERS	LITHEST	LOUSILY	OOZIEST

ORATING	RAGGING	RATTIER	RIGHTLY	ROILING
ORDERED	RAIDERS	RATTISH	RIMLESS	ROLLIES
ORDERER	RAIDING	RATTLED	RIMMERS	ROMANCE
ORDURES	RAILING	RATTLES	RIMMING	ROOKIES
OTHERED	RAINIER	REACHED	RINGERS	ROOKING
OWLLIKE	RAINILY	REACHER	RINGING	ROOMIER
RABBLED	RAINING	REACHES	RISKING	ROOMING
RABBLER	RAISING	READING	ROACHED	RUSHERS
RABBLES	RAMBLED	REAMING	ROACHES	RUSHIER
RACHETS	RAMBLES	REEDING	ROADWAY	RUSHING
RACHIAL	RANCHED	REGMATA	ROASTED	UTTERED
RACINGS	RANCHES	RICKING	ROCKETS	
RACKETS	RANDIES	RIDGING	ROGUERY	
RADDING	RASHEST	RIGHTER	ROGUISH	

With front hook C

ABLINGS	HEDARIM	LAGGING	LOPPING	RANKEST
AMASSES	HERRIES	LAMBERS	LOSABLE	RANKING
ANNULAR	HEWABLE	LAMMING	LOSINGS	RANKISH
APSIDAL	HICKORY	LAMPERS	LOTTING	RANKLED
AROUSAL	HILDING	LAMPING	LOURING	RANKLES
AROUSED	HILLERS	LANKIER	LOUTING	RAPPERS
AROUSER	HILLIER	LAPPERS	LUBBERS	RAPPING
AROUSES	HILLING	LAPPING	LUCKING	RASHERS
ARRACKS	HINKIER	LASHERS	LUMBERS	RATCHES
ASHLESS	HIPPIER	LASHING	LUMPERS	RAVENED
ENSURED	HIPPIES	LATTERS	LUMPIER	RAVENER
ENSURER	HIPPING	LAWLESS	LUMPING	RAVINGS
ENSURES	HITTERS	LAWLIKE	LUMPISH	REAMERS
ENTERED	HOCKING	LEANERS	LUNKERS	REAMING
HADARIM	HOKIEST	LEANEST	LUSTERS	REELING
HALLAHS	HOPPERS	LEANING	OCREATE	REMAINS
HALLOTH	HOPPIER	LEAVERS	OFFERED	REMATED
HAMPERS	HOPPING	LEAVING	OLDNESS	REMATES
HANDLER	HORDING	LICKERS	ORACLES	RESTING
HANGERS	HOUSERS	LICKING	OSMOSES	RIBBERS
HANGING	HOUSING	LIMBERS	OUCHING	RIBBING
HANTING	HUCKLES	LIMBING	OVARIES	RICKETS
HAPPING	HUFFIER	LINGERS	OVERAGE	RICKING
HARKING	HUFFING	LINGIER	OVERALL	RIMMERS
HARMERS	HUGGERS	LINKERS	OVERING	RIMPLED
HARMING	HUGGING	LINKING	OVERLET	RIMPLES
HARRIER	HUMMING	LIPPERS	OVERTLY	RINGERS
HASTENS	HUMPING	LIPPING	RACKERS	RINGING
HATTERS	HUNKIER	LITORAL	RACKING	RIPPLED
HATTING	HUNTERS	LITTERS	RAFTERS	RIPPLER
HAUNTED	HUPPAHS	LOBBERS	RAFTING	RIPPLES
HAUNTER	HUTZPAH	LOCKERS	RAMMERS	RITTERS
HAZANIM	HUTZPAS	LOCKING	RAMMING	ROCHETS
HAZZANS	INCHING	LOGGERS	RAMPING	ROCKERY
HEATERS	LACKERS	LOGGIER	RANCHED	ROCKETS
HEATING	LACKING	LOGGING	RANCHES	ROCKING

ROOKERY	ROUPIER	RUMBLES	RUSHERS	UMBERED
ROOKING	ROUPILY	RUMMIER	RUSHING	UNIFORM
ROQUETS	ROWDIES	RUMMIES	RUSTIER	UPPINGS
ROTCHES	RUDDIER	RUMPLED	RUSTILY	
ROUCHES	RUMBLED	RUMPLES	RUSTING	

With back hook C

AMMONIA	BULIMIA	DACTYLI	SYLLABI	TYMPANI
AMNESIA	CHIASMI	ELENCHI	THALAMI	
APHASIA	CHORAGI	EPIGONI	TSUNAMI	

With front hook D

ADDLING	ELUSION	ICKIEST	RAFTING	RIPPERS
ALLYING	ELUSIVE	INKIEST	RAGGING	RIPPING
ANGERED	ELUSORY	ITCHING	RAGGLES	ROLLING
ANGLERS	EMERGED	JELLABA	RAINING	ROVINGS
ANGLING	EMERGES	JIBBAHS	RAMMING	RUBBERS
ASHIEST	EMITTED	OLOROSO	RATTING	RUBBING
AWNINGS	EMOTING	ONENESS	READING	RUGGING
EDUCING	EMOTION	OUCHING	REAMERS	RUMBLED
EJECTED	ENOUNCE	RABBETS	REAMING	RUMBLES
ELATING	EPILATE	RABBLED	RIBBING	RUMMERS
ELATION	EVOLVED	RABBLES	RIBLETS	WELLING
ELUDERS	EVOLVES	RAFFISH	RIFTING	WINDLED
ELUDING	HURRIES	RAFTERS	RILLING	WINDLES

With back hook D

ABRIDGE	ANODIZE	AZOTISE	BESIEGE	CAPSULE
ABSCISE	ANTIQUE	AZOTIZE	BESLIME	CAPTURE
ABSOLVE	APPEASE	BACCATE	BESMILE	CAPUCHE
ACCRETE	APPRISE	BACKHOE	BESMOKE	CAROUSE
ACERATE	APPRIZE	BAGPIPE	BICYCLE	CASCADE
ACETATE	APPROVE	BALANCE	BIVALVE	CASEATE
ACHIEVE	ARABIZE	BANDAGE	BRABBLE	CAUDATE
ACQUIRE	ARCHIVE	BAPTISE	BRAILLE	CAYENNE
ACTUATE	ARCUATE	BAPTIZE	BRAMBLE	CENSURE
ACYLATE	ARRANGE	BARRAGE	BRATTLE	CHALICE
ADJUDGE	ARTICLE	BECRIME	BREATHE	CHARQUI
ADULATE	ASCRIBE	BECURSE	BRIGADE	CHELATE
ADVANCE	ASPERSE	BEDRAPE	BRINDLE	CHICANE
AGATIZE	ASSUAGE	BEDUNCE	BRISTLE	CHORTLE
AGENIZE	ASSWAGE	BEEHIVE	BRITTLE	CHUCKLE
AGGRADE	ATOMISE	BEELINE	BROCADE	CILIATE
AGITATE	ATOMIZE	BEGRIME	BROMATE	CITRATE
AGONISE	ATTACHE	BEGUILE	BROMIZE	CLEANSE
AGONIZE	ATTRITE	BEHOOVE	CABBAGE	CLOSURE
ANALYSE	AUDIBLE	BELIEVE	CADENCE	CLOTURE
ANALYZE	AUREOLE	BEREAVE	CALCINE	COCKADE
ANIMATE	AURICLE	BERHYME	CALIBRE	COCKEYE
ANODISE	AVERAGE	BESHAME	CAPSIZE	COGNISE

108

COGNIZE	CUNEATE	DISSAVE	ESPOUSE	GRADATE
COLLAGE	CURETTE	DISYOKE	ESQUIRE	GRAPPLE
COLLATE	CUSPATE	DIVERGE	EXAMINE	GRECIZE
COLLIDE	CYANIDE	DIVORCE	EXAMPLE	GRIDDLE
COLLUDE	CYCLIZE	DIVULGE	EXCLUDE	GRIMACE
COLOGNE	DEALATE	DIVULSE	EXCRETE	GRIZZLE
COMBINE	DEBRIDE	DOGGONE	EXECUTE	GRUMBLE
COMMOVE	DECEASE	DRABBLE	EXPENSE	GRUNTLE
COMMUNE	DECEIVE	DRAGGLE	EXPIATE	GUMSHOE
COMMUTE	DECLARE	DRIBBLE	EXPLODE	GUTTATE
COMPARE	DECLINE	DRIZZLE	EXPLORE	HACHURE
COMPERE	DECUPLE	DRUMBLE	EXPULSE	HALTERE
COMPETE	DECURVE	DUALISE	EXPUNGE	HAMBONE
COMPILE	DEFENCE	DUALIZE	EXTRUDE	HERBAGE
COMPOSE	DEFENSE	DWINDLE	FALCATE	HEROIZE
COMPUTE	DEFLATE	EBONISE	FATIGUE	HYDRATE
CONCAVE	DEFORCE	EBONIZE	FEATURE	IDOLISE
CONCEDE	DEGLAZE	ECLIPSE	FELLATE	IDOLIZE
CONDOLE	DEGRADE	EDUCATE	FENAGLE	IMAGINE
CONDONE	DEHISCE	EFFULGE	FERRULE	IMBLAZE
CONDUCE	DELEAVE	EGOTIZE	FILIATE	IMBRUTE
CONFIDE	DELOUSE	ELEGISE	FINAGLE	IMITATE
CONFINE	DEMERGE	ELEGIZE	FINANCE	IMMERGE
CONFUSE	DENTATE	ELEVATE	FINESSE	IMMERSE
CONFUTE	DEPLANE	EMANATE	FISSURE	IMPASTE
CONJURE	DEPLETE	EMBLAZE	FLAMBEE	IMPINGE
CONNIVE	DEPLORE	EMBRACE	FLOUNCE	IMPLODE
CONNOTE	DEPLUME	EMBRUTE	FOLIAGE	IMPLORE
CONSOLE	DEPRAVE	EMPLACE	FOLIATE	IMPROVE
CONSUME	DEPRIVE	EMPLANE	FORBODE	IMPULSE
CONTUSE	DERANGE	EMPLOYE	FORTUNE	INCENSE
CONVENE	DESCALE	EMULATE	FOVEATE	INCLINE
CONVOKE	DESERVE	ENCHASE	FRAZZLE	INCLOSE
COPPICE	DESPISE	ENCLAVE	FRECKLE	INCLUDE
CORNICE	DESPITE	ENCLOSE	FRIBBLE	INCURVE
CORNUTE	DESTINE	ENDORSE	FRIZZLE	INDORSE
CORRADE	DETERGE	ENFLAME	FROGEYE	INDULGE
CORRODE	DETRUDE	ENFORCE	FROUNCE	INFLAME
COSTUME	DEVALUE	ENFRAME	FULMINE	INFLATE
COTTAGE	DEVIATE	ENGORGE	FURCATE	INNERVE
COWHIDE	DEVOICE	ENGRAVE	FURNACE	INQUIRE
CRACKLE	DEVOLVE	ENHANCE	GABELLE	INSNARE
CRANKLE	DIALYSE	ENLARGE	GALEATE	INSPIRE
CREMATE	DIALYZE	ENNOBLE	GALOSHE	INSTATE
CRENATE	DICTATE	ENOUNCE	GAROTTE	INTERNE
CREVICE	DIFFUSE	ENPLANE	GARROTE	INTITLE
CRIMPLE	DISABLE	ENQUIRE	GAVOTTE	INTRUDE
CRINKLE	DISCASE	ENSLAVE	GAZETTE	INTWINE
CRIPPLE	DISEASE	ENSNARE	GEMMATE	INVERSE
CRUMBLE	DISLIKE	ENTHUSE	GESTATE	INVOICE
CRUMPLE	DISPOSE	ENTITLE	GESTURE	INVOLVE
CRUSADE	DISPUTE	ENTWINE	GLIMPSE	INWEAVE
CUITTLE	DISRATE	EPILATE	GLOBATE	IRONISE
CULTURE	DISROBE	EROTIZE	GRABBLE	IRONIZE

ISOLATE	MORTICE	PACKAGE	PRELUDE	REGLAZE
ITEMISE	MORTISE	PALMATE	PREMISE	REGORGE
ITEMIZE	MURIATE	PALPATE	PREPARE	REGRADE
ITERATE	NARRATE	PANCAKE	PREPAVE	REGRATE
JAWBONE	NECROSE	PANICLE	PREPOSE	REHINGE
KEYNOTE	NICTATE	PANTILE	PRESAGE	REHOUSE
KNUCKLE	NITRATE	PARBAKE	PRESIDE	REIMAGE
KYANISE	NITRIDE	PASSAGE	PRESUME	REISSUE
KYANIZE	NURTURE	PASTURE	PRETAPE	REJOICE
LABIATE	OBELISE	PATINAE	PRETYPE	REJUDGE
LACTATE	OBELIZE	PECTIZE	PREVISE	RELAPSE
LAICISE	OBLIQUE	PEDICLE	PREWIRE	RELEASE
LAICIZE	OBSCURE	PENANCE	PRICKLE	RELIEVE
LATTICE	OBSERVE	PENNATE	PROBATE	REMERGE
LECTURE	OBTRUDE	PEPTIZE	PROCURE	RENEGUE
LEISURE	OBVIATE	PERDURE	PRODUCE	REPLACE
LIBRATE	OCCLUDE	PERFUME	PROFANE	REPLATE
LICENCE	OCTUPLE	PERFUSE	PROFILE	REPRICE
LICENSE	ODORIZE	PERJURE	PROMISE	REPRISE
LINEATE	OPERATE	PERMUTE	PROMOTE	REPROBE
LIONISE	OUTBAKE	PERVADE	PRONATE	REPROVE
LIONIZE	OUTCROW	PETIOLE	PROPINE	REPULSE
LIQUATE	OUTDARE	PHILTRE	PROPONE	REQUIRE
MACHINE	OUTDATE	PHONATE	PROPOSE	REQUITE
MANACLE	OUTFACE	PICKAXE	PRORATE	RERAISE
MANDATE	OUTFIRE	PICRATE	PROVIDE	REROUTE
MASSAGE	OUTGAZE	PICTURE	PROVOKE	RESCALE
MEASURE	OUTHEAR	PILEATE	PULSATE	RESCORE
MEDIATE	OUTLINE	PILLAGE	PURPOSE	RESEIZE
MESSAGE	OUTLIVE	PINNATE	PUSTULE	RESERVE
MIDSIZE	OUTLOVE	PIPETTE	QUIBBLE	RESHAPE
MIDWIFE	OUTMODE	PISTOLE	RADIATE	RESHAVE
MIGRATE	OUTMOVE	PLACATE	RAILCAR	RESHINE
MISCITE	OUTPACE	PLICATE	RAMPAGE	RESLATE
MISCODE	OUTRACE	PLUMAGE	RAPTURE	RESOLVE
MISDATE	OUTRAGE	POETISE	RAWHIDE	RESPACE
MISFILE	OUTRATE	POETIZE	REALISE	RESPADE
MISFIRE	OUTRAVE	POLEAXE	REALIZE	RESPIRE
MISGAGE	OUTSIZE	POLLUTE	REARGUE	RESPITE
MISHEAR	OUTVOTE	PORTAGE	REAWAKE	RESTAGE
MISLIKE	OUTWILE	POSTURE	RECEIVE	RESTATE
MISLIVE	OVERAGE	POTHOLE	RECLINE	RESTOKE
MISMATE	OVERAWE	PRATTLE	RECOUPE	RESTORE
MISMOVE	OVERDYE	PREBAKE	RECRATE	RESTYLE
MISNAME	OVERSEE	PRECEDE	RECURVE	RESURGE
MISPAGE	OVERUSE	PRECISE	RECYCLE	RETASTE
MISRATE	OVULATE	PRECODE	REDLINE	RETINUE
MISRULE	OXALATE	PRECURE	REEVOKE	RETITLE
MISTIME	OXIDATE	PREDATE	REFENCE	RETRACE
MISTUNE	OXIDISE	PREFACE	REFEREE	REUNITE
MISTYPE	OXIDIZE	PREFADE	REFLATE	REVALUE
MISYOKE	OZONATE	PREFILE	REFORGE	REVENGE
MONOCLE	OZONISE	PREFIRE	REFRAME	REVENUE
MONTAGE	OZONIZE	PREGAME	REGAUGE	REVERSE

REVOICE	SINUATE	SUBLIME	TRINDLE	UPGRADE
REVOLVE	SITUATE	SUBSIDE	TROUBLE	UPHEAVE
REWEAVE	SKIFFLE	SUBSUME	TROUNCE	UPRAISE
RIPOSTE	SKYDIVE	SUBVENE	TRUCKLE	UPROUSE
ROMANCE	SMOOTHE	SUFFICE	TRUFFLE	UPSCALE
ROSETTE	SMUGGLE	SUFFUSE	TRUNDLE	UPSTAGE
RUINATE	SNAFFLE	SUICIDE	TRUSTEE	UPSTARE
RUMMAGE	SNARFLE	SULCATE	TUMESCE	UPSURGE
RUPTURE	SNIFFLE	SULFATE	TWADDLE	URINATE
SALVAGE	SNIGGLE	SUMMATE	TWANGLE	UTILISE
SARDINE	SNOOZLE	SUPPOSE	TWATTLE	UTILIZE
SATIATE	SNUFFLE	SURBASE	TWEEDLE	VALANCE
SCABBLE	SNUGGLE	SURFACE	TWIDDLE	VALUATE
SCEPTRE	SOLVATE	SURMISE	TWINKLE	VAMOOSE
SCOURGE	SOUFFLE	SURNAME	ULULATE	VANDYKE
SCRIEVE	SPACKLE	SURVIVE	UNAWAKE	VARIATE
SCROUGE	SPANGLE	SUSPIRE	UNBRACE	VENTURE
SCRUPLE	SPARKLE	SWADDLE	UNBRAKE	VERDURE
SCUFFLE	SPECKLE	SWINDLE	UNCHOKE	VESTURE
SCUMBLE	SPICATE	SWINGLE	UNCLOSE	VIBRATE
SCUTTLE	SPINDLE	SWIZZLE	UNCRATE	VIOLATE
SECLUDE	SPLODGE	SYNAPSE	UNDERGO	VITIATE
SECONDE	SPLURGE	SYRINGE	UNDRAPE	WALLEYE
SECRETE	SPRINGE	TALLAGE	UNFENCE	WARGAME
SELVAGE	SQUEEZE	TAMARIN	UNGLOVE	WARSTLE
SENESCE	STARTLE	TEENAGE	UNHINGE	WELCOME
SENSATE	STATURE	TERRACE	UNHORSE	WHEEDLE
SERIATE	STEEPLE	TEXTURE	UNHOUSE	WHEEPLE
SERRATE	STICKLE	TITRATE	UNITIZE	WHIFFLE
SERVICE	STIPPLE	TONSURE	UNLOOSE	WHISTLE
SHACKLE	STIPULE	TORTURE	UNMITRE	WHITTLE
SHAMBLE	STOPPLE	TRACHLE	UNNERVE	WOODBIN
SHEATHE	STRIATE	TRADUCE	UNQUOTE	WRANGLE
SHINGLE	STUBBLE	TRAIPSE	UNREEVE	WRASSLE
SHMOOZE	STUMBLE	TRAMPLE	UNSTATE	WRASTLE
SHRIEVE	STYLISE	TREADLE	UNTWINE	WREATHE
SHUFFLE	STYLIZE	TREDDLE	UNVOICE	WRESTLE
SHUTTLE	SUBDUCE	TREMBLE	UPCURVE	WRIGGLE
SILENCE	SUBLATE	TRICKLE	UPCYCLE	WRINKLE

With front hook E

CAUDATE	MENDERS	QUALITY	SPECIAL	UPHROES
CLOSING	MENDING	QUIPPED	SPOUSAL	VALUATE
COTYPES	MERGING	QUIPPER	SPOUSED	VENTERS
DENTATE	MIGRANT	RADIATE	SPOUSES	VENTING
IRENICS	MIGRATE	RASURES	SQUIRED	VERSION
LAPSING	MISSION	RECTORS	SQUIRES	VICTORS
LECTION	MISSIVE	SCALADE	STATING	VOCABLE
LECTORS	MOTIONS	SCALLOP	STOPPED	VOLUTES
LEGISTS	NATIONS	SCAPING	STOVERS	
LEVATOR	NERVATE	SCARPED	STRANGE	
MAILING	PHORATE	SERINES	STRAYED	

With back hook E

ABSINTH	COCHLEA	FRACTUR	MARCHES	PLIMSOL	STAMPED
ACALEPH	COLICIN	FUCHSIN	MARQUIS	POTLACH	STEARIN
ACANTHA	COMPLIN	FURCULA	MATELOT	POULARD	STROBIL
ACICULA	COURANT	GELATIN	MAXILLA	PRACTIC	SUCCUBA
ACQUIRE	CRANNOG	GINGIVA	MEDULLA	PRECAVA	SULPHID
ACTINIA	CREATIN	GIRASOL	MEGAPOD	PREMIER	SUNBATH
AGLYCON	CROCEIN	GLIADIN	MESQUIT	PREPUPA	SYMBIOT
ALEURON	CYPSELA	GRAMARY	METAMER	PROLONG	SYNONYM
ALKALIN	CYSTEIN	GRANDAM	MEZQUIT	PROMISE	TABORIN
ALKALIS	DAUPHIN	GRAPLIN	MICELLA	PROTEAS	TACHISM
AMPHORA	DEBOUCH	GRATINE	MINUTIA	PROTEGE	TACHIST
AMPULLA	DECIDUA	GRAVIDA	MISWRIT	PROTEID	TESSERA
ANCILLA	DECLASS	HALIDOM	MONILIA	PTERYLA	THERMIT
ANETHOL	DEVELOP	HEGUMEN	MONOPOD	PTOMAIN	THIAMIN
ANTENNA	DEXTRIN	HEMATIN	MORPHIN	QUADRAT	THIAZIN
ANTIGEN	DIVORCE	HETAERA	MUSICAL	REHEARS	THIAZOL
ARMILLA	DOMICIL	HOMININ	NARCEIN	RELEASE	THIONIN
ATROPIN	DOVECOT	HUSHABY	NARWHAL	RHABDOM	TOLIDIN
AUREOLA	DRACHMA	INDAMIN	NEGLIGE	ROCKABY	TRACHEA
AUTOMAT	DUVETYN	INDIGEN	NEURULA	SALICIN	TRAVOIS
AVELLAN	ECDYSON	INDORSE	NICOTIN	SALVAGE	TRIAZIN
BABESIA	ECHIDNA	INDULIN	NOCTURN	SAPHENA	TRICORN
BACKBIT	EMERITA	INERTIA	OOTHECA	SAPONIN	TRIOXID
BARYTON	EMPLOYE	INFAUNA	OUTCAST	SARCINA	TRIPTAN
BENEFIC	ENDORSE	INHUMAN	OUTCHID	SAUTOIR	URETHAN
BESTRID	ENVELOP	INTERNE	OUTRANG	SCAPULA	URETHRA
BOMBARD	ESCALOP	ISOCHOR	OUTWRIT	SCHMOOS	VACCINE
BROADAX	EULOGIA	JACINTH	OXYPHIL	SCOPULA	VALVULA
CABEZON	EXAMINE	KERMESS	PAPILLA	SCURRIL	VERRUCA
CAESURA	EXHEDRA	LAMBAST	PARVENU	SECONDE	VITAMIN
CAFFEIN	FILARIA	LAMELLA	PATELLA	SEQUELA	WANNABE
CANNULA	FIMBRIA	LANOLIN	PENSION	SILICON	WOODBIN
CARABIN	FINALIS	LARGESS	PEROXID	SILIQUA	XANTHIN
CARACOL	FISTULA	LICENCE	PERSONA	SMARAGD	XYLIDIN
CAVEOLA	FLUORID	LICENSE	PFENNIG	SOLANIN	ZOOGLEA
CHALAZA	FLUORIN	LIGROIN	PICOLIN	SPICULA	ZYMOGEN
CHLORID	FOLKMOT	LINGULA	PINNULA	SPINULA	
CHLORIN	FORMULA	LOCUSTA	PISCINA	SPIRULA	
CINEAST	FOVEOLA	MAMILLA	PLANULA	SQUILLA	

With front hook F

ACTIONS	ARROWED	LABELLA	LASHERS	LEECHES
AIRIEST	EARLESS	LACKING	LASHING	LEERING
AIRINGS	EASTERS	LAGGERS	LATTENS	LENSING
AIRWAYS	EASTING	LAGGING	LATTERS	LETCHED
ALLOWED	ESTIVAL	LAKIEST	LAWLESS	LETCHES
ALTERED	ETCHERS	LAMMING	LECTION	LICKERS
ALTERER	ETCHING	LAPPERS	LEDGIER	LICKING
ARMINGS	IRELESS	LAPPING	LEECHED	LIGHTED

LINGERS
LINTIER
LINTING
LIPPERS
LIPPIER
LIPPING
LITTERS
LOCKING
LOGGERS
LOGGING
LOPPERS

LOPPIER
LOPPING
LOURING
LOUTING
LOWERED
LUBBERS
LUFFING
LUMPING
LUNKERS
LUSHEST
LUSHING

LUSTERS
LUTINGS
LUTISTS
OREBODY
OXTAILS
RACKING
RAGGING
RANKERS
RANKEST
RANKING
RAPPING

RAZZLES
REEDMAN
REEDMEN
RETTING
RIGGING
RIGHTED
RIGIDLY
RILLING
RINGING
RISKERS
RISKIER

RISKILY
RISKING
RITTERS
ROCKING
RUGGING
UNCTION
UNHOUSE
USELESS
UTILITY

With front hook G

ALLIUMS
ALLYING
AMBLERS
AMBLING
ANGLING
ARGLING
ASKINGS
EARINGS
EARLESS
ELATING
ELATION
ENTRIES
ESTATED
ESTATES
HARRIES
HOSTING
INNINGS
IZZARDS
LABELLA
LAIRIER
LAIRING
LAMMING

LANCERS
LANCING
LANDERS
LASSIES
LAZIEST
LEANERS
LEANING
LIMMERS
LINTIER
LINTING
LISTENS
LISTERS
LITTERS
LITTERY
LOAMING
LOBATED
LOBULAR
LOBULES
LOOMING
LOOPIER
LOPPIER
LOPPING

LOUTING
LOWERED
LUGGING
LUMPIER
LUMPILY
LUNCHED
LUNCHES
NATTIER
OATIEST
OATLIKE
OFFERED
ONENESS
RABBLED
RABBLER
RABBLES
RAFTERS
RAFTING
RAINIER
RAINING
RANGERS
RANTERS
RANTING

RANULAR
RASPERS
RASPING
RATINGS
RAVELED
RAVELLY
REEDIER
REEDILY
RIDDERS
RIDDING
RIDDLED
RIDDLES
RIEVERS
RIFTING
RILLING
RIMIEST
RINDING
RINNING
RIPPERS
RIPPING
RITTERS
ROOMERS

ROOMING
ROUCHES
ROUNDED
ROUNDER
ROUPING
ROUSERS
ROUSING
ROUTERS
ROUTING
ROWABLE
RUBBERS
RUBBING
RUFFING
RUMBLED
RUMBLER
RUMBLES
RUMMEST
UNLOCKS
UNSHIPS
UNSIGHT
UTTERED

With back hook G

ASPIRIN
CHITLIN
CREATIN

FINIKIN
GELATIN
MAHJONG

MORPHIN
RAVELIN
RELAXIN

RESILIN
SCULPIN
SPONGIN

TABORIN
UNDERDO

With front hook H

AGGADAH
AGGADAS
AGGADIC
AGGADOT
AIRBALL
AIRIEST
AIRLESS

AIRLIKE
AIRLINE
AIRLOCK
ALATION
ALLOWED
ALTERED
AMBONES

ANGRIER
APLITES
ARBORED
ARBOURS
ARMLESS
ARROWED
ARUSPEX

AUTEURS
EARINGS
EATABLE
EATINGS
EDGIEST
EIGHTHS
EXAMINE

EXARCHY
INKIEST
ITCHING
OROLOGY
OSTLERS
OVERFLY
OVERING

With back hook H

AGGADOT	HAFTARA	KABBALA	MESHUGA	SHAMMAS
BEGORRA	HAGGADA	KASHRUT	MEZUZOT	TZITZIT
CABBALA	HALAKHA	MADRASA	NARGILE	VERANDA
CHALLOT	HOSANNA	MASTABA	SAVANNA	YESHIVA
CHUTZPA	HYDRANT	MEGILLA	SHAHADA	

With front hook I

CONICAL	SLANDER	SOLATED	SOLATES

With back hook I

CALAMAR	COTHURN	MACARON	QUADRAT	TROCHIL
CONCEPT	DRACHMA	MARCHES	SIGNIOR	ZECCHIN
CONCERT	DUUMVIR	PARCHES	STROBIL	
CORNETT	HETAIRA	PENSION	TANDOOR	

With front hook J

ANGLERS	APERIES	OUSTERS	OWLIEST	UNCTION
ANGLING	OSTLERS	OUSTING	UDDERED	

With front hook K

ALEWIFE	LATCHES	NICKERS	NUBBIER
ETAMINE	LISTERS	NIGHTLY	NURLING
ICKIEST	NAPPERS	NOBBIER	RIMMERS
INKIEST	NAPPING	NOCKING	VETCHES

With back hook K

ALMANAC	FORERAN	POLITIC	SHOEPAC
BALDRIC	OVERRAN	SHELLAC	TAMARIS

With front hook L

ABILITY	AWFULLY	EGGIEST	IONISED	ITERATE
ACERATE	AZURITE	ENDINGS	IONISER	OBELIAS
AIRIEST	EARNERS	EPIDOTE	IONISES	OMENTUM
ANGUISH	EARNING	ETCHING	IONIZED	ONENESS
ASHLESS	EDGIEST	IGNEOUS	IONIZER	OWLIEST
AUREATE	EERIEST	IGNITES	IONIZES	UMBERED

With back hook L

ABOMASA	ANTENNA	BRECCIA	CHALAZA	DECIDUA
ACROMIA	AQUARIA	BRIMFUL	CHIASMA	DILUVIA
AECIDIA	ARCHAEA	CAESURA	CHRISMA	DIPTERA
ALLODIA	BASIDIA	CANDIDA	COMITIA	DUODENA
ALLUVIA	BIENNIA	CAROUSE	CONIDIA	DYSPNEA
AMPHORA	BRACHIA	CEREBRA	CORPORA	ENTHRAL

ENTOZOA	HYPOGEA	METHOXY	PRECAVA	STRIATA
EROTICA	ILLUVIA	MINUTIA	PREPUPA	SULFURY
EXCRETA	IMPERIA	MYCELIA	PROSOMA	SYNOVIA
EXORDIA	INDUSIA	NOUMENA	PUDENDA	TEGMINA
FILARIA	INERTIA	OOGONIA	PUPARIA	TESSERA
FIMBRIA	INFAUNA	OOTHECA	PYGIDIA	TRACHEA
GALANGA	INTHRAL	PATAGIA	PYREXIA	TYMPANA
GANGLIA	LIXIVIA	PERIDIA	RESIDUA	URETHRA
GERMINA	LOCUSTA	PERINEA	SKILFUL	VACCINA
GINGIVA	MALARIA	PERSONA	SPECTRA	VIATICA
GONIDIA	MANDRIL	PISCINA	SPLENIA	VISCERA
HYDROXY	MARSHAL	PLIMSOL	STAMINA	ZOOGLEA
HYMENIA	METAZOA	PODAGRA	STOMATA	

With front hook M

ACERATE	ARCHERS	EAGERLY	ETHOXYL	ORALITY
ADWOMAN	ARCHING	EMETICS	ETHYLIC	ORATORY
ADWOMEN	ARGENTS	ENDINGS	IFFIEST	ORRISES
AGNATES	ARROWED	ENOLOGY	ISOGAMY	OTHERED
ALIGNED	ASKINGS	ERISTIC	OATLIKE	OUCHING
ALIGNER	AXILLAE	ETHANAL	OMENTUM	UTTERED
ANGLERS	AXILLAS	ETHANES	ORALISM	UTTERER
ANGLING	EAGERER	ETHANOL	ORALIST	

With back hook M

CLASSIS	FINALIS	KATSINA	TELECOM

With front hook N

APERIES	ATRIUMS	EOLITHS	OVATION
ARROWED	EARLIER	IFFIEST	UMBERED

With back hook N

ACTINIA	DILUVIA	LEATHER	OUTGNAW	RESHAVE
ALFAQUI	DIPTERA	MAGNETO	OUTGROW	RESPOKE
APHELIA	ECTOZOA	MALARIA	OVERSEE	ROSARIA
AQUARIA	ELECTRO	METAZOA	OVERSEW	SMOOTHE
ARCADIA	ENTOZOA	MISDRAW	PANACEA	SOUTHER
ARCHAEA	FEDAYEE	MISGIVE	PARTAKE	THROMBI
ASCIDIA	FILARIA	MISGROW	PELORIA	UNBROKE
BESPOKE	FLYBLOW	MISKNOW	PRESHOW	UNFROZE
BESTREW	FORESEE	MISTAKE	QUARTER	UNLOOSE
BESTROW	FORGIVE	MYCELIA	REAWAKE	UNSPOKE
BOHEMIA	FORSAKE	NORTHER	REAWOKE	UPTHROW
CODRIVE	GALLICA	OUTDRAW	RECHOSE	VITELLI
COLLAGE	HACKSAW	OUTFLOW	REDRIVE	WHIPSAW
CONIDIA	HYPOGEA	OUTGIVE	REFROZE	WREATHE

With front hook O

CARINAS	ESTRINS	MICRONS	OLOGIST	VARIOLE
CHERISH	ESTRIOL	MIKRONS	PINIONS	VERBIDS
DONATES	ESTRONE	MISSION	POSSUMS	VERSETS
ECOLOGY	ESTROUS	MISSIVE	RANGIER	ZONATED
EDEMATA	ESTRUAL	NANISMS	RATIONS	
ENOLOGY	ESTRUMS	OLOGIES	STOMATE	

With back hook O

ARMIGER	CORNETT	GENIPAP	POLITIC
CLASSIC	COURANT	INTAGLI	RANCHER
COMMAND	EXPRESS	LEGGIER	SOMBRER
CONCERT	FLAMING	PERFECT	ZECCHIN

With front hook P

ACTIONS	LASHERS	LUMPISH	REBOOKS	REFIXES
ADDLING	LASHING	LUNGERS	REBOUND	REFOCUS
AIRINGS	LASTERS	LUNGING	REBUILD	REFORMS
AIRWISE	LATINAS	LUNKERS	REBUILT	REFROZE
ALIMONY	LATTERS	LUSHEST	RECASTS	REFUNDS
ALLIUMS	LAYOFFS	LYINGLY	RECEDED	REGNANT
ALTERED	LEACHED	ORTOLAN	RECEDES	REHEATS
ALTERER	LEACHES	OSTMARK	RECEPTS	REJUDGE
ANELING	LEADERS	OTHERED	RECHECK	RELATES
ANTHERS	LEADING	OUCHING	RECHOSE	RELIVES
ARABLES	LEASERS	RAISERS	RECIPES	RELOADS
ARCHING	LEASING	RAISING	RECITED	REMAKES
ARTICLE	LEATHER	RANGING	RECLEAN	REMISED
ARTIEST	LEDGERS	RANKING	RECODED	REMISES
ARTISAN	LESSORS	RANKISH	RECODES	REMIXED
EARLIER	LIGHTED	RATTLED	RECOOKS	REMIXES
ECTASES	LIGHTER	RATTLER	REDATED	REMOLDS
ENCHANT	LINKERS	RATTLES	REDATES	REMORSE
ENOLOGY	LINKING	REACHED	REDRAFT	RENAMES
EONISMS	LOPPING	REACHER	REDRIED	REORDER
HARMERS	LOTTERS	REACHES	REDRIES	REPACKS
HARMING	LOTTING	REACTED	REDRILL	REPAVED
HONEYED	LOWBOYS	READAPT	REEDITS	REPAVES
ICKIEST	LOWLAND	READMIT	REELECT	REPLACE
IMPINGS	LUCKIER	READOPT	REENACT	REPLANS
INCHERS	LUCKILY	REALLOT	REERECT	REPLANT
INCHING	LUCKING	REALTER	REFACED	REPOSED
INFOLDS	LUGGERS	REAPPLY	REFACES	REPOSES
INKIEST	LUGGING	REARMED	REFECTS	REPPING
ITCHIER	LUMBAGO	REAVERS	REFIGHT	REPRESS
ITCHILY	LUMBERS	REBILLS	REFILED	REPRICE
ITCHING	LUMPENS	REBINDS	REFILES	REPRINT
LACINGS	LUMPERS	REBIRTH	REFIRED	RESALES
LANCHES	LUMPIER	REBOARD	REFIRES	RESCIND
LANNERS	LUMPING	REBOILS	REFIXED	RESCORE

RESELLS	RESORTS	RETRAIN	REVISIT	ROBANDS
RESENTS	RESPLIT	RETREAT	REVISOR	RODDING
RESERVE	RESTAMP	RETRIAL	REWARMS	ROOFERS
RESHAPE	RESTERS	RETRIMS	REWEIGH	ROOFING
RESHIPS	RESTORE	RETYPED	REWIRED	ROSIEST
RESHOWN	RESUMED	RETYPES	REWIRES	SALTERS
RESHOWS	RESUMER	REUNION	REWORKS	SALTERY
RESIDED	RESUMES	REUNITE	REWRAPS	SHAWING
RESIDER	RETAPED	REVALUE	RICKETS	UNITIVE
RESIDES	RETAPES	REVERBS	RICKING	URGINGS
RESIFTS	RETASTE	REVIEWS	RIGGING	UTTERED
RESOAKS	RETELLS	REVISED	RILLING	UTTERER
RESOLVE	RETESTS	REVISES	RIMMING	

With back hook P

MINICAM

With front hook R

ADDLING	EDUCING	EMAILED	ESTATES	HEMATIC
ALLYING	EDUCTOR	EMENDED	ETCHING	ICTUSES
AMBLERS	EJECTED	EMERGED	EVERTED	OILIEST
AMBLING	EJECTOR	EMERGES	EVOKERS	OUSTERS
AMENTUM	ELAPSED	EMITTED	EVOKING	OUSTING
ANKLING	ELAPSES	EMITTER	EVOLUTE	OYSTERS
ANTINGS	ELATERS	EMOTION	EVOLVED	UNROUND
APHIDES	ELATING	ENOUNCE	EVOLVER	URALITE
APTNESS	ELATION	EQUITES	EVOLVES	
EARINGS	ELATIVE	ESTATED	EVULSED	

With back hook R

ABRIDGE	ARRANGE	BRAWLIE	COLLEGE	CONSOLE
ABSOLVE	ASPERSE	BREATHE	COLLIDE	CONSUME
ACHIEVE	ASSUAGE	BRITTLE	COLLUDE	CONVENE
ACICULA	ATOMISE	BROWNIE	COMBINE	CONVOKE
ACQUIRE	ATOMIZE	BRUSQUE	COMMUNE	COSTUME
ADVANCE	ATTACHE	CANNULA	COMMUTE	COTTAGE
AGITATO	AUSTERE	CAPABLE	COMPARE	COUTHIE
AIRLINE	BAGPIPE	CAPTURE	COMPILE	COWRITE
AMPULLA	BALANCE	CAROUSE	COMPOSE	CRACKIE
ANALYSE	BANDAGE	CAVEOLA	COMPUTE	CRAPPIE
ANALYZE	BAPTIZE	CENSURE	CONCEDE	CREEPIE
ANIMATE	BEGUILE	CHICANE	CONCISE	CRIPPLE
ANIMATO	BELIEVE	CHIPPIE	CONDOLE	CRUMMIE
ANODISE	BEREAVE	CHORTLE	CONDONE	CRUSADE
ANODIZE	BESIEGE	CHUCKLE	CONDUCE	CULCHIE
ANTIQUE	BICYCLE	CINGULA	CONFIDE	CULSHIE
APPEASE	BLASTIE	CLEANSE	CONFINE	CUTESIE
APPRISE	BRABBLE	COCHLEA	CONFUTE	DECEIVE
APPRIZE	BRAILLE	CODRIVE	CONJURE	DECLARE
APPROVE	BRASSIE	COGNIZE	CONNIVE	DECLINE

DEFLATE	FINAGLE	LECTURE	POLLUTE	RUMMAGE
DEFORCE	FISTULA	LICENCE	POSTURE	SALVAGE
DEGRADE	FLOSSIE	LICENSE	POTHOLE	SANDBUR
DELOUSE	FORESEE	LINGULA	PRATTLE	SCAPULA
DEMERGE	FORGIVE	LIONISE	PRECISE	SCOURGE
DEPLETE	FORSAKE	LIONIZE	PREFACE	SCUFFLE
DEPLORE	FOVEOLA	LOWLIFE	PRELUDE	SECONDE
DEPRAVE	FRENULA	MACABRE	PREPARE	SECRETE
DEPRIVE	FRIBBLE	MASSAGE	PREPPIE	SERVICE
DERANGE	FRIZZLE	MEASURE	PRESAGE	SHACKLE
DESERVE	FURCULA	MEDULLA	PRESIDE	SHEATHE
DESPISE	GANGLIA	MICELLA	PRESUME	SHEENIE
DETERGE	GAROTTE	MIDLIFE	PRIVATE	SHINGLE
DIALYSE	GARROTE	MILLINE	PROCURE	SHMOOZE
DIALYZE	GESTURE	MISLIKE	PRODUCE	SHUFFLE
DIFFUSE	GLASSIE	MISTAKE	PROFANE	SHUTTLE
DISABLE	GLIMPSE	MODERNE	PROFILE	SILENCE
DISLIKE	GRABBLE	MORTICE	PROMISE	SINCERE
DISPOSE	GRAPPLE	MORTISE	PROMOTE	SKYDIVE
DISPUTE	GREENIE	MUNCHIE	PROPOSE	SMOOTHE
DISROBE	GRIMACE	NARRATE	PROVIDE	SMUGGLE
DISSAVE	GRIZZLE	NEURULA	PROVOKE	SNIFFLE
DIVORCE	GRUMBLE	NURTURE	QUIBBLE	SNIGGLE
DIVULGE	HAGRIDE	OBSCENE	RAMPAGE	SNUFFLE
DOGGONE	HEXAPLA	OBSCURE	REALISE	SPARKLE
DRIBBLE	HOTLINE	OBSERVE	REALIZE	SPATULA
DRUGGIE	IDOLISE	OBTRUDE	RECEIVE	SPECULA
ECLIPSE	IDOLIZE	ODORIZE	RECLINE	SPICULA
EMBLAZE	IGNOBLE	OUTLINE	RECYCLE	SPINDLE
EMBRACE	IMAGINE	OUTLIVE	REDLINE	SPLURGE
EMPLOYE	IMMENSE	OUTRIDE	REISSUE	SPRINGE
ENCHASE	IMPINGE	OUTSIDE	REJOICE	SPUNKIE
ENCLOSE	IMPLORE	OVERDYE	RELAPSE	SQUEEZE
ENDORSE	IMPROVE	OVERSEE	RELEASE	STAGGIE
ENFORCE	INCLINE	OXIDISE	RELIEVE	STARTLE
ENGRAVE	INCLOSE	OXIDIZE	REPLACE	STEAMIE
ENHANCE	INDORSE	OZONISE	REPROVE	STEELIE
ENLARGE	INDULGE	OZONIZE	REPULSE	STICKIE
ENNOBLE	INFLAME	PACKAGE	REQUIRE	STICKLE
ENQUIRE	INFLATE	PAPILLA	REQUITE	STIPPLE
ENSLAVE	INQUIRE	PARTAKE	RESERVE	STRANGE
ENSNARE	INSNARE	PASTURE	RESHAPE	STUMBLE
EPISTLE	INSPIRE	PATELLA	RESOLVE	STYLISE
ESPOUSE	INTENSE	PECULIA	RESTORE	STYLIZE
EXAMINE	INTRUDE	PEPTIZE	RETRACE	SUBLIME
EXCLUDE	INVOLVE	PERFUME	REUNITE	SUBSIDE
EXCRETE	ITEMISE	PERJURE	REVENGE	SUBTILE
EXECUTE	ITEMIZE	PERVADE	REVENUE	SUFFICE
EXEMPLA	JAWBONE	PILLAGE	REVERSE	SUPPOSE
EXPLODE	JOYRIDE	PINNULA	REVOLVE	SUPREME
EXPLORE	KEYNOTE	PLACATE	REWRITE	SURFACE
EXPUNGE	KILLDEE	PLANULA	ROMANCE	SURMISE
EXTREME	KNUCKLE	POETISE	ROSEOLA	SURNAME
EXTRUDE	LAMELLA	POETIZE	RUBEOLA	SURVIVE

SWINDLE	TRICKIE	UPGRADE	VENTURE	WHEEDLE
SWIZZLE	TROUBLE	UPHEAVE	VEXILLA	WHIFFLE
TEENAGE	TROUNCE	UPRAISE	VIBRATO	WHISTLE
TITCHIE	TRUCKLE	UPSTAGE	VILLAGE	WHITTLE
TOPSIDE	TRUNDLE	UPSTATE	VINCULA	WINSOME
TORTURE	TWADDLE	UTILISE	VINTAGE	WRANGLE
TRADUCE	TWANGLE	UTILIZE	VIOLATE	WREATHE
TRAMPLE	TWIDDLE	VALVULA	WARGAME	WRESTLE
TREADLE	TWINKLE	VARIOLA	WARSTLE	WRIGGLE
TREMBLE	UNITIZE	VASCULA	WELCOME	

With front hook S

ADDLING	CRAPPER	HACKLES	HOTTING	LIPLESS
ALLOWED	CRAWLED	HADDOCK	HOVELED	LIPPERS
ALLYING	CRAWLER	HAFTING	HUNTERS	LIPPIER
ANGUINE	CREAKED	HAGGING	HUNTING	LIPPING
ASHLESS	CREAMED	HALLOWS	HUSHING	LITTERS
CABBING	CREAMER	HAMMERS	HUTTING	LIVERED
CAMPERS	CREWING	HAMMING	KELPING	LOBBERS
CAMPING	CRIMPED	HANKING	KELTERS	LOGGERS
CANDENT	CRIMPER	HARKING	KERRIES	LOGGING
CANNERS	CRUMPLE	HARPERS	KETCHES	LOPPIER
CANNING	CRUNCHY	HARPIES	KIDDERS	LOPPING
CANTING	CUFFING	HARPING	KIDDING	LOTTERS
CARIOUS	CULCHES	HATTERS	KILLING	LOTTING
CARLESS	CULLERS	HAULING	KINKING	LOWDOWN
CARPERS	CULLING	HEALING	KINLESS	LOWNESS
CARPING	CULLION	HEARERS	KIPPERS	LUBBERS
CARRIER	CUMMERS	HEARING	KIPPING	LUFFING
CARTING	CUMMING	HEATHER	KITTLES	LUGGERS
CATTIER	CUNNERS	HEAVING	KOOKUMS	LUGGING
CATTILY	CUPPERS	HELLERS	LACKERS	LUMBERS
CATTING	CURRIED	HELLING	LACKING	LUMPIER
CHILLER	CURRIES	HELVING	LAGGING	LUMPING
COFFERS	CURVIER	HERRIED	LAMMING	LUSHING
COFFING	CUTCHES	HERRIES	LANDERS	MARTENS
COLLOPS	CUTTERS	HILLING	LAPPERS	MARTING
COOCHES	CUTTLED	HINNIED	LAPPING	MASHERS
COOPERS	CUTTLES	HINNIES	LASHERS	MASHING
COOPING	CUTWORK	HIPLESS	LASHING	MATTERS
COOTERS	EATINGS	HIPPING	LATCHES	MELLING
COPULAE	EDGIEST	HITLESS	LATHERS	MELTERS
COPULAS	EDITION	HITTERS	LEAVING	MELTING
CORNERS	EDUCING	HITTING	LICKERS	MIRKIER
CORNING	ELECTED	HOCKERS	LICKING	MIRKILY
COUTERS	ELECTEE	HOCKING	LIGHTED	MITHERS
COUTHER	ELECTOR	HOGGING	LIGHTER	MOCKING
COWLING	ENTRIES	HOOTERS	LIGHTLY	MOLDERS
CRAGGED	EXPERTS	HOOTING	LIMIEST	MOOCHED
CRAMMED	HACKING	HOPPERS	LIMMERS	MOOCHER
CRAPING	HACKLED	HOPPIER	LINGERS	MOOCHES
CRAPPED	HACKLER	HOPPING	LINKING	MOTHERS

MOTHERY	PARRIER	PRINTER	TIPPLES	WADDLED
MOULDER	PARRING	PUDDING	TITCHES	WADDLES
MUSHING	PATTERS	PUNKIER	TOCCATA	WAGGERS
MUTCHES	PATTING	PUNKIES	TOCKING	WAGGING
NAGGERS	PAWNERS	PURRING	TONIEST	WALLOWS
NAGGIER	PAWNING	PUTTERS	TOOLING	WAMPISH
NAGGING	PEAKING	QUADDED	TOPPERS	WANKING
NAILING	PECKIER	QUASHED	TOPPING	WANNING
NAPLESS	PECKING	QUASHER	TOPPLED	WAPPING
NAPPERS	PECTATE	QUASHES	TOPPLES	WARDING
NAPPIER	PEELING	QUIFFED	TOTTING	WARMERS
NAPPING	PEERING	QUIRING	TOWABLE	WARMING
NARKIER	PELTERS	QUIRTED	TOWAGES	WASHERS
NIBBING	PENDING	TABBING	TOWAWAY	WASHING
NICKERS	PILINGS	TABLING	TRAINED	WATCHES
NICKING	PILLAGE	TACKERS	TRAINER	WAYBACK
NIFFERS	PILLING	TACKING	TRAPPED	WEARERS
NIFFIER	PINIEST	TAGGERS	TRAPPER	WEARING
NIFFING	PINLESS	TAGGING	TRASSES	WEENIES
NIGGERS	PINNERS	TAKEOUT	TRESSED	WEEPERS
NIGGLED	PINNIES	TALKERS	TRESSES	WEEPIER
NIGGLER	PINNING	TALKIER	TRICKLE	WEEPING
NIGGLES	PITTING	TALKING	TRIDENT	WEETING
NIPPERS	PLASHED	TAMPERS	TRIPPED	WELLING
NIPPIER	PLASHER	TAMPING	TRIPPER	WELTERS
NIPPILY	PLASHES	TANGING	TROKING	WIGGERS
NIPPING	PLATTED	TARRIER	TROLLED	WIGGING
NITTIER	PLATTER	TARRING	TROLLER	WILLERS
NOBBIER	PLAYING	TARTING	TROPHIC	WILLING
NOBBILY	PONGIER	TEAMING	TROWING	WINDLED
NOGGING	PONGING	TENCHES	TRUMPET	WINDLES
NUBBERS	PONTOON	TICKERS	TUBBIER	WINGERS
NUBBIER	POOLERS	TICKING	TUBBING	WINGIER
OFTENER	POOLING	TICKLED	TUMBLED	WINGING
ORDINES	PORTERS	TICKLER	TUMBLER	WINGMAN
PACIEST	PORTING	TICKLES	TUMBLES	WINGMEN
PACINGS	POTTERS	TIFFING	TUMPING	WINKING
PALLING	POTTIER	TILLAGE	TUNNING	WISHERS
PANNERS	POTTING	TILLING	ULLAGES	WISHING
PANNING	POUTERS	TILTING	UNBAKED	WITCHED
PARABLE	POUTING	TINGING	UNBELTS	WITCHES
PARGING	PRATTLE	TINKERS	UNBLOCK	WITHERS
PARKERS	PRAYERS	TINTERS	UNBURNT	WOOSHED
PARKIER	PRAYING	TINTING	UNCHOKE	WOOSHES
PARKING	PRIGGED	TIPPLED	UNDRESS	WOTTING
PARLING	PRINTED	TIPPLER	UNROOFS	WOUNDED

With back hook S

ABALONE	ABETTER	ABIGAIL	ABLEIST	ABRADER
ABANDON	ABETTOR	ABJURER	ABLUENT	ABREACT
ABDOMEN	ABFARAD	ABLATOR	ABORTER	ABRIDGE
ABETTAL	ABHENRY	ABLEISM	ABOULIA	ABROSIA

ABSCISE	ADHIBIT	AIRBALL	ALIENER	AMNIOTE
ABSCOND	ADIPOSE	AIRBASE	ALIENOR	AMORIST
ABSENCE	ADJOINT	AIRBOAT	ALIGNER	AMOROSO
ABSINTH	ADJOURN	AIRCREW	ALIMENT	AMOSITE
ABSOLVE	ADJUDGE	AIRDATE	ALIQUOT	AMOTION
ABSTAIN	ADJUNCT	AIRDROP	ALKANET	AMPHORA
ABUTTAL	ADJURER	AIRFARE	ALLAYER	AMPOULE
ABUTTER	ADJUROR	AIRFLOW	ALLEGER	AMPUTEE
ACADEME	ADMIRAL	AIRFOIL	ALLEGRO	AMREETA
ACALEPH	ADMIRER	AIRGLOW	ALLHEAL	AMTRACK
ACAPNIA	ADOPTEE	AIRHEAD	ALLICIN	AMYLASE
ACARINE	ADOPTER	AIRHOLE	ALLOBAR	AMYLENE
ACCEDER	ADORNER	AIRLIFT	ALLONGE	AMYLOID
ACCIDIA	ADRENAL	AIRLINE	ALLONYM	AMYLOSE
ACCIDIE	ADULATE	AIRLOCK	ALLOVER	ANAEMIA
ACCLAIM	ADVANCE	AIRMAIL	ALLOXAN	ANAGOGE
ACCOUNT	ADVISEE	AIRPARK	ALLSEED	ANAGRAM
ACCRETE	ADVISER	AIRPLAY	ALLURER	ANALGIA
ACCRUAL	ADVISOR	AIRPORT	ALMANAC	ANALYSE
ACCUSAL	AERADIO	AIRPOST	ALMEMAR	ANALYST
ACCUSER	AERATOR	AIRSHED	ALMONER	ANALYTE
ACEQUIA	AEROBAT	AIRSHIP	ALPHORN	ANALYZE
ACEROLA	AEROBIC	AIRSHOT	ALTERER	ANAPEST
ACETATE	AEROGEL	AIRSHOW	ALTHAEA	ANAPHOR
ACETONE	AEROSAT	AIRSIDE	ALTHORN	ANATASE
ACHIEVE	AEROSOL	AIRTIME	ALTOIST	ANCHUSA
ACHIOTE	AFFAIRE	AIRTRAM	ALUMINA	ANCIENT
ACHOLIA	AFFIANT	AIRWAVE	ALUMINE	ANCILLA
ACICULA	AFFICHE	AKRASIA	ALUNITE	ANDANTE
ACOLYTE	AFFIXER	AKVAVIT	ALYSSUM	ANDIRON
ACONITE	AFFLICT	ALAMEDA	AMALGAM	ANDROID
ACQUEST	AFFRONT	ALAMODE	AMANITA	ANEMONE
ACQUIRE	AFGHANI	ALANINE	AMARONE	ANERGIA
ACRASIA	AGAMETE	ALASTOR	AMASSER	ANEROID
ACRASIN	AGAROSE	ALATION	AMATEUR	ANETHOL
ACREAGE	AGATIZE	ALBIZIA	AMAUTIK	ANEURIN
ACROBAT	AGEMATE	ALBUMEN	AMBIENT	ANGAKOK
ACROGEN	AGENDUM	ALBUMIN	AMBOINA	ANGARIA
ACRONYM	AGENIZE	ALCAIDE	AMBOYNA	ANGIOMA
ACRYLIC	AGGADAH	ALCALDE	AMBROID	ANGLING
ACTINIA	AGGRADE	ALCAYDE	AMBSACE	ANHINGA
ACTINON	AGINNER	ALCAZAR	AMENDER	ANILINE
ACTUATE	AGITATE	ALCOHOL	AMENTIA	ANIMATE
ACYLATE	AGLYCON	ALCOPOP	AMERCER	ANIMATO
ACYLOIN	AGNOMEN	ALEMBIC	AMESACE	ANIMISM
ADAMANT	AGNOSIA	ALENCON	AMIDASE	ANIMIST
ADAPTER	AGONISE	ALEURON	AMIDINE	ANISEED
ADAPTOR	AGONISM	ALEXINE	AMIDONE	ANISOLE
ADDUCER	AGONIST	ALFALFA	AMIRATE	ANNATTO
ADELGID	AGONIZE	ALFAQUI	AMMETER	ANNELID
ADENINE	AGRAFFE	ALFORJA	AMMONAL	ANNOYER
ADENOID	AILERON	ALGEBRA	AMMONIA	ANNULET
ADENOMA	AILMENT	ALIDADE	AMNESIA	ANODISE
ADHERER	AINSELL	ALIENEE	AMNESIC	ANODIZE

ANODYNE	ARAWANA	ASSAGAI	AUTOMAT	BAHADUR
ANOLYTE	ARBITER	ASSAULT	AUTONYM	BAILIFF
ANOPSIA	ARCADIA	ASSAYER	AUTOPEN	BAILOUT
ANOSMIA	ARCANUM	ASSEGAI	AUXETIC	BAKLAVA
ANTACID	ARCHFOE	ASSHOLE	AVARICE	BAKLAWA
ANTBEAR	ARCHINE	ASSUAGE	AVENGER	BALAFON
ANTENNA	ARCHING	ASSUMER	AVERAGE	BALANCE
ANTHILL	ARCHIVE	ASSURED	AVERTER	BALDRIC
ANTIGEN	ARCHWAY	ASSURER	AVIATOR	BALLADE
ANTILOG	ARCSINE	ASSUROR	AVIONIC	BALLAST
ANTIQUE	AREAWAY	ASSWAGE	AVOCADO	BALLBOY
ANTLION	ARENITE	ASTANGA	AVODIRE	BALLOON
ANTONYM	ARIETTA	ASTASIA	AVOIDER	BALLUTE
APAGOGE	ARIETTE	ASTERIA	AWAITER	BALONEY
APANAGE	ARMBAND	ASTILBE	AWARDEE	BAMBINO
APAREJO	ARMHOLE	ASTOUND	AWARDER	BANDAGE
APATITE	ARMIGER	ASTRICT	AWLWORT	BANDANA
APHAGIA	ARMILLA	ATAGHAN	AXILLAR	BANDEAU
APHASIA	ARMLOAD	ATALAYA	AXOLOTL	BANDING
APHASIC	ARMLOCK	ATAVISM	AXONEME	BANDITO
APHONIA	ARMOIRE	ATAVIST	AZIMUTH	BANDORA
APHONIC	ARMORER	ATELIER	AZOTISE	BANDORE
APLANAT	ARMREST	ATEMOYA	AZOTIZE	BANDSAW
APLASIA	ARNATTO	ATHEISM	AZULEJO	BANDURA
APOCARP	ARNOTTO	ATHEIST	AZURITE	BANGKOK
APOCOPE	AROUSAL	ATHLETE	BAALISM	BANKING
APOLUNE	AROUSER	ATHODYD	BAASKAP	BANKSIA
APOMICT	AROWANA	ATOMISE	BABASSU	BANNOCK
APOSTIL	ARRAIGN	ATOMISM	BABBITT	BANQUET
APOSTLE	ARRANGE	ATOMIST	BABBLER	BANSHEE
APOTHEM	ARRAYAL	ATOMIZE	BABESIA	BANSHIE
APPARAT	ARRAYER	ATRESIA	BABICHE	BANTENG
APPAREL	ARRIVAL	ATROPIN	BABYSIT	BAPTISE
APPEASE	ARRIVER	ATTABOY	BACALAO	BAPTISM
APPLAUD	ARSENAL	ATTACHE	BACCALA	BAPTIST
APPLIER	ARSENIC	ATTAINT	BACCARA	BAPTIZE
APPOINT	ARTICLE	ATTEMPT	BACKBAR	BARBELL
APPOSER	ARTISAN	ATTRACT	BACKFAT	BARBULE
APPRISE	ARTISTE	ATTRITE	BACKFIT	BARCHAN
APPRIZE	ARTWORK	AUBERGE	BACKHOE	BARCODE
APPROVE	ARUGOLA	AUCTION	BACKING	BARGAIN
APPULSE	ARUGULA	AUDIBLE	BACKLOG	BARGOON
APRAXIA	ASCARID	AUDIENT	BACKLOT	BARILLA
APRICOT	ASCETIC	AUDITEE	BACKOUT	BARISTA
APYRASE	ASCRIBE	AUDITOR	BACKSAW	BARKEEP
AQUAFIT	ASHCAKE	AUGMENT	BACKSET	BARMAID
AQUATIC	ASHFALL	AUGURER	BACULUM	BARONET
AQUAVIT	ASHRAMA	AUREOLA	BADLAND	BARONNE
AQUIFER	ASHTRAY	AUREOLE	BAFFLER	BAROQUE
ARABESK	ASOCIAL	AURICLE	BAGASSE	BARRACK
ARABICA	ASPERSE	AUSFORM	BAGGAGE	BARRAGE
ARABIZE	ASPHALT	AUSPICE	BAGGING	BARRIER
ARANEID	ASPIRER	AUSTRAL	BAGPIPE	BARROOM
ARAROBA	ASPIRIN	AUTARCH	BAGWORM	BARTEND

BARWARE	BECRUST	BELTWAY	BICORNE	BIVOUAC
BARYTON	BECURSE	BEMADAM	BICYCLE	BIZARRE
BASCULE	BEDDING	BENCHER	BIDARKA	BIZARRO
BASENJI	BEDEVIL	BENEFIT	BIDDING	BIZNAGA
BASHING	BEDGOWN	BENISON	BIFIDUM	BLABBER
BASHLYK	BEDHEAD	BENOMYL	BIFOCAL	BLACKEN
BASINET	BEDIGHT	BENTHON	BIGFOOT	BLADDER
BASMATI	BEDIZEN	BENZENE	BIGGING	BLADING
BASSETT	BEDLAMP	BENZINE	BIGHEAD	BLAGGER
BASSIST	BEDMATE	BENZOIN	BIGHORN	BLANKET
BASSOON	BEDOUIN	BENZOLE	BIGUINE	BLANKIE
BASTARD	BEDPOST	BENZOYL	BIKEWAY	BLARNEY
BASTILE	BEDRAIL	BEPAINT	BILAYER	BLASTER
BASTING	BEDRAPE	BEQUEST	BILEVEL	BLASTIE
BASTION	BEDREST	BEREAVE	BILLBUG	BLATHER
BATCHER	BEDROCK	BERETTA	BILLING	BLATTER
BATFOWL	BEDROLL	BERGERE	BILLION	BLAUBOK
BATGIRL	BEDROOM	BERHYME	BILSTED	BLEATER
BATHING	BEDSIDE	BERLINE	BILTONG	BLEEDER
BATHMAT	BEDSOCK	BERSEEM	BIMETAL	BLEEPER
BATHTUB	BEDSORE	BERSERK	BIMORPH	BLELLUM
BATISTE	BEDTICK	BESCOUR	BINDING	BLENDER
BATTING	BEDTIME	BESHAME	BINGING	BLESBOK
BATTLER	BEDUNCE	BESHOUT	BINOCLE	BLESSER
BAULKER	BEDWARD	BESHREW	BIOCHIP	BLETHER
BAUXITE	BEDWARF	BESIEGE	BIOCIDE	BLINDER
BAWCOCK	BEEFALO	BESLIME	BIOFILM	BLINKER
BAWDRIC	BEEHIVE	BESMEAR	BIOFUEL	BLINTZE
BAYONET	BEELINE	BESMILE	BIOHERM	BLISTER
BAYSIDE	BEERNUT	BESMOKE	BIOTECH	BLITHER
BAYWOOD	BEETLER	BESPEAK	BIOTITE	BLITZER
BAZOOKA	BEEYARD	BESTEAD	BIOTOPE	BLOATER
BEADING	BEFLECK	BESTREW	BIOTRON	BLOCKER
BEAGLER	BEGLOOM	BESTROW	BIOTYPE	BLOGGER
BEALING	BEGONIA	BESWARM	BIPLANE	BLOOMER
BEANBAG	BEGRIME	BETAINE	BIRDDOG	BLOOPER
BEARCAT	BEGROAN	BETHANK	BIRDING	BLOSSOM
BEARHUG	BEGUILE	BETHINK	BIRETTA	BLOTTER
BEARING	BEGUINE	BETHORN	BIRIANI	BLOUSON
BEARPAW	BEHAVER	BETHUMP	BIRLING	BLOWGUN
BEASTIE	BEHOOVE	BETOKEN	BIRYANI	BLOWJOB
BEATING	BEIGNET	BETROTH	BISCUIT	BLOWOFF
BEATNIK	BEJEWEL	BETTING	BISMUTH	BLOWOUT
BEBEERU	BELABOR	BEVELER	BISNAGA	BLUBBER
BEBLOOD	BELAYER	BEVOMIT	BISTORT	BLUCHER
BECHALK	BELCHER	BEZIQUE	BITCOIN	BLUDGER
BECHARM	BELDAME	BEZZANT	BITRATE	BLUECAP
BECLASP	BELIEVE	BHANGRA	BITTERN	BLUEFIN
BECLOAK	BELLBOY	BHISTIE	BITTING	BLUEGUM
BECLOUD	BELLEEK	BIBBING	BITTOCK	BLUEING
BECLOWN	BELLHOP	BIBCOCK	BITUMEN	BLUEJAY
BECRAWL	BELLING	BIBELOT	BITURBO	BLUFFER
BECRIME	BELOVED	BIBLIST	BIVALVE	BLUNDER
BECROWD	BELTING	BICOLOR	BIVINYL	BLUNGER

BLURTER	BOOZING	BRADOON	BROKING	BULLPEN
BLUSHER	BORAZON	BRAGGER	BROMATE	BULWARK
BLUSTER	BORDURE	BRAHMAN	BROMIDE	BUMBLER
BOARDER	BOREDOM	BRAIDER	BROMINE	BUMBOAT
BOASTER	BORKING	BRAILLE	BROMISM	BUMELIA
BOATFUL	BORNEOL	BRAMBLE	BROMIZE	BUMMALO
BOATING	BORNITE	BRANDER	BRONCHO	BUMPKIN
BOBECHE	BORONIA	BRANNER	BRONZER	BUNCHER
BOBSLED	BOROUGH	BRASIER	BROODER	BUNDIST
BOBSTAY	BORSCHT	BRASSIE	BROOKIE	BUNDLER
BOBTAIL	BORSTAL	BRATTLE	BROTHEL	BUNGLER
BODHRAN	BOSCAGE	BRAVADO	BROTHER	BUNHEAD
BOFFOLA	BOSHBOK	BRAVURA	BROWNER	BUNRAKU
BOGBEAN	BOSKAGE	BRAWLER	BROWNIE	BUNTING
BOGGLER	BOSQUET	BRAZIER	BROWSER	BUOYAGE
BOGHOLE	BOSSDOM	BREADTH	BRUCINE	BURBLER
BOGLAND	BOSSISM	BREAKER	BRUCITE	BURDOCK
BOGWOOD	BOTCHER	BREAKUP	BRUISER	BURETTE
BOGYISM	BOTTLER	BREATHE	BRUITER	BURGAGE
BOHEMIA	BOTULIN	BRECCIA	BRULYIE	BURGEON
BOHRIUM	BOUCHEE	BRECHAM	BRULZIE	BURGHER
BOILOFF	BOUDOIR	BRECHAN	BRUSHER	BURGLAR
BOLIVAR	BOULDER	BREEDER	BRUSHUP	BURGOUT
BOLIVIA	BOUNCER	BREKKIE	BRUTISM	BURKITE
BOLLARD	BOUNDER	BREVIER	BRUXISM	BURLESK
BOLOGNA	BOUQUET	BREWAGE	BUBBLER	BURNING
BOLONEY	BOURBON	BREWING	BUBINGA	BURNOUT
BOLSHIE	BOURDON	BREWPUB	BUCKEEN	BURRITO
BOLSTER	BOURREE	BREWSKI	BUCKEYE	BURSEED
BOMBARD	BOURSIN	BRICKLE	BUCKLER	BURSTER
BOMBAST	BOUTADE	BRICOLE	BUCKRAM	BURTHEN
BOMBING	BOUVIER	BRIDLER	BUCKSAW	BURWEED
BOMBLET	BOWHEAD	BRIDOON	BUCOLIC	BUSGIRL
BOMBORA	BOWHUNT	BRIEFER	BUDDING	BUSHIDO
BONANZA	BOWKNOT	BRIGADE	BUDWOOD	BUSHING
BONDAGE	BOWLDER	BRIGAND	BUDWORM	BUSHLOT
BONDING	BOWLFUL	BRIMMER	BUFFALO	BUSHPIG
BONEBED	BOWLINE	BRINDLE	BUFFOON	BUSHTIT
BONESET	BOWLING	BRINGER	BUGABOO	BUSHWAH
BONFIRE	BOWSHOT	BRIOCHE	BUGBANE	BUSKING
BONIATO	BOWWOOD	BRIQUET	BUGBEAR	BUSLOAD
BONNOCK	BOXBALL	BRISKET	BUGSEED	BUSSING
BONTBOK	BOXHAUL	BRISTLE	BUILDER	BUSTARD
BOOBIRD	BOXWOOD	BRISTOL	BUILDUP	BUSTIER
BOODLER	BOYCHIK	BRITSKA	BULBLET	BUSTLER
BOOKBAG	BOYCOTT	BRITTLE	BULGHUR	BUTANOL
BOOKEND	BOYHOOD	BRITZKA	BULIMIA	BUTCHER
BOOKFUL	BRABBLE	BROADEN	BULIMIC	BUTTOCK
BOOKING	BRACERO	BROCADE	BULKAGE	BUTYRAL
BOOKLET	BRACHET	BROCKET	BULLACE	BUTYRIN
BOOMKIN	BRACING	BROCOLI	BULLBAT	BUTYRYL
BOOMLET	BRACKEN	BROIDER	BULLDOG	BUYBACK
BOOSTER	BRACKET	BROILER	BULLION	BUZZARD
BOOTLEG	BRADAWL	BROKAGE	BULLOCK	BUZZCUT

124

BUZZING	CALLUNA	CAPITAL	CARRELL	CATTALO
BUZZWIG	CALOMEL	CAPITOL	CARRIER	CATWALK
BYLINER	CALORIC	CAPORAL	CARRION	CAUDATE
CABARET	CALORIE	CAPPING	CARRYON	CAULKER
CABBAGE	CALOTTE	CAPRESE	CARTAGE	CAUSTIC
CABBALA	CALOYER	CAPRICE	CARTFUL	CAUTION
CABEZON	CALPACK	CAPROCK	CARTOON	CAVALLA
CABILDO	CALPAIN	CAPSIZE	CARVING	CAVETTO
CABINET	CALTRAP	CAPSTAN	CASCADE	CAVIARE
CABLING	CALTROP	CAPSULE	CASCARA	CAVILER
CABOMBA	CALUMET	CAPTAIN	CASEASE	CAYENNE
CABOOSE	CALYCLE	CAPTCHA	CASEATE	CAZIQUE
CABOVER	CALYPSO	CAPTION	CASELAW	CEDILLA
CACHACA	CALZONE	CAPTIVE	CASEOSE	CEILIDH
CACIQUE	CAMBISM	CAPTURE	CASERNE	CEILING
CACKLER	CAMBIST	CAPUCHE	CASETTE	CELADON
CACODYL	CAMBIUM	CARABAO	CASHIER	CELESTA
CACONYM	CAMBRIC	CARABID	CASSABA	CELESTE
CADAVER	CAMCORD	CARABIN	CASSATA	CELLIST
CADDICE	CAMELIA	CARACAL	CASSAVA	CELLULE
CADELLE	CAMELID	CARACOL	CASSENA	CELOSIA
CADENCE	CAMISIA	CARACUL	CASSENE	CEMBALO
CADENZA	CAMORRA	CARAMEL	CASSINA	CENACLE
CADMIUM	CAMPHOL	CARAVAN	CASSINE	CENSURE
CAESIUM	CAMPHOR	CARAVEL	CASSINO	CENTARE
CAESURA	CAMPING	CARAWAY	CASSOCK	CENTAUR
CAFFEIN	CAMPION	CARBARN	CASTING	CENTAVO
CAGEFUL	CAMPONG	CARBIDE	CASTOFF	CENTILE
CAGOULE	CAMPOUT	CARBINE	CASUIST	CENTIME
CAISSON	CAMWOOD	CARBORA	CATAGEN	CENTIMO
CAITIFF	CANAKIN	CARCASE	CATALOG	CENTNER
CAJAPUT	CANASTA	CARDIAC	CATALPA	CENTRAL
CAJEPUT	CANDELA	CARDING	CATARRH	CENTRUM
CAJOLER	CANDIDA	CARDOON	CATAWBA	CEPHEID
CAJUPUT	CANDLER	CARFARE	CATBIRD	CERAMAL
CALAMAR	CANDOUR	CARIBOO	CATBOAT	CERAMIC
CALCINE	CANELLA	CARIBOU	CATCALL	CERATIN
CALCITE	CANIKIN	CARIOCA	CATCHER	CERESIN
CALCIUM	CANNING	CARIOLE	CATCHUP	CERUMEN
CALDERA	CANNOLI	CARJACK	CATCLAW	CERVEZA
CALDRON	CANNULA	CARLINE	CATECHU	CESSION
CALECHE	CANTALA	CARLING	CATERAN	CESSPIT
CALIBER	CANTATA	CARLOAD	CATERER	CESTODE
CALIBRE	CANTDOG	CARMINE	CATFACE	CESTOID
CALICHE	CANTEEN	CARNAGE	CATFALL	CEVICHE
CALICLE	CANTINA	CAROCHE	CATHEAD	CHABOUK
CALIPEE	CANTRAP	CAROLER	CATHECT	CHACHKA
CALIPER	CANTRIP	CAROTID	CATHODE	CHAEBOL
CALKING	CANZONA	CAROTIN	CATJANG	CHAFFER
CALLANT	CANZONE	CAROUSE	CATLING	CHAGRIN
CALLBOY	CAPELAN	CARPING	CATMINT	CHAINER
CALLING	CAPELET	CARPOOL	CATSPAW	CHALAZA
CALLOSE	CAPELIN	CARPORT	CATSUIT	CHALCID
CALLOUT	CAPERER	CARRACK	CATTAIL	CHALICE

125

CHALLAH	CHECKER	CHOLERA	CITATOR	CLOSURE
CHALLIE	CHECKUP	CHOLINE	CITHARA	CLOTBUR
CHALONE	CHEDDAR	CHOMPER	CITHERN	CLOTURE
CHALUPA	CHEDITE	CHOOSER	CITHREN	CLOUTER
CHAMADE	CHEEPER	CHOPINE	CITIZEN	CLOWDER
CHAMBER	CHEERER	CHOPPER	CITRATE	CLUBBER
CHAMFER	CHEERIO	CHORALE	CITRINE	CLUCKER
CHAMISA	CHEETAH	CHORINE	CITTERN	CLUMBER
CHAMISE	CHEFDOM	CHORION	CLABBER	CLUMPER
CHAMISO	CHELATE	CHORIZO	CLACHAN	CLUMPET
CHAMPAC	CHELOID	CHOROID	CLACKER	CLUNKER
CHAMPAK	CHEMISE	CHORTEN	CLADISM	CLUPEID
CHAMPER	CHEMISM	CHORTLE	CLADIST	CLUSTER
CHANCEL	CHEMIST	CHOUSER	CLADODE	CLUTTER
CHANCER	CHEQUER	CHOWDER	CLAIMER	CLYSTER
CHANCRE	CHEROOT	CHRISOM	CLAMBER	COACHER
CHANGER	CHERVIL	CHROMYL	CLAMMER	COACTOR
CHANNEL	CHETRUM	CHRONIC	CLAMOUR	COADMIT
CHANOYU	CHEVIOT	CHRONON	CLAMPER	COAEVAL
CHANSON	CHEVRET	CHUCKER	CLANGER	COAGENT
CHANTER	CHEVRON	CHUCKLE	CLANGOR	COALBIN
CHANTEY	CHEWINK	CHUDDAH	CLAPPER	COALPIT
CHANTOR	CHIANTI	CHUDDAR	CLAQUER	COAMING
CHAPATI	CHIASMA	CHUDDER	CLARION	COARSEN
CHAPEAU	CHIBOUK	CHUGGER	CLARKIA	COASTER
CHAPLET	CHICANE	CHUKKAR	CLASHER	COATING
CHAPPAL	CHICANO	CHUKKER	CLASPER	COAXING
CHAPPIE	CHICKEE	CHUNDER	CLASSER	COBBLER
CHAPTER	CHICKEN	CHUNNEL	CLASSIC	COCAINE
CHARADE	CHIFFON	CHUNTER	CLASSON	COCCOID
CHARGER	CHIGGER	CHUPPAH	CLASTIC	COCHAIR
CHARIOT	CHIGNON	CHURNER	CLATTER	COCHLEA
CHARISM	CHILIAD	CHUTIST	CLAUGHT	COCKADE
CHARKHA	CHILLER	CHUTNEE	CLAVIER	COCKEYE
CHARLEY	CHILLUM	CHUTNEY	CLAYPAN	COCKNEY
CHARLIE	CHIMERA	CHUTZPA	CLEANER	COCKPIT
CHARMER	CHIMERE	CHYMIST	CLEANSE	COCOMAT
CHARNEL	CHIMLEY	CHYTRID	CLEANUP	COCONUT
CHARPAI	CHIMNEY	CIBOULE	CLEARER	COCOTTE
CHARPOY	CHINONE	CICHLID	CLEAVER	COCOYAM
CHARQUI	CHINOOK	CICOREE	CLICKER	CODDLER
CHARTER	CHINWAG	CIGARET	CLIMATE	CODEINA
CHASING	CHIPPER	CILIATE	CLIMBER	CODEINE
CHASTEN	CHIPPIE	CINEAST	CLINGER	CODICIL
CHATEAU	CHIPSET	CINEOLE	CLINKER	CODLING
CHATTEL	CHIRPER	CINERIN	CLIPPER	CODRIVE
CHATTER	CHIRRUP	CIPOLIN	CLITTER	COELIAC
CHAUFER	CHITLIN	CIRCLER	CLOBBER	COELOME
CHAYOTE	CHITTER	CIRCLET	CLOCKER	COENACT
CHAZZAN	CHLORAL	CIRCUIT	CLOGGER	COENURE
CHAZZEN	CHLORID	CISSOID	CLONING	COEQUAL
CHEAPEN	CHLORIN	CISTERN	CLONISM	COERCER
CHEAPIE	CHOLATE	CISTRON	CLOSEUP	COERECT
CHEATER	CHOLENT	CITADEL	CLOSING	COESITE

COEXERT	COMPLOT	CONTEND	CORRADE	COWHAND
COEXIST	COMPORT	CONTENT	CORRECT	COWHERB
COFFRET	COMPOSE	CONTEST	CORRIDA	COWHERD
COFOUND	COMPOST	CONTEXT	CORRODE	COWHIDE
COGNATE	COMPOTE	CONTORT	CORRUPT	COWLICK
COGNISE	COMPUTE	CONTOUR	CORSAGE	COWLING
COGNIZE	COMRADE	CONTROL	CORSAIR	COWPLOP
COHABIT	COMSYMP	CONTUSE	CORSLET	COWPOKE
COHERER	CONCAVE	CONVECT	CORTEGE	COWPUNK
COINAGE	CONCEAL	CONVENE	CORTINA	COWRITE
COINFER	CONCEDE	CONVENT	CORULER	COWSHED
COINTER	CONCEIT	CONVERT	CORVINA	COWSKIN
COITION	CONCENT	CONVICT	COSINES	COWSLIP
COLICIN	CONCEPT	CONVOKE	COSMISM	COWTOWN
COLLAGE	CONCERN	COOKING	COSMIST	COXCOMB
COLLARD	CONCERT	COOKOFF	COSSACK	COZENER
COLLATE	CONCHIE	COOKOUT	COSTARD	CRABBER
COLLECT	CONCOCT	COOKTOP	COSTING	CRACKER
COLLEEN	CONCORD	COOLANT	COSTREL	CRACKIE
COLLEGE	CONDEMN	COONCAN	COSTUME	CRACKLE
COLLIDE	CONDOLE	COONTIE	COTERIE	CRACKUP
COLLIER	CONDONE	COPAIBA	COTHURN	CRADLER
COLLOID	CONDUCE	COPEPOD	COTINGA	CRAFTER
COLLUDE	CONDUCT	COPIHUE	COTTAGE	CRAMMER
COLOGNE	CONDUIT	COPILOT	COTTIER	CRAMPIT
COLONEL	CONDYLE	COPPICE	COUCHER	CRAMPON
COLONIC	CONFECT	COPYBOY	COUGHER	CRANIUM
COLORED	CONFIDE	COPYCAT	COULOIR	CRANKLE
COLORER	CONFINE	COPYIST	COULOMB	CRANNOG
COLUMEL	CONFIRM	COQUINA	COULTER	CRAPOLA
COMAKER	CONFORM	COQUITO	COUNCIL	CRAPPER
COMATIK	CONFUSE	CORACLE	COUNSEL	CRAPPIE
COMBINE	CONFUTE	CORANTO	COUNTER	CRASHER
COMBING	CONGEAL	CORBEIL	COUPLER	CRAVING
COMBUST	CONGEST	CORBINA	COUPLET	CRAWDAD
COMFORT	CONIFER	CORDAGE	COURAGE	CRAWLER
COMFREY	CONIINE	CORDIAL	COURANT	CRAZING
COMMAND	CONJOIN	CORDING	COURIER	CREAMER
COMMEND	CONJURE	CORDITE	COURLAN	CREASER
COMMENT	CONLANG	CORDOBA	COURSER	CREATIN
COMMODE	CONNECT	COREIGN	COURTER	CREATOR
COMMOVE	CONNIVE	CORELLA	COUTURE	CREEPER
COMMUNE	CONNOTE	CORKAGE	COUVADE	CREEPIE
COMMUTE	CONQUER	CORMLET	COVERER	CREMATE
COMPACT	CONSENT	CORNCOB	COVERUP	CREMINI
COMPARE	CONSIGN	CORNETT	COVETER	CREOSOL
COMPART	CONSIST	CORNICE	COWBANE	CRESSET
COMPEER	CONSOLE	CORNROW	COWBELL	CREVICE
COMPEND	CONSORT	CORNUTO	COWBIND	CREWCUT
COMPERE	CONSULT	COROLLA	COWBIRD	CRIBBER
COMPETE	CONSUME	CORONAL	COWFLAP	CRICKET
COMPILE	CONTACT	CORONEL	COWFLOP	CRICOID
COMPING	CONTAIN	CORONER	COWGIRL	CRIMINI
COMPLIN	CONTEMN	CORONET	COWHAGE	CRIMMER

CRIMPER	CUDDLER	CYANATE	DAUPHIN	DECURVE
CRIMPLE	CUDWEED	CYANIDE	DAWDLER	DEFACER
CRIMSON	CUISINE	CYANINE	DAWNING	DEFAMER
CRINGER	CUITTLE	CYANITE	DAYBOOK	DEFAULT
CRINGLE	CULCHIE	CYCASIN	DAYCARE	DEFENCE
CRINITE	CULICID	CYCLASE	DAYGLOW	DEFENSE
CRINKLE	CULLION	CYCLING	DAYMARE	DEFICIT
CRINOID	CULOTTE	CYCLIST	DAYPACK	DEFILER
CRIOLLO	CULPRIT	CYCLIZE	DAYROOM	DEFINER
CRIPPLE	CULSHIE	CYCLOID	DAYSAIL	DEFLATE
CRISPEN	CULTISM	CYCLONE	DAYSIDE	DEFLECT
CRISPER	CULTIST	CYMLING	DAYSTAR	DEFORCE
CRITTER	CULTURE	CYPRIAN	DAYTIME	DEFRAUD
CRITTUR	CULVERT	CYSTEIN	DAYWORK	DEFROCK
CROAKER	CUMARIN	CYSTINE	DAZZLER	DEFROST
CROCEIN	CUMQUAT	CYSTOID	DEADEYE	DEFUSER
CROCHET	CUMSHAW	CYTOSOL	DEADPAN	DEGLAZE
CROCKET	CUNNING	CZARDOM	DEALATE	DEGRADE
CROFTER	CUPCAKE	CZARINA	DEALIGN	DEHISCE
CROONER	CUPELER	CZARISM	DEALING	DEICIDE
CROPPER	CUPPING	CZARIST	DEAREST	DEICTIC
CROPPIE	CUPRITE	DABBLER	DEBACLE	DEIFIER
CROQUET	CURACAO	DABSTER	DEBASER	DELAINE
CROSIER	CURACOA	DADAISM	DEBATER	DELATOR
CROSSER	CURATOR	DADAIST	DEBEARD	DELAYER
CROTALE	CURBING	DAGLOCK	DEBONER	DELEAVE
CROUTON	CURCUMA	DAGWOOD	DEBRIDE	DELIGHT
CROWBAR	CURDLER	DALAPON	DEBRIEF	DELIMIT
CROWDER	CURETTE	DALLIER	DECAGON	DELIVER
CROWDIE	CURLING	DAMAGER	DECALOG	DELOUSE
CROWNER	CURRACH	DAMFOOL	DECAPOD	DELTOID
CROWNET	CURRAGH	DAMIANA	DECAYER	DELUDER
CROZIER	CURRANT	DAMNEST	DECEASE	DEMAGOG
CRUCIAN	CURRENT	DAMOSEL	DECEIVE	DEMENTI
CRUISER	CURRIER	DAMOZEL	DECIARE	DEMERGE
CRULLER	CURSIVE	DAMPING	DECIBEL	DEMERIT
CRUMBER	CURTAIL	DANAZOL	DECIDER	DEMESNE
CRUMBLE	CURTAIN	DANDLER	DECIDUA	DEMETON
CRUMBUM	CURTANA	DANGLER	DECIMAL	DEMIGOD
CRUMMIE	CURTSEY	DANSEUR	DECKING	DEMINER
CRUMPET	CUSHION	DAPHNIA	DECKLES	DEMIREP
CRUMPLE	CUSTARD	DAPSONE	DECLAIM	DEMOTIC
CRUNODE	CUTAWAY	DARIOLE	DECLARE	DEMOUNT
CRUPPER	CUTBACK	DARLING	DECLINE	DENDRON
CRUSADE	CUTBANK	DARNEST	DECODER	DENIZEN
CRUSADO	CUTDOWN	DARNING	DECOLOR	DENTINE
CRUSHER	CUTICLE	DARSHAN	DECORUM	DENTIST
CRUZADO	CUTLINE	DASHEEN	DECOYER	DENTURE
CRYOGEN	CUTOVER	DASHIKI	DECREER	DENUDER
CRYONIC	CUTTAGE	DASHPOT	DECRIAL	DEODAND
CRYSTAL	CUTTING	DASTARD	DECRIER	DEODARA
CUBICLE	CUTWORK	DASYURE	DECROWN	DEORBIT
CUCKOLD	CUTWORM	DAUNDER	DECRYPT	DEPAINT
CUDBEAR	CUVETTE	DAUNTER	DECUPLE	DEPLANE

DEPLETE	DEWCLAW	DIMORPH	DISSECT	DOUBLER
DEPLORE	DEWDROP	DINETTE	DISSENT	DOUBLET
DEPLUME	DEWFALL	DINGBAT	DISSERT	DOUBTER
DEPOSAL	DEXTRAL	DIOCESE	DISTAFF	DOUCEUR
DEPOSER	DEXTRAN	DIOPTER	DISTAIN	DOURINE
DEPOSIT	DEXTRIN	DIOPTRE	DISTEND	DOVECOT
DEPRAVE	DHANSAK	DIORAMA	DISTICH	DOVEKEY
DEPRIVE	DHOOTIE	DIORITE	DISTILL	DOVEKIE
DEPSIDE	DHOURRA	DIOXANE	DISTOME	DOWAGER
DERAIGN	DHURRIE	DIOXIDE	DISTORT	DOWNBOW
DERANGE	DIABASE	DIPLOID	DISTURB	DOWSING
DERECHO	DIABOLO	DIPLOMA	DISYOKE	DOYENNE
DERIDER	DIAGRAM	DIPLONT	DITCHER	DOZENTH
DERIVER	DIALECT	DIPNOAN	DIURNAL	DRABBET
DERMOID	DIALING	DIPSHIT	DIVERGE	DRABBLE
DERRICK	DIALIST	DIPTYCA	DIVIDER	DRACENA
DESCALE	DIALLER	DIPTYCH	DIVINER	DRACHMA
DESCANT	DIALYSE	DIRTBAG	DIVISOR	DRAFTEE
DESCEND	DIALYZE	DISABLE	DIVORCE	DRAFTER
DESCENT	DIAMIDE	DISAVOW	DIVULGE	DRAGGER
DESERVE	DIAMINE	DISBAND	DIVULSE	DRAGGLE
DESIRER	DIAMOND	DISCANT	DJIBBAH	DRAGNET
DESKILL	DIAPSID	DISCARD	DOCKAGE	DRAGOON
DESKTOP	DIARIST	DISCASE	DODOISM	DRAINER
DESMOID	DIASTEM	DISCEPT	DOESKIN	DRAUGHT
DESPAIR	DIASTER	DISCERN	DOGBANE	DRAWBAR
DESPISE	DIATRON	DISCOID	DOGCART	DRAWING
DESPITE	DIAZINE	DISCORD	DOGEDOM	DRAWLER
DESPOIL	DIAZOLE	DISDAIN	DOGFACE	DRAYAGE
DESPOND	DIBBLER	DISEASE	DOGGONE	DREAMER
DESSERT	DICAMBA	DISEUSE	DOGGREL	DREDGER
DESTAIN	DICOTYL	DISGUST	DOGSKIN	DREIDEL
DESTINE	DICTATE	DISHELM	DOGSLED	DRESSER
DESTROY	DICTION	DISHFUL	DOGTAIL	DRIBBLE
DESUGAR	DIDDLER	DISHPAN	DOGTROT	DRIBLET
DETENTE	DIDDLEY	DISHRAG	DOGVANE	DRIFTER
DETERGE	DIEBACK	DISJECT	DOGWOOD	DRILLER
DETINUE	DIEHARD	DISJOIN	DOLPHIN	DRINKER
DETRACT	DIESTER	DISLIKE	DOMAINE	DRIPPER
DETRAIN	DIETHER	DISLIMN	DOMICIL	DRIVING
DETRUDE	DIFFUSE	DISMAST	DOMINIE	DRIZZLE
DEUTZIA	DIGAMMA	DISOBEY	DONATOR	DROMOND
DEVALUE	DIGGING	DISPART	DONEGAL	DROPLET
DEVELOP	DIGICAM	DISPEND	DONGOLA	DROPOUT
DEVIANT	DIGITAL	DISPLAY	DONSHIP	DROPPER
DEVIATE	DIGOXIN	DISPORT	DOODLER	DROPTOP
DEVISAL	DIGRAPH	DISPOSE	DOORMAT	DROSERA
DEVISEE	DILATER	DISPUTE	DOORWAY	DROUGHT
DEVISER	DILATOR	DISRATE	DORHAWK	DROVING
DEVISOR	DILEMMA	DISROBE	DORNECK	DROWNER
DEVOICE	DILUENT	DISROOT	DORNICK	DRUBBER
DEVOLVE	DILUTER	DISRUPT	DORNOCK	DRUDGER
DEVOTEE	DILUTOR	DISSAVE	DOSSIER	DRUGGET
DEWATER	DIMETER	DISSEAT	DOTTREL	DRUGGIE

DRUMBLE	EARDROP	EGOTIZE	EMPEROR	ENPLANE
DRUMLIN	EARDRUM	EIDETIC	EMPIRIC	ENQUIRE
DRUMMER	EARFLAP	EIDOLON	EMPLACE	ENROBER
DRUTHER	EARHOLE	EIGHTVO	EMPLANE	ENSLAVE
DRYLAND	EARLDOM	EINKORN	EMPLOYE	ENSNARE
DRYSUIT	EARLOBE	EIRENIC	EMPOWER	ENSNARL
DRYWALL	EARLOCK	EISWEIN	EMPRISE	ENSUITE
DRYWELL	EARMARK	EJECTOR	EMPRIZE	ENSURER
DUALISE	EARMUFF	EKISTIC	EMPTIER	ENTASIA
DUALISM	EARNEST	EKPWELE	EMPYEMA	ENTENTE
DUALIST	EARNING	ELASTIC	EMULATE	ENTERER
DUALIZE	EARPLUG	ELASTIN	ENABLER	ENTERIC
DUALLIE	EARRING	ELATION	ENACTOR	ENTERON
DUBBING	EARSHOT	ELATIVE	ENAMINE	ENTHRAL
DUBNIUM	EARWORM	ELECTEE	ENAMOUR	ENTHUSE
DUBSTEP	EASTING	ELECTOR	ENATION	ENTICER
DUCKPIN	EATABLE	ELECTRO	ENCHAIN	ENTITLE
DUCTING	EBONISE	ELEGIAC	ENCHANT	ENTRAIN
DUCTULE	EBONITE	ELEGISE	ENCHASE	ENTRANT
DUDETTE	EBONIZE	ELEGIST	ENCLASP	ENTREAT
DUDGEON	ECBOLIC	ELEGIZE	ENCLAVE	ENTRUST
DUELING	ECDYSON	ELEMENT	ENCLOSE	ENTWINE
DUELIST	ECHELLE	ELEVATE	ENCODER	ENTWIST
DUELLER	ECHELON	ELFLOCK	ENCRUST	ENVELOP
DUKEDOM	ECHIDNA	ELISION	ENCRYPT	ENVENOM
DULCIAN	ECHOISM	ELITISM	ENDEMIC	ENVIRON
DULLARD	ECLIPSE	ELITIST	ENDGAME	ENWHEEL
DUMPING	ECLOGUE	ELLIPSE	ENDLEAF	EOBIONT
DUNGEON	ECOCIDE	ELMWOOD	ENDNOTE	EPAULET
DUNKING	ECOGIFT	ELOINER	ENDOGEN	EPAZOTE
DUNNAGE	ECORCHE	ELUSION	ENDOPOD	EPEEIST
DUNNITE	ECOTAGE	ELUTION	ENDORSE	EPERGNE
DUOTONE	ECOTONE	ELUVIUM	ENDOWER	EPHEDRA
DUPATTA	ECOTOUR	EMANATE	ENDPLAY	EPICARP
DURABLE	ECOTYPE	EMBLAZE	ENDURER	EPICENE
DURAMEN	ECOZONE	EMBOSOM	ENERGID	EPICURE
DURANCE	ECTOPIA	EMBOWEL	ENFEOFF	EPIDERM
DURMAST	ECUMENE	EMBOWER	ENFEVER	EPIDOTE
DUSTBIN	EDAMAME	EMBRACE	ENFLAME	EPIGONE
DUSTING	EDIFICE	EMBROIL	ENFORCE	EPIGRAM
DUSTOFF	EDIFIER	EMBROWN	ENFRAME	EPILATE
DUSTPAN	EDITION	EMBRUTE	ENGAGER	EPIMERE
DUSTRAG	EDUCATE	EMBRYON	ENGORGE	EPISCIA
DUUMVIR	EDUCTOR	EMENDER	ENGRAFT	EPISODE
DUVETYN	EELPOUT	EMERALD	ENGRAIL	EPISOME
DWELLER	EELWORM	EMERITA	ENGRAIN	EPISTLE
DWINDLE	EFFACER	EMEROID	ENGRAVE	EPITAPH
DYEWEED	EFFENDI	EMETINE	ENHANCE	EPITHET
DYEWOOD	EFFULGE	EMIRATE	ENJOYER	EPITOME
DYNAMIC	EFTSOON	EMITTER	ENLARGE	EPITOPE
DYSPNEA	EGALITE	EMOCORE	ENLIVEN	EPOXIDE
DYSURIA	EGGHEAD	EMOTION	ENNOBLE	EPSILON
EANLING	EGOTISM	EMPALER	ENOLASE	EQUATOR
EARACHE	EGOTIST	EMPANEL	ENOUNCE	ERASION

ERASURE	EUPNOEA	EXTERNE	FARMING	FETCHER
ERECTER	EUSTELE	EXTINCT	FARRAGO	FETLOCK
ERECTOR	EVACUEE	EXTRACT	FARRIER	FETTLER
EREMITE	EVANGEL	EXTREME	FARSIDE	FEUDIST
EREPSIN	EVASION	EXTRUDE	FARTLEK	FIANCEE
ERISTIC	EVENING	EXUDATE	FASCINE	FIBRATE
ERLKING	EVENTER	EXURBIA	FASCISM	FIBROID
EROSION	EVERTOR	EYEBALL	FASCIST	FIBROIN
EROTICA	EVICTEE	EYEBEAM	FASHION	FIBROMA
EROTISM	EVICTOR	EYEBOLT	FASTING	FIBSTER
EROTIZE	EVOLUTE	EYEBROW	FATBACK	FICTION
ERRATIC	EVOLVER	EYEFOLD	FATBIRD	FIDDLER
ERRHINE	EXABYTE	EYEHOLE	FATHEAD	FIDEISM
ESCALOP	EXACTER	EYEHOOK	FATIGUE	FIDEIST
ESCAPEE	EXACTOR	EYELIFT	FATLING	FIEFDOM
ESCAPER	EXALTER	EYESHOT	FATWOOD	FIELDER
ESCHEAT	EXAMINE	EYESORE	FAUNIST	FIFTEEN
ESCOLAR	EXAMPLE	EYESPOT	FAUVISM	FIGHTER
ESCUAGE	EXCERPT	EYEWINK	FAUVIST	FIGMENT
ESERINE	EXCIMER	FACEOFF	FAVELLA	FIGTREE
ESPARTO	EXCIPLE	FACIEND	FAVORER	FIGURER
ESPOUSE	EXCITER	FACTICE	FAZENDA	FIGWORT
ESQUIRE	EXCITON	FACTION	FEASTER	FILAREE
ESSAYER	EXCITOR	FACTOID	FEATHER	FILBERT
ESSENCE	EXCLAIM	FACTURE	FEATURE	FILCHER
ESTHETE	EXCLAVE	FADDISM	FEDERAL	FILIATE
ESTREAT	EXCLUDE	FADDIST	FEEDBAG	FILIBEG
ESTRIOL	EXCRETE	FADEOUT	FEEDING	FILLING
ESTRONE	EXCUSER	FAGOTER	FEEDLOT	FILMDOM
ETAGERE	EXECUTE	FAIENCE	FEELING	FILMSET
ETAMINE	EXEGETE	FAILING	FEIGNER	FINAGLE
ETATISM	EXERGUE	FAILURE	FELAFEL	FINANCE
ETCHANT	EXHAUST	FAINTER	FELLATE	FINBACK
ETCHING	EXHIBIT	FAIRING	FELSITE	FINDING
ETERNAL	EXHUMER	FAIRWAY	FELSPAR	FINESSE
ETESIAN	EXOCARP	FAITOUR	FELTING	FINFOOT
ETHANAL	EXODERM	FALAFEL	FELUCCA	FINMARK
ETHANOL	EXOTISM	FALBALA	FELWORT	FIREARM
ETHICAL	EXPANSE	FALLING	FENAGLE	FIREBUG
ETHINYL	EXPENSE	FALLOFF	FENCING	FIREDOG
ETHMOID	EXPIATE	FALLOUT	FENLAND	FIREPAN
ETHOXYL	EXPIRER	FANATIC	FENURON	FIREPIT
ETHYNYL	EXPLAIN	FANCIER	FEOFFEE	FIREPOT
EUCAINE	EXPLANT	FANFARE	FEOFFER	FISHEYE
EUCLASE	EXPLODE	FANFOLD	FEOFFOR	FISHGIG
EUCRITE	EXPLOIT	FANGIRL	FERMATA	FISHING
EUDEMON	EXPLORE	FANTAIL	FERMENT	FISHNET
EUGENIA	EXPOSAL	FANTASM	FERMION	FISHWAY
EUGENIC	EXPOSER	FANTAST	FERMIUM	FISSION
EUGENOL	EXPOSIT	FANWORT	FERRATE	FISSURE
EUGLENA	EXPOUND	FANZINE	FERRITE	FISTFUL
EULOGIA	EXPULSE	FARADAY	FERRULE	FISTING
EUPHROE	EXPUNGE	FARCEUR	FERVOUR	FISTULA
EUPLOID	EXSCIND	FARINHA	FESTOON	FITCHET

131

FITCHEW	FLOSSIE	FOOTLER	FRANKUM	FUNCTOR
FITMENT	FLOTAGE	FOOTLES	FRAUGHT	FUNDING
FITTING	FLOTSAM	FOOTPAD	FRAYING	FUNERAL
FIXATIF	FLOUNCE	FOOTSIE	FRAZZLE	FUNFAIR
FIXTURE	FLOUTER	FOOTWAY	FRECKLE	FUNFEST
FLAGGER	FLOWAGE	FOOZLER	FREEBEE	FUNGOID
FLANEUR	FLUBBER	FORAGER	FREEBIE	FUNICLE
FLANGER	FLUBDUB	FORAMEN	FREEDOM	FUNSTER
FLANKER	FLUERIC	FORAYER	FREEGAN	FURBALL
FLANNEL	FLUFFER	FORBEAR	FREESIA	FURCATE
FLAPPER	FLUIDIC	FORBODE	FREEWAY	FURLONG
FLAREUP	FLUNKER	FOREARM	FREEZER	FURNACE
FLASHER	FLUNKEY	FOREBAY	FREIGHT	FURRIER
FLASKET	FLUNKIE	FOREGUT	FRESHEN	FURRING
FLATBED	FLUORID	FORELEG	FRESHER	FURTHER
FLATCAP	FLUORIN	FOREPAW	FRESHET	FUSILLI
FLATCAR	FLUSHER	FORERUN	FRESNEL	FUSSPOT
FLATLET	FLUSTER	FORESEE	FRETSAW	FUSTIAN
FLATTEN	FLUTING	FORETOP	FRETTER	FUTHARC
FLATTER	FLUTIST	FOREVER	FRIBBLE	FUTHARK
FLATTIE	FLUTTER	FORFEIT	FRIGATE	FUTHORC
FLATTOP	FLUXION	FORFEND	FRIJOLE	FUTHORK
FLAVINE	FLYAWAY	FORGING	FRILLER	FUTTOCK
FLAVONE	FLYBELT	FORGIVE	FRISBEE	GABBARD
FLAVOUR	FLYBLOW	FORGOER	FRISEUR	GABBART
FLEABAG	FLYBOAT	FORKFUL	FRISKER	GABBLER
FLEAPIT	FLYLINE	FORMANT	FRISKET	GABELLE
FLEECER	FLYOVER	FORMATE	FRISSON	GABFEST
FLEHMEN	FLYPAST	FORMICA	FRITTER	GADROON
FLENSER	FLYTIER	FORMULA	FRIZZER	GADWALL
FLESHER	FLYTING	FORSAKE	FRIZZLE	GAGSTER
FLEURON	FLYTRAP	FORTUNE	FROGEYE	GAHNITE
FLEXION	FOALING	FORWARD	FROGLET	GAINSAY
FLEXURE	FOCUSER	FOSSICK	FROMAGE	GALABIA
FLICKER	FOGGAGE	FOUETTE	FRONTAL	GALANGA
FLINDER	FOGGING	FOULARD	FRONTON	GALATEA
FLINGER	FOGHORN	FOULING	FROSTED	GALETTE
FLIPPER	FOGYDOM	FOUNDER	FROTHER	GALILEE
FLIRTER	FOGYISM	FOURGON	FROUNCE	GALIPOT
FLITTER	FOILIST	FOVEOLA	FROWNER	GALLANT
FLIVVER	FOLACIN	FOVEOLE	FRUITER	GALLATE
FLOATEL	FOLDOUT	FOWLING	FRUSTUM	GALLEIN
FLOATER	FOLIAGE	FOXFIRE	FUCHSIA	GALLEON
FLOGGER	FOLIATE	FOXHOLE	FUCHSIN	GALLETA
FLOKATI	FOLKMOT	FOXHUNT	FUCKOFF	GALLICA
FLOODER	FOLKWAY	FOXSKIN	FUCKWIT	GALLIOT
FLOORER	FONDANT	FOXTAIL	FUEHRER	GALLIUM
FLOOSIE	FONDLER	FOXTROT	FUELLER	GALLNUT
FLOOZIE	FONTINA	FRACTAL	FUGUIST	GALLOON
FLOPPER	FOOTAGE	FRACTUR	FULCRUM	GALLOOT
FLOREAT	FOOTBAG	FRAENUM	FULFILL	GALOSHE
FLORIST	FOOTBED	FRAKTUR	FULMINE	GALUMPH
FLORUIT	FOOTBOY	FRAMING	FUMBLER	GAMBADE
FLOSSER	FOOTING	FRANKER	FUMETTE	GAMBADO

GAMBIER	GENLOCK	GLIMMER	GOSSOON	GREYLAG
GAMBLER	GENOISE	GLIMPSE	GOTHITE	GRIBBLE
GAMBOGE	GENOMIC	GLISTEN	GOUACHE	GRIDDER
GAMBREL	GENSENG	GLISTER	GOURAMI	GRIDDLE
GAMELAN	GENTIAN	GLITTER	GOURMET	GRIEVER
GAMINES	GENTILE	GLOATER	GRABBER	GRIFFIN
GANACHE	GEODUCK	GLOBOID	GRABBLE	GRIFFON
GANGREL	GEORGIC	GLOBULE	GRACILE	GRIFTER
GANGSTA	GERBERA	GLOCHID	GRACKLE	GRILLER
GANGWAY	GERENUK	GLONOIN	GRADATE	GRIMACE
GANTLET	GESTALT	GLOSSER	GRADINE	GRINDER
GARBAGE	GESTAPO	GLUCOSE	GRADUAL	GRINNER
GARBLER	GESTATE	GLUEPOT	GRAFTER	GRIPPER
GARBLES	GESTURE	GLUTTON	GRAINER	GRISKIN
GARBOIL	GETAWAY	GLYCINE	GRAMMAR	GRISTER
GARGLER	GHARIAL	GLYPTIC	GRANDAD	GRISTLE
GARIGUE	GHERKIN	GNAWING	GRANDAM	GRITTER
GARLAND	GHILLIE	GNOMIST	GRANDEE	GRIZZLE
GARMENT	GHOULIE	GNOSTIC	GRANDMA	GROANER
GAROTTE	GIARDIA	GOBBLER	GRANDPA	GROGRAM
GARPIKE	GIFTING	GOBIOID	GRANGER	GROMMET
GARROTE	GIGABIT	GODDAMN	GRANITA	GROOMER
GASKING	GIGATON	GODETIA	GRANITE	GROOVER
GASOHOL	GIGGLER	GODHEAD	GRANNIE	GROSSER
GASSING	GILBERT	GODHOOD	GRANOLA	GROUPER
GASTREA	GILDING	GODLING	GRANTEE	GROUPIE
GASTRIN	GILLNET	GODROON	GRANTER	GROUSER
GATCHER	GIMMICK	GODSEND	GRANTOR	GROUTER
GATELEG	GINGALL	GODSHIP	GRANULE	GROWLER
GATEWAY	GINGELI	GODWARD	GRAPHIC	GROWNUP
GAUCHER	GINGHAM	GOGGLER	GRAPLIN	GRUBBER
GAUFFER	GINGILI	GOLDARN	GRAPNEL	GRUDGER
GAVOTTE	GINNING	GOLDBUG	GRAPPLE	GRUELER
GAWMOGE	GINSENG	GOLDEYE	GRASPER	GRUMBLE
GAZANIA	GIRAFFE	GOLDURN	GRATING	GRUMMET
GAZELLE	GIRASOL	GOLFING	GRAUPEL	GRUNGER
GAZETTE	GIRDLER	GOLIARD	GRAVIDA	GRUNION
GEARING	GIROLLE	GOLIATH	GRAVURE	GRUNTER
GEEKDOM	GIROSOL	GOLOSHE	GRAYLAG	GRUNTLE
GELATIN	GISARME	GOMBEEN	GRAYOUT	GRUYERE
GELCOAT	GITTERN	GOMERAL	GRAZIER	GRYPHON
GELDING	GIZZARD	GOMEREL	GRAZING	GUANACO
GELLANT	GJETOST	GOMERIL	GREASER	GUANASE
GEMMATE	GLACIER	GONDOLA	GREATEN	GUANINE
GEMMULE	GLADDEN	GOODBYE	GRECIZE	GUARANA
GEMSBOK	GLAMOUR	GOOMBAH	GREENIE	GUARANI
GENERAL	GLANCER	GOOMBAY	GREENTH	GUARDER
GENERIC	GLASSIE	GORCOCK	GREETER	GUAYULE
GENETIC	GLAZIER	GORDITA	GREISEN	GUDGEON
GENETTE	GLAZING	GORILLA	GREMIAL	GUERDON
GENIPAP	GLEAMER	GORMAND	GREMLIN	GUESSER
GENISTA	GLEANER	GOSHAWK	GREMMIE	GUILDER
GENITAL	GLEYING	GOSLING	GRENADE	GUIPURE
GENITOR	GLIADIN	GOSPORT	GREYHEN	GUISARD

GUMBALL	HALACHA	HARPING	HEDONIC	HILDING
GUMBOIL	HALAKAH	HARPIST	HEELING	HILLOCK
GUMBOOT	HALAKHA	HARPOON	HEELTAP	HILLTOP
GUMDROP	HALALAH	HARRIER	HEGEMON	HINDGUT
GUMLINE	HALAVAH	HARSHEN	HEGUMEN	HIPBONE
GUMMITE	HALBERD	HARSLET	HEIGHTH	HIPLINE
GUMMOSE	HALBERT	HARUMPH	HEIRDOM	HIPSTER
GUMSHOE	HALCYON	HARVEST	HEISTER	HIRUDIN
GUMTREE	HALFWIT	HASHTAG	HEKTARE	HISSING
GUMWEED	HALIBUT	HASSIUM	HELIAST	HISTONE
GUMWOOD	HALIDOM	HASSOCK	HELICON	HITCHER
GUNBOAT	HALLWAY	HATBAND	HELIPAD	HOARDER
GUNFIRE	HALOGEN	HATCHEL	HELISKI	HOARSEN
GUNLOCK	HALTERE	HATCHER	HELLCAT	HOATZIN
GUNNERA	HALVING	HATCHET	HELLERI	HOBBLER
GUNNING	HALYARD	HATRACK	HELLION	HOBNAIL
GUNPLAY	HAMATSA	HAUBERK	HELPING	HOBOISM
GUNPORT	HAMBONE	HAULAGE	HEMAGOG	HOECAKE
GUNROOM	HAMBURG	HAULIER	HEMATIC	HOEDOWN
GUNSHIP	HAMMADA	HAULING	HEMATIN	HOGBACK
GUNSHOT	HAMMOCK	HAULOUT	HEMIOLA	HOGMANE
GUNWALE	HAMSTER	HAUNTER	HEMLINE	HOGNOSE
GURGLET	HANAPER	HAUTBOY	HEMLOCK	HOGWEED
GURNARD	HANDBAG	HAUTEUR	HENBANE	HOISTER
GUTTLER	HANDCAR	HAVARTI	HENCOOP	HOLDALL
GUYLINE	HANDFUL	HAVEREL	HENPECK	HOLDING
GUZZLER	HANDGUN	HAVIOUR	HEPARIN	HOLDOUT
GWEDUCK	HANDLER	HAWKING	HEPATIC	HOLIBUT
GYMNAST	HANDLES	HAYCOCK	HEPTANE	HOLIDAY
GYMSLIP	HANDOFF	HAYFORK	HEPTOSE	HOLLAND
GYPLURE	HANDOUT	HAYLAGE	HERBAGE	HOLMIUM
GYPSTER	HANDSAW	HAYLOFT	HERDING	HOLSTER
GYRATOR	HANDSEL	HAYRACK	HERETIC	HOLYDAY
HABITAN	HANDSET	HAYRICK	HERITOR	HOMAGER
HABITAT	HANGDOG	HAYRIDE	HEROINE	HOMBURG
HABITUE	HANGING	HAYSEED	HEROISM	HOMEBOY
HACHURE	HANGOUT	HAYWARD	HEROIZE	HOMINES
HACKBUT	HANGTAG	HAYWIRE	HERRING	HOMINID
HACKING	HANUMAN	HEADEND	HESSIAN	HOMININ
HACKLER	HAPKIDO	HEADFUL	HESSITE	HOMMOCK
HACKNEY	HAPLITE	HEADING	HETAERA	HOMOLOG
HACKSAW	HAPLOID	HEADPIN	HETAIRA	HOMONYM
HADDOCK	HAPLONT	HEADSET	HEXAGON	HONOREE
HAFNIUM	HAPTENE	HEADWAY	HEXAPLA	HONORER
HAFTARA	HARBOUR	HEALING	HEXAPOD	HOOCHIE
HAGGADA	HARDHAT	HEARING	HEXEREI	HOODLUM
HAGGARD	HARDPAN	HEARKEN	HEXOSAN	HOOKING
HAGGLER	HARDTOP	HEARSAY	HIBACHI	HOOKLET
HAGRIDE	HARELIP	HEARTEN	HIDALGO	HOOSGOW
HAHNIUM	HARIANA	HEATHEN	HIDEOUT	HOPEFUL
HAIRCAP	HARICOT	HEATHER	HIGGLER	HOPHEAD
HAIRCUT	HARIJAN	HEATING	HIGHBOY	HOPLITE
HAIRNET	HARISSA	HECKLER	HIGHTOP	HOPPING
HAIRPIN	HARMINE	HECTARE	HIGHWAY	HOPSACK

HOPTOAD	HYGEIST	IMPLORE	INFLATE	INTRUDE
HORDEIN	HYGIENE	IMPOSER	INFLECT	INTRUST
HORIZON	HYMNIST	IMPOUND	INFLICT	INTWINE
HORMONE	HYPERON	IMPOWER	INFRACT	INTWIST
HORNDOG	HYPONEA	IMPREGN	INFUSER	INUKSUK
HORNING	HYPONYM	IMPRESA	INGENUE	INULASE
HORNIST	HYPOXIA	IMPRESE	INGRAFT	INVADER
HORNITO	ICEBERG	IMPREST	INGRAIN	INVALID
HOSANNA	ICEBOAT	IMPRINT	INGRATE	INVEIGH
HOSPICE	ICEFALL	IMPROVE	INGROUP	INVERSE
HOSTAGE	ICEWINE	IMPULSE	INHABIT	INVITEE
HOSTILE	ICEWORM	IMPUTER	INHALER	INVITER
HOSTLER	ICHNITE	INBEING	INHERIT	INVOICE
HOTCAKE	ICTERIC	INBOARD	INHIBIN	INVOKER
HOTFOOT	IDLESSE	INBOUND	INHIBIT	INVOLVE
HOTHEAD	IDOLISE	INBREED	INHUMER	INWEAVE
HOTLINE	IDOLISM	INBURST	INITIAL	IODIZER
HOTLINK	IDOLIZE	INCENSE	INJURER	IONISER
HOTSHOT	IDYLIST	INCIPIT	INKBLOT	IONIZER
HOTSPOT	IGNATIA	INCISOR	INKHORN	IONOGEN
HOTSPUR	IGNITER	INCITER	INKLING	IONOMER
HOUNDER	IGNITOR	INCLASP	INKWELL	IPOMOEA
HOUNGAN	IGNORER	INCLINE	INKWOOD	IRIDIUM
HOUSING	IGUANID	INCLOSE	INLAYER	IRONING
HOVERER	IKEBANA	INCLUDE	INNERVE	IRONISE
HRYVNIA	ILLEGAL	INCOMER	INOSINE	IRONIST
HRYVNYA	ILLOGIC	INCONNU	INOSITE	IRONIZE
HUDDLER	IMAGINE	INCRUST	INQUEST	ISAGOGE
HUMBLER	IMAGING	INCURVE	INQUIET	ISATINE
HUMDRUM	IMAGISM	INDAMIN	INQUIRE	ISOBARE
HUMERAL	IMAGIST	INDEXER	INSCAPE	ISOBATH
HUMIDOR	IMAMATE	INDICAN	INSCULP	ISOCHOR
HUMMOCK	IMBIBER	INDICIA	INSIDER	ISOFORM
HUNDRED	IMBLAZE	INDIGEN	INSIGHT	ISOGONE
HUNTING	IMBOSOM	INDITER	INSNARE	ISOGRAM
HURDLER	IMBOWER	INDORSE	INSPECT	ISOGRIV
HURLING	IMBROWN	INDOXYL	INSPIRE	ISOHYET
HURRIER	IMBRUTE	INDRAFT	INSTALL	ISOLATE
HURTLES	IMITATE	INDUCER	INSTANT	ISOLEAD
HUSBAND	IMMERGE	INDULGE	INSTATE	ISOLINE
HUSKING	IMMERSE	INDULIN	INSTILL	ISOPACH
HUSTLER	IMPAINT	INDWELL	INSULAR	ISOSPIN
HUSWIFE	IMPALER	INEARTH	INSULIN	ISOTACH
HUTMENT	IMPANEL	INERTIA	INSURED	ISOTONE
HUTZPAH	IMPASSE	INFANTA	INSURER	ISOTOPE
HYALINE	IMPASTE	INFANTE	INTEGER	ISOTYPE
HYALITE	IMPASTO	INFARCT	INTERIM	ISOZYME
HYALOID	IMPEARL	INFAUNA	INTERNE	ITCHING
HYDATID	IMPEDER	INFEOFF	INTHRAL	ITEMISE
HYDRANT	IMPERIL	INFERNO	INTITLE	ITEMIZE
HYDRASE	IMPINGE	INFIDEL	INTONER	ITERATE
HYDRATE	IMPLANT	INFIELD	INTRANT	JACAMAR
HYDRIDE	IMPLEAD	INFIGHT	INTREAT	JACINTH
HYDROID	IMPLODE	INFLAME	INTROIT	JACKDAW

JACKLEG	JOURNAL	KEESTER	KIPSKIN	LACUNAR
JACKPOT	JOURNEY	KEGELER	KISTFUL	LADANUM
JACOBIN	JOUSTER	KEGLING	KITCHEN	LADDISM
JACONET	JOYANCE	KEISTER	KITHARA	LADHOOD
JACUZZI	JOYRIDE	KEITLOA	KITLING	LADRONE
JADEITE	JUBILEE	KENNING	KLAVERN	LADYBUG
JALAPIN	JUDOIST	KERAMIC	KLEAGLE	LADYKIN
JAMBEAU	JUGGLER	KERATIN	KLEZMER	LAGGARD
JANGLER	JUGHEAD	KERMODE	KLISTER	LAGGING
JANITOR	JUGULAR	KERNING	KNACKER	LAICISE
JARGOON	JUJITSU	KERNITE	KNAIDEL	LAICISM
JARHEAD	JUJUISM	KEROGEN	KNAPPER	LAICIZE
JARLDOM	JUJUIST	KERYGMA	KNEADER	LAIRAGE
JASMINE	JUJUTSU	KESTREL	KNEECAP	LAKEBED
JAVELIN	JUMBLER	KETCHUP	KNEELER	LALIQUE
JAWBONE	JUMBUCK	KEYCARD	KNEEPAD	LALLAND
JAWLINE	JUMPING	KEYHOLE	KNEEPAN	LAMBADA
JAYBIRD	JUMPOFF	KEYNOTE	KNEIDEL	LAMBAST
JAYWALK	JUNIPER	KEYSTER	KNESSET	LAMBERT
JEEPNEY	JUSSIVE	KEYWORD	KNIFING	LAMBING
JEJUNUM	JUSTICE	KHADDAR	KNITTER	LAMBKIN
JELLABA	JUVENAL	KHALIFA	KNOCKER	LAMELLA
JEMADAR	KABADDI	KHAMSIN	KNOLLER	LAMINAL
JEMIDAR	KABBALA	KHANATE	KNOTTER	LAMININ
JEOPARD	KABOCHA	KHEDIVE	KNOWING	LAMPION
JERREED	KACHINA	KHIRKAH	KNUCKLE	LAMPOON
JESTING	KAINITE	KIBITKA	KOKANEE	LAMPREY
JETBEAD	KAJEPUT	KICKING	KOLBASI	LAMSTER
JETFOIL	KAKIVAK	KICKOFF	KOMATIK	LANDING
JETPACK	KALIMBA	KIDSKIN	KOPIYKA	LANDLER
JETPORT	KAMOTIK	KIESTER	KOTOWER	LANEWAY
JEWELER	KAMOTIQ	KILLDEE	KOUPREY	LANGLEY
JEZEBEL	KAMPONG	KILLICK	KREMLIN	LANGREL
JIBBOOM	KAMSEEN	KILLING	KREUZER	LANGUET
JIGABOO	KANTELE	KILLJOY	KRIMMER	LANGUOR
JILLION	KAOLINE	KILLOCK	KRULLER	LANIARD
JINGALL	KARAKUL	KILOBAR	KRYPTON	LANITAL
JINGLER	KARAOKE	KILOBIT	KUMQUAT	LANOLIN
JOBNAME	KARTING	KILORAD	KUNZITE	LANTANA
JOCKDOM	KASHMIR	KILOTON	KYANISE	LANTERN
JODHPUR	KASHRUT	KILTING	KYANITE	LANYARD
JOGGING	KATCINA	KIMCHEE	KYANIZE	LAPWING
JOGGLER	KATHODE	KINDLER	LABARUM	LARDOON
JOGTROT	KATHUMP	KINDLES	LABELER	LARIGAN
JOHNNIE	KATSINA	KINDRED	LABIATE	LASAGNA
JOHNSON	KATSURA	KINESIC	LABORER	LASAGNE
JOINDER	KATYDID	KINETIC	LABROID	LASHING
JOINING	KAYAKER	KINETIN	LACQUER	LASHKAR
JOINTER	KEBBOCK	KINFOLK	LACQUEY	LASSOER
JOLLIER	KEBBUCK	KINGCUP	LACTASE	LASTING
JONQUIL	KEELAGE	KINGDOM	LACTATE	LATAKIA
JOSHING	KEELSON	KINGLET	LACTEAL	LATCHET
JOSTLER	KEENING	KINGPIN	LACTONE	LATERAL
JOTTING	KEEPING	KINSHIP	LACTOSE	LATHING

LATILLA	LETDOWN	LITHIUM	LUNATIC	MALANGA
LATOSOL	LETTUCE	LIVENER	LUNCHER	MALARIA
LATRINE	LEUCINE	LIVEYER	LUNETTE	MALEATE
LATTICE	LEUCISM	LOADING	LUNGFUL	MALISON
LAUGHER	LEUCITE	LOAFING	LUPANAR	MALLARD
LAUNDER	LEUCOMA	LOANING	LUPULIN	MALLING
LAUWINE	LEUKOMA	LOATHER	LURCHER	MALMSEY
LAVROCK	LEVATOR	LOBBYER	LURDANE	MALODOR
LAWBOOK	LEVELER	LOBEFIN	LUSTRUM	MALTASE
LAWSUIT	LEVERET	LOBELIA	LUTFISK	MALTING
LAYAWAY	LEVULIN	LOBSTER	LUTHERN	MALTOSE
LAYETTE	LEXICON	LOBTAIL	LUTHIER	MALWARE
LAYOVER	LIAISON	LOBWORM	LYCOPOD	MAMASAN
LAZARET	LIBELEE	LOCATER	LYDDITE	MAMMOCK
LEACHER	LIBELER	LOCATOR	LYNCHER	MAMMOTH
LEADING	LIBERAL	LOCKAGE	LYRICON	MANACLE
LEADOFF	LIBRATE	LOCKJAW	LYSOGEN	MANAGER
LEAFAGE	LICENCE	LOCKNUT	LYTHRUM	MANAKIN
LEAFLET	LICENSE	LOCKOUT	MACADAM	MANATEE
LEAGUER	LICKING	LOCKRAM	MACAQUE	MANCHET
LEAKAGE	LIFEWAY	LOCKSET	MACARON	MANDALA
LEANING	LIFTOFF	LOCOISM	MACHACA	MANDATE
LEARNER	LIGHTEN	LODGING	MACHETE	MANDOLA
LEASING	LIGHTER	LOGBOOK	MACHINE	MANDORA
LEATHER	LIGNITE	LOGGING	MACHREE	MANDREL
LEAVING	LIGROIN	LOGROLL	MACHZOR	MANDRIL
LECTERN	LIMACON	LOGWOOD	MACRAME	MANGLER
LECTION	LIMBECK	LONGBOW	MACUMBA	MANGOLD
LECTURE	LIMEADE	LONGING	MADEIRA	MANHOLE
LECYTHI	LIMITED	LOOKISM	MADONNA	MANHOOD
LEEWARD	LIMITER	LOOKIST	MADRASA	MANHUNT
LEFTISM	LIMPKIN	LOOKOUT	MADRONA	MANIHOT
LEFTIST	LINALOL	LOOTING	MADRONE	MANIKIN
LEGATEE	LINDANE	LORDING	MADRONO	MANILLA
LEGATOR	LINEAGE	LORDOMA	MADWORT	MANILLE
LEGGING	LINECUT	LORGNON	MADZOON	MANIOCA
LEGHOLD	LINGCOD	LORIMER	MAESTRO	MANIPLE
LEGHORN	LINGUAL	LORINER	MAFFICK	MANITOU
LEGROOM	LINKAGE	LOUNGER	MAFIOSO	MANKIND
LEGUMIN	LINKBOY	LOVEBUG	MAGALOG	MANNITE
LEGWORK	LINOCUT	LOWBALL	MAGENTA	MANNOSE
LEHAYIM	LINSANG	LOWBROW	MAGNATE	MANROPE
LEISTER	LINSEED	LOWDOWN	MAGNETO	MANSARD
LEISURE	LINURON	LOWLAND	MAHATMA	MANSION
LEMMING	LIONISE	LOWLIFE	MAHJONG	MANTEAU
LEMPIRA	LIONIZE	LOZENGE	MAHONIA	MANTLET
LENDING	LIPPING	LUCARNE	MAHUANG	MANTRAM
LENSING	LIPREAD	LUCENCE	MAILBAG	MANTRAP
LENTISK	LIQUATE	LUCERNE	MAILING	MANUMIT
LENTOID	LIQUEUR	LUCIFER	MAILLOT	MANURER
LEOPARD	LIRIOPE	LUGGAGE	MAINTOP	MANWARD
LEOTARD	LISPING	LUGSAIL	MAJAGUA	MAPPING
LEPORID	LISTING	LUGWORM	MALACCA	MAQUILA
LESBIAN	LITERAL	LUMBAGO	MALAISE	MARABOU

MARANTA	MAYPOLE	MESQUIT	MINIBAR	MISMEET
MARASCA	MAYWEED	MESSAGE	MINICAB	MISMOVE
MARBLER	MAZURKA	MESSIAH	MINICAM	MISNAME
MARCATO	MAZZARD	MESTESO	MINICAR	MISPAGE
MARCHER	MEANDER	MESTINO	MINIKIN	MISPART
MARCONI	MEANING	MESTIZA	MINILAB	MISPLAN
MARGATE	MEASURE	MESTIZO	MINIMAL	MISPLAY
MARGENT	MECHOUI	METAMER	MINIMUM	MISRATE
MARIMBA	MEDDLER	METATAG	MINISKI	MISREAD
MARINER	MEDEVAC	METHANE	MINIVAN	MISRULE
MARKHOR	MEDIANT	METICAL	MINIVER	MISSEAT
MARKING	MEDIATE	METISSE	MINORCA	MISSEND
MARLINE	MEDICAL	METONYM	MINSTER	MISSILE
MARLING	MEDIGAP	METOPON	MINTAGE	MISSION
MARLITE	MEDIVAC	METRIST	MINUEND	MISSIVE
MARMITE	MEDRESE	MEZQUIT	MIRACLE	MISSORT
MARPLOT	MEDULLA	MEZUZAH	MIRADOR	MISSOUT
MARQUEE	MEDUSAN	MICELLE	MISAVER	MISSTEP
MARQUES	MEERKAT	MICROBE	MISBILL	MISSTOP
MARRANO	MEETING	MICROHM	MISBIND	MISSUIT
MARRIED	MEGABAR	MIDCULT	MISCALL	MISTAKE
MARRIER	MEGABIT	MIDDLER	MISCAST	MISTBOW
MARSALA	MEGAHIT	MIDIRON	MISCITE	MISTEND
MARSHAL	MEGAPOD	MIDLAND	MISCODE	MISTERM
MARTIAN	MEGASSE	MIDLINE	MISCOIN	MISTIME
MARTINI	MEGATON	MIDLIST	MISCOOK	MISTRAL
MARTLET	MEGILLA	MIDMOST	MISDATE	MISTUNE
MASCARA	MEGILPH	MIDNOON	MISDEAL	MISTYPE
MASKING	MEISTER	MIDRIFF	MISDEED	MISUSER
MASQUER	MELAENA	MIDSHIP	MISDEEM	MISWORD
MASSAGE	MELANGE	MIDSOLE	MISDIAL	MISYOKE
MASSEUR	MELANIC	MIDTERM	MISDOER	MITERER
MASTABA	MELANIN	MIDTOWN	MISDRAW	MITOGEN
MASTIFF	MELILOT	MIDWEEK	MISEASE	MITSVAH
MASTOID	MELISMA	MIDWIFE	MISEDIT	MITZVAH
MATADOR	MELODIA	MIDYEAR	MISFEED	MIXDOWN
MATCHER	MELTAGE	MIGRANT	MISFILE	MIXTAPE
MATCHUP	MEMENTO	MIGRATE	MISFIRE	MIXTURE
MATELOT	MEMETIC	MILEAGE	MISFOLD	MOBBISM
MATILDA	MENACER	MILFOIL	MISFORM	MOBSTER
MATINEE	MENAZON	MILITIA	MISGAGE	MOCHILA
MATTING	MENDIGO	MILKSOP	MISGIVE	MODELER
MATTOCK	MENDING	MILLAGE	MISGROW	MODERNE
MATTOID	MENFOLK	MILLDAM	MISHEAR	MODICUM
MATURER	MENORAH	MILLIER	MISJOIN	MODISTE
MATZOON	MENTHOL	MILLIME	MISKEEP	MODULAR
MAULING	MENTION	MILLINE	MISKICK	MOFETTE
MAUNDER	MERCADO	MILLING	MISKNOW	MOIDORE
MAXILLA	MERGING	MILLION	MISLEAD	MOISTEN
MAXIMAL	MERMAID	MILLRUN	MISLIKE	MOJARRA
MAXIMIN	MERONYM	MINARET	MISLIVE	MOLDING
MAXIMUM	MEROPIA	MINDSET	MISMAKE	MOLLUSC
MAXWELL	MESCLUN	MINERAL	MISMARK	MOLLUSK
MAYBIRD	MESHING	MINGLER	MISMATE	MOMENTO

138

MONACID	MOURNER	MUTATOR	NEPHRON	NOMBRIL
MONARCH	MOUSAKA	MUZZLER	NERVINE	NOMINAL
MONARDA	MOUSING	MYALGIA	NERVING	NOMINEE
MONAXON	MOUTHER	MYELINE	NERVULE	NONACID
MONERAN	MOVABLE	MYELOMA	NERVURE	NONAGON
MONEYER	MOVIOLA	MYLODON	NESTFUL	NONBANK
MONGREL	MOZETTA	MYNHEER	NESTLER	NONBOOK
MONIKER	MUDBANK	MYOMERE	NETBALL	NONCOLA
MONITOR	MUDDLER	MYOSOTE	NETBOOK	NONFACT
MONOCLE	MUDFLAP	MYOTOME	NETIZEN	NONPAST
MONOCOT	MUDFLAT	NACELLE	NETSUKE	NONPLAY
MONOFIL	MUDFLOW	NAGGING	NETSURF	NONSKED
MONOLOG	MUDHOLE	NAGWARE	NETTING	NONSTOP
MONOMER	MUDLARK	NAILSET	NETTLER	NONSUIT
MONOPOD	MUDPACK	NAIVETE	NETWORK	NONUPLE
MONOSKI	MUDROCK	NAMETAG	NEURINE	NONUSER
MONSOON	MUDROOM	NANDINA	NEUROMA	NONWORD
MONSTER	MUDSILL	NANKEEN	NEURONE	NOONDAY
MONTAGE	MUEDDIN	NANOBOT	NEURULA	NOONING
MONTANE	MUEZZIN	NAPHTHA	NEUSTON	NORLAND
MONTERO	MUFFLER	NAPHTOL	NEUTRAL	NORTENA
MONURON	MUGGING	NARCEIN	NEUTRON	NORTENO
MOOCHER	MUGSHOT	NARCISM	NEWBORN	NORTHER
MOONBOW	MUGWORT	NARCIST	NEWSBOY	NOSEBAG
MOONDOG	MUGWUMP	NARCOMA	NIAGARA	NOSEGAY
MOONEYE	MUKHTAR	NARCOSE	NIBBLER	NOSTRIL
MOONLET	MULATTO	NARGILE	NIBLICK	NOSTRUM
MOONSET	MULLEIN	NARRATE	NICOTIN	NOTABLE
MOORAGE	MULLION	NARWHAL	NICTATE	NOTATOR
MOORHEN	MULLITE	NATRIUM	NIGELLA	NOTCHER
MOORING	MULLOCK	NATURAL	NIGGARD	NOTELET
MOPHEAD	MULTURE	NAVARIN	NIGGLER	NOTEPAD
MORAINE	MUMBLER	NAVETTE	NIGHTIE	NOTHING
MORDANT	MUMMING	NEATNIK	NILGHAI	NOTICER
MORDENT	MUNCHER	NECKING	NILGHAU	NOVELLA
MORELLE	MUNCHIE	NECKLET	NINEPIN	NOWHERE
MORELLO	MUNNION	NECKTIE	NIOBATE	NUCLEIN
MORNING	MUNSTER	NECROSE	NIOBITE	NUCLEON
MOROCCO	MUNTING	NEEDFUL	NIOBIUM	NUCLIDE
MORPHIA	MUNTJAC	NEEDLER	NIRVANA	NUDNICK
MORPHIN	MUNTJAK	NEEDLES	NITCHIE	NUMERAL
MORRION	MUONIUM	NEGATER	NITERIE	NUMERIC
MORTICE	MURIATE	NEGATON	NITINOL	NUNATAK
MORTISE	MURRAIN	NEGATOR	NITPICK	NUNCHUK
MOSCATO	MURTHER	NEGLECT	NITRATE	NUPTIAL
MOSELLE	MUSETTE	NEGLIGE	NITRIDE	NURSING
MOSHING	MUSHING	NEGROID	NITRILE	NURTURE
MOSTEST	MUSHRAT	NEGRONI	NITRITE	NUTCASE
MOTTLER	MUSICAL	NELUMBO	NOBBLER	NUTGALL
MOUFLON	MUSKRAT	NEMATIC	NOCTUID	NUTMEAT
MOULAGE	MUSPIKE	NEMESIA	NOCTULE	NUTPICK
MOULDER	MUSTANG	NEOLITH	NOCTURN	NUTTING
MOULTER	MUSTARD	NEONATE	NOGGING	NUTWOOD
MOUNTER	MUTAGEN	NEOTYPE	NOMARCH	NUZZLER

NYLGHAI	OILSEED	ORPHREY	OUTGROW	OUTSULK
NYLGHAU	OILSKIN	ORTOLAN	OUTHAUL	OUTSWIM
NYMPHET	OINOMEL	OSMUNDA	OUTHEAR	OUTTAKE
OARLOCK	OLDSTER	OSSETRA	OUTHOWL	OUTTALK
OATCAKE	OLEFINE	OSSICLE	OUTHUNT	OUTTASK
OATMEAL	OLESTRA	OSTEOID	OUTJUMP	OUTTELL
OBELISE	OLICOOK	OSTEOMA	OUTKEEP	OUTTROT
OBELISK	OLIVINE	OSTIOLE	OUTKICK	OUTTURN
OBELISM	OLOGIST	OSTMARK	OUTKILL	OUTVOTE
OBELIZE	OLOROSO	OTALGIA	OUTLAND	OUTWAIT
OBLIGEE	OMENTUM	OTOCYST	OUTLAST	OUTWALK
OBLIGER	OMICRON	OTOLITH	OUTLEAD	OUTWARD
OBLIGOR	OMIKRON	OTTOMAN	OUTLEAP	OUTWEAR
OBLIQUE	OMITTER	OUABAIN	OUTLIER	OUTWEEP
OBSCURE	ONANISM	OUGUIYA	OUTLINE	OUTWILE
OBSERVE	ONANIST	OUTBACK	OUTLIVE	OUTWILL
OBTRUDE	ONBOARD	OUTBAKE	OUTLOOK	OUTWIND
OBVERSE	ONOMAST	OUTBARK	OUTLOVE	OUTWORK
OBVIATE	OOMIACK	OUTBAWL	OUTMODE	OUTYELL
OCARINA	OOPHYTE	OUTBEAM	OUTMOVE	OUTYELP
OCCIPUT	OOSPERM	OUTBRAG	OUTPACE	OVATION
OCCLUDE	OOSPORE	OUTBULK	OUTPLAN	OVERACT
OCTAGON	OPALINE	OUTBURN	OUTPLAY	OVERAGE
OCTANOL	OPENING	OUTCALL	OUTPLOD	OVERALL
OCTETTE	OPERAND	OUTCAST	OUTPLOT	OVERARM
OCTOPOD	OPERANT	OUTCOME	OUTPOLL	OVERAWE
OCTUPLE	OPERATE	OUTCOOK	OUTPORT	OVERBET
OCULIST	OPINION	OUTCROP	OUTPOST	OVERBID
ODALISK	OPOSSUM	OUTCROW	OUTPOUR	OVERBUY
ODDBALL	OPPIDAN	OUTDARE	OUTPRAY	OVERCUT
ODDMENT	OPPOSER	OUTDATE	OUTPULL	OVERDOG
ODONATE	OPSONIN	OUTDOER	OUTRACE	OVERDUB
ODORANT	OPTIMUM	OUTDOOR	OUTRAGE	OVERDYE
ODORIZE	OPUNTIA	OUTDRAG	OUTRANK	OVEREAT
ODYSSEY	OQUASSA	OUTDRAW	OUTRATE	OVERJOY
OENOMEL	ORALISM	OUTDROP	OUTRAVE	OVERLAP
OERSTED	ORALIST	OUTDUEL	OUTREAD	OVERLAY
OESTRIN	ORATION	OUTEARN	OUTRIDE	OVERLET
OESTRUM	ORATURE	OUTFACE	OUTRING	OVERLIE
OFFBEAT	ORBITAL	OUTFALL	OUTROAR	OVERMAN
OFFCAST	ORBITER	OUTFAST	OUTROCK	OVERPAY
OFFENCE	ORCHARD	OUTFAWN	OUTROLL	OVERRUN
OFFENSE	ORCINOL	OUTFEEL	OUTROOT	OVERSEA
OFFEREE	ORDERER	OUTFIND	OUTSAIL	OVERSEE
OFFERER	ORDINAL	OUTFIRE	OUTSELL	OVERSET
OFFEROR	OREGANO	OUTFLOW	OUTSERT	OVERSEW
OFFICER	ORGANIC	OUTFOOL	OUTSIDE	OVERSUP
OFFLOAD	ORGANON	OUTFOOT	OUTSING	OVERTIP
OFFRAMP	ORGANUM	OUTGAIN	OUTSIZE	OVERTOP
OFFSIDE	ORGANZA	OUTGAZE	OUTSOAR	OVERUSE
OGREISM	ORGIAST	OUTGIVE	OUTSOLE	OVERWET
OILBIRD	ORIFICE	OUTGLOW	OUTSPAN	OVICIDE
OILCAMP	ORIGAMI	OUTGNAW	OUTSTAY	OVIDUCT
OILHOLE	ORPHISM	OUTGRIN	OUTSTEP	OVOIDAL

OVULATE	PALLIUM	PARGING	PAYLOAD	PEONAGE
OXALATE	PALMFUL	PARKADE	PAYMENT	PEONISM
OXAZINE	PALMIER	PARKING	PAYROLL	PEOPLER
OXAZOLE	PALMIST	PARKOUR	PAYSLIP	PEPSINE
OXBLOOD	PALMTOP	PARKWAY	PAYWALL	PEPTALK
OXHEART	PALMYRA	PARLOUR	PEACHER	PEPTIDE
OXIDANT	PALOOKA	PAROLEE	PEACOAT	PEPTIZE
OXIDASE	PALPATE	PARONYM	PEACOCK	PEPTONE
OXIDATE	PALSHIP	PAROTID	PEAFOWL	PERACID
OXIDISE	PAMPEAN	PARQUET	PEARLER	PERCALE
OXIDIZE	PAMPERO	PARRIER	PEASANT	PERCENT
OXYACID	PANACEA	PARSLEY	PEASCOD	PERCEPT
OXYPHIL	PANACHE	PARSNIP	PECCAVI	PERCHER
OXYSALT	PANCAKE	PARTAKE	PECTASE	PERCOID
OXYSOME	PANDECT	PARTIAL	PECTATE	PERDURE
OXYTONE	PANDOOR	PARTIER	PECTIZE	PEREION
OZONATE	PANDORA	PARTING	PEDAGOG	PERFECT
OZONIDE	PANDORE	PARTITA	PEDALER	PERFORM
OZONISE	PANDOUR	PARTLET	PEDDLER	PERFUME
OZONIZE	PANDURA	PARTNER	PEDICAB	PERFUSE
PABULUM	PANGENE	PARTYER	PEDICEL	PERGOLA
PACHISI	PANGRAM	PARVENU	PEDICLE	PERIAPT
PACHUCO	PANICLE	PARVISE	PEDOCAL	PERIDOT
PACKAGE	PANICUM	PASCHAL	PEEBEEN	PERIGEE
PACKING	PANNIER	PASQUIL	PEELING	PERIGON
PACTION	PANNIST	PASSADE	PEENING	PERILLA
PADDING	PANOCHA	PASSADO	PEERAGE	PERIQUE
PADDLER	PANOCHE	PASSAGE	PEKEPOO	PERIWIG
PADDOCK	PANPIPE	PASSING	PELAGIC	PERJURE
PADLOCK	PANTHER	PASSION	PELICAN	PERLITE
PADRONA	PANTILE	PASSIVE	PELISSE	PERMUTE
PADRONE	PANTOUM	PASSKEY	PELORIA	PEROGIE
PADSHAH	PAPADAM	PASTERN	PELOTON	PEROXID
PAESANO	PAPADOM	PASTEUP	PELTAST	PERPEND
PAGEANT	PAPADUM	PASTIME	PEMBINA	PERPENT
PAGEBOY	PAPASAN	PASTINA	PEMICAN	PERSALT
PAGEFUL	PAPERER	PASTING	PENANCE	PERSIST
PAGURID	PAPHIAN	PASTURE	PENDANT	PERSONA
PAHLAVI	PAPOOSE	PATAMAR	PENDENT	PERTAIN
PAILFUL	PAPRICA	PATCHER	PENGUIN	PERTURB
PAINTER	PAPRIKA	PATELLA	PENICIL	PERUSAL
PAIRING	PARABLE	PATHWAY	PENLITE	PERUSER
PAISANA	PARADER	PATIENT	PENNAME	PERVADE
PAISANO	PARADOR	PATRIOT	PENNANT	PERVERT
PAISLEY	PARAGON	PATROON	PENNINE	PETCOCK
PALABRA	PARAPET	PATTERN	PENOCHE	PETIOLE
PALADIN	PARASOL	PAVIOUR	PENSION	PETRALE
PALATAL	PARATHA	PAVISER	PENSTER	PETTING
PALAVER	PARBAKE	PAVISSE	PENTANE	PETUNIA
PALAZZO	PARBOIL	PAVLOVA	PENTENE	PEYTRAL
PALETOT	PARDNER	PAWNAGE	PENTODE	PEYTREL
PALETTE	PAREIRA	PAYABLE	PENTOSE	PFENNIG
PALFREY	PARETIC	PAYBACK	PENUCHE	PHAETON
PALIKAR	PARFAIT	PAYDOWN	PENUCHI	PHANTOM

PHARAOH	PIGTAIL	PLACATE	PLUGGER	POMPANO
PHARMER	PIGWEED	PLACEBO	PLUGOLA	PONIARD
PHASMID	PILGRIM	PLACING	PLUMAGE	PONTIFF
PHELLEM	PILLAGE	PLACKET	PLUMBER	PONTOON
PHENATE	PILLBUG	PLACOID	PLUMBUM	POOFTAH
PHILTER	PILLION	PLAFOND	PLUMMET	POOFTER
PHILTRE	PILLOCK	PLAGUER	PLUMPEN	POPCORN
PHISHER	PILSNER	PLAITER	PLUMPER	POPEDOM
PHONATE	PIMENTO	PLANCHE	PLUMULE	POPOVER
PHONEME	PIMPING	PLANNER	PLUNDER	POPSTER
PHORATE	PINBALL	PLANTER	PLUNGER	PORCINI
PHOTINO	PINBONE	PLASHER	PLUNKER	PORKPIE
PHYTANE	PINCHER	PLASMID	PLUVIAL	PORTAGE
PIAFFER	PINCURL	PLASMIN	PLYWOOD	PORTEND
PIANISM	PINESAP	PLASMON	POACHER	PORTENT
PIANIST	PINFOLD	PLASTER	POBLANO	PORTICO
PIANOLA	PINHEAD	PLASTIC	POCHARD	PORTION
PIASABA	PINHOLE	PLASTID	POCOSEN	PORTRAY
PIASAVA	PINITOL	PLATANE	POCOSIN	POSTAGE
PIASTER	PINKEYE	PLATEAU	POCOSON	POSTBAG
PIASTRE	PINKING	PLATINA	PODAGRA	POSTBOY
PIBROCH	PINNACE	PLATING	PODCAST	POSTDOC
PICACHO	PINNULE	PLATOON	PODESTA	POSTEEN
PICADOR	PINOCLE	PLATTER	POETISE	POSTERN
PICCATA	PINSPOT	PLAUDIT	POETIZE	POSTING
PICCOLO	PINTADA	PLAYACT	POGONIA	POSTURE
PICKAXE	PINTADO	PLAYBOY	POGONIP	POTABLE
PICKEER	PINTAIL	PLAYDAY	POINTER	POTBOIL
PICKING	PINTANO	PLAYLET	POITREL	POTENCE
PICKLER	PINTUCK	PLAYOFF	POLARON	POTHEAD
PICKNEY	PINWALE	PLAYPEN	POLEAXE	POTHEEN
PICKOFF	PINWEED	PLAYSET	POLECAT	POTHERB
PICOLIN	PINWORK	PLEADER	POLEMIC	POTHOLE
PICOTEE	PINWORM	PLEASER	POLENTA	POTHOOK
PICQUET	PIONEER	PLEATER	POLICER	POTICHE
PICRATE	PIPEAGE	PLEDGEE	POLITIC	POTLINE
PICRITE	PIPEFUL	PLEDGER	POLLACK	POTLUCK
PICTURE	PIPETTE	PLEDGET	POLLARD	POTSHOT
PIDDLER	PIRAGUA	PLEDGOR	POLLING	POTTAGE
PIDDOCK	PIRANHA	PLENISM	POLLIST	POTTEEN
PIEBALD	PIROGUE	PLENIST	POLLOCK	POULARD
PIECING	PIROQUE	PLEOPOD	POLLUTE	POULTER
PIEFORT	PISCINA	PLEROMA	POLOIST	POUNCER
PIEHOLE	PISHOGE	PLESSOR	POLYBAG	POUNDAL
PIERCER	PISMIRE	PLIMSOL	POLYCOT	POUNDER
PIERROT	PISSANT	PLINKER	POLYENE	POUSSIE
PIETISM	PISSOIR	PLISKIE	POLYGON	POUTINE
PIETIST	PISTOLE	PLODDER	POLYMER	PRAETOR
PIFFLER	PITAPAT	PLONKER	POLYNYA	PRAIRIE
PIGBOAT	PITCHER	PLOSION	POLYOMA	PRAISER
PIGMENT	PITFALL	PLOSIVE	POLYPED	PRALINE
PIGNOLI	PITHEAD	PLOTTER	POLYPOD	PRANCER
PIGSKIN	PITTING	PLOWBOY	POMATUM	PRATTLE
PIGSNEY	PLACARD	PLUCKER	POMFRET	PRAWNER

142

PREAVER	PRESAGE	PROCEED	PSALTER	PYRRHIC
PREBAKE	PRESALE	PROCTOR	PSAMMON	PYRROLE
PREBEND	PRESELL	PROCURE	PSCHENT	QABALAH
PREBILL	PRESENT	PRODDER	PSYCHIC	QAMUTIK
PREBIND	PRESHIP	PRODRUG	PSYLLID	QAWWALI
PREBOIL	PRESHOW	PRODUCE	PTOMAIN	QUADRAT
PREBOOK	PRESIDE	PRODUCT	PTYALIN	QUADRIC
PRECAST	PRESIFT	PROETTE	PUBBING	QUAFFER
PRECEDE	PRESOAK	PROFANE	PUCCOON	QUAHAUG
PRECENT	PRESORT	PROFFER	PUDDING	QUANTIC
PRECEPT	PRESSER	PROFILE	PUDDLER	QUARREL
PRECIPE	PRESSOR	PROGGER	PUGAREE	QUARTAN
PRECISE	PRESTER	PROGRAM	PUGGING	QUARTER
PRECODE	PRESUME	PROJECT	PUGGREE	QUARTET
PRECOOK	PRETAPE	PROLINE	PUGMARK	QUARTIC
PRECOOL	PRETEEN	PROLONG	PULLMAN	QUASHER
PRECURE	PRETELL	PROMINE	PULLOUT	QUASSIA
PREDATE	PRETEND	PROMISE	PULPING	QUASSIN
PREDAWN	PRETERM	PROMOTE	PULSATE	QUAYAGE
PREDICT	PRETEST	PRONATE	PULSION	QUELLER
PREDUSK	PRETEXT	PRONOUN	PUMICER	QUERIDA
PREEDIT	PRETRIM	PROOFER	PUMMELO	QUERIER
PREEMIE	PRETYPE	PROPANE	PUMPKIN	QUERIST
PREEMPT	PRETZEL	PROPEND	PUNCHER	QUESTER
PREENER	PREVAIL	PROPENE	PUNNING	QUESTOR
PREFACE	PREVENT	PROPHET	PUNSTER	QUETZAL
PREFADE	PREVERB	PROPINE	PURFLER	QUIBBLE
PREFECT	PREVIEW	PROPJET	PURGING	QUICKEN
PREFILE	PREVISE	PROPONE	PURITAN	QUICKIE
PREFIRE	PREWARM	PROPOSE	PURLIEU	QUIETEN
PREFORM	PREWARN	PROPYNE	PURLINE	QUIETER
PREFUND	PREWIRE	PRORATE	PURLING	QUILLAI
PREGAME	PREWORK	PROSECT	PURLOIN	QUILLET
PREHEAT	PREWRAP	PROSOMA	PURPORT	QUILLOW
PRELATE	PREZZIE	PROSPER	PURPOSE	QUILTER
PRELECT	PRICKER	PROSSIE	PURPURA	QUINELA
PRELOAD	PRICKET	PROSTIE	PURPURE	QUININA
PRELUDE	PRICKLE	PROTEAN	PURSUER	QUININE
PREMAKE	PRIMAGE	PROTECT	PURSUIT	QUINNAT
PREMIER	PRIMATE	PROTEGE	PURVIEW	QUINOID
PREMISE	PRIMERO	PROTEID	PUSHPIN	QUINONE
PREMIUM	PRIMINE	PROTEIN	PUSHROD	QUINTAL
PREMOLD	PRIMING	PROTEND	PUSSLEY	QUINTAN
PRENAME	PRIMULA	PROTEST	PUSTULE	QUINTAR
PREPACK	PRINCES	PROTIST	PUTAMEN	QUINTET
PREPARE	PRINKER	PROTIUM	PUTDOWN	QUINTIC
PREPAVE	PRINTER	PROTYLE	PUTLOCK	QUINTIN
PREPLAN	PRISERE	PROVERB	PUTTIER	QUINZIE
PREPOSE	PRIVATE	PROVIDE	PUZZLER	QUIPPER
PREPPIE	PROBAND	PROVISO	PYAEMIA	QUITTER
PREPREG	PROBANG	PROVOKE	PYRALID	QUITTOR
PREPUCE	PROBATE	PROVOST	PYRAMID	QUIXOTE
PREPUPA	PROBLEM	PROWLER	PYREXIA	QUIZZER
PREQUEL	PROCARP	PRURIGO	PYROGEN	QUOMODO

143

RABASKA	RATAFEE	RECHEAT	REFFING	RELIEVE
RABBLER	RATAFIA	RECHECK	REFIGHT	RELIEVO
RABBONI	RATATAT	RECITAL	REFINER	RELIGHT
RACCOON	RATCHET	RECITER	REFLATE	RELIQUE
RACEWAY	RATFINK	RECLAIM	REFLECT	RELLENO
RACKFUL	RATHOLE	RECLAME	REFLOAT	REMAKER
RACQUET	RATLINE	RECLASP	REFLOOD	REMERGE
RADIANT	RATTAIL	RECLEAN	REFORGE	REMIXER
RADIATE	RATTEEN	RECLINE	REFOUND	REMNANT
RADICAL	RATTLER	RECLUSE	REFRACT	REMODEL
RADICEL	RATTOON	RECOLOR	REFRAIN	REMORSE
RADICLE	RATTRAP	RECOUNT	REFRAME	REMOULD
RAFFLER	RAVAGER	RECOVER	REFRONT	REMOUNT
RAFTING	RAVELER	RECRATE	REFUGEE	REMOVAL
RAGDOLL	RAVELIN	RECROWN	REFUSAL	REMOVER
RAGGING	RAVENER	RECRUIT	REFUSER	RENEGER
RAGHEAD	RAVIOLI	RECURVE	REFUTAL	RENEGUE
RAGTIME	RAWHIDE	RECUSAL	REFUTER	RENEWAL
RAGWEED	REACHER	RECYCLE	REGALER	RENEWER
RAGWORM	REACTOR	REDBAIT	REGATTA	RENNASE
RAGWORT	READAPT	REDBIRD	REGAUGE	RENTIER
RAILBED	READING	REDBONE	REGIMEN	REOCCUR
RAILCAR	READMIT	REDCOAT	REGLAZE	REOFFER
RAILING	READOPT	REDHEAD	REGORGE	REORDER
RAILWAY	READORN	REDLINE	REGOSOL	REPAINT
RAIMENT	READOUT	REDNECK	REGRADE	REPANEL
RAINBOW	REAGENT	REDOUBT	REGRAFT	REPAPER
RAINOUT	REALGAR	REDOUND	REGRANT	REPINER
RAISING	REALIGN	REDPOLL	REGRATE	REPLACE
RAKEOFF	REALISE	REDRAFT	REGREEN	REPLANT
RALLIER	REALISM	REDREAM	REGREET	REPLATE
RAMBLER	REALIST	REDRILL	REGRIND	REPLEAD
RAMEKIN	REALIZE	REDRIVE	REGROOM	REPLETE
RAMILIE	REALLOT	REDROOT	REGROUP	REPLICA
RAMPAGE	REALTER	REDSKIN	REGULAR	REPLIER
RAMPART	REALTOR	REDTAIL	REHINGE	REPLUMB
RAMPIKE	REARGUE	REDUCER	REHOUSE	REPOINT
RAMPION	REARING	REDWARE	REIFIER	REPOSAL
RAMPOLE	REAVAIL	REDWING	REIMAGE	REPOSER
RANCHER	REAWAKE	REDWOOD	REINCUR	REPOSIT
RANCOUR	REBATER	REEDING	REINTER	REPOWER
RANKING	REBEGIN	REEJECT	REISSUE	REPRICE
RANKLES	REBIRTH	REELECT	REITBOK	REPRINT
RANPIKE	REBLEND	REELING	REIVING	REPRISE
RANSACK	REBLOOM	REENACT	REJOICE	REPROBE
RANTING	REBOARD	REENDOW	REJUDGE	REPROOF
RAPHIDE	REBOUND	REENJOY	RELABEL	REPROVE
RAPPORT	REBRAND	REENTER	RELAPSE	REPTILE
RAPTURE	REBREED	REEQUIP	RELATER	REPULSE
RAREBIT	REBUILD	REERECT	RELATOR	REQUEST
RASBORA	REBUKER	REEVOKE	RELAXER	REQUIEM
RASPING	RECEIPT	REEXPEL	RELAXIN	REQUIRE
RASSLER	RECEIVE	REFENCE	RELEARN	REQUITE
RATABLE	RECHART	REFEREE	RELEASE	RERAISE

144

REROUTE	RETIREE	RIDDLER	ROOFING	RUNAWAY
RESCALE	RETIRER	RIDOTTO	ROOFTOP	RUNBACK
RESCIND	RETITLE	RIFFAGE	ROOMFUL	RUNDLET
RESCORE	RETOTAL	RIFFLER	ROOSTER	RUNDOWN
RESCUEE	RETRACE	RIFLING	ROOTAGE	RUNNING
RESCUER	RETRACK	RIGGING	ROOTCAP	RUNOVER
RESEIZE	RETRACT	RIGHTER	ROOTKIT	RUPTURE
RESERVE	RETRAIN	RIKISHA	ROOTLES	RUSHING
RESHAPE	RETREAD	RIKSHAW	ROOTLET	RUSSULA
RESHAVE	RETREAT	RIMFIRE	ROPEWAY	RUSTLER
RESHINE	RETRIAL	RIMLAND	RORQUAL	RUSTLES
RESHOOT	RETSINA	RIMROCK	ROSACEA	SABATON
RESIDER	RETWEET	RIMSHOT	ROSEBAY	SABAYON
RESIDUE	RETWIST	RINGGIT	ROSEBUD	SABBATH
RESIGHT	REUNION	RINGLET	ROSEHIP	SACATON
RESILIN	REUNITE	RINGTAW	ROSELLA	SACCADE
RESLATE	REUTTER	RINSING	ROSELLE	SACCULE
RESMELT	REVALUE	RIOTING	ROSEOLA	SACKBUT
RESOJET	REVELER	RIPCORD	ROSETTE	SACKFUL
RESOLVE	REVENGE	RIPENER	ROSINOL	SACKING
RESOUND	REVENUE	RIPIENO	ROSOLIO	SACRING
RESPACE	REVERER	RIPOSTE	ROSTRUM	SACRIST
RESPADE	REVERIE	RIPPLER	ROTATOR	SADDLER
RESPEAK	REVERSE	RIPPLET	ROTIFER	SADIRON
RESPECT	REVERSO	RIPSTOP	ROTUNDA	SAFFRON
RESPELL	REVILER	RIPTIDE	ROUGHEN	SAFROLE
RESPIRE	REVISAL	RISIBLE	ROUGHER	SAGGARD
RESPITE	REVISER	RISOTTO	ROUILLE	SAGUARO
RESPLIT	REVISIT	RISSOLE	ROULADE	SAHIWAL
RESPOND	REVISOR	RIVETER	ROULEAU	SAHUARO
RESPOOL	REVIVAL	RIVIERA	ROUNDEL	SAILING
RESPRAY	REVIVER	RIVIERE	ROUNDER	SALCHOW
RESTACK	REVOICE	RIVULET	ROUNDUP	SALICIN
RESTAFF	REVOKER	ROADBED	ROUSTER	SALIENT
RESTAGE	REVOLVE	ROADWAY	ROUTINE	SALLIER
RESTAMP	REVUIST	ROAMING	ROWBOAT	SALPIAN
RESTART	REWAKEN	ROARING	ROWLOCK	SALTERN
RESTATE	REWEAVE	ROASTER	ROYSTER	SALTIER
RESTOCK	REWEIGH	ROBINIA	RUBABOO	SALTINE
RESTOKE	REWIDEN	ROBOTIC	RUBASSE	SALTING
RESTORE	REWRITE	ROBUSTA	RUBBING	SALTIRE
RESTUFF	REYNARD	ROCKOON	RUBDOWN	SALTPAN
RESTYLE	RHABDOM	ROEBUCK	RUBELLA	SALUTER
RESUMER	RHENIUM	ROISTER	RUBEOLA	SALVAGE
RESURGE	RHIZOID	ROLLICK	RUCHING	SAMADHI
RETABLE	RHIZOME	ROLLING	RUCTION	SAMBHAR
RETABLO	RHODIUM	ROLLMOP	RUDDOCK	SAMBHUR
RETAKER	RHODORA	ROLLOUT	RUDERAL	SAMBUCA
RETASTE	RHUBARB	ROLLWAY	RUFFIAN	SAMBUKE
RETHINK	RIBBAND	ROMAINE	RUFFLER	SAMISEN
RETICLE	RIBBING	ROMANCE	RUINATE	SAMOVAR
RETINAL	RIBWORT	ROMAUNT	RUMBLER	SAMOYED
RETINOL	RICKSHA	RONDURE	RUMMAGE	SAMPLER
RETINUE	RICOTTA	RONTGEN	RUMPLES	SAMSARA

SAMURAI	SAWBILL	SCOPULA	SEAWARE	SERVICE
SANCTUM	SAWBUCK	SCORING	SEAWEED	SERVING
SANDBAG	SAWDUST	SCORNER	SECEDER	SESSION
SANDBAR	SAWMILL	SCOTOMA	SECLUDE	SESTINA
SANDBUR	SAXHORN	SCOTTIE	SECONAL	SESTINE
SANDDAB	SAXTUBA	SCOURER	SECONDE	SETBACK
SANDHOG	SCABBLE	SCOURGE	SECRETE	SETLINE
SANDLOT	SCALADE	SCOUTER	SECTION	SETTING
SANDPIT	SCALADO	SCOWDER	SECULAR	SETTLER
SANGRIA	SCALAGE	SCOWLER	SECURER	SETTLOR
SANICLE	SCALARE	SCRAICH	SEDUCER	SEVENTH
SANTERA	SCALENE	SCRAIGH	SEEDBED	SEVERAL
SANTERO	SCALEUP	SCRAPER	SEEDPOD	SEVICHE
SANTOKU	SCALING	SCRAPIE	SEEMING	SEVRUGA
SANTOOR	SCALLOP	SCRAVEL	SEEPAGE	SEXPERT
SANTOUR	SCALPEL	SCREWER	SEGMENT	SEXTAIN
SANYASI	SCALPER	SCREWUP	SEINING	SEXTANT
SAPAJOU	SCAMMER	SCRIBER	SEISING	SEXTILE
SAPHEAD	SCAMPER	SCRIEVE	SEISURE	SEXTING
SAPHENA	SCANDAL	SCROOGE	SEIZING	SFUMATO
SAPIENT	SCANDIA	SCROTUM	SEIZURE	SHACKLE
SAPLING	SCANNER	SCROUGE	SELFDOM	SHADING
SAPONIN	SCAPULA	SCRUPLE	SELLOFF	SHADOOF
SAPPHIC	SCARFER	SCUFFER	SELLOUT	SHAGGER
SAPPING	SCARLET	SCUFFLE	SELTZER	SHAHADA
SAPROBE	SCARPER	SCULKER	SELVAGE	SHAHDOM
SAPSAGO	SCATTER	SCULLER	SEMINAR	SHAHEED
SAPWOOD	SCAUPER	SCULPIN	SEMIPRO	SHAITAN
SARANGI	SCEPTER	SCUMBAG	SENATOR	SHAKEUP
SARCASM	SCEPTIC	SCUMBLE	SENDOFF	SHALLOP
SARCINA	SCEPTRE	SCUMMER	SENECIO	SHALLOT
SARCOID	SCHAPPE	SCUNNER	SENESCE	SHALLOW
SARCOMA	SCHEMER	SCUPPER	SENHORA	SHALWAR
SARDANA	SCHERZO	SCUTAGE	SENOPIA	SHAMBLE
SARDINE	SCHLEPP	SCUTTER	SENSATE	SHAMMER
SARMENT	SCHLOCK	SCUTTLE	SENTIMO	SHAMPOO
SARSNET	SCHLONG	SEABIRD	SEPPUKU	SHANTEY
SASHIMI	SCHLUMP	SEABOOT	SEPTAGE	SHANTIH
SATCHEL	SCHMEAR	SEACOCK	SEPTIME	SHAPEUP
SATIATE	SCHMEER	SEAFOAM	SEQUENT	SHARIAH
SATINET	SCHMUCK	SEAFOOD	SEQUOIA	SHARIAT
SATSANG	SCHNEID	SEAFOWL	SERFAGE	SHARKER
SATSUMA	SCHNOOK	SEAGULL	SERFDOM	SHARPEN
SATYRID	SCHOLAR	SEAKALE	SERGING	SHARPER
SAUCIER	SCHTICK	SEALANT	SERIATE	SHARPIE
SAUNTER	SCIATIC	SEALIFT	SERICIN	SHASLIK
SAURIAN	SCIENCE	SEALING	SERIEMA	SHATTER
SAUSAGE	SCISSOR	SEAMARK	SERINGA	SHAVING
SAUTOIR	SCIURID	SEAPORT	SEROVAR	SHEARER
SAVANNA	SCOFFER	SEASIDE	SERPENT	SHEATHE
SAVARIN	SCOLDER	SEATING	SERPIGO	SHEBANG
SAVELOY	SCOLLOP	SEAWALL	SERRANO	SHEBEAN
SAVIOUR	SCOOPER	SEAWANT	SERRATE	SHEBEEN
SAVORER	SCOOTER	SEAWARD	SERVANT	SHEDDER

SHEENEY	SHORTIA	SINKAGE	SLANDER	SNARLER
SHEENIE	SHORTIE	SINKFUL	SLAPPER	SNEAKER
SHEEPLE	SHOTGUN	SINOPIA	SLASHER	SNEERER
SHEETER	SHOUTER	SINUATE	SLATHER	SNEEZER
SHEHNAI	SHOWING	SIRLOIN	SLATING	SNICKER
SHEITAN	SHOWOFF	SIROCCO	SLAYING	SNIFFER
SHEITEL	SHRIEVE	SISTRUM	SLEDDER	SNIFFLE
SHELLAC	SHRIVEL	SITTING	SLEEKEN	SNIFTER
SHELLER	SHRIVER	SITUATE	SLEEKER	SNIGGER
SHELTER	SHTETEL	SIXTEEN	SLEEPER	SNIGGLE
SHELTIE	SHUCKER	SIZZLER	SLEIGHT	SNIGLET
SHELVER	SHUDDER	SJAMBOK	SLICKEN	SNIPING
SHEMALE	SHUFFLE	SKANKER	SLICKER	SNIPPER
SHERBET	SHUNNER	SKATING	SLIMMER	SNIPPET
SHEREEF	SHUNTER	SKATOLE	SLINGER	SNOGGER
SHERIFF	SHUSHER	SKEETER	SLIPOUT	SNOOKER
SHEROOT	SHUTEYE	SKELLUM	SLIPPER	SNOOPER
SHIATSU	SHUTOFF	SKELTER	SLIPWAY	SNOOZER
SHIATZU	SHUTOUT	SKEPTIC	SLITHER	SNOOZLE
SHICKER	SHUTTER	SKIDDER	SLITTER	SNORING
SHICKSA	SHUTTLE	SKIDDOO	SLOBBER	SNORKEL
SHIFTER	SHYLOCK	SKIDPAD	SLOGGER	SNORTER
SHIKARA	SHYSTER	SKIDWAY	SLOTTER	SNOWCAP
SHIKARI	SIAMANG	SKIFFLE	SLUBBER	SNOWCAT
SHIKKER	SIAMESE	SKILLET	SLUGGER	SNUBBER
SHIKSEH	SIBLING	SKIMMER	SLUMBER	SNUFFER
SHIMMER	SIBSHIP	SKIMMIA	SLUMGUM	SNUFFLE
SHINDIG	SICKBAY	SKINFUL	SLUMISM	SNUGGLE
SHINGLE	SICKBED	SKINKER	SLUMMER	SOAKAGE
SHINNEY	SICKOUT	SKINNER	SMACKER	SOAKING
SHINOLA	SIDEARM	SKIPPER	SMARAGD	SOARING
SHIPLAP	SIDEBAR	SKIPPET	SMARTEN	SOCAGER
SHIPPEN	SIDECAR	SKIRRET	SMARTIE	SOCCAGE
SHIPPER	SIDEWAY	SKIRTER	SMASHER	SOCKEYE
SHIPPON	SIENITE	SKITTER	SMASHUP	SOFABED
SHIPWAY	SIEVERT	SKITTLE	SMATTER	SOILAGE
SHIRKER	SIFTING	SKOOKUM	SMEARER	SOILURE
SHITAKE	SIGANID	SKREEGH	SMEDDUM	SOJOURN
SHITBAG	SIGHTER	SKREIGH	SMELLER	SOLACER
SHITCAN	SIGMOID	SKULKER	SMELTER	SOLANIN
SHITTAH	SIGNAGE	SKYDIVE	SMIDGEN	SOLANUM
SHITTER	SIGNING	SKYGLOW	SMIDGIN	SOLDIER
SHITTIM	SIGNIOR	SKYHOOK	SMIRKER	SOLERET
SHIVITI	SIGNORA	SKYJACK	SMOKING	SOLFEGE
SHMATTE	SILENCE	SKYLARK	SMOLDER	SOLICIT
SHMOOZE	SILESIA	SKYLINE	SMOOTHE	SOLITON
SHOCKER	SILICLE	SKYSAIL	SMOTHER	SOLOIST
SHOEPAC	SILICON	SKYSURF	SMUGGLE	SOLUBLE
SHOOTER	SILIQUE	SKYWALK	SNACKER	SOLVATE
SHOPBOY	SILURID	SKYWARD	SNAFFLE	SOLVENT
SHOPHAR	SIMITAR	SLABBER	SNAGGER	SOMEONE
SHOPPER	SIMULAR	SLACKEN	SNAGGLE	SOMEWAY
SHORING	SINGING	SLACKER	SNAPPER	SONANCE
SHORTEN	SINGLET	SLAMMER	SNARFLE	SONHOOD

147

SONSHIP	SPELLER	SPURNER	STEAMER	STOOPER
SOOTHER	SPELTER	SPURRER	STEAMIE	STOPGAP
SOPHISM	SPELUNK	SPURREY	STEARIN	STOPING
SOPHIST	SPENCER	SPURTER	STEELIE	STOPOFF
SOPRANO	SPENDER	SPURTLE	STEEPEN	STOPPER
SORBATE	SPHERIC	SPUTNIK	STEEPER	STOPPLE
SORBENT	SPICULE	SPUTTER	STEEPLE	STORAGE
SORBOSE	SPIEGEL	SPYWARE	STEERER	STOUTEN
SORDINE	SPIELER	SQUALOR	STEMMER	STOWAGE
SORGHUM	SPILING	SQUARER	STEMSON	STRAFER
SOROCHE	SPILITE	SQUEEZE	STENCIL	STRANGE
SORTING	SPILLER	SQUILLA	STENGAH	STRATUM
SOUBISE	SPINAGE	SRADDHA	STENTOR	STRAYER
SOUFFLE	SPINDLE	STABBER	STEPDAD	STRETTA
SOUNDER	SPINNER	STABILE	STEPMOM	STRETTO
SOUPCON	SPINNEY	STABLER	STEPPER	STREWER
SOURGUM	SPINOFF	STACKER	STEPSON	STRIATE
SOURSOP	SPINOUT	STACKUP	STERANE	STRIDER
SOUSLIK	SPINULE	STADDLE	STERLET	STRIDOR
SOUTANE	SPIRAEA	STADIUM	STERNUM	STRIGIL
SOUTHER	SPIRANT	STAFFER	STEROID	STRIKER
SOWBACK	SPIREME	STAGGER	STERTOR	STRIPER
SOYBEAN	SPIRULA	STAGGIE	STETSON	STRIVER
SOYMEAL	SPITTER	STAGING	STEWARD	STROBIL
SOYMILK	SPITTLE	STAINER	STEWBUM	STROKER
SPACING	SPLICER	STAITHE	STEWPAN	STROPHE
SPACKLE	SPLODGE	STALKER	STEWPOT	STROYER
SPAEING	SPLURGE	STAMINA	STHENIA	STRUDEL
SPALLER	SPOILER	STAMMEL	STIBINE	STUBBLE
SPAMBOT	SPONDEE	STAMMER	STIBIUM	STUDDIE
SPAMMER	SPONGER	STAMPER	STICKER	STUDENT
SPANCEL	SPONGIN	STANDBY	STICKIE	STUDIER
SPANGLE	SPONSON	STANDEE	STICKLE	STUFFER
SPANIEL	SPONSOR	STANDER	STICKUM	STUIVER
SPANKER	SPOOFER	STANDUP	STICKUP	STUMBLE
SPANNER	SPOOLER	STANINE	STIFFEN	STUMPER
SPARGER	SPOONER	STANNUM	STIFFIE	STUNNER
SPARKER	SPOONEY	STAPLER	STIFLER	STUTTER
SPARKLE	SPOORER	STARDOM	STINGER	STYLING
SPAROID	SPORRAN	STARKER	STINKER	STYLISE
SPARROW	SPORTER	STARLET	STINTER	STYLIST
SPASTIC	SPORTIF	STARTER	STIPEND	STYLITE
SPATTER	SPORULE	STARTLE	STIPPLE	STYLIZE
SPATULA	SPOTTER	STARTUP	STIPULE	STYLOID
SPATZLE	SPOUSAL	STARVER	STIRRER	STYPTIC
SPAWNER	SPOUTER	STATICE	STIRRUP	STYRENE
SPEAKER	SPRAYER	STATION	STOCKER	SUASION
SPEARER	SPRIGHT	STATISM	STOLLEN	SUBADAR
SPECIAL	SPRINGE	STATIST	STOMACH	SUBAREA
SPECKLE	SPUDDER	STATIVE	STOMATE	SUBATOM
SPECTER	SPUDGEL	STATURE	STOMPER	SUBBASE
SPECTRE	SPUMONE	STATUTE	STONKER	SUBBING
SPEEDER	SPUMONI	STEALER	STOOKER	SUBCELL
SPEEDUP	SPUNKIE	STEALTH	STOOLIE	SUBCLAN

SUBCODE	SUCRASE	SURTOUT	SYMBIOT	TALLBOY
SUBCOOL	SUCROSE	SURVEIL	SYMPTOM	TALLIER
SUBCULT	SUCTION	SURVIVE	SYNAGOG	TALLITH
SUBDEAN	SUFFARI	SUSPECT	SYNANON	TALLYHO
SUBDUAL	SUFFICE	SUSPEND	SYNAPSE	TALOOKA
SUBDUCE	SUFFUSE	SUSPIRE	SYNCARP	TAMANDU
SUBDUCT	SUGARER	SUSTAIN	SYNCHRO	TAMARAO
SUBDUER	SUGGEST	SWABBER	SYNCOPE	TAMARAU
SUBEDIT	SUICIDE	SWABBIE	SYNFUEL	TAMARIN
SUBERIN	SUITING	SWADDLE	SYNONYM	TAMASHA
SUBFILE	SULFATE	SWAGGER	SYNOVIA	TAMBALA
SUBFUSC	SULFIDE	SWAGGIE	SYNTAGM	TAMBOUR
SUBGOAL	SULFITE	SWALLOW	SYNTONE	TAMBURA
SUBHEAD	SULFONE	SWAMPER	SYNTYPE	TAMPALA
SUBIDEA	SULLAGE	SWANPAN	SYRETTE	TAMPING
SUBITEM	SULPHID	SWAPPER	SYRINGA	TAMPION
SUBJECT	SULPHUR	SWARMER	SYRINGE	TANAGER
SUBJOIN	SULTANA	SWASHER	SYRPHID	TANBARK
SUBLATE	SUMMAND	SWATHER	SYSTOLE	TANDOOR
SUBLIME	SUMMATE	SWATTER	TABANID	TANGELO
SUBLINE	SUMOIST	SWEARER	TABARET	TANGENT
SUBMENU	SUMPTER	SWEATER	TABBING	TANGLER
SUBPART	SUNBATH	SWEENEY	TABETIC	TANGRAM
SUBPENA	SUNBEAM	SWEEPER	TABLEAU	TANKAGE
SUBPLOT	SUNBELT	SWEETEN	TABLING	TANKARD
SUBRACE	SUNBIRD	SWEETIE	TABLOID	TANKFUL
SUBRENT	SUNBURN	SWELTER	TABORER	TANKINI
SUBRING	SUNCARE	SWERVER	TABORET	TANNAGE
SUBRULE	SUNDECK	SWIDDEN	TABORIN	TANNATE
SUBSALE	SUNDIAL	SWIFTER	TABOULI	TANNING
SUBSECT	SUNDOWN	SWIFTIE	TACHISM	TANTARA
SUBSERE	SUNGLOW	SWIGGER	TACHIST	TANTRUM
SUBSIDE	SUNLAMP	SWILING	TACHYON	TANYARD
SUBSIST	SUNLAND	SWILLER	TACKLER	TAPERER
SUBSITE	SUNRISE	SWIMMER	TACKLES	TAPETUM
SUBSOIL	SUNROOF	SWINDLE	TACNODE	TAPHOLE
SUBSUME	SUNROOM	SWINGBY	TACRINE	TAPIOCA
SUBTASK	SUNSPOT	SWINGER	TACTION	TAPPING
SUBTEEN	SUNSTAR	SWINGLE	TADPOLE	TAPROOM
SUBTEND	SUNSUIT	SWINNEY	TAENITE	TAPROOT
SUBTEST	SUNTRAP	SWIPPLE	TAFFETA	TAPSTER
SUBTEXT	SUNWARD	SWISHER	TAGGANT	TARDYON
SUBTONE	SUPPORT	SWITHER	TAGLINE	TARRIER
SUBTYPE	SUPPOSE	SWIZZLE	TAGMEME	TARSIER
SUBUNIT	SUPREME	SWOBBER	TAILFAN	TARTANA
SUBVENE	SUPREMO	SWOONER	TAILFIN	TARTLET
SUBVERT	SURBASE	SWOOPER	TAILING	TARTUFE
SUBZONE	SURCOAT	SWOPPER	TAILLES	TARTUFO
SUCCEED	SURFACE	SWOTTER	TAKEOFF	TARWEED
SUCCOUR	SURFEIT	SYENITE	TAKEOUT	TASKBAR
SUCCUBA	SURFING	SYLPHID	TALIPED	TASTING
SUCCUMB	SURGEON	SYLVINE	TALIPOT	TATHATA
SUCKLER	SURMISE	SYLVITE	TALKING	TATOUAY
SUCKLES	SURNAME	SYMBION	TALLAGE	TATTING

TATTLER	TERRINE	THYMOMA	TOLLWAY	TOURACO
TAUNTER	TERROIR	THYROID	TOLUATE	TOURING
TAURINE	TERTIAL	TICKING	TOLUENE	TOURISM
TAUTAUG	TERTIAN	TICKLER	TOLUIDE	TOURIST
TAVERNA	TESTATE	TIDDLER	TOLUOLE	TOURNEY
TAXABLE	TESTING	TIDERIP	TOMBACK	TOWAWAY
TAXICAB	TESTOON	TIDEWAY	TOMBOLA	TOWBOAT
TAXIWAY	TESTUDO	TIEBACK	TOMBOLO	TOWHEAD
TEABOWL	TETANIC	TIERCEL	TOMFOOL	TOWLINE
TEACAKE	TETOTUM	TIGHTEN	TOMPION	TOWMOND
TEACART	TETRODE	TILAPIA	TONEARM	TOWMONT
TEACHER	TETROSE	TILLAGE	TONETIC	TOWNLET
TEAROOM	TEXTILE	TILLITE	TONETTE	TOWPATH
TEASHOP	TEXTURE	TIMARAU	TONIGHT	TOWROPE
TEATIME	THALWEG	TIMBALE	TONNAGE	TOWSACK
TEAWARE	THANAGE	TIMBREL	TONNEAU	TOXEMIA
TECHNIC	THANKER	TIMEOUT	TONSURE	TOYLAND
TECTITE	THAWING	TIMOLOL	TONTINE	TOYSHOP
TEENDOM	THEATER	TINAMOU	TOOLBAR	TOYTOWN
TEETHER	THEATRE	TINFOIL	TOOLING	TRACHEA
TEKTITE	THEELIN	TINGLER	TOOLSET	TRACHLE
TELECOM	THEELOL	TINHORN	TOOTLER	TRACING
TELEOST	THENAGE	TINKLER	TOOTSIE	TRACKER
TELERAN	THEOLOG	TINTING	TOPCOAT	TRACTOR
TELFORD	THEORBO	TINTYPE	TOPICAL	TRADING
TELOGEN	THEOREM	TINWARE	TOPKICK	TRADUCE
TELPHER	THERIAC	TINWORK	TOPKNOT	TRAFFIC
TEMBLOR	THERIAN	TIPCART	TOPLINE	TRAILER
TEMPERA	THERMAL	TIPPLER	TOPMAST	TRAINEE
TEMPEST	THERMEL	TIPSTER	TOPONYM	TRAINER
TEMPLAR	THERMIT	TITANIA	TOPPING	TRAIPSE
TEMPLET	THIAMIN	TITHING	TOPSAIL	TRAITOR
TEMPTER	THIAZIN	TITLARK	TOPSIDE	TRAJECT
TEMPURA	THIAZOL	TITLIST	TOPSOIL	TRAMCAR
TENDRIL	THICKEN	TITRANT	TOPSPIN	TRAMELL
TENFOLD	THICKET	TITRATE	TOPWORK	TRAMMEL
TENNIST	THIMBLE	TITULAR	TORCHON	TRAMPER
TENONER	THINKER	TOADLET	TORMENT	TRAMPLE
TENSION	THINNER	TOASTER	TORNADO	TRAMWAY
TENTAGE	THIONIN	TOBACCO	TORPEDO	TRANCHE
TEPACHE	THIONYL	TOCCATA	TORQUER	TRANGAM
TEQUILA	THISTLE	TODDLER	TORRENT	TRANNIE
TERAOHM	THORITE	TOECLIP	TORSADE	TRANSIT
TERBIUM	THORIUM	TOEHOLD	TORSION	TRANSOM
TERGITE	THOUGHT	TOENAIL	TORTONI	TRAPEZE
TERMITE	THRIVER	TOESHOE	TORTURE	TRAPPER
TERNION	THROWER	TOFUTTI	TOSSPOT	TRASHER
TERPENE	THRUPUT	TOGGLER	TOSTADA	TRAVAIL
TERRACE	THRUWAY	TOKAMAK	TOSTADO	TRAWLER
TERRAIN	THUGGEE	TOKOMAK	TOSTONE	TRAWLEY
TERRANE	THULIUM	TOLIDIN	TOUCHER	TRAYFUL
TERREEN	THUMPER	TOLLAGE	TOUCHUP	TREACLE
TERRENE	THUNDER	TOLLBAR	TOUGHEN	TREADER
TERRIER	THYMINE	TOLLING	TOUGHIE	TREADLE

TREASON	TROCHEE	TUNNAGE	TZARISM	UNLEARN
TREATER	TROCHIL	TUPPING	TZARIST	UNLEVEL
TREDDLE	TROFFER	TURACOU	TZIGANE	UNLOOSE
TREETOP	TROLAND	TURBETH	UKELELE	UNMAKER
TREFOIL	TROLLER	TURBINE	UKULELE	UNMITER
TREHALA	TROLLEY	TURBITH	ULEXITE	UNMITRE
TREKKER	TROLLOP	TURFSKI	ULTISOL	UNMOULD
TREMBLE	TROMMEL	TURGITE	ULULATE	UNNERVE
TREMOLO	TROOPER	TURISTA	UMBRAGE	UNPLAIT
TRENAIL	TROPINE	TURMOIL	UNAKITE	UNQUIET
TREPANG	TROPISM	TURNING	UNAWARE	UNQUOTE
TRESSEL	TROTTER	TURNKEY	UNBLIND	UNRAVEL
TRESTLE	TROUBLE	TURNOFF	UNBLOCK	UNREEVE
TRIACID	TROUNCE	TURNOUT	UNBOSOM	UNRIVET
TRIADIC	TROUPER	TURPETH	UNBRACE	UNROUND
TRIAZIN	TROUSER	TURTLER	UNBRAID	UNSCREW
TRIBADE	TRUCKER	TUSSOCK	UNBRAKE	UNSHELL
TRIBUNE	TRUCKLE	TUSSORE	UNBUILD	UNSHIFT
TRIBUTE	TRUDGEN	TUSSUCK	UNCHAIN	UNSIGHT
TRICKER	TRUDGER	TUTELAR	UNCHAIR	UNSLING
TRICKLE	TRUFFLE	TUTOYER	UNCHOKE	UNSNARL
TRICLAD	TRUMPET	TWADDLE	UNCLAMP	UNSPEAK
TRICORN	TRUNDLE	TWANGER	UNCLASP	UNSPOOL
TRIDENT	TRUNNEL	TWANGLE	UNCLOAK	UNSTACK
TRIDUUM	TRUSSER	TWASOME	UNCLOSE	UNSTATE
TRIFFID	TRUSTEE	TWATTLE	UNCLOUD	UNSTEEL
TRIFLER	TRUSTER	TWEEDLE	UNCOVER	UNSTICK
TRIGGER	TRUSTOR	TWEENER	UNCRATE	UNSTRAP
TRIGRAM	TRUTHER	TWEENIE	UNCROWN	UNSWEAR
TRILITH	TRYPSIN	TWEETER	UNCTION	UNTHINK
TRILLER	TRYSAIL	TWEEZER	UNDOING	UNTRACK
TRIMMER	TRYSTER	TWELFTH	UNDRAPE	UNTREAD
TRIMPOT	TSARDOM	TWIBILL	UNEARTH	UNTRUTH
TRINDLE	TSARINA	TWIDDLE	UNEQUAL	UNTWINE
TRINKET	TSARISM	TWINJET	UNFAITH	UNTWIST
TRIOLET	TSARIST	TWINKIE	UNFENCE	UNVOICE
TRIOXID	TSATSKE	TWINKLE	UNFROCK	UNWEAVE
TRIPACK	TSUNAMI	TWINSET	UNGLOVE	UPALONG
TRIPLET	TUATARA	TWIRLER	UNGROUP	UPBRAID
TRIPOLI	TUATERA	TWISTER	UNGUARD	UPBUILD
TRIPPER	TUBAIST	TWISTOR	UNGUENT	UPCHUCK
TRIPPET	TUBULAR	TWITTER	UNHINGE	UPCLIMB
TRIPTAN	TUBULIN	TWIZZLE	UNHORSE	UPCURVE
TRIREME	TUCKING	TWOFOLD	UNHOUSE	UPCYCLE
TRISECT	TUFTING	TWOONIE	UNIBROW	UPDATER
TRISEME	TUGBOAT	TWOSOME	UNICORN	UPDRAFT
TRISHAW	TUGHRIK	TYCHISM	UNIFACE	UPFLING
TRISOME	TUITION	TYLOSIN	UNIFIER	UPGRADE
TRITIUM	TUMBLER	TYPEBAR	UNIFORM	UPHEAVE
TRITOMA	TUMBREL	TYPESET	UNITAGE	UPHOARD
TRITONE	TUMBRIL	TYPHOID	UNITARD	UPLIGHT
TRIUMPH	TUMESCE	TYPHOON	UNITIZE	UPRAISE
TRIVIUM	TUMMLER	TZARDOM	UNJOINT	UPRIGHT
TROCHAR	TUNICLE	TZARINA	UNKNOWN	UPRISER

UPRIVER	VAMOOSE	VESTING	VOLTAGE	WARSLER
UPROUSE	VAMPIRE	VESTURE	VOLUTIN	WARSTLE
UPSCALE	VANDYKE	VETERAN	VOMITER	WARTHOG
UPSHIFT	VANILLA	VETIVER	VORLAGE	WARTIME
UPSHOOT	VANLOAD	VIADUCT	VOUCHEE	WARWORK
UPSILON	VANPOOL	VIBRANT	VOUCHER	WASHBAG
UPSKILL	VANTAGE	VIBRATE	VOUDOUN	WASHDAY
UPSLOPE	VAPORER	VIBRATO	VOUVRAY	WASHING
UPSTAGE	VAQUERO	VIBRION	VOYAGER	WASHOUT
UPSTAIR	VARIANT	VICEROY	VULGATE	WASHRAG
UPSTAND	VARIATE	VICOMTE	VULTURE	WASHTUB
UPSTARE	VARIOLA	VICTUAL	WABBLER	WASSAIL
UPSTART	VARIOLE	VICUGNA	WADDING	WASTAGE
UPSTATE	VARMENT	VIDALIA	WADDLER	WASTREL
UPSURGE	VARMINT	VIDETTE	WADMAAL	WASTRIE
UPSWEEP	VASEFUL	VIDICON	WADMOLL	WATCHER
UPSWELL	VAULTER	VIEWING	WAESUCK	WATERER
UPSWING	VAUNTER	VIHUELA	WAFFLER	WATTAGE
UPTEMPO	VAVASOR	VILAYET	WAFTAGE	WATTAPE
UPTHROW	VEDALIA	VILLAGE	WAFTURE	WATTLES
UPTREND	VEDETTE	VILLAIN	WAGERER	WAVELET
URAEMIA	VEHICLE	VILLEIN	WAGONER	WAVEOFF
URALITE	VEILING	VINASSE	WAGTAIL	WAVERER
URANIDE	VEINING	VINEGAR	WAISTER	WAVICLE
URANISM	VEINLET	VINTAGE	WAITING	WAXBILL
URANITE	VEINULE	VINTNER	WAITRON	WAXWEED
URANIUM	VELIGER	VIOLATE	WAKANDA	WAXWING
URETHAN	VELOUTE	VIOLIST	WAKENER	WAXWORK
URETHRA	VENDACE	VIOLONE	WALKING	WAXWORM
URIDINE	VENISON	VIRELAI	WALKOUT	WAYBACK
URINATE	VENOMER	VIRELAY	WALKWAY	WAYBILL
URODELE	VENTAGE	VIREMIA	WALLEYE	WAYMARK
UROGRAM	VENTAIL	VIRGATE	WALTZER	WAYSIDE
UROLITH	VENTRAL	VIRGULE	WAMEFOU	WEASAND
USAUNCE	VENTURE	VISCOSE	WAMEFUL	WEATHER
USURPER	VENTURI	VISIBLE	WANGLER	WEAVING
UTENSIL	VERANDA	VISITER	WANIGAN	WEAZAND
UTILISE	VERBENA	VISITOR	WANNABE	WEBBING
UTILIZE	VERBILE	VITAMER	WANTAGE	WEBCAST
UTOPIAN	VERDICT	VITAMIN	WARBIRD	WEBINAR
UTOPISM	VERDURE	VITESSE	WARBLER	WEBPAGE
UTOPIST	VERISMO	VITIATE	WARFARE	WEBSITE
UTRICLE	VERMEIL	VITRAIN	WARGAME	WEBSTER
UTTERER	VERMUTH	VITRINE	WARHEAD	WEBWORK
VACCINA	VERNIER	VITRIOL	WARISON	WEBWORM
VACCINE	VERONAL	VIVERID	WARLOCK	WEBZINE
VACUOLE	VERRUCA	VLOGGER	WARLORD	WEDDING
VAGRANT	VERSANT	VOCABLE	WARMING	WEDLOCK
VALANCE	VERSINE	VOCALIC	WARNING	WEEDBED
VALENCE	VERSION	VOCODER	WARPAGE	WEEKDAY
VALIANT	VERTIGO	VODCAST	WARPATH	WEEKEND
VALONIA	VERVAIN	VOGUING	WARRANT	WEEPING
VALUATE	VESICLE	VOICING	WARRIOR	WEIGELA
VALVULE	VESTIGE	VOLCANO	WARSHIP	WEIGHER

WEIRDIE	WHIPPIT	WINDLES	WORKTOP	YELLING
WELCHER	WHIPRAY	WINDROW	WORLDER	YESHIVA
WELCOME	WHIPSAW	WINDWAY	WORRIER	YIELDER
WELFARE	WHIRLER	WINESAP	WORSHIP	YODELER
WELSHER	WHISKER	WINESOP	WORSTED	YOGHURT
WELTING	WHISKEY	WINGBOW	WRANGLE	YOGOURT
WENCHER	WHISPER	WINGLET	WRAPPER	YOHIMBE
WENDIGO	WHISTLE	WINGNUT	WRASSLE	YOUNGER
WERGELD	WHITING	WINGTIP	WRASTLE	YOUNKER
WERGELT	WHITLOW	WINKLER	WREAKER	YOUTHEN
WERGILD	WHITTER	WINNING	WREATHE	YPERITE
WESSAND	WHITTLE	WINNOCK	WRECKER	YTTRIUM
WESTERN	WHIZZER	WIPEOUT	WRENTIT	ZACATON
WESTING	WHOLISM	WIRETAP	WRESTER	ZAMARRA
WETBACK	WHOOMPH	WIREWAY	WRESTLE	ZAMARRO
WETLAND	WHOOPEE	WISEGUY	WRIGGLE	ZAPATEO
WETSUIT	WHOOPER	WITHOUT	WRINGER	ZAPTIAH
WETTING	WHOOPIE	WITLING	WRINKLE	ZAPTIEH
WETWARE	WHOOPLA	WITLOOF	WRISTER	ZAREEBA
WHACKER	WHOPPER	WITTING	WRITHER	ZEBRANO
WHALING	WHORING	WOBBLER	WRITING	ZEBRINE
WHANGEE	WHORTLE	WOLFRAM	WRONGER	ZECCHIN
WHAPPER	WICKAPE	WOMMERA	WRYNECK	ZELKOVA
WHATNOT	WICKING	WOODBIN	XANTHAN	ZEMSTVO
WHATSIT	WICKIUP	WOODCUT	XANTHIN	ZENAIDA
WHEATEN	WICKYUP	WOODHEN	XIPHOID	ZEOLITE
WHEEDLE	WIDENER	WOODLOT	XYLIDIN	ZEPPOLE
WHEELER	WIDEOUT	WOODRAT	XYLITOL	ZIKURAT
WHEELIE	WIDGEON	WOODSIA	YACHTER	ZILLION
WHEEPLE	WIDOWER	WOOLHAT	YACHTIE	ZINCATE
WHEEZER	WIELDER	WOOLLEN	YAMALKA	ZINCITE
WHETTER	WIFEDOM	WOOMERA	YAMULKA	ZITHERN
WHICKER	WIGGING	WOONERF	YARDAGE	ZOISITE
WHIFFER	WIGGLER	WOORALI	YARDARM	ZOOGLEA
WHIFFET	WILDCAT	WOORARI	YASHMAC	ZORILLA
WHIFFLE	WILDING	WORDAGE	YASHMAK	ZORILLE
WHIMPER	WINCHER	WORDING	YATAGAN	ZORILLO
WHIMSEY	WINDAGE	WORKBAG	YAWPING	ZYMOGEN
WHINGER	WINDBAG	WORKDAY	YEALING	ZYMOSAN
WHIPPER	WINDIGO	WORKING	YEAREND	ZYZZYVA
WHIPPET	WINDING	WORKOUT	YEARNER	

With front hook T

ABLINGS	ANNATES	ENFOLDS	HATCHER	HORNING
ACNODES	ANTRUMS	ENTERED	HATCHES	HUMPERS
ACONITE	APELIKE	ENURING	HEATERS	HUMPING
ACTIONS	ARTIEST	ERBIUMS	HEMATIC	ILLITES
ALIPEDS	AUTONYM	ESTATES	HERMITS	INKLING
ALLOWED	EARDROP	HACKING	HICKEST	IRELESS
ALLYING	EARLESS	HANKERS	HICKISH	ISSUING
ANGLERS	EASELED	HANKING	HORNIER	ITCHIER
ANGLING	EENSIER	HATCHED	HORNILY	OCHERED

153

OMENTUM	READERS	ROLLERS	RUSTIER	WIDDLED
OUCHING	READING	ROLLIES	RUSTILY	WIDDLES
RACINGS	REASONS	ROLLING	RUSTING	WIGGIER
RACKERS	REDDLED	ROMPING	RUTHFUL	WIGGING
RACKING	REDDLES	ROTTERS	UPPINGS	WIGLESS
RAILERS	RENAILS	ROTTING	URGENCY	WIGLIKE
RAILING	RENDING	ROUBLES	WADDLED	WILLING
RAINING	RICKING	ROUPING	WADDLER	WINGING
RAMMING	RIFLERS	ROUSERS	WADDLES	WINIEST
RAMPING	RIFLING	ROUTING	WANGLED	WINKLED
RANCHES	RIGGERS	ROWELED	WANGLER	WINKLER
RANKING	RIGGING	RUCKING	WANGLES	WINKLES
RANSOMS	RILLING	RUCKLED	WATTLED	WINNING
RAPPERS	RIMMERS	RUCKLES	WATTLES	WISTING
RAPPING	RIMMING	RUFFLED	WEEDIER	WITCHED
RASHERS	RIPPERS	RUFFLES	WEEDILY	WITCHES
RAVELED	RIPPING	RUNDLES	WEENIES	WITTERS
RAVELER	ROCKING	RUNNELS	WEETING	WITTING

With back hook T

APPLIES	DIRTIES	HIPPIES	MEALIES	PRIVIES
ARTSIES	DISJOIN	HISSIES	MICKLES	PUNKIES
BACCARA	DIVINES	HOODIES	MINUTES	PURPLES
BAGGIES	DIZZIES	HOOKIES	MISDEAL	PUSSIES
BALLIES	DOGGIES	HORSIES	MISPLAN	RANDIES
BANDIES	DOWDIES	HUMBLES	MUCKLES	READIES
BASEMEN	DRIBBLE	HUMPIES	MUDDIES	REDREAM
BAWDIES	DUCKIES	HUNKIES	MUMSIES	REGIMEN
BLONDES	EMPTIES	HUSKIES	MUSKIES	RELEARN
BONNIES	FAIRIES	IMMUNES	NANCIES	REMOTES
BOSSIES	FANCIES	INDICAN	NAPPIES	RIBBIES
BRASHES	FATTIES	INDIGEN	NASTIES	ROOKIES
BRINIES	FINALIS	INTERNE	NEWSIES	ROOMIES
BUGGIES	FLUSHES	IRONIES	NIFTIES	ROWDIES
BULLIES	FOLKIES	IVORIES	OCTUPLE	RUDDIES
BUSHIES	FOOTIES	JAGGIES	OPAQUES	RUMMIES
BUTCHES	FOVEOLE	JAMMIES	OUTBURN	SALTIES
CANZONE	FRESHES	JEHADIS	OUTLEAP	SASSIES
CATTIES	FRONTES	JERKIES	PALSIES	SAVAGES
CHOICES	FUNNIES	JETTIES	PAPPIES	SAVVIES
CHOKIES	GAUCHES	JIHADIS	PARTIES	SECURES
CLASSIS	GAUDIES	JOLLIES	PASTIES	SEDATES
COCKIES	GAWKIES	JUNKIES	PHONIES	SEMIMAT
CONJOIN	GENTLES	KITTLES	PIGGIES	SERENES
CONTRAS	GIDDIES	LADDIES	PINKIES	SHIPMEN
CRAZIES	GIRLIES	LAMBIES	PLANCHE	SILKIES
CROSSES	GOONIES	LEGGIES	PLATIES	SILLIES
DANDIES	GROSSES	LITTLES	PLUSHES	SIMPLES
DICKIES	HABITAN	LOONIES	POPPIES	SISSIES
DINGIES	HANDCAR	LUCKIES	PORKIES	SMILIES
DINKIES	HARDIES	MARABOU	POTTIES	SMOKIES
DIPLOMA	HEAVIES	MATURES	PREPLAN	SOOTHES

SPARKLE	SWISHES	TECHIES	WEDGIES	WORDIES
SPRUCES	SYMBION	TEGUMEN	WEENIES	WUSSIES
SQUARES	TALKIES	UNIQUES	WEEPIES	YUMMIES
STABLES	TARDIES	UNLEARN	WHITIES	
SULKIES	TARRIES	VEINULE	WITHIES	
SUNBURN	TATTIES	VETIVER	WOODIES	
SUPPLES	TAWNIES	WEARIES	WOOLIES	

With front hook U

PENDING	PLINKED	PRAISER	PRATING
PLIGHTS	PRAISED	PRAISES	PRISING

With front hook V

AGILITY	ENTAILS	ICELIKE	OUCHING
ENATION	ERISTIC	LOGGERS	ROOMING
ENOLOGY	ICELESS	LOGGING	

With front hook W

ADDLING	EENSIER	HINGING	HOPPERS	RACKFUL
AGELESS	HACKERS	HINNIED	HOPPING	RACKING
ALLOWED	HACKING	HINNIES	HUMPING	RAPPERS
AMBLING	HAMMING	HIPLESS	INCHERS	RAPPING
ANGLERS	HANGING	HIPLIKE	INCHING	RASSLED
ANGLING	HAPPING	HIPPIER	INDIGOS	RASSLES
ARMINGS	HEELERS	HIPPING	INDOWED	RECKING
ARTIEST	HEELING	HISTING	INKLING	RESTERS
ARTLESS	HEEZING	HITTERS	INNINGS	RESTING
ASHIEST	HELMING	HOLISMS	IRELESS	RETCHED
ASSAILS	HELPING	HOOFING	ITCHIER	RETCHES
EANLING	HERRIED	HOOPERS	ITCHING	RICKING
EASELED	HERRIES	HOOPING	OORALIS	RINGERS
EDGIEST	HINGERS	HOOPLAS	OOZIEST	RINGING

With back hook W

RICKSHA

With back hook X

BANDEAU	COUTEAU	MORCEAU	RONDEAU	TRUMEAU
BATTEAU	FABLIAU	OCTUPLE	ROULEAU	
CHAPEAU	JAMBEAU	PLATEAU	TABLEAU	
CHATEAU	MANTEAU	PURLIEU	TONNEAU	

With front hook Y

ATAGHAN	EARNERS	EASTING
EANLING	EARNING	OURSELF

With back hook Y

ACTRESS	CREAMER	HEXAPOD	POLYPOD	SNUGGER
ADVISOR	CROOKER	HILLOCK	PRINTER	SOLDIER
ANTILOG	CRYOGEN	HOMOLOG	PSALTER	SOVKHOZ
ANTONYM	CURRIER	HOMONYM	PUDDING	SPINACH
APOCARP	CUSHION	HUMMOCK	PUPILAR	SPINNER
AUDITOR	CUSTARD	HYDROPS	RECOVER	SPLOTCH
AUTARCH	DELIVER	HYPONYM	REFINER	SPOOFER
AXILLAR	DEMAGOG	INCISOR	REVISOR	SPUTTER
BASILAR	DILATOR	JEALOUS	RINGLET	SQUELCH
BASTARD	DIPLOID	JEOPARD	ROLLICK	SQUOOSH
BISCUIT	DRAUGHT	JUGGLER	ROTATOR	STAGGER
BLADDER	DROLLER	KETCHUP	RUBBISH	STEALTH
BLANKET	DROUGHT	KNACKER	SACRIST	STEMMER
BLISTER	DRUDGER	KOLKHOS	SADDLER	STOMACH
BLOOMER	ENACTOR	KOLKHOZ	SAFFRON	STRETCH
BLOSSOM	ENDARCH	LACUNAR	SAVAGER	SULPHUR
BLUBBER	ENDOGEN	LAMINAR	SAWDUST	SUNBEAM
BLUSTER	ENTREAT	LEATHER	SCHLEPP	SYNCARP
BOTCHER	EUPLOID	LYSOGEN	SCHLOCK	SYNONYM
BOULDER	FARRIER	MERONYM	SCHLUMP	THEOLOG
BROIDER	FASHION	METONYM	SCHMALZ	THICKET
BULLOCK	FEATHER	MONARCH	SCHMUCK	THUNDER
BURGLAR	FLATTER	MONITOR	SCRATCH	TITULAR
BUTCHER	FLAVOUR	MONOLOG	SCREECH	TOPONYM
CABBAGE	FLICKER	MONOPOD	SCRUNCH	TOURIST
CACONYM	FLUTTER	MULLOCK	SCULLER	TRICKER
CAJOLER	FRILLER	MUSTARD	SEAWEED	TROLLOP
CALAMAR	FURRIER	NEBBISH	SEMINAR	TUSSOCK
CARTOON	GARBAGE	NEGATOR	SHIMMER	TUTELAR
CENTAUR	GIMMICK	NITPICK	SHMALTZ	TWITTER
CHANCER	GLAZIER	NOMARCH	SHUDDER	UNCLOUD
CHATTER	GLITTER	OUTWEAR	SIGNIOR	VARNISH
CHEDDAR	GLUTTON	OVERMAN	SKITTER	VAVASOR
CHIRRUP	GREENER	PARONYM	SLABBER	VILLAGE
CIRCUIT	GRILLER	PEACOCK	SLIPPER	VILLAIN
CITATOR	GRINDER	PEASANT	SLITHER	VINEGAR
CLATTER	GYRATOR	PEDAGOG	SLOBBER	WARRANT
CLUSTER	HAPLOID	PEDDLER	SLUMBER	WHISKER
CLUTTER	HATCHER	PIZZAZZ	SMELTER	WHISPER
COLLIER	HEATHER	PLASTER	SMOTHER	
COSTUME	HEGEMON	PLUMBER	SNICKER	
COTTAGE	HEGUMEN	POLYGON	SNIPPET	

With front hook Z

INCITES	ONETIME	OOLOGIC	OOPHYTE	OOSPERM	OOSPORE

Chapter 6: Words having the same front and back hooks

With front or back hook A

BET	HOY	LUM	SPIC	TAP
DIT	KIN	MAS	SPIRE	VIATIC
DOS	LOOF	MASS	STERN	

With front or back hook B

LAMB

With front or back hook C

ILIA

With front or back hook D

ACE	ELATE	EVOLVE	RAKE	ROGUE	WINE
ADDLE	ELUDE	HOLE	RAPE	ROVE	
ANGLE	EMERGE	ICE	RAVE	RUMBLE	
EAVE	EMOTE	IRE	READ	UNITE	
EDUCE	ENOUNCE	OPE	REE	WALE	
EKE	EPILATE	RABBLE	RIVE	WINDLE	

With front or back hook E

ARS	ELS	MAIL	MIR	POS	SPRIT
CRUS	GAL	MERGE	MUS	RAS	STOP
DIT	GEST	MIC	PIC	SCAR	TAS

With front or back hook F

LEA	REE

With front or back hook G

RAN	RIN

With front or back hook H

AGGADA	ALMA	EIGHT	UMP
AGGADOT	EAT	OKE	

With front or back hook I

CON	MID

With front or back hook K

BAR

With front or back hook L

ATRIA	AURA	EAR	EASE	OMENTA

With front or back hook M

ALAR

With front or back hook N

ALA	EAR	EVE	OPE

With front or back hook O

KAY	MEN	PES	PING

With front or back hook P

LEA	LUM	RAM	REP	ROM

With front or back hook R

AGA	AMBLE	ANCHO	AVE	EMOTE	EVOLVE
AGE	AMI	APE	ELATE	EVOKE	USE

With front or back hook S

ABLE	ANGA	CAPE	COOPER	CRAPPER	CUP
ADDER	ANGER	CAR	COOT	CRAWL	CUPPER
ADDLE	ARK	CARE	COOTER	CRAWLER	CURF
AGA	ASSES	CARER	COP	CREAK	CUT
AGE	ATE	CARES	COPE	CREAM	CUTE
AGER	AUGER	CARING	COPING	CREAMER	CUTTER
AGGER	AVE	CARP	COPULA	CREED	CUTTLE
AID	AVER	CARPER	CORE	CREW	CUTWORK
AIL	AWN	CARPING	CORER	CRIMP	EAR
AIN	CAB	CARRIER	CORN	CRIMPER	EARING
ALE	CAD	CART	CORNER	CRIP	EAT
ALINE	CALL	CAT	COT	CRUMPLE	EATER
ALL	CAM	CENT	COUTER	CRYER	EATING
ALLOW	CAMP	CHILLER	COUTH	CUD	EDGE
ALP	CAMPER	CION	COW	CUFF	EDILE
ALT	CAMPING	COFF	COWL	CULL	EDITION
ALTER	CAN	COFFER	COWLING	CULLER	EDUCE
AMBO	CANNER	COLD	CRAG	CULLION	EEL
AMP	CANNING	COLLOP	CRAM	CUM	EGGAR
AND	CANT	CONE	CRAP	CUMMER	EGO
ANE	CANTER	COOP	CRAPE	CUNNER	ELECT

ELECTEE	HEARER	IDLER	LAW	LUNK	NIPPER
ELECTOR	HEARING	IGNORE	LAY	MACK	NIT
ELL	HEATH	ILK	LAYER	MALL	NOB
EME	HEATHER	ILL	LEAVE	MALT	NOG
ENATE	HEAVE	IMP	LEAVING	MART	NOGGING
END	HELL	INGLE	LEDGE	MARTEN	NOOK
ENDER	HELLER	INK	LEEK	MASHER	NOOSE
ENDING	HELVE	INKER	LEET	MATTER	NOW
EPIC	HEN	INNER	LENDER	MAZE	NUB
ERA	HENT	INNING	LICK	MELL	NUBBER
ETA	HERD	INTER	LICKER	MELT	NUFF
EVEN	HERO	IRE	LICKING	MELTER	NUG
EWER	HEUCH	IZAR	LID	MERK	OAK
EXIST	HEUGH	KAT	LIER	MEW	OAR
EXPERT	HEW	KEEN	LIGHT	MIDGE	OBA
HACK	HEWER	KEET	LIGHTER	MILE	OCA
HACKING	HILL	KEG	LIME	MILER	ODA
HACKLE	HIM	KELP	LIMMER	MILING	ODIUM
HACKLER	HIN	KELTER	LING	MIRK	OIL
HADDOCK	HIP	KEP	LINGER	MITE	OKE
HADE	HIRE	KID	LINK	MITER	OLD
HAFT	HIST	KIDDER	LIP	MITTEN	OLE
HAG	HIT	KIER	LIPPER	MOCK	OMA
HAH	HITTER	KILL	LIPPING	MOG	OMBER
HAKE	HIVE	KILLING	LIT	MOKE	OMBRE
HALE	HOCK	KIN	LITTER	MOLDER	ONE
HALIER	HOCKER	KINK	LIVER	MOLT	OOT
HALL	HOD	KIP	LOB	MOOCHER	ORB
HALLOW	HODDEN	KIPPER	LOBBER	MOTE	ORE
HALT	HOE	KIS	LOG	MOTHER	ORT
HAM	HOER	KIT	LOGAN	MOULDER	OUGHT
HAMAL	HOG	KITE	LOGGER	MUG	OUR
HAME	HONE	KITING	LOGGING	MUGGER	OUTER
HAMMER	HOOK	KITTLE	LOID	MUSHING	OWN
HANK	HOOT	KOOKUM	LOOP	MUT	PACE
HARD	HOOTER	LAB	LOP	NAG	PACER
HARE	HOP	LACK	LOPE	NAGGER	PACING
HARK	HOPPER	LACKER	LOPER	NAGGING	PAIL
HARP	HOPPING	LAG	LOT	NAIL	PALE
HARPER	HORN	LAGGING	LOTTER	NAP	PALL
HARPING	HOT	LAHAL	LOUGH	NAPPER	PAM
HAT	HOVEL	LAKE	LOW	NARK	PAN
HATTER	HOVER	LAKER	LOWDOW	NEAP	PANG
HAUGH	HOW	LAKING	N	NECK	PANNER
HAUL	HUCK	LAM	LOWER	NIB	PAR
HAULING	HUN	LANDER	LOWING	NICK	PARABLE
HAVE	HUNT	LAP	LUBBER	NICKER	PARE
HAVEN	HUNTER	LAPPER	LUFF	NIDE	PARER
HAVER	HUNTING	LASHER	LUG	NIFF	PARGE
HAW	HUT	LASHING	LUGGER	NIFFER	PARGING
HAY	ICE	LAT	LUM	NIGGER	PARING
HEAL	ICK	LATHER	LUMBER	NIGGLE	PARK
HEALING	ICKER	LAVE	LUMP	NIGGLER	PARKER
HEAR	IDLE	LAVER	LUNG	NIP	PARKING

PARRIER	PLAY	TACK	TILLER	TRIPPER	WANKER
PARSE	POKE	TACKER	TILT	TROKE	WAP
PARSER	PONTOON	TAG	TIME	TROLL	WARD
PARTAN	POOF	TAGGER	TING	TROLLER	WARE
PAS	POOL	TAIN	TINGE	TROVE	WARM
PAT	POOLER	TAKE	TINKER	TROW	WARMER
PATE	POON	TAKEOUT	TINT	TROY	WARMING
PATTER	PORE	TAKER	TINTER	TRUCK	WART
PAVIN	PORT	TAKING	TINTING	TRUMPET	WASHER
PAWN	PORTER	TALE	TIPPLE	TUB	WASHING
PAWNER	POT	TALER	TIPPLER	TUCK	WAT
PAY	POTTER	TALK	TOCCATA	TUFF	WAY
PEAK	POUT	TALKER	TOCK	TUM	WAYBACK
PEAN	POUTER	TALKING	TOKE	TUMBLE	WEAR
PEAR	PRANG	TALL	TOKER	TUMBLER	WEARER
PEC	PRAT	TAMP	TOLE	TUMP	WEEP
PECK	PRATTLE	TAMPER	TONE	TUN	WEEPER
PECTATE	PRAY	TAMPING	TONER	TUNG	WEEPING
PED	PRAYER	TANG	TOOL	TYE	WEET
PEEL	PREE	TANK	TOOLING	UGH	WELL
PEELING	PRIER	TAR	TOP	ULLAGE	WELTER
PEER	PRIEST	TARE	TOPE	ULU	WIG
PEISE	PRIG	TARRIER	TOPER	UMMA	WIGGER
PELT	PRINT	TART	TOPPER	UMP	WIGGING
PELTER	PRINTER	TAT	TOPPING	UNBELT	WILE
PEND	PROG	TATE	TOPPLE	UNBLOCK	WILL
PERM	PRYER	TATER	TORE	UNCHOKE	WILLER
PEW	PUD	TAW	TOT	UNROOF	WINDLE
PIC	PUDDING	TEAK	TOUR	UNSET	WINDLES
PICA	PUN	TEAL	TOUT	UPPER	WINE
PICK	PUNK	TEAM	TOUTER	UPPING	WING
PIER	PUNKIE	TEEL	TOW	URD	WINGER
PIKE	PUR	TEIN	TOWAGE	URGE	WINK
PIKER	PURGE	TELE	TOWAWAY	URGER	WIPE
PILE	PUTTER	TENT	TRAIN	URGING	WIPER
PILING	QUAD	TERN	TRAINER	WAB	WISHER
PILL	QUARK	TET	TRAIT	WADDLE	WITHE
PILLAGE	QUASHER	TEW	TRAP	WAG	WITHER
PIN	QUID	TICK	TRAPPER	WAGE	WIVE
PINE	QUILL	TICKER	TRAY	WAGER	WOP
PINNER	QUINT	TICKING	TRICK	WAGGER	WORD
PINTO	QUIRE	TICKLE	TRICKLE	WAIL	WOT
PIT	QUIRT	TICKLER	TRIDENT	WAIN	WOUND
PITTING	TAB	TIFF	TRIKE	WALE	
PLASHER	TABBING	TILE	TRINE	WALLOW	
PLAT	TABLE	TILL	TRIP	WAN	
PLATTER	TABLING	TILLAGE	TRIPE	WANK	

With front or back hook T

ABLES	HIGH	RAP	REF	RUNDLE	WAS
HAE	HIN	RASHES	RES	SADIS	WAT
HEN	HIS	REES	RIPES	SORES	WEE

WEENIES   WOS

With front or back hook W

ANE

With front or back hook Y

ARROW   AWN   EGG   ILL   OWL

Chapter 7: New NWL18 Words with Hooks

With Front Hook B

OTHERED   OWIE

With Front Hook D

OWIE

With Front Hook F

EELING   OTHERED

With Front Hook H

AIRBALL   EELING

With Front Hook J

EELING

With Front Hook K

EELING

With Front Hook M

OTHERED

With Front Hook P

EELING   OTHERED

With Front Hook R

EELING   OWIE   OWIES

With Front Hook S

EELING   NUBBER   NUBBERS   WAYBACK

With Front Hook T

OWIE   OWIES

With Front Hook Y

OWIE   OWIES

With Front Hook Z

OWIE

With Back Hook D

BARCODE   MISGAGE   PUGGLE   UPCYCLE   VAPE   YUKE

With Back Hook E

CAVEOLA

With Back Hook H

TEREFA

With Back Hook I

MACARON

With Back Hook L

METICA   UNSEE

With Back Hook N

UNSAW   UNSEE

With Back Hook R

CAVEOLA   VAPE   WALIE   WORDIE

With Back Hook S

AGYRIA	BITCOIN	COTIJA	MISFOLD	RETWEET	UPCYCLE
AIRBALL	BITRATE	DHOLL	MISGAGE	ROOTKIT	VAPE
ANAGEN	BITURBO	DIDYMO	NONI	SANTOKU	VAPER
ANTIFA	BIZJET	EELING	NONKIN	SCHNEID	VAPING
ARAWANA	BOKEH	EMOJI	NUBBER	SEROMA	WALIE
AROWANA	BOTNET	EXOME	NUTJOB	SHEEPLE	WAYBACK
ARUANA	CANKLE	FARRO	OWIE	TELOGEN	WORDIE
ASIAGO	CAPCOM	FIBRATE	PAPASAN	THETRI	YUKE
AUDISM	CAPTCHA	LEUCISM	PREMAKE	TOGROG	ZEN
AUDIST	CATAGEN	LOOGIE	PUGGLE	TRUTHER	
BARCODE	CHYRON	MACARON	QAPIK	TWERK	
BESTIE	CONLANG	METICA	RAGDOLL	UNSEE	

With Back Hook T

ANTIFA   WORDIES

With Back Hook W

FARRO

Take Both Front or Back S Hook

EELING   NUBBER   WAYBACK

About the Author

Norman Wei is an environmental consultant and Scrabble player living in Cape Coral, Florida. He is the author of Anagram Cartoon - a Fun Way to Learn Anagrams - a book with over 800 cartoons depicting close to 2000 anagrams.

A copy of his cartoon book can be purchased from his website www.normanwei.com and at amazon.com worldwide. It is also available at www.bookdepository.com worldwide.

Smaller collections (around 100 cartoons) are also available on Amazon Kindle worldwide in Kindle format.

Beside Scrabble, Norman's other hobbies are scuba diving, underwater and wildlife photography, charcoal drawings, standup paddle board and flying drones.

His underwater and wildlife (humming birds, eagles, ospreys, caracara, owls, Amazon parrots, etc) photos are available from his website www.photosbynormanwei.com.

He can be reached at Scrabble@normanwei.com.

Made in the USA
Columbia, SC
10 June 2019